Indigenous Australia

2nd Edition

by Larissa Behrendt

Foreword by Stan Grant

for
dummies®
A Wiley Brand

Indigenous Australia For Dummies®, 2nd Edition

Published by
Wiley Publishing Australia Pty Ltd
42 McDougall Street
Milton, Qld 4064
www.dummies.com

Copyright © 2021 Wiley Publishing Australia Pty Ltd

The moral rights of the author have been asserted.

ISBN: 978-0-730-39027-5

 A catalogue record for this book is available from the National Library of Australia

Cover image: © Daphne Marks/Copyright Agency, 2020

Typeset by SPi

10 9 8 7 6 5 4 3 2 1

READERS OF THIS BOOK SHOULD BE AWARE THAT, IN SOME ABORIGINAL AND TORRES STRAIT ISLANDER COMMUNITIES, SEEING IMAGES OF DECEASED PERSONS IN PHOTOGRAPHS MAY CAUSE SADNESS OR DISTRESS AND, IN SOME CASES, OFFEND AGAINST STRONGLY HELD CULTURAL PROHIBITIONS. THIS BOOK CONTAINS IMAGES OF PEOPLE WHO ARE DECEASED.

Contents at a Glance

Table of Contents

Foreword by Stan Grant

There is a place where Australia disappears. It is a holy place and an ancient place. It is a place where once people lived and laughed and loved; where they traded and danced. It is a place where a boy was born who would grow to be a powerful man; a leader of his people. When he died this man was given a ceremonial burial. His body was smeared in ochre and his arms folded gently across his chest and he was lowered into the ground. Forty thousand years later he would be 'discovered' and given a name. He is Mungo Man and he is our connection to a time before time that today lives in time. He is a connection to what the famed anthropologist William H Stanner once called 'the Everywhen'. We might call it the Dreaming. Mungo Man is the oldest human remains ever found on our continent.

I go there sometimes, to the dried-up shores of Lake Mungo. I have been there with old men who keep old stories. I have slept under the magical sky alongside my cousins and we have carved sacred totems into the ground. It is not my traditional country but my great-grandfather had kinship ties here and he spoke the languages of the Muthi Muthi and the Barkandji as well as his own Wiradjuri. It is a special place; not a place of bones and stones as scientists might see it but a living, breathing place. Away from the roads and the power lines and fences, where there is just openness and timelessness, I know there is something that beats eternal; that is older than any nation. No flag or border or anthem can capture what exists here; it is for us to feel and to know and to respect. It is for us to belong.

How many of us can say we truly belong in our country? Can we say we know our country? Are we alive to the stories and rhythms and the sounds of this place we now call Australia? We live in a land where the true stories have been silenced. We live in a land where old voices speaking old tongues have vanished. What does it do to a place to lose its sound; to lose its people? There is sadness here, deep sadness. But there is life too if we care to listen and feel.

There are places like Lake Mungo everywhere; 'Everyplaces' for the 'Everywhen'. You can find them by our riverbanks, under the stars, in our rocks and fields. Larissa Behrendt invites you to take that journey. She will take you into an Australia we think we know but remain so ignorant of, and we are poorer for that. Who are these First People of our land? How many languages were spoken here? What is their art and politics and music and ceremony? Larissa will open up a new country for you. And you will find that there is a place here more magical than you could know. But it demands something of you. Are you ready to face our history? Do you know what really happened when the British came? Are you ready to learn about invasion and colonisation and what it does to a people to lose their place in their own country?

Australia is a hard place. It is a place still seeking peace with itself. The journey for justice is a road half travelled. 'Sorry' isn't enough when the First People of this land die younger and suffer more than any other Australians. Reconciliation and recognition and Treaty are the business we have not finished. But, oh how my people sing. And how we play. We are the living story of this land and it is a story just waiting for you.

The bones of our ancestors are buried in this soil, but they rest uneasy. It is for us to bring this land peace. That work starts here with this book. Larissa Behrendt calls it Indigenous Australia For Dummies – yep that's about right; we are still just learning. But read this and be smarter.

Stan Grant
Television news and political journalist, television presenter,
filmmaker and bestselling author
November 2020

Introduction

U nderstanding the history and culture of Australia is impossible without understanding the country's Indigenous peoples. And understanding Australia's Indigenous peoples is reliant on understanding their history, traditional and contemporary cultural values, worldviews and experiences.

Indigenous Australia For Dummies looks at the experiences of Indigenous people, including their political activism and aspirations, and seeks to debunk some of the myths, especially the negative stereotypes, that still exist in Australian society about Indigenous people. Indigenous history and contemporary issues are very political matters in Australia. This book often looks at these matters from an Indigenous perspective, as well as canvassing alternative views.

About This Book

Indigenous Australia For Dummies is a general reference book targeting audiences who don't know much about Australia's Indigenous peoples but are keen to know more. It looks at both historical and contemporary issues. The book is designed to give readers a good general knowledge of all the relevant issues and hopefully inspire them to then read more detailed writings on what can be very complex topics. This book can be read straight through or read selectively by topic, because each chapter is self-contained.

Australia's Indigenous peoples are made up of Aboriginal people — who live all around the country — and Torres Strait Islanders, who settled the many small islands to the north of Cape York Peninsula in Queensland.

Terminology is complex when it comes to Indigenous identity in Australia. The term *Indigenous* is used in this book to describe both Aboriginal people and Torres Strait Islanders. The term *Aboriginal* is used when referring to matters that apply only to Aboriginal people; similarly with the use of the term *Torres Strait Islanders*. The fact that some Aboriginal people don't like to be called 'Indigenous' is also important to remember. Increasingly, the preferred term is *First Nations*. Others prefer to be referred to through their nation or clan affiliation.

Because Indigenous languages in Australia were originally oral languages — not written — nation or clan names often have multiple spellings. Regional variations on pronunciation have also led to more than one spelling for other words. Throughout the text, when referring to specific nations or clans, I have adopted the most commonly used spelling.

Note: As both the author of this book and an Aboriginal person myself, if it sounds like I'm telling the story as an insider, I am.

On a different note, to help you get the information you need as quickly as possible, this book uses several conventions:

>> **Bold** words make the key terms and phrases in bulleted lists jump out and grab your attention.

>> *Italics* signal that a word is an important defined term.

>> Monofont is used to signal a web address.

>> Sidebars, text separated from the rest of the type in grey boxes, are interesting but generally optional reading. You won't miss anything critical if you skip the sidebars. If you choose to read the sidebars, though, you can benefit from some additional and interesting information.

Foolish Assumptions

This book assumes the following about you, the reader:

>> That you have a rudimentary understanding of Australian history — such as that Australia was colonised by the British in 1788

>> That you have a basic knowledge of Australian geography — or that at least you're able to look up different places on a map!

Icons Used in This Book

Throughout this book, the following icons are used to help you identify when you're about to learn something special, quirky or significant.

CULTURAL PROTOCOLS

This is important information about Indigenous cultures that allows you to better understand Indigenous people.

MYTH BUSTER

Many myths, misunderstandings and stereotypes about Indigenous people have become widespread since European settlement of Australia. This information straightens out a few of those things.

REMEMBER

Information adjacent to this icon helps to give a deeper understanding of the topic being discussed.

TECHNICAL STUFF

This is specialised information, often legal in nature, that explains terms or gives the background to a topic.

TIP

This icon denotes a piece of advice about the subject matter being discussed that helps you to learn more.

Where to Go from Here

You can approach this book any way you like. You can read from start to finish — and perhaps skip some things along the way that you already know or are less interested in. Or you can go straight to the topics you're most interested in and dive right in there. For an overview of the diversity and richness of Indigenous cultures both before and after colonisation, for example, head to Chapters 1 to 4.

Chapters 5 to 9 look at the growth of the British colonies in Australia and the impact on and reactions of Indigenous people. The chapters in Part 3 are all about Indigenous activism, while Chapters 16 to 20 highlight the rich tradition of art, storytelling, dance and music that's as vibrant today as it was before colonisation.

And if it's the current issues you'd like to jump in and tackle, head to Chapters 21 and 22.

You can use the table of contents to find topics quickly. The glossary lets you cut to the chase on any terms you may want to clarify.

For Dummies books are meant to be fun to read as well as informative, so go ahead and enjoy!

1

An Ancient People: Then and Now

Understand the extensive history of Indigenous peoples, going back over 65,000 years.

Work out why it's important to understand rich and diverse Indigenous history, cultures and values, both traditional and contemporary.

Find out about Indigenous worldviews, bush tucker and languages.

Get to know protocols when addressing Indigenous people or holding an event on traditional lands.

Chapter **1**

Understanding Indigenous Australia

The Aboriginal people of Australia are said to be the custodians of the world's oldest living culture. Indigenous Australians — Aboriginal people and Torres Strait Islanders — have worldviews that focus on the interconnectedness between people and their environment, and the bonds they have with each other. They are also an important part of the Australian story. Modern Australia can't be understood without also considering the significance of its Indigenous peoples and their cultures in that story.

The colonisation of Australia devastated Indigenous people and cultures — populations were decimated, traditional lands and means of self-sufficiency were taken, and government policies aimed at assimilation legitimised the taking of Indigenous children from their families so they could grow up as 'white' Australians. But, although this was a difficult period, the story of how Indigenous people — and their cultures — survived is inspiring.

In this chapter, I provide an overview of Australia's history through Indigenous eyes, covering how government practices were able to control the lives of Indigenous people, even up until recent times, and what they did to defend themselves, their rights and their country. This chapter gives you a quick look at the breadth of contemporary Indigenous culture and political action that celebrates their very survival. And it also looks briefly at how Indigenous people are tackling some of the major challenges they face today — lower levels of literacy, higher levels of unemployment, higher levels of poverty and poorer health than other Australians.

Understanding these aspects of Indigenous history and cultures enables you to gain a greater insight into who Indigenous people are and what their cultures are like, what issues they face today and some of the solutions being employed to meet these challenges.

Indigenous Cultures: Then and Now

More than 500 different Aboriginal nations existed at the time the British colonised Australia — possibly up to one million people in total. They had lived on this land for over 65,000 years, adjusting to dramatic changes in the environment and landscape. The arrival of the British in 1788, however, had a fundamental impact on Indigenous cultures. Over the next century, as colonies spread far and wide, Aboriginal people were separated from their traditional lands, affecting their ability to care for their country, support themselves and their families and practise traditional ceremonies. But Indigenous cultures were resilient and, even in the face of such overwhelming change, they still adapted.

Today, Indigenous people live across Australia in communities in urban, rural and remote areas. Although they were once considered by non-Indigenous Australians to be a dying, inferior race, their increasing populations and continuing cultural practices show that contemporary Indigenous cultures are vibrant and still very much alive. Chapter 2 outlines the initial decline and later growth of the Indigenous population since colonisation, as well as the cultural protocols of how to address Indigenous people in different areas of Australia.

Ancient traditions

Indigenous cultures across Australia had strong connections to their traditional land. They relied on it to provide them with everything they needed to survive — food, shelter, tools and medicine. And they needed each other as well. Nations were divided into *clans*, which were large extended families, perhaps as small as 30 people in some cases. In such small groups, everyone had to pitch in and people were very reliant on each other.

These circumstances gave rise to cultural values that focused on this interconnectedness. Through complex totemic systems, Indigenous people were reminded of their connection with nature, each other and their ancestors. They also believed in respect and responsibility for country, and respect for the wisdom and authority of Elders. Chapter 4 delves into traditional practices and beliefs, and Chapter 23 describes some of the cultural sites that remain important for Indigenous peoples today.

Diversity, diversity and more diversity

Although Indigenous cultures around Australia shared many values and had similar worldviews, great diversity was also present, explained to a large extent by the vastly different environments and climates across Australia. Indigenous communities living by the ocean had different ways of life, different technologies and different practices from Indigenous communities living in the middle of Australia in arid desert areas. However, across the country, large gatherings of several clans took place for ceremonial purposes, and trading routes spread across the continent. See Chapter 3 for more on cultural diversity, in both traditional and contemporary contexts.

REMEMBER

Indigenous cultures have remained strong and vibrant across Australia. Even in contemporary forms — using new technology or incorporating aspects of other cultures — they maintain a strong connection to traditional practices. Chapter 25 examines, and debunks, some of the myths that have developed over the years about Indigenous people.

Contemporary painting, singing and dancing

Art, song and dance were key aspects of traditional cultural practice, mostly engaged in for ceremonial purposes, and they retain a central position in contemporary cultures.

Indigenous art has become a worldwide sensation, with some pieces attracting prices in the tens, even hundreds of thousands of dollars. This industry hasn't, however, translated into wealth for the artists. Chapter 16 looks in detail at some of the successes in the Indigenous art world.

Indigenous songs were one of the most fragile parts of Indigenous cultures, being some of the first things that were lost with colonisation. Today, however, Indigenous people are strongly engaged with music — particularly country and western music! Younger Indigenous people have also embraced hip-hop music and rap as a way of expressing their views and aspirations. Indigenous dance has emerged as a leading contemporary Indigenous art form, blending traditional dancing with more modern styles. Indigenous dance companies have flourished around Australia. See Chapter 17 for some of the best of Indigenous Australia's musicians and dancers.

Old and new ways of storytelling

Indigenous cultures have a storytelling tradition, and Indigenous people have embraced new ways of getting their message across. Indigenous playwrights, theatre directors and filmmakers have also employed Indigenous actors to tell Indigenous stories. Indigenous people have also set up their own national radio service and television service, both complementing the many regional radio and television services set up by Indigenous communities. See Chapter 19 for more on the development of these media, as well as the establishment of the National Black Theatre, one of Australia's first political theatres.

Although Indigenous cultures originally had an oral tradition with no written languages, Indigenous storytellers have now turned their hand to the written word. For a long time, Indigenous people had stories written about them by white anthropologists, linguists, historians and writers but, since the 1970s, Indigenous people have had an increasing desire to tell their own stories themselves. Since then, Indigenous writing has crossed over into many genres, including crime novels and women's popular fiction. Chapter 18 covers Indigenous writing and publishing in detail.

And they can kick a ball!

Australia's Indigenous peoples lived hunter-gatherer lifestyles. This meant they spent a lot of time moving and had a nutritious, balanced diet. It was a way of life that kept people strong and healthy. Perhaps because of this traditional way of life, Indigenous people have excelled as athletes. Across many sports — but especially football and athletics — Indigenous people have made a sizeable contribution to Australia's sporting prowess. Sportspeople are good role models for Indigenous young people and often work in Aboriginal and Torres Strait Islander communities as mentors, assisting with building confidence and self-esteem, and encouraging young people to be active, fit and healthy. You can find more information on leading Indigenous sportspeople and the work they do in Chapter 20.

There Goes the Neighbourhood

Understanding contemporary Indigenous cultures and worldviews is largely reliant on understanding how Australia's Indigenous peoples have been treated during the country's comparatively brief European history.

Lieutenant James Cook (later Captain) claimed the eastern coast of Australia for the British in 1770. At the time, the agreement among the large, powerful colonising countries such as Britain, Spain and France was that lands such as Australia, populated only by natives who were seen to be inferior, could be claimed by the colonial power that found them first. This was known as the *doctrine of discovery*. (Chapter 5 examines this concept and some of the European explorations that led to it.) Indigenous people could have had no idea that, after 1770, their world would change as it did.

The takeover begins

In 1778, the First Fleet arrived in Sydney Cove and established a penal colony. The settlement was designed to assist with the problem of overcrowding in British prisons — grown worse since the American revolution stopped prisoners being sent there — and to establish a claim to the territory against other colonial powers, especially the French. With the establishment of the colony, life for Indigenous Australians would never be the same again. Chapter 6 explores the ramifications of this first colony.

The colony spreads

The colony at Sydney Cove soon spread. The colony needed agricultural industries such as wheat, sheep and cattle to survive, and for that it needed land. The British eventually set up colonies around the country, including:

>> Van Diemen's Land, which became known as Tasmania

>> Port Phillip District, in what is now Victoria

>> Moreton Bay, near what is now Brisbane

>> Adelaide, in South Australia

REMEMBER

The impact on Aboriginal people of the establishment of these colonies was profound. One of the initial problems for them was the effect of the diseases brought by the British. Aboriginal people had no immunity to smallpox, colds, flu and measles, and populations were decimated as these diseases spread. Chapter 7 looks in detail at the impact of this expansion.

Loss of land

As the colonies were established and spread out from their initial boundaries, Aboriginal people were pushed off their land. They also lost their livelihoods — their ability to feed and shelter themselves and their families — and cultural practices were disrupted. This led inevitably to conflict — often violent conflict — as Aboriginal people resisted, as best they could, the attempts to dispossess them of their land. Although this resistance (mostly setting fire to buildings and infra-structure, and killing stock), did stall the expansion of the frontier in some places, eventually the colonists, with their superior firepower and increasing numbers, gained the upper hand.

In many places, Aboriginal people found themselves pushed to the margins of towns and forced to live on specially designated reserves. In some cases, Aboriginal people were able to live on their traditional lands on pastoral stations and were given very basic rations, in exchange for work for the station owner. See Chapter 8 for more on this uneasy alliance.

And children taken too

As the colonists got the upper hand, they attempted to assimilate Aboriginal people into European cultural ways. They believed that one of the most effective ways to do this was to remove Aboriginal children from their families and bring them up away from them and their culture, sometimes placing them in institutions, other times adopting them into white families. This also affected Torres Strait Islander people, after missions were established in the Torres Strait in the late 1800s and as Torres Strait Islanders began to settle on the mainland.

All states and territories had laws that permitted the removal of Indigenous children from their families. Some people administering the policy genuinely believed that removing Indigenous children from their families would give them a better life. Despite those good intentions, the practice often had devastating consequences for the children taken away and the families they left behind. Chapter 9 examines this painful issue in detail.

Fighting Back

From the very start of the colonisation process, Aboriginal people resisted the infringement of their rights to their lands and the impact on their communities and cultures. Over the years, Aboriginal communities continued to assert their rights to their lands and to protest their unequal treatment. Torres Strait Islanders soon joined them.

The right to be equal

When the British established their colony at Sydney Cove, they transported their laws as well as their people. Although it was asserted that the laws and their protections applied equally to Aboriginal people and colonists, in practice this wasn't the case.

Not only were Aboriginal people's rights to their lands denied, but they were also rarely offered protection from frontier violence. They were subject to regulations about where they could live, who they could marry, and whether and where they could work. They weren't entitled to the same wages as other workers doing the same jobs. In most places, they couldn't vote.

Aboriginal people sought to challenge these restrictions, petitioning governments and even the British Crown. A key focus of their advocacy was equal treatment — particularly the rights to own and farm their own land and to have the same rights to citizenship as other Australians. Chapter 10 covers some of the more notable examples of Indigenous people's claims to citizenship rights, and some of the early organisations set up to fight for them. That chapter also lists some of the Indigenous leaders who emerged throughout the fight for the right to be equal.

Changing the playing field

By the 1960s, Indigenous communities around Australia were experiencing third-world conditions. Many Australians — black and white — believed that this was unacceptable. As a result of a decade-long grassroots campaign, over 90 per cent of Australians voted in 1967 to change the Constitution to empower the federal government to make laws for Indigenous people. At the time, people genuinely believed that this change would herald a new era of non-discrimination, because people thought that the federal government would act in a way that would benefit Indigenous people. Although reality later proved this assumption wrong, the vote was a significant moment in Australia's history, when such a large majority of Australians believed that the improved treatment of Indigenous people was important for the country. Chapter 11 looks at the referendum in more detail.

'We want our land back'

Land rights have been a key focus for Indigenous political movements ever since 1788. The land rights movement gained momentum in the 1960s and 1970s. Several land rights regimes were set up — in the Northern Territory and New South Wales, in particular — though aspirations for a national scheme never eventuated. These schemes were set up by governments under different legislation and varied in terms of how they established land councils and the provisions they made for the return of land to Indigenous people. Rights to land were also given a boost in 1992, when the High Court of Australia recognised that, in some circumstances, Indigenous people could claim a 'native title' right to their traditional land. See Chapter 12 for information about the land rights movement.

Reconciliation, practical reconciliation and intervention

Governments still struggle to work out how to address systemic problems of Indigenous disadvantage. In the early 1990s, a national agenda of reconciliation was established that sought to, over a ten-year period, consult with Indigenous people about the best ways they could work together to overcome Indigenous disadvantage. This was replaced by a subsequent government with a program of 'practical reconciliation' that, it said, would focus on the areas of health, housing, education and employment. This approach didn't produce tangible results, however, and, in 2007, the federal government began a policy of intervention in the Northern Territory, where it sought to impose further change in the communities.

To date, no significant inroads have been made into reducing the difference between the disadvantaged circumstances of the broad Indigenous community and the living standards of other Australians. Chapters 13 and 14 examine the political response to this socioeconomic divide.

'Sorry' — and then what?

On 13 February 2008, Prime Minister Kevin Rudd delivered a historic address in the federal parliament, where he apologised to Indigenous Australians for past wrongs committed by governments against them, particularly for the removal of children from their families. This apology was seen as an act of enormous symbolic importance. Since then, the Australian government has also endorsed the United Nations Declaration on the Rights of Indigenous Peoples, which supports self-determination for Indigenous peoples. Indigenous people continue to fight for that right in practice by seeking to be centrally involved in the policies and programs that affect their community.

The extent to which the symbolic changes will facilitate changes in the actual lives of Indigenous Australians still remains to be seen. Chapter 15 looks at the ramifications of the apology and Chapter 22 looks closely at the current issues surrounding the concept of self-determination.

New Problems for an Old Culture

The impact of colonisation on Indigenous peoples was profound. Traditional ways of life were completely disrupted; the consequences of dispossession, segregation and racist policies left an unhappy legacy. This legacy is clear in the statistics, showing that Indigenous people are much more disadvantaged in areas of health, education outcomes and employment. These statistics pose a challenge in the goal to create a level playing field for all Australians, with Indigenous communities themselves playing an active and effective role in trying to find solutions. Chapter 24 looks at some of the achievements of Indigenous people — those who were the first to break through the barrier of these disadvantages.

Breaking the cycle of poverty

Indigenous life expectancy is lower than that of other Australians, health poorer, home ownership levels lower and housing conditions worse than those of other Australians. Indigenous people also have lower levels of education and higher levels of unemployment than their non-Indigenous counterparts. Much has been done to try to remedy this situation. Indigenous people have set up their own medical services and are training to be nurses and doctors to address pressing health needs in their communities. Chapter 21 has more information on Indigenous health.

That Indigenous disadvantage won't be overcome without improving the education levels of Indigenous people is well understood. Literacy levels and school attendance rates are a key focus in this area. Indigenous people have developed special programs that help to engage Indigenous children with learning how to read and write, and innovative programs have been designed to improve the education of Indigenous adults.

Of course, a correlation exists between education levels and unemployment levels. Another barrier to entering the workforce for Indigenous people is the remoteness of some communities. These challenges around education and employment, and examples of effective programs that have been developed to address these issues, are also explored in Chapter 21.

Challenging the rules and regulations

Aboriginal and Torres Strait Islander communities had their own laws and governance structures. Some of these survive today. But, when the British colonised Australia, they imposed their rules and governance systems, with no recognition of the rights of Indigenous Australians.

British law was supposed to protect Indigenous people. In practice, it was a weapon that hastened their dispossession. It was also used to control Indigenous people by dictating where Indigenous people could live, the conditions of their employment, whether they could vote and sometimes even if they could marry. It also legalised theft of their land and removal of their children. Indigenous people also came into contact with the criminal justice system, being targeted by the police, charged with offences that non-Indigenous people wouldn't have been charged with, and were more likely to be refused bail and given longer sentences compared with non-Indigenous people.

All this led to an overrepresentation of Indigenous people in prisons and to the charge that systemic racism exists in the criminal justice system. The Royal Commission into Aboriginal Deaths in Custody confirmed the bias in the legal system and made many recommendations.

REMEMBER

Very few of the recommendations made by the Royal Commission have been implemented, and Indigenous Australians continue to be overrepresented in prisons. Chapter 22 explores governance issues in the context of Australia's legal and political systems and Chapter 26 outlines ten key legal decisions affecting Indigenous people.

Setting up Indigenous enterprises

Indigenous people haven't stayed idle in the face of the problems that face their communities. Throughout this book are many instances of Indigenous people developing effective solutions to their own problems. One area in which Indigenous people are continuing to try to find new opportunities for their communities is in business and economic development. From ecotourism and cultural tours to partnerships with mining companies, bush tucker restaurants and Indigenous-owned holiday resorts, Indigenous people are finding new ways to try to enter the economy. This is an important strategy in overcoming Indigenous disadvantage. You can find more detail about how this strategy is being implemented in Indigenous communities across Australia in Chapters 3 and 21.

Doing It for Ourselves

Despite such serious disadvantage throughout the history of Indigenous Australia, communities across the country have also had their successes in finding solutions to intractable problems. These solutions are often simple, like providing drying-out shelters or rehabilitation programs to deal with issues of alcohol abuse and violence, bilingual language models that assist in improving educational outcomes and night patrols that keep the peace in Indigenous communities. All along, Indigenous people have said that, if they had the tools to be able to deal with the issues within their own communities, they would do a better job than governments. Plenty of evidence attests that this is the case and Indigenous claims to the right to self-determination remain a central part of their political agenda. Chapter 22 looks at these issues in more depth.

Chapter **2**

Rich Past, Strong Traditions

boriginal culture has been acknowledged as the world's oldest surviving culture. Its rich traditions and spiritual beliefs, and its complex social organisation, derive from many thousands of years of living history. Despite the decimation of early populations through introduced disease, frontier violence and alienation from traditional lands, culture and language, the social cohesion and cultural strength of Indigenous communities has survived.

The Torres Strait Islands have an equally rich culture. With evidence of occupation dating back 2,500 years, cultural practices and values have been influenced by reliance on the sea and then by the trading that took place with the Macassans, from the islands of what is now Indonesia, to the north. Life began to change for Torres Strait Islanders with the establishment of missions on the islands from the late 1800s.

In today's Australia, much confusion surrounds the make-up of the Indigenous population and the correct protocols in addressing Indigenous people. This chapter sets out a little of the history of Indigenous Australia and tackles the issue of the correct terminology for the diverse communities that exist around the country.

The First Australians

Given Australia's geological status as the oldest continent in the world, the fact that the country is also the home of the world's oldest surviving culture and religion is perhaps not surprising. Aboriginal people believe that they and their ancestors have occupied Australia since the beginning of time. Dreamtime stories relate to a creation period — when the Earth was shaped, stars were made and animals developed. These stories explain, for example, how an echidna got its spikes or how a particular bird became flightless.

Archaeological findings and developments in DNA technology have led to current estimates that modern humans — *Homo sapiens* — evolved in Africa about 190,000 years ago, moving to the Middle East about 120,000 years ago and arriving in Australia via Asia over 65,000 years ago. Europe was populated about 40,000 years ago and the American continent about 14,000 years ago.

The discovery at Lake Mungo of 'Mungo Lady' in 1969 and 'Mungo Man' in 1974 challenged the 'out of Africa' theory of the spread of modern humans. Their remains have been estimated to be around 40,000 years old. DNA tests showed that they didn't share ancestry with modern human beings. Some scientists have speculated that this means migration to Australia didn't occur in one wave. See Chapter 23 for more on this site. More recently, Madjedbebe, a sandstone rock shelter in Arnhem Land in the Northern Territory, dates human presence to over 65,000 years ago.

The Torres Strait Islands are to the north-east of Australia — between the mainland and Papua New Guinea — and have been considered as part of Queensland since 1879. More than 270 islands dot this area, though only 17 are inhabited. The Torres Strait Islands are believed to have been first inhabited by people migrating from Papua at least 2,500 years ago. Evidence may be found in the future that dates settlement earlier, possibly up to around 4,000 years ago.

65,000 Years of Tradition

Archaeological evidence suggests that Aboriginal people arrived in Australia at least 65,000 years ago. Three areas have been identified as likely places where people travelling from South-East Asia arrived in Australia — the Kimberley region in the north of Western Australia, Arnhem Land in the Top End of the Northern Territory and Cape York at the northern tip of Queensland. These areas contain rock shelters that have been used as places to live. Their floors are littered with the charcoal and ash remnants of campfires, the remains of food such as shells and bones, and other reminders of human life such as tools and ochre. Stone tools and ochre are the most resilient of these materials and they can be used to ascertain the dates human activity occurred. (*Ochre* comes from soft varieties of iron oxide minerals, ranging in colour from pale yellow to deep rust red, and was used in ceremonial activities such as the painting of rockfaces and the painting of faces and bodies.)

With Australia being relatively isolated, the technology of Aboriginal people and Torres Strait Islanders didn't evolve in the same way as it did in other parts of the world. Aboriginal people didn't develop through ages of pottery, bronze and iron; stone technology was used into the 1960s. Use of stone technology and painting with ochre pigments are practices that date back to at least 60,000 years ago, evidenced from the dating of ochre fragments from the floor of a rock shelter in Arnhem Land.

Aboriginal cultures in Australia were the first to develop ground edges on cutting tools and the first to grind seeds. Archaeological work at Madjedbebe (once referred to as Malakunanja II) and Nauwalabila I has uncovered pieces of ground ochre, bone fragments, shells, tool fragments and evidence of food processing. Carbon dating of the lowest layers that showed human activity places them conservatively at 65,000 years ago.

A cave on Barrow Island, off the coast of Western Australia, shows presence from 50,000 years ago. Ochre found at other sites around Australia has been dated from 10,000 to 40,000 years ago. A fragment of painting in a limestone rock shelter at Carpenter's Gap, near Windjana National Park in the Kimberley (Western Australia), was dated at 40,000 years using carbon-dating technology. Rock art dating back 30,000 years exists on the Burrup Peninsula, also in Western Australia.

MYTH BUSTER

Aboriginal people were once thought to have been on Australia for as long as 40,000 years. After more recent archaeological work, that was moved to 50,000 years. It is now accepted to be *at least* 65,000 — but this might even prove to be longer in the future.

Evidence of the duration of Aboriginal presence in Australia comes from many sources. Rock art was a common way of recording cultural practices, with some examples depicting animals that became extinct up to 40,000 years ago. Some of the oldest rock paintings, found in shelters in northern Australia, depict ceremonies that are still performed and ceremonial decorations that are still worn today — evidence of the continuation of Aboriginal cultural practices.

In the Torres Strait Islands, technology focused on using materials from the sea — fish bones, turtle shells, pearl shells and other shells. These were carved for use in ceremonies and as ornamental objects, and for tools, spearheads and fish hooks.

THE GREAT SOUTHERN LAND: HOW DID IT GET THERE?

Australia, the world's largest island — and a continent in itself — has rocks that date to over 3,000 million years ago. Experts estimate it began its journey across the Earth's surface as an isolated continent between 55 million and 10 million years ago. Australia continues to move to the north by about seven centimetres per year.

Australia's shape is largely due to the movement of the Earth's tectonic plates and long-term changes to sea levels, but the landscape has also been shaped by wind and water erosion. About half of Australia's rivers run inland and end in salt lakes. These draining patterns have a very long history, with some valleys maintaining their positions for millions of years. For example, the salt lakes of the Yilgarn region in Western Australia are the remains of a river drainage system that was active before the continental drift separated Australia from Antarctica.

The land mass that is now Australia started near the South Pole and was covered in ice caps. When the ice melted, parts of the continent subsided, forming sedimentary basins. By the Cretaceous Period (145 million to 65 million years ago) Australia was so flat that rising sea levels created a shallow sea that spread across the continent and divided it into three land masses.

During the Paleogene Period (65 million to 23 million years ago) and the Neogene Period (23 million to 2 million years ago), Australia experienced volcanic activity that continued in what is now Victoria and Queensland up until several thousand years ago. The most recent volcanic activity was at Mt Gambier in South Australia, which erupted about 6,000 years ago.

Around 30,000 years ago, Australia had a pleasant climate with abundant water, plenty of plants, snow-covered mountains and large animals — megafauna — roaming around. This had changed 10,000 years later, when the most recent ice age came. It lasted about 5,000 years. The middle of Australia was covered in large sand dunes during this time. Rainfall levels were half what they are today and the temperature was approximately ten degrees lower.

During its lowest level, the sea receded, and Australia, Tasmania and New Guinea formed one large land mass. When the ice age ended and temperatures started to rise, a surge in plant growth took place and the area where people could live in a hunter-gatherer lifestyle increased. It was during this rise in sea level that Tasmania was created (so, that's about 11,000 years ago!) by the island becoming separated from the mainland. New Guinea was cut off from Australia by rising sea levels around 8,000 years ago.

By around 5,000 years ago, the islands of the Torres Strait resembled those that now exist — the Torres Strait Islands — including high islands of volcanic rock to the west and small flat islands typical of the central and eastern areas, as well as sand cays and small volcanic islands in the far north of the strait, and large silt islands adjacent to the Papuan coast.

Aboriginal and Torres Strait Islander Populations Today

Aboriginal peoples and Torres Strait Islanders are still identified as distinct populations within the Australian community. Just as they did long ago, Aboriginal people and Torres Strait Islanders live in diverse circumstances across Australia, adapting to different environments and circumstances.

Torres Strait Islander culture is also distinct from Aboriginal cultures and, as would be expected of island communities, is largely focused on the sea. Various languages are spoken throughout the Torres Strait, including English and Torres Strait Creole. The traditional languages of the Torres Strait are divided between Meriam Mir in the eastern islands and Kala Lagaw Ya in the central and western islands. The latter has four dialects, including Mabuiag. See Chapter 3 for more on Indigenous languages.

Defining who is an Indigenous person

A person's identity is a personal thing. Identity goes to the heart of how all people feel about their ancestry and the environment in which they grew up. Many Aboriginal people and Torres Strait Islanders have mixed heritage but choose to identify as being an Aboriginal or a Torres Strait Islander person.

When governments and organisations have to assess whether a person is Aboriginal or Torres Strait Islander, they generally use three criteria, all of which must be fulfilled. In their view, the person must

>> Be of Aboriginal descent or Torres Strait Islander descent

>> Identify as an Aboriginal person or as a Torres Strait Islander

>> Be accepted as an Aboriginal person or as a Torres Strait Islander by the Aboriginal or Torres Strait Islander community in which she lives

The benefits of these criteria are that they include a component that looks at the way the person defines herself, as well as giving the community a role in determining who's considered to be Aboriginal or Torres Strait Islander for official purposes. Importantly, the test doesn't look at the percentage of Aboriginal or Torres Strait Islander heritage — or *blood quantum* — that a person has. If a person meets the requirements of the criteria, what 'percentage' of Aboriginal or Torres Strait Islander heritage she has doesn't matter. This definition gives some power to the Indigenous community about who is considered to be Aboriginal and Torres Strait Island.

RECOGNISING THE FLAGS

The Aboriginal flag was designed by Harold Thomas in 1971. The flag was displayed on 12 July 1971, National Aborigines' Day, at Victoria Square in Adelaide, and was also used at the Tent Embassy in Canberra in 1972. The flag has a horizontal stripe of black to represent Aboriginal people and a red stripe to represent the land and the blood that has been spilt on it. It also has a large yellow circle in the middle that represents the sun and symbolises the eternal joining of Aboriginal people to their land. It was given legal status as a flag of Australia in 1995.

In 2019, conflict emerged about the use of the flag on products (initiated by one of the companies Thomas had licenced to reproduce the image on clothing). In 2020, negotiations continued to allow the flag to be used more freely, while also taking commercial considerations into account.

The Torres Strait Islander flag was designed by Bernard Namok of Thursday Island. The flag has a representation of a white Dhari — a ceremonial headdress — which represents the people of the Torres Strait. It has a five-pointed star to symbolise peace and the five major island groups. A green horizontal stripe represents the land, a black stripe the people and a blue stripe the sea. It was also given legal status as a flag of Australia in 1995.

Aboriginal and Torres Strait Islander peoples don't embrace the term 'half-caste'. Even Aboriginal people of mixed ancestry usually say 'I am Aboriginal' — rather than 'I am part-Aboriginal', for example. For this reason, it may cause offence to Aboriginal people and Torres Strait Islanders if asked, 'What percentage of Aboriginal blood are you?'

Counting the Indigenous population in Australia

In the 2016 Australian census, the Indigenous population was estimated to be 798,365 people. This is about 3.3 per cent of the Australian population. The Australian Bureau of Statistics (ABS), which collects population data, understands that keeping accurate statistics is problematic, because not all Indigenous people fill in the census form and not all enrol to vote. For this reason, the official population is assumed to be an underestimation of the actual number of Indigenous people.

Estimates of the Indigenous population across Australia at the time Britain established its colony in Sydney Cove are between 750,000 and 1 million people.

A national referendum in 1967 overwhelmingly voted to alter the Constitution to allow Indigenous people to be included in the census (see Chapter 11 for more on the referendum). But, before 1971, the census didn't seek to include Indigenous people who lived beyond settled areas. Estimates obtained by authorities responsible for the welfare of Indigenous people were given but accurate numbers weren't available. However, Indigenous people were identified as part of population counts from 1901. This information was collected but Indigenous people 'of more than half blood' weren't included in the official figures.

After declining since the colonisation of Australia began, the national Indigenous population has been steadily climbing since the 1950s. Table 2-1 shows population figures from the ABS.

Indigenous populations had been decimated from the arrival of the British colonists due to the impact of disease, dislocation from traditional country and from food and water supplies, frontier massacres and the separation of families. By 1901, many non-Indigenous Australians assumed that Aboriginal and Torres Strait Islander peoples were dying races. This trend started to reverse in the mid-1950s. Although not all Indigenous people were included in the census figures until after 1967, the increases prior to that suggest the population had already begun to grow.

TABLE 2-1

National Indigenous Population since 1901

Year	National Indigenous Population
1901	93,000
1921	72,000
1933	81,000
1947	76,000
1954	75,000
1961	84,000
1966	102,000
1971	115,953
1976	160,915
1981	159,897
1986	227,645
1991	265,492
1996	386,000
2001	458,500
2006	517,200
2011	548,400
2016	798,365

After 1967, it still took many years to have the total population recorded accurately. Apart from the inclusion of more Indigenous people in the census, the increase in population is attributed to a higher reproduction rate within the Indigenous community, with Indigenous families having more children on average than other Australians. The increase is also linked to more people identifying with their Indigenous ancestry. In 2016, 798,365 people identified at Indigenous. Of that number, 727,485 (91 per cent) identified as Aboriginal, 38,660 (5 per cent) identified as Torres Strait Islander and 32,220 (4 per cent) identified as both Aboriginal and Torres Strait Islander.

REMEMBER

The profile of Aboriginal and Torres Strait Islander communities is much younger than that of the rest of the Australian population. The median age of the Indigenous population is 23; for the total Australian population, it's 37.8. For Aboriginal and Torres Strait Islander populations, 274, 333 are under 15 years of age; 34,012 are over 65 years. This means that Indigenous Australians under 15 are 34 per cent of the Indigenous population (compared to 18 per cent for non-Indigenous Australians) and over 65s are 4 per cent of the Indigenous population (compared with 16 per cent for non-Indigenous Australians).

It is projected that that Indigenous population of Australia will be 1.1 million by 2031.

Locating where Indigenous people live today

Indigenous populations were spread across Australia and the Torres Strait Islands at the time of the establishment of the Sydney Cove colony. But with the spread of settlement, many Aboriginal communities were shifted off their traditional lands and eventually clustered on missions and reserves, the edges of larger towns and in communities within urban areas. Torres Strait Island communities were left largely intact, although the establishment of missions there from 1871 also affected their cultural practices.

Today, although many people imagine that most Indigenous people live in remote communities, the reality is quite different. Of the total Indigenous population, 37.4 per cent live in the cities (the largest Aboriginal community in Australia is in western Sydney), 45 per cent in regional parts of Australia and 17.6 per cent in remote areas.

The Torres Strait Islander population in 2016 was 70,880, about 9 per cent of the total Indigenous population. Only 28 per cent of Torres Strait Islander people live in the Torres Strait, with a large diaspora of Torres Strait Islander people living on the mainland, largely in Queensland but also in other parts of Australia. Torres Strait Islander people finish high school at higher rates than Aboriginal people. They also have higher employment rates and higher household incomes on average than Aboriginal people. And, interestingly, Torres Strait Islander people who actually live in the Torres Strait are more likely to finish high school and be employed than Torres Strait Islanders living in other parts of Australia.

Table 2-2 shows Australia's Indigenous population by state, with the largest Indigenous populations in New South Wales and Queensland. However, in the Northern Territory, Indigenous people are by far the highest percentage of total population compared with other states. Interestingly, Tasmania has a relatively high percentage (given the common misconception that Tasmanian Aboriginal people were wiped out in the 1800s — see Chapters 7 and 25) and Victoria has the lowest.

TABLE 2-2 ## Indigenous Population by State, 2016

State or Territory	Indigenous Population	Total Population	Percentage of Total Population	Percentage of Australian Total Indigenous Population
Australian Capital Territory	7,513	403,104	1.9%	0.9%
New South Wales	265,685	7,732,858	3.4%	33.3%
Northern Territory	74,546	245,678	30.0%	9.3%
Queensland	221,276	4,845,152	4.6%	27.7%
South Australia	42,265	1,712,843	2.5%	5.3%
Tasmania	28,537	517,514	5.5%	3.6%
Victoria	57,767	6,173,172	0.9%	7.2%
Western Australia	100,512	2,555,978	3.9%	12.6%
Total	798,365	24,190,907	3.3%	

Source: All data from the Australian Bureau of Statistics.

MYTH BUSTER

Many people assume that Aboriginal people and Torres Strait Islanders who live in cities are assimilated, losing their connection with community and culture. However, even in the urban areas of Australia, cohesive cultural relationships are strong.

Cultural is seen as important to the wellbeing of Indigenous Australians, according to data from the ABS and contained in the National Aboriginal and Torres Strait Islander Social Survey. It found that, among Indigenous Australians aged 15 years and over:

>> 18 per cent spoke an Indigenous language, another 20 per cent spoke some words of their language, and 11 per cent spoke an Australian Indigenous language at home as their main language (see Chapter 3 for more on languages)

>> 62 per cent of Indigenous people knew the name of the clan they're descended from (79 per cent in remote areas; 58 per cent in other areas)

>> 63 per cent of Indigenous people over 15 years and 70 per cent of children aged between 3 and 14 were involved in cultural events, ceremonies or organisations

>> 31 per cent of Indigenous children aged 3 to 14 years spent at least one day a week with an Indigenous Elder or leader

A Note about the Torres Strait Islands

Possession Island, in the Torres Strait, is where Lieutenant James Cook 'took possession' of the whole of the east coast of Australia 'together with all the . . . islands situated upon the said coast' in 1770, so it was always part of the territory claimed for Britain. However, apart from a few Europeans establishing a pearling industry, the Islanders were left to their own devices until the London Missionary Society established its first mission on Erub (Darnley Island) in 1871. Queensland formally annexed the Torres Strait in 1879, so it was subject to all the laws of that state, even though many of the islands are just off the coast of New Guinea.

Today, each island community elects its own council to run affairs on that island, a product of Queensland legislation in 1939. The administration for the region is based on Thursday Island. Fishing is the main economic activity and many families also have small farms. Pearl shells, turtle shells, feathers and canoes were traditionally bartered with neighbours and this trade still forms a basis for economic activity.

In 1978, Australia and Papua New Guinea signed a treaty to define the boundary between the two countries. (Papua New Guinea had gained its independence from Australia in 1975.) The Torres Strait Islands Treaty allows for the free movement — without visas or passports — of Torres Strait Islanders and people from specific coastal villages in Papua New Guinea for traditional activities such as fishing, hunting, ceremonies and traditional trade within a defined zone of the Torres Strait Islands. Business and employment aren't considered traditional activities under the treaty and some quarantine restrictions apply.

REMEMBER

In 1982, a group of Torres Strait Islanders, including Eddie Mabo, made a claim for native title over their lands on the island of Mer, part of the Murray Islands group in the Torres Strait. The case went all the way to the High Court, succeeding in 1992 and providing a basis for Aboriginal people across Australia to make similar claims for their land. See Chapter 12 for more.

In 1994, a Torres Strait Regional Authority was established to allow Torres Strait Islanders greater ability to manage their own affairs. This body has representatives elected from the islands and allows management of affairs according to *ailan kastom* ('island custom' in Torres Creole). And autonomy for the region is still on the political agenda.

In 2010, Justice Paul Finn of the Federal Court recognised the native title rights of Torres Strait Islanders over about 37,800 square kilometres of sea between the Cape York Peninsula and Papua New Guinea. These rights include the right to access, remain in and use the sea in those areas and to take resources, but not for commercial purposes. The finding doesn't exclude others from using the sea.

Saying G'Day

Many non-Indigenous Australians are confused as to the correct terminology to use when addressing, or talking or writing about, Indigenous people. And that's understandable. Many different terms have been used by and about Indigenous people over the years, some downright offensive, some reflecting changing political attitudes and contexts, and some simply a matter of personal preference.

When you meet and get to know an Indigenous person, the most appropriate thing to do is ask how that person prefers to be described or addressed. Sometimes acknowledgement of a person's race isn't appropriate at all, but if you do need to refer to it, verbally or in writing, it's good to know what may or may not cause offence.

'Aboriginal', 'Torres Strait Islander', 'First Nations' or 'Indigenous'?

Torres Strait Islanders come from the Torres Strait to the north of Cape York in Queensland. The term *Aboriginal* applies to Indigenous people from all other parts of Australia.

The term *Indigenous* is commonly used to encompass both Aboriginal people and Torres Strait Islanders. When writing this term, using a capital 'I' is important — like Greek, Italian or Spanish — to designate that it's a nationality. Always capitalising *Aboriginal* is also important.

The letters *ATSI* are often used in abbreviations of organisations such as the Aboriginal and Torres Strait Islander Commission. However, using *ATSI* as an abbreviation for Aboriginal and Torres Strait Islanders is not acceptable.

Some Aboriginal people don't like the term Indigenous — because it fails to convey diversity — and prefer to be called Aboriginal. This can require the use of the term *Aboriginal people and Torres Strait Islanders* rather than *Indigenous people*. Increasingly, some Indigenous people are using the term *First Nations* to describe their unique relationship between themselves and the Australian state.

Some Aboriginal people prefer the use of the term Aboriginal *peoples*, rather than Aboriginal *people*, because this notes the diversity of Aboriginal cultures across the country. And some Aboriginal people don't like the term *Aboriginal* either. Because it's a European construct (simply a word referring to a country's original people), they prefer to be referred to by their tribe or nation name or by an Aboriginal word (read on).

TIP

If you are addressing or introducing an Aboriginal or Torres Strait Islander person, ask how they would like to referred to. They'll most likely appreciate the opportunity to define themselves rather than having someone do it for them.

'Aboriginal' or 'Aborigine'?

Although 'correct English' would have you believe otherwise, when describing an individual, saying, 'She is an Aboriginal' instead of 'She is an Aborigine', is more acceptable. Generally, Aboriginal people say, 'I am an Aboriginal person', or 'I am Aboriginal', instead of 'I am an Aborigine'. Think of it in terms of the use of the word *Australian*; for example, 'I am an Australian' or 'I am Australian' are quite acceptable in 'correct English'.

Aboriginal people and Torres Strait Islanders generally find the term *native* offensive. And, although Aboriginal and Torres Strait Islander people may call each other *blackfellas*, it's generally not a term used by whitefellas — unless they know those blackfellas really well.

Us mob: Koori, Goori or Murri; Noongar or Nunga?

Across Australia, Aboriginal people refer to themselves using words from Aboriginal languages. These aren't always tribe names but words that translate to terms like *us people*, such as:

>> *Koori*, *Goori* or *Murri*, used in New South Wales

>> *Koori*, used in the Australian Capital Territory

>> *Koorie*, used in Victoria

>> *Noongar* or *Nyoongar*, used in southern Western Australia

>> *Nunga*, used in the southern part of South Australia

>> *Murri*, used in Queensland and northern New South Wales

>> **Palawa**, **Punta** or **Paganna**, used in Tasmania

>> **Yolngu**, used in central and eastern Arnhem Land in the Northern Territory and **Anangu** in Central Australia

In New South Wales, Aboriginal people sometimes refer to white people as *gubbas*. Experts believe this was a corruption of the term *governor*. Another word used to describe white people in the south-east is *wundas*. This is an Aboriginal word for *ghost*. In the Top End of the Northern Territory, white people are sometimes called *balanda* (originally referring to the Hollanders — the Dutch — known to the Macassans who visited the region from Indonesia) and, in the Kimberley, *watjella* (perhaps an aberration of whitefella).

Opening an Event: Welcome to Country

A *welcome to country* is a common protocol whereby the traditional owners welcome people onto their land. *Traditional owners* are those who are acknowledged as being of direct descent of the original custodians of that land. The welcome can take many forms; although usually through a speech, it can also include dance or a smoking ceremony. It's often delivered in traditional language.

The practice of having a welcome to country at public events has become a part of mainstream Australian protocol in the last decade. But Aboriginal people have been practising this custom for thousands of years; they had clear understandings of where the boundaries for their traditional lands were and crossing onto someone else's land required permission — like a visa. In some Aboriginal societies, for example, lighting a fire on the boundary was the custom if you wished to pass over someone else's land. If members of the other group were going to permit you to enter, they'd light a fire in return. Another custom was for gifts to be exchanged as a welcome to country. Permission to enter the land of another group was given with the understanding that that group's rules and protocols would be respected.

Welcome or acknowledgement?

Often times, a traditional owner of the area isn't present at an event to deliver the welcome to country. This means that a welcome to country can't be given because only the traditional owners can give that. Instead, an *acknowledgement of country* is given. This is a way of showing respect for the traditional owners and their relationship to their land.

Not all Indigenous people can give a welcome to country. Indigenous people can give a welcome only on their own traditional land. If they aren't on their traditional lands, they're required to give an acknowledgement of country.

What do I say?

Many Australians and visitors deliver an acknowledgement of country before they begin the business of the event. A simple form of words for an acknowledgement of country would be

I acknowledge that I am on the land of [insert name of traditional owners] and pay my respects to their Elders past and present.

Or

I would like to acknowledge that the traditional lands that we are meeting on today are the lands of the [insert name of traditional owners] and pay my respects to their spiritual relationship with this country. I acknowledge their cultural beliefs and heritage and that they are the custodians of this land.

If the traditional owners aren't known, a generic acknowledgement is acceptable:

I acknowledge the original inhabitants of this land, the traditional owners, and pay my respect to their Elders past and present.

Or

I would like to acknowledge that this meeting is being held on Aboriginal land and recognise the strength, resilience and capacity of Aboriginal people in this land.

Or

We acknowledge and respect the traditional custodians whose ancestral land we are meeting on today. We acknowledge the deep feelings of attachment that Aboriginal people have to country.

Acknowledgement of country sometimes also includes an acknowledgement that this land and/or sovereignty was never ceded. See Chapter 22 for more on these ideas of sovereignty.

Whose land am I on?

Because no maps were drawn up in 1788 and so many Aboriginal nations were dispossessed in the following decades, exactly who the traditional owners of a particular area are and what its actual boundaries were isn't always clear — and sometimes disputes arise. However, even in the cities, traditional owners are identified.

Here's a list of some of the prominent language groups in the capital cities:

>> **Adelaide:** You're on the land of the Kaurna people.

>> **Brisbane:** You're on land of the Turrbal or the Jagera (also spelled Yuggera) people.

>> **Canberra:** You're on the land of the Ngunnawal people.

>> **Darwin:** You're on the land of the Larrakia people.

>> **Hobart:** You're on the land of the Nuenonne people.

>> **Melbourne:** You're on the land of the Wurundjeri people of the Kulin nation.

>> **Perth:** You're on the land of the Noongar people.

>> **Sydney:** You're on the land of the Gadigal people of the Eora nation. (This is only in the CBD area — it's a big city! The Eora nation is made up of 29 clans in total.)

One way to find out the traditional owners of a particular place is to check the website of the local Aboriginal and Torres Strait Islander organisations, particularly the land council. The website of the local council will often have information about the local Aboriginal community. In New South Wales, you can also phone the local Aboriginal Land Council; in the Northern Territory, you can contact the Northern Land Council or the Central Land Council; in north Queensland, the Cape York Land Council; in the north of Western Australia, the Kimberley Land Council. Land councils, as such, don't exist in every state but some Indigenous cultural organisations may be able to assist.

TIP

Another way to find the traditional owners is to check the *Aboriginal Australia* map published by the Australian Institute of Aboriginal and Torres Strait Islander Studies (AIATSIS). It's a large map and by no means easy to read in this format, but this gives you an idea of just how many nations and clans have existed. To purchase a copy of the map, go to the website at www.aiatsis.gov.au (under the Explore tab, click on the A Map of Diversity option).

REMEMBER

Indigenous languages were oral languages so correct spellings didn't exist. That's why more than one spelling of an Aboriginal nation or a Torres Strait Island people is often used. Variations in pronunciation among similar dialects also add to the confusion. For example, the Sydney people are the Gadigal people, also sometimes spelled Gaddigal or Cadigal.

Defining the Identity of an Aboriginal Person or a Torres Strait Islander

Governments have tried to define Aboriginal peoples and Torres Strait Islanders in order to determine whether they should be subject to certain laws and regulations. In the past, this practice has been mostly to control Indigenous people — where they could live, whether they could marry and whether their children should be removed.

But, however governments defined Aboriginality in the past and however they treated Aboriginal people and Torres Strait Islanders, Indigenous people have their own way of defining themselves. Identity is a product of family history and experience, languages and heritage, treatment by the rest of society and acceptance by the Indigenous community as being an Aboriginal person or a Torres Strait Islander. Aboriginality for Aboriginal people and Torres Strait Islanders is much more about their relationships than their percentage of blood.

The definition of Aboriginal people and Torres Strait Islanders for official purposes has changed over time. Although three criteria are used today (refer to the section 'Defining who is an Indigenous person', earlier in this chapter), for decades, definitions were based on percentages of blood. 'Full-bloods' and 'half-castes' were treated very differently. From 1910 to the 1940s, people were defined as 'full-blood' if they had no white blood, 'half-caste' if they had one white parent, a 'quadroon' or 'quarter-caste' if they had an Indigenous grandfather or grandmother or an 'octoroon' if their great-grandmother or great-grandfather was Indigenous. Today, these terms are considered offensive and racist by Indigenous people.

Proposals that genetic testing be used to identify who is Indigenous have been rejected on the grounds that race and ethnicity are social, cultural and political constructs so can't be tested in this manner.

ABORIGINAL OR NOT?

Consistency wasn't always a hallmark of how Aboriginal people were treated. In 1996, at the Aboriginal Citizenship Conference in Canberra, historian Peter Read described the experiences of one Aboriginal person who was caught between two worlds:

> In 1935, a fair-skinned Aboriginal man of part-Indigenous heritage was ejected from a hotel for being Aboriginal. He returned home on the mission station to find himself refused entry because he was not Aboriginal. He tried to remove his children but could not because he was told they were Aboriginal. He walked to the next town where he was arrested for being an Aboriginal vagrant and placed on the local reserve. During World War II he tried to enlist but was told he could not because he was Aboriginal. He went interstate and joined up as a non-Aboriginal. After the war he could not acquire a passport without permission because he was Aboriginal. He received exemption from the Aborigines Protection Act — and was told he could no longer visit his relations on the reserve because he was not Aboriginal. He was denied entry to the RSL Club because he was Aboriginal.

This example shows how people could be refused access to services or other opportunities because they were Aboriginal, while also being controlled in other ways because they were 'not Aboriginal enough'.

Even when these barriers have been overcome by changing the laws, discrimination can be encountered. For example, a law now exists that prohibits landlords from refusing to rent places to people simply because they're Indigenous. However, Indigenous people in some areas still find renting a house hard because they're always turned down and told that a place is unsuitable or it went to someone else. In some instances, to prove that the basis of the discrimination is actually their race, Indigenous people have gone into a real estate office and asked if rental accommodation was available. After being told nothing was available, they have sent a white relative in to ask the same question, with that person handed a list of available houses. This circumstance is a breach of the law but that doesn't stop practices of discrimination from occurring.

Stereotypes of Indigenous people

Stereotypes are caricatures of a group of people — usually races or nationalities — that oversimplify and assert that those people display certain inherent characteristics. They're usually negative and, because they generalise and are meant unkindly, are usually considered offensive.

Indigenous culture is seen as positive for tourism. Overseas visitors are interested in learning more about Indigenous cultures, and Aboriginal peoples and Torres

Strait Islanders and their cultures feature prominently in tourism commercials and other material. On the other hand, Indigenous people hear many negative comments from people who don't really know them.

MYTH BUSTER

These negative stereotypes have no correlation to the lived experiences of the vast majority of Indigenous people. Although some Indigenous communities have social problems, these generalisations — that Indigenous people are lazy and don't want to work, that they're alcoholics, that they're violent — are inaccurate and offensive. Table 2-3 looks at the reality of some of these labels. See Chapter 25 for more on these and other myths about Indigenous people.

TABLE 2-3 **Negative Stereotypes versus Reality**

The Negative Stereotype	The Reality
Indigenous people are lazy and don't want to work.	Indigenous people are successful in areas as diverse as medicine, design and architecture, art, law, the public service and stockbroking.
Indigenous cultures are primitive and violent.	Indigenous cultures teach positive values like respect for country and respect for Elders. They frown on violence, especially against women and children. These are the world's oldest living cultures.
Indigenous people, especially in the cities, have lost their culture.	Indigenous people, even in the cities, retain the positive values of their culture and keep cultural practices alive and vibrant.
Indigenous people get more than whites.	Indigenous people have poorer health, lower levels of education, lower life expectancy, higher levels of poverty and lower incomes than other Australians. They don't get free houses and free cars.
Indigenous people are alcoholics.	Problems with alcohol are experienced within Indigenous communities but the communities themselves are at the forefront of dealing with this social problem. Many have banned alcohol from their communities and have community-based programs to deal with alcohol abuse and its associated problems. Per capita, more Indigenous people are teetotallers than are white people.

REMEMBER

Stereotypes aren't always negative. Positive stereotypes are caricatures that over-simplify and assert positive characteristics. Some positive stereotypes made about Indigenous people describe them as a kind of 'noble savage' — that they're very spiritual, untouched by materialism, in touch with nature and telepathic, with the ability to communicate with animals! Most people find these positive stereotypes just as offensive as negative stereotypes because, even though they're not meant unkindly, they're still generalisations, so are misleading and untrue.

But some of us have blond hair and blue eyes!

Some Aboriginal people from mixed heritage are very light-skinned. Some even have blond hair and blue eyes! This means that they aren't easily identified as Aboriginal people by non-Indigenous people.

Some Aboriginal people find speculation about their genetics offensive — and understandably so. In the past genetics was explored only so it could be used to prove theories of white racial superiority. Some Australians say that light-skinned Aboriginal people aren't 'real' Aboriginal people or that they just choose to be Aboriginal people because they can get benefits or it's trendy. These views don't appreciate the complexity of Aboriginal and Torres Strait Islander identities.

For Aboriginal people, their heritage is not just about skin colour. Their Aboriginality is also defined by their feeling part of the Aboriginal community and the Aboriginal community accepting them as Aboriginal as well. These additional aspects of being Aboriginal are recognised by the three criteria now used to define Aboriginality (refer to the section 'Defining who is an Indigenous person', earlier in this chapter). As Indigenous woman Georgia Mantle has written: 'To me, my culture is not surprising . . . it is simply an intrinsic part of who I am. My Aboriginal identity is not represented through my pale skin, but rather through my very essence and being.'

Chapter **3**

A Land of Cultural Diversity

Concepts of ownership didn't exist in traditional Indigenous societies in the same way as they did in European cultures. Aboriginal people and Torres Strait Islanders thought of their relationship to the land as being more like one of guardianship than that of a landlord or owner. They believe they had — and continue to have — an obligation to their traditional land. To have the world's oldest living culture, surviving over 65,000 years, they must be doing a lot of things right!

This strong attachment to traditional country is an inherent characteristic of Aboriginal and Torres Strait Islander cultures across Australia. But across the diverse landscapes and ecosystems of the Australian continent were rich and varied nations. More than 500 different Aboriginal nations or language groups flourished, and their diversity of lifestyle was often shaped by the local environment.

Aboriginal nations living in coastal areas had a different way of surviving than those living in the desert. Though spread out across the country, Indigenous groups still connected with each other. Through ceremonies and trade, they maintained links with each other, and these trade routes and songlines spanned the whole country.

In this chapter, I explore those special relationships between Indigenous people and their country, and with each other. I also look at the kinship systems that various groups maintained to assist their social and cultural cohesion, as well as the different languages and dialects that existed across the country — and which of them have survived.

REMEMBER

With over 500 different nations and language groups, a lot of diversity exists across Australia. Within any general discussion about Aboriginal and Torres Strait Islander peoples, this diversity and nuance must be kept in mind.

Exploring the Indigenous Relationship to Land

Indigenous people have a strong attachment to their land. They had — and retain — a strong spiritual relationship with it, as well as relying on it for their food, shelter and livelihood. Indigenous societies didn't entertain concepts of ownership commonplace among European cultures. Their relationship to the land was more one of custodianship than of ownership. In other words, the relationship of Indigenous people to their traditional land was defined by their responsibilities to that land. Indigenous people believed they had responsibility to look after their country, to conduct particular ceremonies and to ensure that the ecosystems were kept in balance. And these responsibilities still exist today.

For Indigenous cultures across Australia, land means more than just something that's essential for physical survival, with spiritual life strongly linked to it too. In this way, ancestral land had personal significance, with each person obliged to look after it. Other people's land had no meaning to someone who was a stranger to it, and conflicts over the boundaries of where one nation's land ended and another's began were rare. Some land was shared between different groups because of its spiritual or ecological importance but, generally, a nation or clan had sole responsibility for each area of country.

CULTURAL
PROTOCOLS

The relationship where Indigenous people believe they are guardians of their country is very different from European concepts of ownership of land, where it can be bought and sold, transferring it from one owner to the next.

Oral title deeds

Indigenous cultures were oral. Attachment to the land was expressed through song, art, dance and painting. People 'inherited' stories and songs, and became their keepers, eventually passing them down to the following generations. Boundaries of tribal areas are fixed and are explained in these cultural stories. Through this storytelling, ancestral land was passed on to younger generations, along with the responsibility to care for this country. Knowledge created an obligation to protect the land, respect the past, not exploit the land's resources, take responsibility for passing the country on to future generations and maintain the religious ceremonies that needed to be performed there.

Accessing another's country

Entry onto the traditional land of another nation or clan was by ceremony and negotiation. A visiting group had to, in return, allow access to or through its lands. This protocol is still seen today in the practice of acknowledging or welcoming outsiders onto country (refer to Chapter 2). These ceremonies symbolise the attachment to the land and the commitment to protect it. Special religious significance is attached to the resting places of great ancestors. These are sacred sites that have importance for women as well as men. In this way, the landscape was richly symbolic for the Indigenous people who lived upon it.

Mythical stories dictated appropriate modes of behaviour and set standards. In this way, mythical beings were lawmakers. These collectively affirmed standards were enforced by applying social pressure to ensure conformity. Children were taught acceptable modes of behaviour through cultural stories and were taught by example rather than by the strict discipline used to rear European children.

Celebrating Cultural Diversity

Aboriginal values and worldviews had similarities right across the country but, as would be expected for such a large continent, regional differences occurred between different clans and nations. Torres Strait Islander values and worldviews are similar to those of Aboriginal people on the mainland but are also influenced by interaction with other cultures such as the Papuans. Differences in language, art, cultural and religious practices, and social order occurred around the country, especially between different climatic regions.

REMEMBER

Australia is a vast but dry continent, and much of its interior is desert. But it's surrounded by coastline and has river systems and pockets of lush rainforest. Aboriginal people lived across the continent, in every corner and climate. They adapted to survive in different environments, by using different plants and food sources, and taking advantage of varying conditions. The Torres Strait Islands lie between the Cape York Peninsula and Papua New Guinea. The culture of the Torres Strait Islanders is defined by their heavy reliance on the sea.

CULTURAL
PROTOCOLS

An example of the different cultures throughout the country is that didgeridoos weren't played across Australia. These wind instruments were traditionally played only in the north of Australia, from Cape York in the east and Arnhem Land in the Top End of the Northern Territory, to the Kimberley in the north-west. And they were played only by men. The didgeridoo's first appearance in rock art is from a period about 2,000 years ago, leading archaeologists and anthropologists to speculate that this is when the instrument was first invented. It's now played by people across Australia — black and white — and appears in many contemporary musical forms, from country music to opera. See Chapter 4 for more on didgeridoos and Chapter 17 for information about Indigenous music.

CULTURAL
PROTOCOLS

The iconic dot painting style wasn't universally used across Australia but was specific to the areas of the Central and Western Deserts in the middle of Australia. This style of painting is now integrated into contemporary art by practising Indigenous artists across the country. See Chapter 16 for more on traditional art styles.

Clans and nations

Nations were large language groups and *clans* were smaller extended family groups within the nation. Each clan had its own territory and totems, and sometimes its own dialect of the common language of the nation. Although a clan had its own territory, members of one clan could live with another. Women who left their clan's country to live with their husband's clan retained their clan association with their father.

CULTURAL
PROTOCOLS

Nations share a common bond and language. Often, within that language the word for 'man' or 'person' is often the word used for the nation. For example, in Arnhem Land, people are from the Yolngu nation and the name for 'man' in their language is yolngu.

More than 500 different nations

Estimates of the number of nations and clans that existed at the time the Sydney Cove colony was established vary. The exact number wasn't known at the time — especially because the British didn't know how big Australia was and thought some of the middle of the country might be filled with an inland sea. Nor did they have a deep understanding of the complex governance structures within Indigenous communities and their complex relationships with each other. However, the commonly agreed estimate of the number of nations around Australia when the British arrived is between 500 and 600.

REMEMBER

An exact number of clans and nations is difficult to arrive at because anthropologists often can't agree on whether a group was a clan or a nation. In some instances, identified clans that were classified as a subgroup of one nation now claim they're a separate nation, not a clan. The most commonly accepted and used map of the nations of Aboriginal Australia was developed by the Australian Institute of Aboriginal and Torres Strait Islander Studies (AIATSIS). Chapter 2 explains how to get a copy.

MYTH
BUSTER

The impact of colonisation on Aboriginal people was so dramatic and their populations decreased so rapidly that by the early 1900s many people assumed that Aboriginal people would eventually die out. In several parts of Australia, particular nations or clans were assumed to have died out. For example, the last Aboriginal Tasmanian was long thought to have died in 1876, which was not the case, as the myriad Tasmanian traditional owners now attest (refer to Chapter 2 for population statistics). In many of these instances, Aboriginal people had survived but moved to other places for sanctuary — to survive. They can today identify their nation or clan and its traditional lands and trace their heritage back to them.

CULTURAL
PROTOCOLS

In the city of Sydney, local Aboriginal clans include the Gadigal and Dharuk people of the Eora nation. In the city of Melbourne, the local Aboriginal clan is the Wurundjeri people of the Kulin nation.

Freshwater people and saltwater people

Another distinction exists among Indigenous nations. Even today, Aboriginal people sometimes distinguish themselves as *freshwater* or *saltwater* people — that is, whether they live by the rivers inland or by the sea in coastal areas. Each has a very different style of living. Torres Strait Islanders, of course, are all saltwater people.

Aboriginal people on the coast were skilled at fishing and used their sea environment and its marine life to assist their survival. Technology to build boats and nets, as well as spears for fishing, developed in these areas. Shells, fish bones and turtle shells were used to assist with the making of these tools. Marine life was also integrated into cultural stories: Turtles, dugongs, crocodiles and different fish all have a presence in the stories and ceremonies of the Aboriginal people and Torres Strait Islanders living off the sea.

Aboriginal people living in the desert also learned how to navigate their environment. For example, people had to remember carefully the location of waterholes and other sources of water; people also dug wells to access water supplies. Knowledge of where these watering spots were located was reinforced through stories and songs. In many desert areas, few, if any, trees exist. Technology was adapted so that spears were made from the long roots of plants, rather than tree branches. Interestingly, the Warlpiri language doesn't have any words for saltwater things such as ocean and waves. As desert people, the words in their language relate to their local area.

Kinship and Totemic Systems

For Aboriginal peoples on the mainland, another important distinction between people existed. The members of a particular nation or clan knew their relationships to others and the universe through their position in the kinship system of that particular group, and then through their identification with specific totems.

For many Aboriginal people, especially those in remote communities that still adhere to traditional law and culture, these kinship systems are still very important. Even in urban communities, relationships, and therefore roles and responsibilities, between people are crucial to social cohesion. And many educated and urban-dwelling Aboriginal people know their skin names and totems.

Moieties and skin names

Moieties (from a Latin word meaning half, definitely not an Aboriginal word!) are a form of kinship system where the people of a nation or clan were divided into two groups. Moieties can be determined by the mother's side (*matrilineal*), from the father's side (*patrilineal*) or can alternate between each generation (*generational*). Each person belonged to one or the other moiety. This was important when it came to marriage, because a person had to marry someone who was the other moiety to them; otherwise, it was considered a 'wrong-way' marriage.

Often, the moieties were then divided into four to eight different kinship groups that designated a specific name for all members of each group — called *kinship names* or *skin names*. These names identified individuals as a member of that kinship group, sometimes with different names for male and female members of the group. Skin names are given at birth, according to the mother's skin name, along with other names. The subsections further identified different relationships within the clan or nation, such as mother to child, or uncle to nephew or niece, or potential marriage partners.

TECHNICAL STUFF

To illustrate how kinships systems work, take, for example, the Kukatja people of Wirrumanu (Balgo) in Western Australia. Here, people with the skin name of Napurrula (female) and Tjupurrula (male) can marry Tjapanangka and Napanangka respectively for a 'straight-skin' marriage. Their children would be Tjapangarti (male) and Napangarti (female), and the children's 'straight-skin' marriage partners would be Nampitjin and Tjampitjin respectively. Napangarti's children would be Tjangala (male) and Nangala (female); Nampitjin's children would be Tjapanangka or Napanangka. And this covers only the basic relationships between six of the eight groups of the Kukatja kinship system. Examining all eight groups identifies all the relationships, and their inherent roles, obligations and responsibilities, across a complex social system. Similar skin names exist in many language groups across Central Australia.

CULTURAL PROTOCOLS

In Aboriginal cultures across Australia, social restrictions exist between some members of a particular group. For example, a man is banned from talking directly to his mother-in-law. Communication would take place through a third party and a mother-in-law would have a separate fire to her son-in-law and his spouse, with the daughter bringing over food. Some think this protocol developed as a way to reduce friction in families!

Some clans or nations used both moieties and subsections; some just one or the other. Pitjantjatjara people, for example, only use moieties. These moieties and skin names give each person their totems (see the next section). Figure 3-1 shows the relationship between these elements.

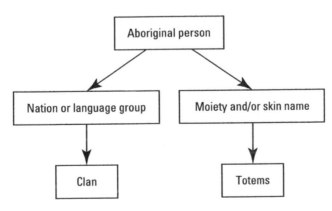

FIGURE 3-1: Geographic organisation is based on language groups, or nations, with social and spiritual organisation based on a kinship system.

DHUWA DREAMING

The Yolngu people of north-eastern Arnhem Land are one of two moieties, Dhuwa and Yirritja, which are then further divided into four skin names for each gender, making eight skin names in all. For people of the Dhuwa moiety, a particular Dreaming story is important. The story concerns the Djang'kawu, who were the major creators of all things Dhuwa. Arriving from heaven in a canoe, the Djang'kawu sisters set off to walk across the land carrying digging sticks. When the sisters touched the ground with these sticks, they created the water, trees, animals and all other features of the Earth. The sisters were always pregnant and their children populated the Earth.

Totems

In addition to their position within the kinship system, Indigenous people have totems. A *totem* is an animal, plant or other object believed to be ancestrally related to a person. People considered themselves to be descended from a totem — they wouldn't eat the meat of any animal of their own totem, for example, and would have to ensure that animal's population was sustained. A totem can also be represented in nature in the form of a large rock, tree, hill, river or other landform.

Indigenous people have three totems:

>> A clan totem that links a person to other people

>> A family or personal totem that links a person to the natural world

>> A spiritual totem that links a person to the universe

Through these totems, Indigenous people realised how they were connected with other people, their land and ancestors, and the universe. Figure 3-2 shows typical totems for a specific individual. The interconnectedness of the natural and the spiritual world with people gave importance to totems as a source of Indigenous identity.

CULTURAL PROTOCOLS

Indigenous people believe they're related to their totems — for example, that their ancestors were mythical beings who had the features of, or became, particular animals or trees.

REMEMBER

Much of Indigenous art is connected with the imagery of totems. Paintings tell stories of ancestral beings that may relate to a totem. Clans have a distinct pattern or marking that may appear in paintings as well. See Chapter 16 for more on Indigenous art.

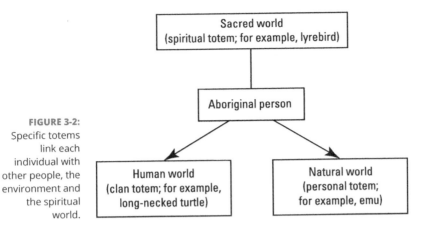

FIGURE 3-2:
Specific totems
link each
individual with
other people, the
environment and
the spiritual
world.

Talking Languages

Indigenous people were skilled linguists. Many people spoke at least two or three languages, often five or more. Some languages were similar — in the same way that Spanish and Italian are — so learning a new language was easy. Others were different so required more skill to learn. Each nation had its own language and often clans would have a regional variation of it. Experts estimate that about 250 broad language groups (some incorporating more than one nation) were in use at the time the Sydney Cove colony was established.

REMEMBER

Aboriginal and Torres Strait Islander cultures had an oral tradition, with nothing written down, explaining why different spellings of Indigenous words are common today, even for the names of Aboriginal nations.

Who speaks what now?

Australians speak more than 400 languages. In 2014, the second National Indigenous Languages Survey found that around 120 of the over 250 Australian Indigenous languages were still spoken. That was down from 145 languages when the first survey was undertaken in 2004. Of those, 100 languages are critically endangered, and 13 were considered strong (still spoken by all age groups and passed down to children). During the period between the two surveys, 30 languages had seen an increase in levels of use, showing a regeneration of Indigenous languages in some parts of Australia.

The 2016 Australian Census showed that 63,754 or, around 10 per cent, of people who identified as Indigenous people reported speaking an Indigenous language at home. For some Indigenous people, English is their second or third language.

The largest Indigenous language groups (not including the various hybrid languages, or *creoles*) are:

>> Tiwi (2,020 speakers), Tiwi Islands

>> Djambarrpuyngu (4,264 speakers), north-east Arnhem Land

>> Pitjantjatjara (3,054 speakers), northern South Australia and into Western Australia

>> Warlpiri (2,276 speakers), north of Alice Springs

>> Noongar/Nyungar (443), south-west Western Australia

>> Wiradjuri (432), central New South Wales

>> Ngarrindjeri (302), south-east of Adelaide

Here's the breakdown of Torres Strait Islander language speakers:

>> Kalaw Kawaw Ya, also spelled Kala Lagaw Ya (1,216 speakers), central and western islands, with four dialects, including Mabuiag

>> Meriam Mir (212 speakers), eastern islands

>> Torres Strait Creole (5,800 speakers) across the islands

>> Other Torres Strait languages (463 speakers)

Vulnerability of languages

Sadly, many Indigenous languages have died out and more continue to be endangered. Of the 120 Indigenous languages spoken today, 100 are listed as 'critically endangered'. This alarming figure has led to the creation of several programs to save languages and for Indigenous publishing houses to concentrate on the publication of materials that foster familiarity with Indigenous languages, such as teaching resources and bilingual books (check out Chapter 18 for details about Indigenous literature and publishing).

Language centres have also been established to promote language in some Indigenous communities. Some of these projects include

>> **Diwurruwurru-Jaru Aboriginal Corporation (Katherine Regional Aboriginal Language Centre**, www.kathlangcentre.org.au): Established in 1992, the centre supports the needs of 32 language groups across 15 major communities in the middle of the Northern Territory.

BILINGUAL EDUCATION

Indigenous children who speak an Indigenous language as their first language can struggle in English-only schools and fall behind in their learning compared with students who speak English as their first language. For this reason, some communities, particularly in the Northern Territory, have developed bilingual educational models. They run a proven, effective model, where teachers learn the local languages and then use those languages to teach English. These bilingual educational models are resource-intensive and not often supported by the government.

>> **Federation of Aboriginal and Torres Strait Islander Languages and Culture** (www.fatsilc.org.au): FATSILC is the national peak body for community-based language programs in Australia. It promotes the maintenance, preservation and revival of Aboriginal and Torres Strait Islander languages and culture.

>> **Muurrbay Aboriginal Language and Culture Co-operative** (www.muurrbay.org.au): The Gumbaynggirr Elders of the Many Rivers area on the northern coast of New South Wales started this cooperative to revive and maintain language and culture in that area. It publishes language dictionaries and teaching materials and supports the Many Rivers Language Centre, which helps those reviving languages from the Tweed to the Hawkesbury Rivers.

>> **Yuwaalaraay gaay–Gamilaraay garay Language Project** (www.yuwaalaraay.org): This project focuses on recording, teaching and preserving Aboriginal languages in the north-west of New South Wales. The project has produced dictionaries and other resources, including CDs and songbooks and online interactive teaching materials.

>> **Bundjalung-Yugambeh Dictionary** (bundjalung.dalang.com.au): This project has been set up to revitalise the language of the Bundjalung community in northern New South Wales and southern Queensland. It includes a dictionary and teaching materials.

>> **Wiradjuri Language** (www.wiradjuri-language.com): This site aims to help to regenerate the Wiradjuri language of central New South Wales, complementing the work of Elder, Stan Grant Snr.

CULTURAL PROTOCOLS

English as a second language for Indigenous people who speak their own language has always been a challenge when they're in court. In the past, many Indigenous people have been convicted of offences when they've been unable to understand what's going on, including the crime they're charged with. These days, courts are supposed to make sure that interpreters of Indigenous languages are available for Indigenous people charged with offences.

Coming Together

Indigenous nations and clans came together for large gatherings and ceremonies on a regular basis but no sense of a national identity had emerged. That came after colonisation when Aboriginal peoples and Torres Strait Islanders joined together at a national level for a stronger political and cultural voice.

REMEMBER

Aboriginal nations and clans had strong networks with each other across the country. These networks were often based on trade. They were also a way in which kin relationships were reinforced. Cultural and spiritual practices also connected nations across the country. People came together to perform ceremonies and exchange stories and songs. A great deal of contact also existed between Aboriginal nations of north Queensland and Torres Strait Islanders, as it does today.

Trade routes

Not surprisingly, Indigenous peoples traded with each other. With established practices of exchange between clans and between nations, trade routes developed around the country. Goods — stones, tools, ochres, shells and fish bones — could find their way from the north of the continent all the way to the south, or travel from the east across to the west. Trade also required people of different clans and nations to respect each other's territorial boundaries. Trade links connected nations right across Australia.

Changes in sea levels sometimes provided new opportunities for exchange. While Australia was an isolated continent, evidence of contact, such as tools, whale bones and shells, between the Torres Strait Islanders and peoples of mainland Australia exists, as well as evidence of contact between the peoples of the Torres Strait and Papua and Indonesia. Finding bones of animals from the northern parts of Australia used in the southern parts, or shells from coastal areas used in the desert, was evidence of trading across large areas of country and by many different nations.

REMEMBER

When Tasmania was cut off from mainland Australia by rising sea levels 11,000 years ago, the Aboriginal people living there became very isolated and lived without contact with the outside world.

Songlines

Tools and cultural items weren't the only things that travelled across the country. In an intricate network of routes that followed the relationships between different nations, ideas, songs and ceremonies were also exchanged.

These routes of cultural exchange are often referred to as *songlines*. These routes would often track the journeys of ancestral beings (Dreaming tracks) and were recorded in traditional songs, painting and dance. A songline could span several nations or language groups.

CULTURAL PROTOCOLS

Songlines are complex cultural connections that are not easily translated into western concepts. A great way to find out more when travelling to different parts of Australia is to go on a cultural tour with a local Aboriginal or Torres Strait Islander guide.

Maintaining Links to Traditional Country

Today, Aboriginal peoples and Torres Strait Islanders maintain their connection to the land in many ways, even if their traditional lifestyles have disappeared or changed. They have maintained this connection through organisations such as land councils and through schemes to buy back control of land. Co-management of natural environments through agreements over national parks is another way in which Indigenous peoples have kept a meaningful connection with their traditional lands. Here are just some of the ways these connections are kept alive:

>> **Ranger programs:** Aboriginal and Torres Strait Islanders across the country are caring for their traditional country through ranger programs. They use a

blend of cultural knowledge and modern technologies to keep the country, waterways and seas healthy and assist in preserving the diversity of ecosystem, flora and fauna. They also undertake important biosecurity work.

>> **Engaging in ecotourism:** As a way to provide an economic base for their communities, some Indigenous people run cultural centres, tour groups that focus on art (such as dance and storytelling performances) or bush tucker, and even luxury resorts at such places as Uluru and Kakadu.

>> **Hunting, gathering and fishing:** Many Indigenous people supplement their diet by hunting, fishing and collecting bush tucker (see Chapter 4 for more on traditional bush foods). Traditional land, waterways and seas, where Indigenous people have some form of land tenure (see Chapter 12), allow Indigenous people to hunt and fish particular species, for personal or community consumption, that are otherwise protected.

>> **Maintaining obligations to care for country:** Some communities partner with government to manage national parks. As mentioned, many Indigenous people are also employed as rangers in national parks and reserves.

>> **Practising ceremonies:** Many different ceremonies are still practised, including welcomes to country (refer to Chapter 2), smoking and *sorry business* (funeral) ceremonies and ceremonies on sacred sites.

Aboriginal land councils

In most states and territories, some tracts of land have been granted back to Aboriginal peoples or Torres Strait Islanders. Sometimes, these grants have restrictions on land use but, in other circumstances, Indigenous people are able to use the land as they wish. This use can be for cultural and ecological purposes (such as performing ceremonies), for hunting, gathering and fishing, or for preserving the environment. Other uses are for economic or community purposes, such as development, tourism, business, community centres and housing.

The return of land rights under land rights legislation is usually done through Aboriginal land councils, organisations through which Aboriginal people can hold, own and manage their interests in land. The largest land council in Australia is the New South Wales Aboriginal Land Council, with more than 23,000 members. This body is statewide but has a network of more than 120 local Aboriginal land councils as part of its structure. With the council executive elected by the Aboriginal members, it's the largest representative body of Aboriginal people.

Other key land councils are the Northern Land Council and Central Land Council in the Northern Territory, the Kimberley Land Council in the north of Western Australia, and Carpentaria Land Council and Cape York Land Council in north Queensland. (For more information on land councils, see Chapter 12.)

Indigenous Land and Sea Corporation

The Indigenous Land and Sea Corporation was established by the federal government to buy land and invest in projects that assist with economic development in Aboriginal communities. It was established in 1995 as part of the government's response to the Mabo native title case brought to the High Court by Torres Strait Islanders, including Eddie Mabo (see Chapter 12). The fund was set up to compensate Indigenous peoples who had been dispossessed so long ago that they could no longer claim native title.

Projects funded by the Indigenous Land and Sea Corporation have included

>> In partnership with the federal government, listing more than 38 Indigenous Protected Areas, covering more than 23 million hectares, where arrangements are in place to ensure Aboriginal involvement in protection of sacred sites, management decisions and employment opportunities, particularly as rangers

>> Jumbun Farm in Queensland, a 244-hectare property that supports a community of 130 Aboriginal people, 26 houses, a community store and a health centre

>> Purchase of the National Black Theatre site in Redfern, Sydney, to be used by local Aboriginal radio and other community organisations (see Chapter 12 for more on Redfern and Chapter 19 for more on the Black Theatre)

>> A commercial fishing venture to support the Ngarrindjeri owned Kuti Co in South Australia, to harvest small clams known as pipis

>> The Kakadu Plum Project, which supports the Indigenous community to engage in commercial harvesting of this unique and highly nutritious food

National parks

Thousands of national parks and other conservation reserves exist in Australia. They protect a huge variety of environments — from deserts to rainforests, and from coral reefs to eucalypt woodlands. Co-management arrangements often include

>> Community involvement in decisions

>> Employment and training as rangers and guides

>> Identification and preservation of sacred sites

Almost all national parks have an Indigenous program and Indigenous rangers so you can find out more about the local environment and its Indigenous history by taking a cultural tour.

SHARING THE RICHES OF ULURU

In November 1983, the Hawke Government announced the title for Uluru-Kata Tjuta National Park (Uluru is also known as Ayers Rock but the park also includes Kata Tjuta, also known as the Olgas) would be handed back to the traditional owners. (The official handover ceremony was held on 26 October 1985.) The traditional owners then leased the land back to the Australian National Parks and Wildlife Service, now the Australian Nature Conservation Agency (ANCA). The traditional owners work jointly with ANCA on the planning and management of the park. This includes managing contemporary use of the park by Aboriginal people, protection of sites of cultural significance and nature conservation.

The Indigenous Land Corporation recently bought the Yulara resort near Uluru. The purchase included all the hotels, tourist and staff accommodation, and the airport. The purchase meant the return of 104,000 hectares of culturally significant freehold land to the traditional owners, the Anangu, who play a continuing role in operating and managing the resort. The Anangu already co-manage the Uluru-Kata Tjuta National Park, which attracts more than 300,000 visitors every year. The purchase of the Yulara resort by the Aboriginal community allows for the provision of a cultural and environmental tourism experience at Uluru-Kata Tjuta National Park. It will also provide jobs and training for Aboriginal people in the local area.

The relationship between the Aboriginal community and tourists hasn't always been an easy one. Climbing the rock was a popular tourist activity but the traditional owners found this offensive, and a desecration of a sacred site. They lobbied to have walking on the rock banned and, on 26 October 2019, the 34th anniversary of the Uluru handback, the climb was officially closed.

CARING FOR COUNTRY, CARING FOR SEA

GhostNets Australia (www.ghostnets.com.au) is an alliance of 22 Aboriginal communities surrounding the Gulf of Carpentaria that retrieve fishing nets that have been discarded at sea, largely from South-East Asia. These 'ghost nets' still trap fish and other marine life, destroying species and habitats. The program has recently been extended across the northern coastline to the Kimberley. The project has removed over 14,000 nets across approximately 1,500 kilometres of coastline, saving some of the trapped marine life. The majority of the animals trapped (52 per cent) are turtles. The rest are predominantly sharks, as well as crocodiles, fish, sea snakes and dugongs. The Aboriginal communities involved see the program as just one way in which they can care for and meet their responsibilities to look after their coastal environment.

IN THIS CHAPTER

» Listening to traditional storytelling

» Appreciating Indigenous outlooks

» Understanding the hunting and gathering lifestyle of Indigenous peoples

» Examining the technology used by Indigenous peoples

» Looking at modern values

Chapter **4**

Traditional Cultural Values and Practices

The relationship that Aboriginal peoples and Torres Strait Islanders had — and continue to have — with their land created particular worldviews and sets of values. The need to survive in a hunter-gatherer lifestyle gave rise to a heavy reliance on the natural environment and the other members of the clan. With this came a strong belief in the importance of reciprocity and interconnectedness.

Indigenous people became very attuned to the world around them, aware of where to find water, food and medicines in the natural world. They also became very skilled at using materials that were at hand to assist with cooking, hunting, fishing and extracting medicine.

In this chapter, I look at the sense of social cohesion that remains a great strength for Australia's Indigenous peoples. I also delve into traditional practices and how they contributed to both survival and the enjoyment of a very harmonious lifestyle in Australia's sometimes challenging environment. And I examine the remarkable technologies that Indigenous people devised in response to their particular regional environments, as well as contemporary values in Indigenous cultures today.

Going Back to the Dreamtime

The *Dreamtime*, sometimes also called the *Dreaming*, is the name now given to the period when, according to Indigenous cultures, the world was created. It is of central significance to Indigenous worldviews and spirituality. Aboriginal people across the country and Torres Strait Islanders in the north share similar concepts, though some practices are specific to one or the other.

Traditional belief was that the Earth and sky always existed and were home to supernatural beings. When the sun first shone, animal shapes emerged in the guise of humans. This element is why, in many Dreamtime stories, people turn into animals and the creatures' features are explained. For example, the stingray was created, according to one story, by a man falling from a cliff onto rocks, explaining why the stingray is flat. His tail, this story explains, is supposed to be the remnants of his spear.

As these beings moved around the Earth, they created the Earth's features and other phenomena like stars and the moon. Their journeys across the landscape are often referred to as *Dreaming tracks*. Some landscapes are linked with the Dreaming of a particular animal, such as Honey Ant Dreaming or Kangaroo Dreaming. These Dreamings have special meaning to people conceived or born in that country. Indigenous people believe they're descended from these supernatural people and creatures, and trace their ancestry back to them.

Many of these beings returned to the Earth, often in important and sacred sites such as waterholes or caves. Others were turned into animals or physical features, such as mountains and rock formations. In this way, the landscape has rich meaning for Indigenous people, who can look out over their country and, in the different formations, see reminders of the stories of their Dreaming.

REMEMBER

Although the Dreamtime refers to a period of creation, it isn't seen as simply occurring a long time ago. Indigenous people have a different concept of time to Europeans, believing that the stories and characters of the Dreamtime are strongly linked to the present and are even believed to assist in determining the future.

TIP

While strong similarities exist among Indigenous cultures, so too do a lot of variations. It's important not to generalise. A good way to appreciate the distinctiveness of an Indigenous culture is to listen to local Elders or take a cultural tour with an Indigenous guide.

Aboriginal leader and Yolngu Elder Silas Roberts described the Dreamtime in this way:

Aboriginals see themselves as part of nature. We see all things natural as part of us. All the things on Earth we see as part human. This is told through the ideas of Dreaming. By Dreaming we mean the belief that, long ago, these creatures started human society. These creatures, these great creatures, are just as much alive today as they were in the beginning. They are everlasting and will never die. They are always part of the land and nature, as we are. Our connection to all things natural is spiritual.

MYTH BUSTER

Dreamtime obviously isn't an Indigenous word. The term is traced back to anthropologist Baldwin Spencer. He noted that the Arrernte word — *altyerre* — means both 'time of creation' and 'dream' and so came up with the word 'Dreamtime'. In most other Aboriginal languages, no similarity exists between the words for dream and creation.

How was the world made?

All Aboriginal and Torres Strait Islander groups had their own theories about how the world came into being and where people came from. Although similarities between these theories exist across the country — universally, for example, everyone had a creation spirit — some differences exist.

It was believed that the sky and Earth always existed but didn't have any features. In many places, the spirit of creation can be found in a snake that wove across the landscape creating its form. In other places, the spirit is a crocodile. In some places, this spirit is linked to the rainbow (and so called the *rainbow serpent*). And, in some places, the spirit was a female spirit (so God really was a woman!).

The southern sky

The sky is also believed to be the dwelling place of ancestral beings and, in some Indigenous cultures, where souls go after death. Just as with creation stories, a wide diversity of stories explains the arrangements of stars in the southern sky.

Different constellations are related to different myths. Many Indigenous groups believe that the Milky Way is a celestial river or stream. In other parts of the country, it is believed to be the sparks and fire from the campfires of ancestral beings that inhabit the sky.

REMEMBER

Indigenous people were as skilled at reading the sky as they were at reading the landscape. Both were used as important tools in navigation. Changes in location and appearance of different objects in the night sky or changes to vegetation and animal habits also indicated seasonal changes.

HOW THE ECHIDNA GOT ITS SPIKES . . .

In the Kammilaroi language, *biggi billa* is the word for echidna. The following story may sound like a simple account of how this creature got its spikes but a bit more is going on:

> *Back in the Dreamtime, there was a terrible drought and the people were hungry. There was little food so, even when people had shared what they had managed to catch and find, they were still hungry. Everyone was getting thinner and thinner, except one old man. So one night, after they had shared some small fish that had been all the food that they could find, the other men followed the old man back to his camp.*

> *From the bushes, they could see the old man over his fire. And they could see, just as they smelt the sweet smell of cooking meat in the air, that the old man was eating a big piece of bundar (kangaroo) from one he had killed and kept to himself.*

> *The men were mad and came to beat the old man who had broken the law with his self-ishness. As he crawled away, his legs broken, the men threw spears at him. The old man crawled over the land, his spears turned to spikes, and his legs faced inwards because of the broken bones. You can see them in the footprints of the biggi billa, who is forever a reminder of the selfishness of the old man.*

The story explains the important value of the need to share with others. It warns of the punishment — and loneliness — that can come of not adhering to the principle of working with the rest of the clan for survival. It also contains a reminder of the distinct tracks left by the echidna in the soil due to the positioning of its feet.

An oral tradition of storytelling

Aboriginal and Torres Strait Islander cultures were rich with storytelling. While Dreamtime stories are often told today as though they're children's stories, they had a sophisticated role and were told with different levels of detail, depending on the sophistication of the listener. Values, laws, responsibilities, history and cultural practices were all recorded in stories told orally, often sitting around a campfire or in ceremonies.

Some stories told of how certain features in the landscape were formed or of how certain animals came to have their distinct characteristics; they could remind people where food or water supplies were, keep note of important relationships with other clans and nations, record how ceremonies were to be conducted and explain important values such as the need to share and the importance of respecting the environment.

CULTURAL PROTOCOLS

Because of the important cultural value of these stories, strict protocols often dictated who could tell and who could hear stories. Some stories could only be told by particular people of certain status within the clan. Others could only be heard by those who had been through certain stages of initiation. If the subject of the stories was about 'women's business' or 'men's business', the stories weren't to be told to people of the opposite sex (see the section 'Separating women's business from men's business', later in this chapter).

Stories may have other purposes too. Scary tales about evil figures or dangerous creatures in a waterhole or lurking in the dark were ways of ensuring that children stayed out of important sources of water, so as not to pollute them, and stayed near the campfire at night so they didn't wander off and get lost or hurt.

CULTURAL PROTOCOLS

Because Indigenous peoples had no written language, messengers were often sent on their errands with a message stick, carved in a way that would assist with memorising the message and also proving that the person delivering the message was genuine.

Indigenous Worldviews

In order to survive, Indigenous people's lives were very closely entwined with their natural environment. They were, therefore, very attuned to what was happening in the world around them — the cycle of the seasons, the paths of the stars, and the migration of fish, birds and animals.

Living so closely with nature, and being so dependent on it for survival, gave rise to a set of values and Indigenous worldviews that reflected the need to work closely with nature, and with each other. These worldviews included principles such as reciprocity, respect for Elders, respect for the distinct roles of women and men, and, of course, respect for the environment.

Aspects of Aboriginal and Torres Strait Islander worldviews can be gleaned from the values and beliefs that shaped traditional culture and continue to shape those communities today.

Sharing based on reciprocity

A strong value within Aboriginal communities and Torres Strait Islander communities was that people should share their resources, tools and food, and help each other when needed. In exchange, people could expect that others would offer help and assistance when it was needed and share what they had.

Given the size of clan groups, often small extended family groups, and the need for families to work together in order to keep everyone fed and looked after, the idea of reciprocity being so significant as a value within the community isn't surprising. This need also placed the key responsibility on the most healthy to look after the more vulnerable within the group — the young, the elderly, the sick. Even today, this concept that you help out others within your family and community is very strong.

Aboriginal people treat extended family the same as immediate family. In traditional culture, the term 'mother' was used for aunts as well as a child's birth mother and 'father' for uncles as well as the natural father. Quite distant relatives are referred to as 'uncle', 'aunt' or 'cousin'. This latter practice still operates today. It makes for a very big family!

Respecting the wisdom of Elders

Older people are seen as the custodians of Indigenous cultures. In traditional society, they were respected for their wisdom. Someone being old didn't automatically ensure that she had status as an Elder. The position came from respect for someone's cultural knowledge and her moral authority. Elders had a strong role to play in the decision-making of the community and were often deferred to for advice. Their role was particularly important in determining cultural matters, such as whether particular people were able to marry each other or not.

Today, strong respect for the wisdom of Elders remains. They are the people who are entitled to do a 'welcome to country' (refer to Chapter 2) and a proper 'acknowledgement of country' acknowledges Elders, past and present. At Aboriginal community events, careful thought is often given to Elders — so, for example, a special 'Elders' tent' may be set up where they can sit in comfort.

When people are revered by the community and given the status of Elder, they are referred to as 'Aunty' or 'Uncle' as a sign of that respect.

Separating women's business from men's business

Indigenous cultures had very specific roles for men, such as hunting, and for women, such as food gathering and childrearing. Cultural stories and spiritual life were also separated into matters for men only and for women only. Decisions around conception and birth were, not surprisingly, the domain of women.

Initiation of boys was, in the main, the responsibility of men, and girls the responsibility of women.

The gender roles of men and women are still referred to as *men's business* and *women's business*. At large communal events, in many Aboriginal communities, the women are commonly seen clustered in one area and the men in another.

REMEMBER

Although male and female roles in Indigenous cultures were very specific, the philosophy behind the separation is not one of women being inferior to men. In Aboriginal society, female Elders can have as much influence — or even more — as male Elders. They participate in key decision-making processes of the community and have moral authority.

The role that women had in traditional Aboriginal culture was challenged by the colonisation of Australia and introduction of European values and views about the role of women. Today, some people claim that Aboriginal culture always tolerated violence and other forms of oppression against women. Others say that the impact and influence of European culture have eroded the power that Aboriginal women enjoyed within their communities.

Respect for the environment

For many Indigenous people, the debates about climate change — whether it exists or not, whether it's human-induced or not — are irrelevant. Living so closely with nature over tens of thousands of years has created a deep feeling of being very interconnected with the environment.

Indigenous people believe that you need to keep the ecosystems that provide the basics for life (food and shelter) healthy because you need them to survive. The air needs to be clean because you breathe it; water needs to be clean because you drink it; food and plant sources need to be sustained because you eat them.

REMEMBER

Even though Indigenous people and their communities are becoming more involved with development on their lands, and more and more Aboriginal people and Torres Strait Islanders live in urban settings, the strong link between people and land remains. Indigenous people are often very concerned about the natural environment and engage in activities that ensure it remains cared for and healthy.

A very key part of Indigenous cultures gives respect to the land in acknowledgement of the role it plays in creating and supporting life.

Living with Nature

As predominantly a hunter-gatherer society, Aboriginal people didn't farm or cultivate the soil for crops in a large-scale way. (While they did grow crops of tubers such as yams, grain such as native millet, macadamia nuts, fruits and berries, their farming has been described as an activity rather than a lifestyle.)

They did, however, have intimate knowledge of their ecosystems and were careful to make sure those systems remained in balance. They also used many things in their natural world to assist with their survival. Torres Strait Islanders, by comparison, did have forms of farming on their islands and their land was clearly allocated to different family groups.

Ecosystems across Australia are vastly different — and geography and climate have changed over time. Indigenous people have adapted to these changes. Around 20,000 years ago, the last Australian ice age reached its coldest peak, lasting for about 5,000 years. This glacial period forced Aboriginal people to shift and change their practices in order to survive, because the world was colder and drier. Aboriginal people moved into all parts of Australia, including the mountains, adapted to the changes and survived.

In the drier areas, groups were smaller and travelled further to find water, but in the colder climates, more emphasis was placed on building shelters and making warm clothes such as possum cloaks. On the coast, where the land was most fertile, the environment could support larger populations and people relied more heavily on the sea and waterways for food and for materials like shells that could be used for tools.

The intimacy of Indigenous peoples' knowledge of their environment included knowing when to burn certain areas to promote new grass growth and so attract kangaroos (see the section 'Fire', later in this chapter, for more on this). It also involved knowing what parts of plants were edible and how to prepare food that may be poisonous to eradicate its toxins. Knowing the medicinal purposes of plants was another important aspect, as well as knowing how to use natural products — bark, wood, grass, seeds and leaves — and parts of animals — bones, tissues and fur — for tools, clothing and shelter.

MYTH BUSTER

Because Indigenous peoples built neither cities nor monuments, European cultures have tended to describe their societies as 'primitive'. This view assesses Indigenous cultures only from a comparison with technology in other parts of the world and fails to appreciate that, although many modern cultures are thousands of years old, Aboriginal cultures have been around for more than 65,000 years and, over that period of time, were able to manage all of the major issues that face a society — social cohesion, environmental destruction and degradation, sustainable population growth and renewable resources. On this assessment, some would argue that Aboriginal cultures are 'advanced' and some other modern cultures are 'developing'.

Hunting and gathering

About 25,000 years ago, the large animals living in Australia — the megafauna — became extinct. These giant marsupials (including rhino-sized wombats, giant kangaroos and koalas), monotremes (such as a sheep-sized echidna), birds (including mallee fowl and flightless birds) and reptiles (supersized snakes, goannas, turtles and crocodiles) disappeared just like the dinosaurs did. Scientists are still speculating on whether this was human-induced extinction or because of dramatic climate change. Regardless, Indigenous people coexisted with the megafauna for many thousands of years before all species became extinct.

Around the same time as the megafauna became extinct, Aboriginal people began using grindstones to make efficient use of seeds and other plant products. The hunter-gatherer lifestyle required deep knowledge of the surrounding environment in order to survive, so the ability to adapt as ecosystems changed was critical. Watching for hawks as they converged on small animals during bushfires helped to find game. In the Northern Territory, people built small horseshoe-shaped hiding places to assist in hunting. Camouflage and imitation were also used in hunting. Bushes, grass and animal skins were worn and human scents disguised by covering the skin with mud.

Even today, many Aboriginal and Torres Strait Islander people supplement their contemporary, store-bought diets with *bush tucker* — plants and small animals gathered for food — or through hunting and fishing. In areas such as Arnhem Land, Cape York and the Torres Strait, between one-quarter and two-thirds of the population engage in hunting and gathering. In these areas, bush tucker also makes a significant contribution to people's health.

Bush food

Indigenous people living in Australia before it was colonised were healthier than they generally are today. They had a better diet and ate more nutritious foods.

Many traditional foods are still eaten today, using knowledge, techniques and skills that have developed over tens of thousands of years. Some foods, like kangaroo, emu and crocodile, have made their way onto fine dining menus around the world. Edible fruits, vegetables, flowers and seeds can all be found in the

Australian bush. Here are some of the foods in the diets of Aboriginal people and Torres Strait Islanders:

>> **Crayfish, yabbies, shrimps, mussels:** Caught with nets and by hand, and cooked in holes in the ground covered in ashes.

>> **Cycad fruit:** Have to be leached, pounded and baked to ensure that the poisons and carcinogens are removed before eating to provide an important staple source of carbohydrate.

>> **Ducks and swans:** Hunted with nets and cooked in coals.

>> **Emus:** Captured with nets, spears, woomeras and boomerangs; their feathers were removed and they were gutted before being cooked in coals or under the ground. Their eggs were a delicacy.

>> **Fish:** Caught using lines, bone hooks, nets, stone traps and spears. They were cased in mud and then cooked in ashes.

>> **Grass and acacia seeds:** Gathered by hand, sometimes ground into a paste, and cooked in ashes.

>> **Honey ants:** Honey ants store honeydew in their abdomens. In Central Australia, Aboriginal women know where to dig to find their underground nests. In the Top End, another type of honey ant, a green ant, also with a sweet abdomen, nests in trees.

>> **Kangaroos:** Hunted with spears, woomeras, clubs and boomerangs, they were gutted and skinned and then cooked in coals or under the ground. The tail was considered one of the tastiest parts of a kangaroo. It's now cooked in a variety of ways, including in honey and soy sauce. The skins were used for clothing and tools.

>> **Mallee fowls, brush turkeys, galahs, pigeons and other small birds:** Caught in nets and cooked in underground ovens.

>> **Nectars:** Flowers from plants like the grevillea, banksia and bottlebrush have nectars that taste sweet. Immersing the flowers in water creates a sweet-tasting drink. Blossoms of some plants are ground in a coolamon (see the section 'Baskets, buckets and coolamons' later in this chapter), with water added to make a drink.

>> **Possums:** Caught in hollow trees, they were gutted, skinned and cooked in coals. Their skin and fur were prized, and used for clothes and tools.

>> **Quandongs:** The quandong tree, found in arid areas, has a large round fruit that can be eaten fresh or dried, with a tart but pleasant taste. The seeds of the fruit have a rough texture and are often strung together and used as body ornaments. The nutritious and oil-rich kernels are sometimes eaten after

roasting or can be ground into a paste and used as a liniment to treat skin disorders or as a skin and hair conditioner.

>> **Snakes, lizards and frogs:** Tracked, often dug out and cooked in coals.

>> **Turtles:** Caught with nets, they were cooked either in holes in the ground covered in ashes or cooked in coals. Their shells were used for tools and ornaments. Eggs were gathered and eaten raw or boiled.

>> **Yams, shoots and wild onions:** Dug out from the ground and eaten raw, boiled or cooked in ashes. Sometimes they were pounded until soft and cooked as a paste.

>> **Water ribbons and water lilies:** Gathered from fresh water, water ribbons are edible tubers and are sweet when steamed. Water lilies have edible pods and seeds.

>> **Wild honey:** Bees (many species) were followed back to their nests high in the trees, which were usually chopped down, with the contents of the hive removed and placed in a paperbark container (later sometimes known as a sugarbag).

>> **Witchetty grubs:** Dug out of red gum trees and cooked in ashes.

>> **Wombats, water rats and small animals:** Caught in traps and nets, they were cooked in holes in the ground filled with ashes.

CULTURAL PROTOCOLS

Mutton-birds and their eggs are a traditional source of food for Aboriginal people in Tasmania. Many of the surrounding islands that have mutton-bird colonies on them have been returned to Aboriginal ownership so this continues to be an important source of food and cultural practice.

Bush medicine

Living a hunter-gatherer lifestyle brings with it many dangers. Burns from fires, eye infections, upset stomachs, headaches, tooth decay, stings from jellyfish and snakebite were all dangers that lay in wait. People also had accidents or were injured in fights or while hunting. It was also believed that serious illness and death could be the result of spirits or sorcery.

Over tens of thousands of years, Aboriginal people have found plants, minerals and other materials from the natural world to assist them in treating injuries and illnesses, and in assisting with good health. The range of remedies used herbs, animal products, hot water, coals, mud and massages. It was also thought that chants or spells and special trinkets had healing powers.

Because people often thought that sorcery or spirits caused illness, some Indigenous people — mostly men but sometimes women — were trained as spiritual doctors. They were trained from an early age on spiritual matters and grew to have great power within their communities. They performed certain rites and were thought to be able to see events in other places and into the future. Though they would sometimes use herbal remedies in their ceremonies, they didn't treat health problems that weren't seen as caused by spirits or sorcery.

Day-to-day medicinal needs were tended to by women who had a vast knowledge of the healing elements in the natural environment around them. Some women were identified as having a particular skill at healing. Healing would often take place in two stages — at the first instance, women in the community would apply their knowledge and then, if that didn't work, a senior woman who specialised in medicine would be consulted.

Here are some common remedies:

>> **Eucalyptus bark:** Could be made into a drink that would stop diarrhoea.

>> **Green plums:** Used to stop toothaches and soothe sore eyes.

>> **Lemongrass:** Used to create a wash to treat fevers and as a drink to treat diarrhoea' Is a more pleasant read this way its root could also be used to help cure sore ears.

>> **Maroon bush, prickly fan flower, currant bush:** Has been used to treat heart disease, intestinal trouble, kidney problems and urinary tract problems. Some people claim it can be beneficial in the treatment of cancer.

>> **Tea-tree, or paperbark trees:** Leaves inhaled to treat colds, applied to the skin to stop stings and crushed in water to treat fevers. The bark was also used as bandages.

REMEMBER

In using medicine, no doses existed. Because medicine was mostly applied externally, with ointments prepared by mixing crushed leaves with animal fat, little chance existed of overdosing.

TIP

Some natural medicines vary in strength, depending on the season. Lemongrasses were picked when they were still green, and green plum leaves were thought to be more potent if used during the dry season.

Tools

Aboriginal people have been living in Australia for an estimated 65,000 years. Archaeological evidence suggests that technology stayed relatively the same until about 10,000 years ago. The tools found from before that time were usually simple ones — stone tools used to carve other tools from wood. The wooden tools don't survive today because they deteriorate but some stone tools have been preserved.

About 5,000 years ago, a radical change in the stone technology occurred, including the production of tools with delicate points and blades. Some speculate that this feature came about because spears with stone points began replacing spears with wooden points. A spear-thrower was also developed.

MYTH BUSTER

Assumptions are often made about the way that Aboriginal people lived thousands of years ago based on the remnants of stone tools and campfires, but other technology was widely used as well. Aboriginal people had to be resourceful and innovative to survive, and used many things in their natural world to assist them. Shells and the resin from trees and plants were the basis of some technologies — like using resins for glue and shells for spearheads. String and rope were made from various fibres and woven into bags, mats and other objects.

Spears, spear-throwers and shields

Spears were used for hunting, fishing and fighting. Some were carved from a single piece of wood; others used attached spearheads made from a variety of materials — stone, shells or wood. These composite spears were the more popular version and found throughout Australia.

Spear-throwers provided extra leverage when throwing a spear, increasing its force. Several different types of spear-throwers were produced but a common feature was a hook or peg fixed at one end onto which the spear was placed. *Woomeras* were a particular type of spear-thrower and were multipurpose tools that could be used for hunting, chopping wood, cutting tree branches and chopping meat.

Shields were also carved from wood, often cutting the wood from the tree without damaging the tree. They were used in hand-to-hand combat as well as for protection against spears thrown from a distance, and were usually highly decorated.

MYTH BUSTER

Far from being inferior weapons, as some may suggest, spears used with a spear-thrower were the fastest weapons in the world before the invention of the self-loading rifle, according to some authoritative sources.

Baskets, buckets and coolamons

Containers were made from many different materials, particularly wood and bark, and were used for carrying food and water. Baskets could be made through a variety of methods, including from two sheets of paperbark being stitched together. Baskets were used mainly as containers for food and for personal possessions.

String bags, a specialised type of basket, were made using a variety of techniques, such as weaving and plaiting, and by using materials such as hair, bark, reeds, grass and palm leaves. They were expandable and collapsible. As well as carrying food, bags could be used to carry infants and, if finely woven, to sift seeds.

Coolamons were a popular type of curved container. They were popular in desert areas and made from the burl of a tree (a dome-shaped growth on the trunk of a tree). Containers could also be made from shells, leaves, bamboo and animal skins — whatever appropriate materials were available in the local environment.

Boomerangs

Boomerangs, tools used for hunting or as weapons, were invented over 10,000 years ago, along with barbed spears. A boomerang could kill a small animal and knock down a larger one. Carved from wood, they were used across most of mainland Australia — but not in the north or in some of the central desert areas (Pitjantjatjara lands) or in Tasmania — and made in a wide variety of shapes.

People in desert areas used the heavy wood of the mulga tree to make boomerangs that assisted in hunting kangaroos. On the New South Wales coast, lighter boomerangs made from mangrove trees were used for duck hunting. Of the two main types — returning and non-returning — the vast majority were of the non-returning variety. The type that returns only comes back if it fails to hit its target.

MYTH BUSTER

Although most people don't associate Indigenous people with modern scientific invention, David Unaipon, an Aboriginal man from South Australia born in 1872, cited the principles of boomerang flight to back up the anticipated invention of the helicopter. As an inventor, he was fascinated with perpetual motion and invented a centrifugal motor and an improved handpiece for sheep shearing. (See Chapter 18 for more on this important Aboriginal writer and inventor.)

Didgeridoos

The *didgeridoo*, also spelled didjeridoo (and sometimes even didjeridu), was a musical instrument made from a hollowed branch, eaten out by termites. It was found only in Arnhem Land, the Kimberley and Pilbara regions. The inside is smoothed out and a resin or gum from trees or plants is added at the narrower end to make the mouthpiece. The didgeridoo was used only in the northern parts of Australia and was played only by men. See Chapter 17 for more on musical instruments.

Canoes

Canoes were used to navigate rivers and coastal areas to assist in hunting and gathering fish, eels, plants, birds and bird eggs. *Canoe trees* are trees with a visible scar from where a canoe was carved out of the bark.

Looking to the Skies

Indigenous people were astronomers with a strong understanding of the skies, and many cultural stories contain knowledge about them. They know the sky as well as they know the land. Stars, the sun and the moon were used by them to navigate across not only water but also land, and to know when the seasons were coming. Rather than seeing constellations as in Western astronomy, objects in the sky often represented beings such as people and animals, and cultural stories around stellar objects ensure knowledge is passed down from one generation to the next.

The Dark Emu

In Indigenous astronomy, the Dark Emu is a formation in the sky that is not made of stars but from the dark space between them. This is an important concept because it means the space between the stars is not empty but full — a theory that links in with recently emerging theories on dark matter and the universe. The position of the emu in the night sky indicates when the emus are nesting and when the best time to collect their eggs is.

TIP

Interest in Indigenous astronomy is increasing. Observatories that have public programs — such as Sydney Observatory — often have lectures or tours by Indigenous astronomers so you can learn more.

Controlling the Environment

Living so closely with the environment, Aboriginal people and Torres Strait Islanders came to understand it. Living a largely hunter-gatherer lifestyle required understanding the cycles and patterns of flora and fauna, the timing of the tides and the cycles and patterns of the seasons. Indigenous people, while living closely with the rhythms of nature around them, also found ways to work with nature, or to get it to work for them, in order to assist with their survival.

Indigenous people developed techniques that helped to control their environment, such as strategically placing rocks in rivers and tidal areas to create fish traps. They also used fire to help keep the ecosystems in balance and adapt the landscape to make food collection easier. Knowledge of the migratory patterns of animals, including birds, insects and fish, also helped ensure an abundant supply of food.

Fire

Bushfires are natural occurrences, usually caused by lightning strikes, but Aboriginal people came to use them as a way of managing their environment. Fire was used across Australia as a way of clearing undergrowth and to encourage regrowth to attract fauna, as well as to flush out game. It was used in a deliberate and systematic way and has been called *firestick farming*. Indigenous fire technology uses a 'cool fire' — one that is easily controlled and burns slowly, and is very different from the 'hot fire' of an out of control bushfire.

In the Arnhem Land region of the Northern Territory, lighting fires during the cooler parts of the year to cut down on destructive fires in the dry months is a continuing customary practice. Some experts believe that this practice, by minimising the occurrence of larger fires, assists with lowering greenhouse gas emissions. Fire was made by two methods:

>> **The friction method:** Friction is created by drilling, sawing or ploughing. *Drilling* is where a pit is made in a softwood stick and another stick — or drill — made of harder wood is fitted vertically into the pit, and the drill is manually spun at a rapid rate. The wood powder created starts to smoulder from the heat produced by the friction and is then tipped onto tinder and blown gently, which ignites it. *Sawing* was a method where the edge of a hardwood stick was drawn rapidly back and forth across a cleft stick, similarly producing heat. *Ploughing* was a way of starting fire where a hardwood stick was rubbed along a groove in a softwood stick. Ploughing wasn't as widely used as the other friction methods.

>> **The percussion method:** In this method, a flint is hit hard against stone, creating a spark. It was a less common method and used only in the central and southern parts of Australia.

Harvesting

Although Indigenous people were hunter-gatherers, they developed techniques to take advantage of seasonal and temporary abundance of some resources. Aboriginal people are thought to have deliberately scattered seeds as they walked across their country in order to harvest the plants the following season.

Some food, such as nuts and kernels, were stored. Strips of kangaroo meat or whale meat were sometimes preserved through drying but, in most cases, food was hunted and gathered for immediate use. Seasonal times of plenty were often times of heightened social interaction and ceremony, involving a large number of people from the region. For example, every spring, the bogong moth migrates from the west and north of New South Wales to the Australian Alps. While the moths gathered in their thousands, people from as far away as the east coast would come to harvest them. Similarly, the bunya nut (like a chestnut and just as tasty) was a traditional food of the Aboriginal people in the rainforests of south-eastern Queensland. Aboriginal people travelled long distances to feast on the nuts that matured in the summer.

TIP

Writer Bruce Pascoe has significantly deepened the understanding of the extent of Indigenous agriculture and aquiculture practices in his book *Dark Emu: Black Seeds: Agriculture or Accident?* Through researching the journals and diaries of early settlers, Pascoe provides compelling evidence about the extent that Indigenous people actively harvested plants and grains.

Fish traps

Large and complex fish traps have been built in different parts of Australia. These complex constructions of stones or plant fibres were built in coastal areas or tidal streams where fish were known to be seasonally abundant. Fish traps are still intact in some places, including the Torres Strait Islands, the Gulf of Carpentaria and in Brewarrina, in the north-west of New South Wales. The same technique of using stone traps to catch fish was used in parts of Victoria to catch eels.

Middens

Middens often show the evidence of community life — where tools were made, fish were killed, shell necklaces woven and meals cooked. In some parts of Australia, middens were deliberate mound-like structures built with the bones of fish, dugongs or other objects.

TIP

These middens have an architectural structure, are of important cultural significance and contain a wealth of information about the practices of Indigenous people over thousands of years.

Shelter

Indigenous people made a range of structures to provide shelters. Natural places of protection from the elements such as caves could be used but a range of different housing structures were also built. These included lean-tos, the weaving of plants together and the use of plants with materials like spinifex to make shelter. In several places such as in Victoria and in the Pilbara, stones were used to make house-like structures. The shelters used varied on the climate and the materials available and highlight the diversity of cultures across Australia.

Contemporary Cultural Values

Today, Indigenous people still live right across Australia in a diversity of circumstances. Close-knit communities thrive in urban areas, clusters of communities have grown on the outskirts of towns where missions or reserves once were (see Chapter 7), and some Aboriginal people live in remote communities and on remote *outstations*, where usually a family group sets up camp (often quite well established) separate from the broader community.

Indigenous people in remote and rural communities still often supplement their diets with traditional food. However, even in the remotest areas, where many traditional practices form a part of everyday life, Indigenous people utilise modern technology. People wear clothes, travel by car — usually four-wheel-drive vehicles — and use mobile phones and satellite technology.

Although changes in technology and living conditions have occurred, key aspects of Indigenous life remain — the interrelatedness and networks among families and communities remain strong. So, too, does connection to land, spiritual beliefs, and cultural and artistic practices. Part 4 covers contemporary culture in detail.

CULTURAL PROTOCOLS

When Indigenous people meet each other, they usually ask, 'Where are you from?' or 'Who's your mob?' This is often a way to see how they may be connected through complex community and extended family relationships.

So, are modern Indigenous and non-Indigenous people really that much different from each other? Characterising the differences between cultures without making generalisations is never easy. However, Table 4-1 shows a few cultural values that Indigenous people have identified to show how their cultures are different from European cultures.

TABLE 4-1   Comparing Indigenous and European Cultural Values

Indigenous Cultural Values	European Cultural Values
People live communally and are interconnected	People are focused more on the individual
Ask 'Where are you from?', 'Who's your mob?'	Ask 'How do you do?', 'What do you do?'
Only certain people can know some things	Knowledge is something for everyone
Women have an equal place around the campfire	Women had to fight for equality
Keep culture alive with storytelling	Write it down!
People are interconnected with their environment	The environment often has to make way for progress

Caring for Country

Today, large areas of Australia are looked after through Aboriginal and Torres Strait Islander ranger programs. These programs are successful in ensuring Indigenous people keep a connection to their traditional country, and meet their cultural responsibilities to care for their country. They also help create employment and ensure that the deep knowledge local communities have of their country are utilised to best care for the land. They use a range of traditional methods and modern technology to track and preserve species, assess the health of ecosystems, undertake fire burning and clean the waterways.

TIP

You can find out more about the many ranger programs across Australia at www. countryneedspeople.org.au.

Invasion

Find out more about the passing contact between Indigenous peoples and foreign voyagers, both from Europe and from the islands to the north.

Examine how the doctrine of discovery, under international law of the time, gave the British what they thought was the right to take the land of Indigenous people — and how Aboriginal people had a very different view.

Trace the spread of the British colony at Sydney Cove, with new colonies established around Australia, and the increasing conflict between Aboriginal people and the colonists as they battled for land, water and food.

Understand the intentions behind policies that took children from their families, and the tragic short- and long-term effects of these policies.

Chapter **5**

First Contacts

When James Cook claimed most of the east coast of Australia for the British in 1770, he was far from the first European to have come into contact with the Indigenous people of the country that would become known as Australia.

Other European powers — the Dutch and the French — had been interested in the great land to the south but hadn't sought to press their claims over it the way the British were determined to do. As well as contact with Europeans, plenty of evidence exists of strong connections with nearer neighbours — the Macassans to the north, from what's now known as Sulawesi in Indonesia, as well as the Papuans, who continue to have close connections with the people of the Torres Strait Islands.

Indigenous people were curious about their visitors but also had an interest in developing trade relationships with those who came to their shores.

In this chapter, I outline some of these early visits and the British intentions for the great southern land, which set the stage for what was to become a strong and independent multicultural nation, though not before great loss for the country's Indigenous people. Here, I also examine what's known of Aboriginal people's response to these first contacts.

Looking for the Unknown Southern Land: Contact before 1770

The British, who established the first colony in Australia, weren't the first to find their way to the Unknown Southern Land (*Terra Australis Incognita*) inhabited by Aboriginal people for the most part, and by Torres Strait Islanders on the islands between Cape York and Papua.

Long before the British arrived, trade links existed with the Macassans and the Papuans. And, as Europeans started to colonise the globe, they found their way to Australia. Dutch seafarers, in particular, sailed and mapped parts of Australia. Historians also believe that explorer Luis Vas de Torres, working for the Spanish Crown, sighted Australia as he sailed through the Torres Strait in 1606. In the 18th century, after Cook's claim on Australia, several French explorers also visited various parts of the continent, including Marc-Joseph Dufresne in 1772, Jean-Francois de Galaup (he added Lapérouse to his name) in 1788 and Bruni d'Entrecasteaux in 1792.

Such encounters saw curiosity from both sides of the cultural fence, even if not all of the encounters were peaceful.

MYTH BUSTER

The possibility that Portuguese sailors knew of the Australian continent is evidenced from 16th-century Portuguese maps showing a land mass similar to Australia called 'Java la Grande'. Similar speculation about visits from the Chinese in the 15th century was sparked by the discovery in 1948 of a statuette from the Ming period near Darwin in the Northern Territory. However, by 1878, the Chinese population was larger than the European population in the Northern Territory. In 1888, the Chinese population numbered 6,122. They were recruited to work on building infrastructure such as the railway lines and also worked on the goldfields. So, the statuette was possibly owned by one of these early migrants rather than Chinese seafarers.

Meet the neighbours: The Macassans

The Macassans are indigenous people from what is now Indonesia and were skilled at sailing and living off the sea. They routinely visited Australia as part of a trading cycle that depended on the seasonal monsoon winds, collecting items such as sea cucumbers (also known as bêche-de-mer or trepang, and a delicacy in Indonesia and China), sea turtles and their shells, and trochus shells.

They sailed to Australia in boats called *praus* and then fished in dugout canoes. Some of these canoes were traded with Aboriginal people and Aboriginal men would sometimes sail with the Macassan fishermen. Tools such as knives and axes, pipes and fishhooks were also traded in exchange for tortoise shells and pearl shells. They collected plants and wood from Australia, especially to assist with repairs of their ships. Macassan words also became part of some Aboriginal dialects, such as words for the points of the compass, some words for tools and words to describe boat parts.

Remains of Macassan campsites on the northern shores of Australia, such as that shown in Figure 5-1, have been dated back to over 800 years. Tamarind trees still mark these spots, where Macassan fishermen dropped the seeds during their visits. Trade between Aboriginal people and the Macassans continued until it was stopped by the Australian government in 1906.

FIGURE 5-1:
A Macassan fireplace at Bremar Island in the Northern Territory.

CULTURAL PROTOCOLS

Aboriginal people and Torres Strait Islanders acknowledged their contact with the Macassans by making reference to them in ceremonies and by representing them in rock paintings.

Papuan people regularly travelled to Arnhem Land, Cape York Peninsula and the Torres Strait. Papuan language and culture had an especially strong influence in the Torres Strait, with canoes, masks, spears and ornamental weapons traded. The Torres Strait Islands Treaty, signed in 1978, formalised this relationship (refer to Chapter 2 for more on this treaty).

The Dutch were here

The first recorded contact between Europeans and Aboriginal people and Torres Strait Islanders in Australia wasn't with the British but, not surprisingly, with the Dutch. Having risen as a superpower and establishing the Dutch East India Company — based in Jakarta, Indonesia — in 1602, the Dutch sailed constantly between Europe and what was then known as the East Indies. In 1605, Willem Janszoon (also known as Jansz), on his ship *Duyfken*, reached the Gulf of Carpentaria in the north-east of the land the Dutch had named New Holland.

The first commemorated landing of a European was that of Captain Dirk Hartog in October 1616 at what is now called Cape Inscription on the west coast of Australia. He left an inscribed pewter plate that was found in 1697 by his countryman Willem de Vlamingh, who was en route to the East Indies.

In 1623, Jan Carstensz was sent to sail around the Gulf of Carpentaria. He and his crew clashed with Aboriginal people and didn't seem to have a high opinion of them. Carstensz wrote that the Aboriginal people were 'more miserable and insignificant than I have ever seen in my life'.

An expedition sponsored by Antonie van Diemen and led by Abel Tasman set out in 1642 to explore the unknown land that lay to the south of the Dutch trading empire. His route took him first to Mauritius, where he was able to stock up on supplies, to make use of the prevailing winds. He then sailed towards the west coast of Australia but, unknowingly, far to the south of the mainland. He found what he dutifully called Van Diemen's Land (after his patron), which is today known as Tasmania, continuing then to New Zealand and north through the southern Pacific back to Batavia. In ten months of exploring, Tasman had circumnavigated the Australian mainland without ever seeing it and, not surprisingly, van Diemen was unimpressed. But Tasman set sail again in 1644 and explored the Gulf of Carpentaria and Arnhem Land in the north of New Holland and sailed some way down the west coast. He observed Aboriginal people as being: 'poor, naked people walking along beaches; without rice or many fruits, very poor and bad tempered people in many places'.

The Dutch didn't seek to establish a colony in the country that would become known as Australia, perhaps because they found nothing of particular value to them.

And then came the English . . .

William Dampier was the first British person to explore New Holland. He came to the north coast of Australia in 1688 and again in 1699. He was a famous English buccaneer who had made a career sailing around the Americas and then the

Pacific. He also gave a negative account of the Aboriginal people when he returned to Britain: 'The Inhabitants of this Country are the miserablest People in the World. Setting aside their Humane Shape, they differ little from Brutes'. Laced with the prejudices of the time, these observations contain the assumption of white superiority and black inferiority that the British believed was the prerequisite to asserting a claim over this country.

TIP

William Dampier wrote that he found the landscape devoid of any riches but took away about 40 samples of native flora. He published *A Voyage to New Holland* in 1703, giving the first published account of what would later become known as Australia.

Landing in Australia: Cook's Arrival

The British asserted a claim over Australia in 1770, during the first Pacific voyage of Lieutenant James Cook (he attained the rank of Captain on completion of his second Pacific voyage in 1775). His ship *Endeavour* sailed the coast of New Zealand, then turned west, sighting the southern coast of New South Wales on 19 April 1770.

He sailed north and, on 29 April 1770, planted the British flag in the soil of Kurnell at what he later named Botany Bay for the specimens collected there. The area is approximately 30 kilometres from what's now the city of Sydney. There, he also carved details recording his arrival into a tree.

The first member of Cook's crew to step foot on Australian soil was Isaac Smith, an 18-year-old midshipman who was also the cousin of Cook's wife, Elizabeth. A small brass plaque now marks the site on the beach.

The Aboriginal people of the area, the Dharawal, were hunting, gathering and fishing that day in their usual manner. They thought the ship looked like a big white bird as it sailed into their cove. Protective of their own food sources, they opposed the landing party by throwing spears. Cook fired a shot, wounding one man, and this dispersed the Aboriginal people, enabling Cook's party to land.

Cook continued to chart the Australian coast all the way north to the tip of Queensland. There, on what became known as Possession Island, just before sunset on Wednesday 22 August 1770, he declared the entire east coast a British possession, later naming it New South Wales. His log records:

At six possession was taken of this country in his Majesty's name and under his colours, fired several volleys of small arms on the occasion and cheer'd three times, which was answer'd from the ship.

Cook had recorded signs that the coast was inhabited during the voyage north, and noted the great number of fires on all the land and islands about them, 'a certain sign they are Inhabited'.

Cook returned to England in May 1771. Cook's journal entries show that he tried to understand the world of the Aboriginal people he observed:

These people may truly be said to be in the pure state of nature, and may appear to some to be the most wretched upon the earth; but in reality they are far happier than . . . we Europeans.

Cook's instructions

Cook had been given instructions that laid out two courses of action for acquiring the continent. The Secret Instructions, contained in the Letterbook carried on the *Endeavour*, included the Additional Instructions that authorised James Cook to take possession of 'a Continent or Land of great extent' thought to exist in southern latitudes.

The letter given to Cook on 30 July 1768 stated that, should he find the land inhabited, he was to 'endeavour by all proper means to cultivate a friendship and alliance with them' and was told 'with the Consent of the Natives to take the possession of convenient situations in the country in the name of the King of Great Britain'.

He was also instructed: 'If you find the Country uninhabited Take Possession for His Majesty by setting up Proper Marks and Inscriptions as first discoverers and possessors'.

TECHNICAL STUFF

Cook's actions — in planting a flag and carving a tree rather than in seeking to engage in any activity that might amount to gaining consent from 'the Natives' — indicate that he chose to assert British claims over Australia by asserting *possession* rather than *conquest*. The British considered the country theirs for the taking but needed to assert their claim to it over other European colonising powers, so these displays of British possession were designed for them. The *Doctrine of Discovery* was a rule of (European designed) international law that gave a European country the right to take land if they discovered it. The land had to be *vacant* — however, that didn't mean *unpeopled*. It just meant not inhabited by Christians. If the indigenous people were considered heathens, they were deemed as not having rights to their own land and so it was 'vacant'.

Joseph Banks' observations

Joseph Banks, the naturalist who accompanied Cook on the voyage, observed: 'This immense tract of land, considerably larger than all of Europe, is thinly inhabited'. He and Cook had seen only a small part of the coast and none of the interior.

MYTH
BUSTER

Banks hypothesised that the interior would be uninhabited because not enough fish would be available and the 'produce of the land' didn't seem to be enough to support a population. He was, of course, wrong about this. The whole continent was populated and the pre-contact Aboriginal population has been estimated as being as high as a million people.

Banks recorded his general impressions of the Australian east coast, noting plants, insects, molluscs, reptiles, birds, fish and animals. He also recorded the Aboriginal customs he observed. The plant material collected and sorted on the voyage was extensive, with the herbarium specimens accounting for about 1,300 new species.

Banks was able to observe: 'Collection of plants was . . . grown so immensely large that it was necessary that some extraordinary care should be taken of them least they should spoil . . .'

REMEMBER

Botany Bay got its name due to the richness and uniqueness of the plants that were found there. Cook, Banks and the rest of the crew spent a week there collecting specimens and assessing the area's suitability for farming.

MYTH
BUSTER

Banks thought the Aborigines would run away and abandon their rights to land. He and Cook were both wrong. Aboriginal people fought many battles, were killed and killed others, such as convicts sent to work in the bush, during raids and ambushes in defence of their land.

The French floating around

The focus on Cook has obscured the presence of French explorers in the region at the time, and their role in charting the mysterious southern land mass and observing its people, flora and fauna. In 1785, King Louis XVI, after reading accounts of Cook's voyage, commissioned Jean-François de Galaup, Comte de La Pérouse, to circumnavigate the Pacific. After sailing to Chile, Alaska, California, East Asia, Japan and the South Pacific, the expedition continued to Australia. By then, news had reached them of an English fleet setting out to establish a penal colony in New South Wales.

La Pérouse sailed in to Botany Bay on 26 January 1788, days after the British fleet arrived. After six weeks, his ships left for New Caledonia and were never seen again. Luckily, his journal and other papers were sent back to France before he disappeared.

Establishing a British Colony

On his return to England, Cook reported that Australia was sparsely populated. Cook and his crew also brought back the view that Aboriginal people in Australia were less technologically advanced than other indigenous populations encountered by the British when building their Empire. They didn't wear clothes. They had small, rudimentary huts and knew 'nothing of Cultivation'. From the accounts of Cook's voyage, Britain viewed Australia as almost empty. In a vast continent with a small, nomadic population, the land was available for possession.

In 1783, James Matra, who had been a midshipman on Cook's voyage, was a leading proponent of establishing a colony in New Holland. The idea became known as the *Matra proposal*. Among its great advantages, Matra listed that the land was 'peopled by only a few black inhabitants, who, in the rudest state of society, knew no other arts than were necessary to their mere animal existence'.

Matra's idea was that the new colony could be established using Americans who had remained loyal to the British during the War of Independence. This argument was rejected but he later amended the proposal to include 'transportees' or convicts among the settlers to relieve Britain's overflowing prisons. He also argued that the land offered an environment for flax cultivation, trade with China and others, and the availability of timber for ships' masts. Sir Joseph Banks supported the proposal.

Seeing through Indigenous Eyes: Perspectives on the Arrival

Europeans who sailed the world, finding people living in different lands and circumstances, would have been used to seeing cultural difference. Although evidence exists of some contact with Europeans who sailed past or ventured inland — intentionally or because they were lost — the cultural differences must have been confronting for Indigenous people. The white skin, blond hair, clothing and new technology must have been strange curiosities.

'We thought they were ghosts'

Some Aboriginal people thought that white people were the ghosts of their ancestors returning from the spirit world.

CULTURAL PROTOCOLS

In many Aboriginal languages, the same word used for 'ghost' was used for Europeans. In Gamillaroi, the word *wunda* means ghost and was used as a name for white people. In South Australia, the Ngarrindjeri used the word *grinkari* for white people, the same word used to describe a human corpse with its skin peeled off. In the south of Western Australia, the Noongar people used the word *djanga* for Europeans, the same word used to describe the spirits of dead people.

'Are they human?'

European clothing was mystifying to Indigenous people, who had never seen such elaborate cloth. Upon meeting Europeans, some Aboriginal men would insist that the newcomers remove their clothes to prove that they were human.

CULTURAL PROTOCOLS

Contact with Europeans was negotiated by the senior men of Aboriginal clans, avoiding, where they could, placing women and children in a position where they would meet the visitors. When outsiders approached islands in the Torres Strait, the women were also hidden, with the men interacting with the visitors. Women weren't allowed to speak with them.

Chapter **6**

The Brits' First Colony: 1788

The reports of Australia from Lieutenant James Cook and his crew planted a seed that the newly acquired territory would make a good place for a penal colony. The settlement would expand the Empire, establish a base in the southern part of the world and provide a place to send prisoners from England's overcrowded prisons. Captain Arthur Phillip set out on the long voyage to Australia, in charge of 11 ships and a population of some 1,500 convicts, crew, marines and civilians, with orders from the British government to establish the colony.

The Aboriginal people were as strange and unfamiliar to the British who arrived on this First Fleet as the landscape, animals and plants. Understandably, they found the environment difficult to adjust to. And the new arrivals were just as strange to the Aboriginal people. Relationships between Aboriginal people and the British quickly became strained as the original inhabitants began to realise that the white people weren't going away.

In this chapter, I look at how the British fared as they established their new colony and how the relationship between Aboriginal people and the new arrivals unfolded.

Captain Phillip and the First Fleet

Britain had transported criminals from its overcrowded prisons to the Americas since the early 1600s. After the American Revolution (1775 to 1783), the United States refused to keep accepting them. Britain then had to find somewhere new. It was also thought that the establishment of a colony would assist in asserting claims over the land against other colonising powers, particularly the French. On 18 August 1786, the decision was made to send a fleet to Botany Bay.

REMEMBER

Captain Arthur Phillip was chosen to lead the First Fleet because he had experience in transporting slaves from Africa to America.

The First Fleet set sail from London on 13 May 1787 for Botany Bay, comprising:

>> Eleven ships, including two naval escort ships, three supply ships and six convict ships

>> Around 1,500 people, including more than 700 convicts (200 of them female convicts and their children), about 250 marines, up to 400 crew, around 50 civilian women and children (the families of the marines) and about 15 officials and passengers

The long trip over

The Fleet crossed the Atlantic, stopping for food, animals and other supplies in the Canary Islands and Rio de Janeiro, and then sailed again, stopping at the Cape of Good Hope at the southern tip of Africa and taking on board further supplies and livestock.

The trip was long and gruelling. It was more than 15,000 miles (24,000 kilometres) and took eight months. Conditions were cramped, food scarce and the smell of humans and animals in such close quarters overwhelming. People became sick but only 23 people, all of them convicts, died.

The ships variously arrived at Botany Bay between 18 and 20 January 1788. Concerns were quickly raised about the spot initially chosen for the settlement because little fresh water was available and the soil was sandy and not fertile enough for farming. Captain Phillip and a small number of his crew sailed north to search for a better location. They found a protected cove in a harbour they named after the British Home Secretary, Lord Sydney. The Fleet landed and began to disembark on this spot on 26 January 1788. A British flag was planted in the ground and the British colony proclaimed.

TECHNICAL STUFF

James Cook had claimed British sovereignty over the east coast of Australia during his voyage in 1770 and Britain considered that it owned a huge part of the country. Because Aboriginal people didn't fence or cultivate the land, the British considered their possession of the land to be justified. But the area that became known as Sydney wasn't vacant land. It was the land of the Gadigal or Cadigal people of the Eora nation. Their interests weren't considered when their lands were claimed as part of the British Empire. In raising the British flag and asserting possession over the land, the British also asserted control over the Aboriginal people, making them British subjects who were expected to obey British laws.

The Captain's orders

Phillip had been instructed to make friendly contact with the Aboriginal people. He was to not only create peaceful relations with them but also see if they could be useful in establishing the colony. Before he set sail, Phillip received his Instructions from King George III. They advised him about managing the convicts, granting and cultivating the land, and exploring the country. They also included specific instruction about how to deal with the Aboriginal people, stating that their lives and livelihoods were to be protected and that friendly relations with them were to be encouraged.

However, the instructions made no mention of protecting or even recognising Aboriginal lands. The British worked on the assumption that the land was now their possession. Although the First Fleet was instructed to establish the colony at Botany Bay, Phillip was separately authorised to choose any other appropriate neighbouring territory.

CULTURAL PROTOCOLS

In his task of making friends with the Aboriginal people, Captain Phillip had an advantage that he didn't realise: A missing front tooth. In Aboriginal culture, a missing front tooth was a symbol of status within society.

TECHNICAL STUFF

By staking a claim on Australia, Britain was relying on the *doctrine of discovery*, a convention that meant that a colonial power that first 'discovered' a land had a right to possession. The doctrine was an understanding between other colonial powers, not with the people of the land being claimed. British claims to Australia would later be justified on the basis that the country was *terra nullius* — vacant or without a government. As neither of those assertions was correct in fact — because Aboriginal people were there and they did have a system of laws and government — this became known as a 'legal fiction' and remained in Australian law until 1992.

Establishing a Penal Colony

The day after the First Fleet arrived in Sydney Cove, male convicts were put to work to clear the land, put up tents, unload the stores, pen the animals, and plant seeds and corn. They then began to build permanent structures. Captain Phillip became the governor of the colony. He oversaw the construction of his own residence, Government House, as well as storehouses, a hospital, huts and a church. By November 1788, another settlement was established at Parramatta, 25 kilometres upstream to the west, where the soil was more fertile. In order to survive in the early years, the British relied on the knowledge of the Aboriginal people in the area. They assisted with identifying where water sources were, what plants and seeds were edible, and how to successfully hunt animals.

REMEMBER

The first conflict between Aboriginal people and the British occurred on 29 May 1788 in the area that's now Rushcutters Bay. Two convicts were killed after they attempted to steal a canoe.

CROSSING CULTURES, BRIEFLY

The first Aboriginal person to be captured by the British was Arabanoo, who was taken in December 1788. The British thought forcing contact would be a way of learning the Aboriginal language of the area and of improving relationships. He was taken to the settlement and a convict was appointed to guard him. Reports say that he was at first pleased by a handcuff on his wrist because he believed it to be an ornament but became angry when he discovered its purpose. He eventually adopted European clothes, learned to speak English and dined regularly with Governor Phillip. He didn't like all of the European customs — he was horrified by the practice of publicly flogging people.

A severe epidemic of smallpox broke out among the Aboriginal population in April 1789. Arabanoo helped to care for two children — Nabaree and Abaroo — and then succumbed to the disease himself and died in May. During his time among the British, he gave them information about the language and customs of his people.

Other Aboriginal people were captured by the early settlers, who had similar goals of learning the language and culture, and forcing closer relationships between the Aboriginal people and the settlers.

First impressions

Many of the white colonists' first impressions of Aboriginal people were not positive. They didn't understand — or value — the culture of the Aboriginal people, even though their knowledge helped the colony to survive. Variously, Aboriginal people were described as 'stupid', 'barbaric' and 'primitive'. Some of the white settlers were afraid of the Aboriginal people and didn't want them near the settlement.

However, other people in this first colony understood that Aboriginal culture, while being very different from European culture, had its own advantages and benefits. They also understood that Aboriginal people were deeply attached to their land and were attempting to resist the presence of the British.

One such person was an officer in the First Fleet, Watkin Tench. He took time to observe the cultural practices and habits of the Aboriginal people. His diary gives insights into the way Aboriginal people lived at the time of the establishment of the colony at Sydney:

It does not appear that these poor creatures have any fixed Habitation;
sometimes sleeping in a Cavern of Rock, which they make as warm as a Oven

by lighting a Fire in the middle of it, they will take up their abode here, for one Night perhaps, then in another the next Night. At other times (and we believe mostly in Summer) they take up their lodgings for a Day or two in a Miserable Wigwam, which they made from Bark of a Tree. There are dispersed about the woods near the water, 2, 3, 4 together; some Oyster, Cockle and Muscle [sic] Shells lie about the Entrance of them, but not in any Quantity to indicate they make these huts their constant Habitation. We met with some that seemed entirely deserted indeed it seems pretty evident that their Habitation, whether Caverns or Wigwams, are common to all, and Alternatively inhabited by different Tribes.

REMEMBER

Upon his arrival, Captain Phillip estimated that the population of Aboriginal people in the Sydney region was 1,500. However, the total population of Aboriginal people in Australia at that time is estimated to be between 750,000 and 1 million, according to the Australian Bureau of Statistics (ABS), based on anthropological minimum figures.

A difficult start

The first years of the colony were difficult and it almost didn't survive. The first harvest produced nothing, so Governor Phillip sent a ship to the Cape of Good Hope for more supplies. In June 1790, the Second Fleet, consisting of six ships, arrived. Its supplies were badly needed but the newly arrived convicts were so ill, with many close to death, that they were more of a drain than a help. Of more than 1,000 convicts who travelled with the Second Fleet, 278 died on the voyage over — compared with 23 of the 1,500 people on the First Fleet — earning it the nickname of 'the Death Fleet'. It had been contracted to private businesses.

The 11 ships of the Third Fleet, carrying some 2,000 convicts (with fewer than 200 dying en route), landed in 1791. (By 1800, another 20 convict ships had arrived, with deaths on board remaining relatively high on most voyages until around 1804, when the figure dropped to a handful each voyage; by 1817, Britain was sending more than ten ships per year, each carrying around 150 to 200 people, until 1840, with another four arriving in 1849.)

Although food was still in short supply, it's fair to say that the colony was well established by 1792. By this time, trading ships were regularly visiting Sydney. A whaling industry had been established and the sheep were producing wool. Released convicts were engaged in farming. However, problems occurred in the colony because of the gender imbalance — with about four men to every woman.

Governor Phillip found establishing relationships with the local Aboriginal people difficult. He and some others in his colony attempted to reach across the cultural divide between people who had different lifestyles, worldviews and languages. But he became frustrated by the lack of results and attempted to facilitate better contact. Aboriginal people seemed generally uninterested in European customs and ways. Phillip's frustrations were exacerbated when he was speared in the shoulder in May 1790 while at Manly Cove, the traditional land of the Cameraigal.

His patience with the local people was further strained when Aboriginal resistance fighter Pemulwuy speared a white colonist. This attack was provoked because the man had killed some Aboriginal people. Phillip wanted his own revenge and ordered the troops to kill ten and capture two Aboriginal people. Fifty troops were sent into the bush, but their lack of skill in the local environment meant that they gave early warning of their presence to the Aboriginal people. As a result, the party failed to capture a single Aboriginal person.

REMEMBER

Conflict occurred between Aboriginal people and the new arrivals due to the pressures placed on the environment by the colony. With local resources, particularly food, running low, some of the local clans found themselves without enough food. This was especially so in the winter months. Some people took up offers from Phillip to move into town, sleeping and eating in the settler's homes.

Governor Phillip returned to London in 1792. By this time, the colony was established. Between 1792 and 1794, the governance of the colony was the responsibility of Major Francis Grose and then Captain William Paterson until Governor Hunter took over in 1795.

Seeing How the Locals Dealt with the New Arrivals

The arrival of the British led to fundamental and irreversible change within the culture, lifestyle, health and spiritual life of Aboriginal people.

Aboriginal people along the east coast of Australia had had contact with white people before. Their ships would sail along the coast and, though they would stop sometimes, they would always move on.

Aboriginal people didn't engage in serious resistance to the new colony at first because they assumed that the white people wouldn't stay. In Aboriginal culture, people had responsibility for their traditional country and their spiritual life was wrapped up in the landscape around them. They assumed that white people would have those responsibilities and worldview too and would have to return to their own land to look after it. The way the Europeans colonised other people's land was a foreign concept to Aboriginal people.

When it became apparent that the white people were going to stay, the attitudes of Aboriginal people began to harden. Many violent acts of resistance occurred as they took a stand against the occupation of their lands and the threats to their culture and way of life. They were particularly concerned about the spoiling of water sources, the impact on food supplies and European practices such as building houses and farming, which appeared to destroy the landscape. Conflict also escalated over the treatment of Aboriginal women by British men and the destruction of sacred sites by the British as their colony grew.

Responses of Aboriginal people to the permanent presence of the British were complex. Some continued to resist — sometimes violently — the continual encroachment onto Aboriginal land. Others interacted with the new arrivals and adopted some of their customs, becoming well-known figures in the colony.

Bennelong

It seems Governor Phillip believed that one way to improve his relationship with the Aboriginal people was through an interpreter of sorts, willing or unwilling. As with Arabanoo's capture in 1788, in November 1789, Bennelong and Colebee were captured and taken to the Governor. Colebee escaped but Bennelong remained in the colony. He adopted some of the habits and customs of the British, dressing in their clothes and learning their language. His portrait appears in Figure 6-1.

FIGURE 6-1: Portrait of Bennelong by an unknown artist, circa 1798.

Bennelong went back to his clan in May 1790 but was seen again in September when he was at the large gathering at Manly where Governor Phillip was speared. He wasn't involved in the incident — which resulted from a misunderstanding — but afterwards he frequently appeared at Sydney Cove to enquire after the Governor's health. This contact continued, with Bennelong reassured that he wouldn't be detained. In 1791, a hut was built for him on the eastern point of Sydney Cove at a place now called Bennelong Point, site of the Sydney Opera House.

Barangaroo, Bennelong's wife, wasn't as impressed, and opposed her husband's conciliatory relationship with the people who were establishing themselves on Aboriginal land. She was encouraged to drink wine and wear European clothes but refused, angering her husband. All she ever wore was a slim bone through her nose, even when dining with the Governor. (See the following section for more on Barangaroo.)

When Governor Phillip returned to London in December 1792, Bennelong went with him — along with another Aboriginal man called Yemmerrawanne — and they were presented to King George III. Yemmerrawanne died in Britain after battling a chest infection. Bennelong returned to Sydney with Governor Hunter in 1795. Reports at that time observe his ill health due to cold, homesickness and the long delay in leaving for Australia. On his return, he seemed to find fitting in or being fully accepted by either his own people or the colonists hard. He began drinking heavily and died in 1813; he was buried at James Squire's orchard at Kissing Point on the Parramatta River.

The British presence in Australia saw the population of the Aboriginal people dramatically drop. This wasn't due to frontier violence, but to the inability of the immune systems of Aboriginal people to cope with the diseases that the British brought with them. With no built-up resistance, smallpox, colds and flu were lethal to Aboriginal people. The drop in population around Sydney Cove was so drastic that bodies were found in the water or on rocks, evidence that the customary burial practices couldn't be carried out because not enough people were alive or well enough to carry them out.

Barangaroo

Barangaroo was an important senior Cammeraygal woman and renowned fisherwoman. Women like her were the main providers of food in the community, and she was a strong figure in the colony. While her husband, Bennelong, interacted with the colonists (refer to the previous section), she continued to assert her rights to her country and rejected the trinkets such as clothing that the colonists tried to tempt her with. She is also recorded as intervening when a convict was being flogged. Appalled at the barbaric act, she threatened to flog the man meting out the punishment. A headland in Sydney Harbour, where the Aboriginal women used to gather, is now named after her.

CULTURAL
PROTOCOLS

As a token of goodwill, the colonists collected 4,000 fish in one day in 1790 as a gift to the Cammeraygal men. This showed both how plentiful the resource was and how little the colonists thought about sustainability. When Barangaroo found out, she was enraged at the waste. But she also understood that the economic power of Aboriginal women was being undermined.

CULTURAL
PROTOCOLS

When she went into labour, Barangaroo wanted to give birth at Government House. This was built on a site that was important to the local Aboriginal people, whose practice was to give birth in such places for cultural and spiritual reasons. Phillip refused her request. Barangaroo didn't want to have her baby in the hospital because she viewed it as a place of death. Phillip persuaded Bennelong to let him take her there, and she died shortly after giving birth. (The child perished in infancy.) Bennelong buried her ashes in the garden of Government House.

REMEMBER

Bennelong and Barangaroo represented the two different approaches that Aboriginal people had to the invaders. Bennelong worked closely with them and attempted to be like them. Barangaroo, on the other hand, continued to resist their presence and the imposition of European culture on Aboriginal people.

Pemulwuy

Pemulwuy was a leader and warrior within the Aboriginal community (see Figure 6-2 for the only known image of him). He came from the Bidjigal clan of the Dharug nation to the south and west of Sydney Cove, around the Georges River and Parramatta area. He came to the attention of the colonists when he speared Phillip's gamekeeper, John McIntire, in September 1790. Around this time, the colonists had started to occupy more and more land, sparking the Hawkesbury and Nepean wars.

Led by Pemulwuy and his son, Tedbury, Aboriginal people raided stations or killed sheep and cattle. They also used fire to burn buildings and destroy crops.

REMEMBER

The various clans made these raids for various reasons. Sometimes the purpose was to obtain food, particularly corn. Other times, the raids were in retaliation for atrocities committed against Aboriginal people, particularly Aboriginal women. This guerrilla war of resistance continued until 1816.

In May 1801, Governor King issued orders that Aboriginal people near Parramatta, Georges River and Prospect could be shot on sight, and in November a proclamation offered a reward for Pemulwuy's death or capture. Pemulwuy was twice shot seriously and survived, giving rise to the myth that he was unable to be killed by bullets. He eventually died from bullet wounds in June 1802 after being shot by two colonists. His head was cut off and sent to England. Aboriginal people continue to be unhappy that a person they consider a resistance fighter hasn't been given a proper burial, but his head has never been found in any British repository. His son, Tedbury, continued the resistance.

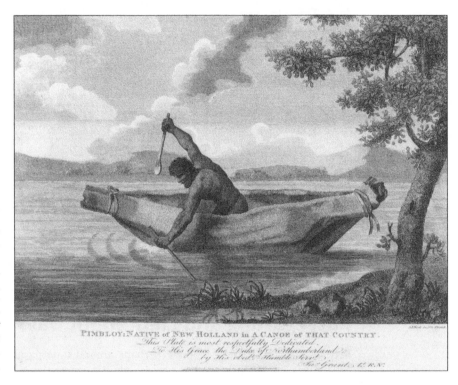

FIGURE 6-2: The only known image of Pemulwuy, by Samuel John Neele (1758–1824), from James Grant's *The Narrative of a Voyage of Discovery in HM Vessel Lady Nelson 1803–1804.*

REMEMBER

Pemulwuy's impact on the colonists in his resistance to their growing settlement is shown in the words of Governor King, who wrote that Pemulwuy was 'a terrible pest to the colony', though he acknowledged that 'he was a brave and independent character'.

CULTURAL PROTOCOLS

While some of the local clan members who survived the impact of the diseases looked to move away from the settlement, other clans came to the Sydney area. Some came to assist with the resistance to British presence and some were curious about the new settlement.

MYTH BUSTER

Even though Sydney Cove was the place of the first European colony in Australia, and the arrival of the British affected the culture and practices of the Aboriginal people who lived there, traces of Aboriginal presence in the area can still be found today. Shell middens and rock carvings can be found around the harbour, as well as further afield, such as the carving shown in Figure 6-3 (from Bundeena, just south of Sydney). Cultural connections between people have also been maintained.

FIGURE 6-3:
Rock art depicts a kangaroo, from Bundeena, Sydney.

Patyegarang and Lieutenant Dawes

Patyegarang was a young woman, perhaps around 15 years old, at the time the colony was established. She has become a well-known figure today because she formed a friendship with one of the engineers in the colonist, Lieutenant Dawes, who was also an astronomer.

Dawes set up a hut at what is now called Dawes Point on Sydney Harbour. He was curious about Aboriginal culture, and particularly their understanding of the skies. Patyegarang was his key teacher and Dawes recorded the words of the Eora language that she taught him in his journals. That language is being revived today with heavy reliance on those journals — a lasting legacy.

Dawes left the colony after a disagreement with Governor Phillip about a punitive expedition to punish the local Aboriginal people after Phillip's gamekeeper was speared. He became heavily involved with the international anti-slavery movement.

The relationship between Patyegarang and Lieutenant Dawes is distinctive because Dawes, unlike his contemporaries who wrongly saw Indigenous people as primitive and stone-aged, was respectful and curious about the knowledge of the local Aboriginal community and wanted to learn from them.

CURIOSITY AND DESECRATION

The skeletal remains of Indigenous people were treated as curiosities by the Europeans. Theories that certain races were inferior to Europeans, which were prevalent at the time, also created scientific interest in remains. Skeletons were collected from burial sites and sent back to universities, museums and private collections in Britain and Europe. Today, Indigenous people advocate strongly for the return of those remains. When they are successful, they give those remains a proper burial.

Chapter **7**

Pushing the Boundaries of the Colony

After the penal colony in Sydney Cove was established in 1788, the settlement first went through a period of stabilisation before starting to grow. The British began colonies across the country and eventually colonised the whole of Australia.

The colonisation of Australia wasn't a peaceful process. Indigenous people describe it as an invasion. But something that the Europeans carried with them had a greater impact on the Aboriginal population than their firearms — diseases against which Aboriginal people had developed no immunity.

The British colonists began granting Aboriginal land to settlers and freed convicts so that they could farm. Europeans took Aboriginal land, destroyed the balance of the environment, destroyed hunting grounds and ceremonial sites, stopped access to waterholes, and depleted resources for food and medicine. This led to inevitable conflict as Aboriginal people attempted to defend their traditional territories and their way of life.

In this chapter, I look at the development of the colonies and its effect on Aboriginal communities around the country. I also examine the legal ramifications of the way the British established their ownership of land for the future of Australia's Indigenous peoples.

Opening Up the Land: White Settlement Spreads

The Sydney settlement spread out quickly to the north and south, and soon to the west. Though the Blue Mountains stopped the expansion for a short period, the range was crossed in 1813, opening up vast new country the colonists thought could be used for farming. Penal colonies were started in Van Diemen's Land (Tasmania) in 1803 and at Moreton Bay in 1824, in what was to become Queensland. Free settlements started in Melbourne, Adelaide and Perth.

By the 1880s, the colonists had reached Central Australia, establishing pastoral stations. Even some of the most remote parts of the country were being settled. The colonies were each separately proclaimed over this period, splitting off from New South Wales, and then uniting as separate states under the banner of the Commonwealth of Australia in 1901. See the section 'Growing the British Colony', later in this chapter, for more on the establishment of the colonies.

In the beginning, Aboriginal people often met the newcomers with hospitality and generosity but, when they realised that the colonists were not going to leave — and would continue to take more and more land — attitudes began to change and conflict was inevitable.

As the colony grew, pressure for more land for the settlement increased. The British had always intended to take over the land when they set up the colony in Sydney Cove. As the penal colony established itself, more people — including freed convicts — wanted to try their hand at developing pastoral properties and the wealth they promised. And the colony needed increased production of food in order to support its growing population. Land grants were given for this purpose and the settlement spread further and further across the lands of Aboriginal people.

Spreading Disease Far and Wide

While colonists tried to attract Aboriginal people to European customs and values, they brought something that would destroy Aboriginal society more quickly than their colonisation processes — their diseases.

Aboriginal people had lived for tens of thousands of years largely without contact with other people, and lived in a very healthy and clean environment. Their immune systems had, therefore, not developed natural resistance to many of the diseases that were common in European society. For this reason, disease was the most lethal thing that the settlers brought with them, quite likely the greatest contributing factor to the drastic reduction of population numbers among Aboriginal people during the period of colonisation. Before contact with Europeans, the chief medical issues for Aboriginal society related to eye and skin complaints.

REMEMBER

The diseases that swept through Aboriginal communities, often proving fatal, included the common cold, influenza, leprosy, measles, smallpox, tuberculosis, venereal disease and whooping cough. Europeans could still die from these diseases in the 18th century but for Aboriginal people with no previous exposure and so no immunity, the death rate was much higher.

In some places on the *frontier* (land that was in the process of being colonised), disease swept through and killed most of the Aboriginal population before any contact with white people was made. Children were particularly susceptible to these imported diseases and some areas reported that the spread of the diseases had killed all of their children.

By 1850, disease had led to a noticeable decline in Aboriginal numbers, dramatically affecting Aboriginal cultural life and society. Older people, as well as children, were vulnerable to diseases, so figures of authority — such as Elders and medicine experts — died, and with them went their knowledge. Kinship systems were also severely affected by the loss of so many people so quickly. Links between generations were also impacted because the tradition of handing down oral knowledge to people was severely disrupted. Traditions, knowledge and languages were lost during this period. By the time Aboriginal people found themselves physically defending their land, they were dealing with depleted numbers, the loss of loved ones and fundamental changes to their cultural and societal structures.

Meeting Aboriginal Resistance

Europeans had assumed that Aboriginal people would appreciate the benefits of European culture. They believed that they had a superior and advanced civilisation and that Aboriginal people were backward and uncivilised, and had a savage culture. But Aboriginal people could see very little point in many European practices when the colonists arrived. They didn't need to farm or keep domestic animals because they survived perfectly well with their hunter-gatherer lifestyle. They also had their own complex worldviews and understandings of the environment around them, so saw little need to adopt European religions and philosophies.

REMEMBER

Many incidents have been reported where Aboriginal people were, in fact, horrified by some British practices — especially on observing the public flogging of convicts as a punishment.

As for the two cultures learning from each other, it seemed, at first, that the colonists were the ones who had more to learn from Aboriginal culture. Aboriginal people showed them how to cut and treat the barks of Australian trees in order to build shelters, how to use bark fibre in order to make ropes and the best timbers for making boats. They also proved to be excellent guides around the land and often assisted Europeans seeking to explore further afield.

Even though the knowledge Aboriginal people had of their environment helped the fledgling colony to survive, some colonists claimed that Aboriginal people were naturally evil, untrustworthy and prone to violence. This was, of course, not true. Aboriginal people were generally peaceful, with fighting usually on a small scale and often stopping when first blood was drawn. Certainly, no wars over land or ideology took place such as those that had occurred in Europe.

Particularly, Aboriginal people didn't understand the way Europeans took others' land. They had a spiritual and cultural attachment to their own traditional territory and assumed that the British would have the same connection with their own country. The idea that you would take over someone else's land was unknown to them.

TECHNICAL
STUFF

For the British, the issue around who owned the land was clear. They believed they had rightfully claimed possession over the land and were entitled to it. Lieutenant Cook had claimed the east coast of Australia in 1770 and the colony had further established the entitlement in 1788 (refer to Chapters 5 and 6). With these actions, the British not only thought they had defeated the claims of all other colonial powers — such as the French and the Dutch — but also that they now had power over Aboriginal people themselves, who had now become British subjects. Some effort was made to communicate this new legal arrangement to Aboriginal people, a challenge made more complex because of the need to communicate across languages and cultures. Attempts were made to communicate these concepts pictorially, most famously in the Proclamation to the Aborigines in 1816 from Governor Thomas Davey in Van Diemen's Land, shown in Figure 7-1.

FIGURE 7-1: Governor Davey's Proclamation to the Tasmanian Aborigines in 1816.

While this position of power was clear to the British, it wasn't so clear to Aboriginal people. They didn't understand British property law and had their own Aboriginal laws that recognised their custodianship of the land and their responsibility to it. They didn't realise they were subject to British law any more than they understood that they had now become British subjects.

REMEMBER

Governor Lachlan Macquarie established an Aboriginal school at Parramatta in 1814. Called the 'Native Institution', its aims were to 'civilise, educate and foster habits of industry and decency in the Aborigines'. Parents, however, removed children from the school after they realised its aim was to distance the children from their culture and families. The school closed in 1820. Macquarie also established a farm that Aboriginal people could work on in Port Jackson, with the aim of them then integrating into white society as farmhands and domestic servants. Similar to the school, the farm eventually failed.

CULTURAL PROTOCOLS

Governor Macquarie shared the frustration of the governors before him that Aboriginal people didn't seem interested in learning the ways of Europeans. He came up with the idea that he would identify a 'king' or 'queen' in different Aboriginal clans as a way of facilitating better relationships with them by having a person who could negotiate on behalf of others. This idea, of course, completely misunderstood the dynamics and structure of Aboriginal society — its decision-making was much more inclusive than the strict hierarchies of European cultures. The naming of a person as 'king' or 'queen' by the colonists didn't elevate that person's power within his or her own clan. Instead, the breastplates Aboriginal people were given to denote their position came to represent attempts to undermine Aboriginal society and a tendency to patronise Aboriginal people.

TECHNICAL STUFF

Within European culture, strong views were held about the racial superiority of white people and the inferiority of all other races. This meant that the British who arrived in Australia thought Aboriginal people were naturally inferior to the British. In fact, in some theories, Aboriginal people were thought to be at the lowest end of the evolutionary chain. Some of the colonists wanted to 'civilise' the Aboriginal people so they would live more like Europeans. Others thought it inevitable that Aboriginal people would die out because they wouldn't be able to withstand European colonisation.

BUNGAREE, ABORIGINAL DIPLOMAT

Aboriginal people and colonists had complex and varied ways of dealing with each other. One Aboriginal figure who became prominent in the Sydney colony was Bungaree.

Originally from the Broken Bay area, he moved to Sydney and walked between the two worlds. Bungaree was intelligent and curious, with a strong sense of humour, impersonating the governors and other local figures. He befriended Governor Macquarie — who built huts for him and his family — and sailed with Matthew Flinders as he circumnavigated Australia from 1801 to 1803. He was a popular figure in the new colony, with news of him appearing regularly in the newspapers, and he was often drawn and painted by artists. He also assisted the colonists in tracking escaped convicts. Governor Macquarie gave him the title of King and he became known as King of Broken Bay. But he was also influential in his own community and looked after his family by selling or bartering fish. Like a diplomat, he navigated and negotiated between the colonists and his own people.

As with several other Aboriginal personalities around Sydney Cove, Bungaree had a wife who was also a colourful local character. Her name was Cora Gooseberry and she became known as the Queen of Sydney to South Head. She was often portrayed wrapped in a government-issued blanket, with a scarf on her head and smoking a pipe. At the time of her death in 1852, at the age of 75, she was thought by the colonists to have been the last member of the Kuring-gai clan; however, historians later discovered that descendants of her clan had joined the remnants of other groups to ensure their survival.

Growing the British Colony

As the colony started to grow, demand for land increased. Between 1788 and 1868 about 150,000 convicts arrived from the United Kingdom. Free settlers started arriving in 1793. Colonists — and eventually freed convicts — wanted to try their hand at the growing sheep and cattle industries. Sometimes people were given land grants by the colonial government; other times they simply took the land. These people became known as *squatters*. They took their sheep and settled in the spacious lands, thought most suitable for pastures, around the Macquarie and Lachlan Rivers. By 1804, most of the Cumberland Plain west of Sydney was occupied by the colonists.

Settlement spread to the north and south of Sydney, and out to the west to the base of the Blue Mountains. Other sites were explored, and new *penal colonies* (specifically, areas developed using convict labour, as well as providing places of imprisonment) and *free settlements* (those built without convicts) were founded over the next 100 years:

>> **1788:** Penal colony at Port Jackson (Sydney Cove) established

>> **1803:** Penal colony at Van Diemen's Land established at Risdon Cove and then Hobart Town in 1804 (prisons operated on the west coast at Sarah Island and Macquarie Harbour, 1822 to 1833 and 1846 to 1847, and on the east coast at Port Arthur, 1833 to 1877); proclaimed as separate colony 1825, name changed to Tasmania 1856

>> **1813:** Blaxland, Wentworth and Lawson crossed the Blue Mountains

>> **1824:** Penal colony at Moreton Bay (Redcliffe Point) established, moved to current site of Brisbane in 1825; Queensland proclaimed 1859

>> **1824 to 1838:** Successive military settlements established along the coast of the Northern Territory (all abandoned by 1849); western border of New South Wales shifted west to include them

>> **1826:** Military settlement established at King George Sound (later site of Albany, Western Australia), extending the British claim to the whole of Australia

>> **1829:** Free settlement established at Perth and western half of Australia named Swan River Colony; Western Australia proclaimed 1839

>> **1831:** Free settlement of Port Phillip (Melbourne) established; Colony of Victoria founded 1851

>> **1836:** Colony of South Australia proclaimed and free settlement of Adelaide established

>> **1863:** Northern Territory annexed to South Australia; Darwin established 1869

>> **1871:** London Missionary Society arrives on Erub (Darnley Island) in the Torres Strait; Torres Strait Islands annexed to Queensland 1879

REMEMBER

When the Torres Strait Islands were annexed to Queensland in 1879, the traditional owners fell under the control of the Queensland government and were covered by its legislation. When the Queensland government passed the first comprehensive legislation dealing with Indigenous people — the *Aboriginal Protection and Restriction of the Sale of Opium Act 1897* — Torres Strait Islanders were subjected to the same policies of protection and segregation that Aboriginal people were and also lost their legal status as British citizens, becoming, in effect, wards of the state.

Figure 7-2 shows the spread of development during the 19th century. In the following sections, I focus on the settlement of the Bathurst region in New South Wales, the Port Arthur and Moreton Bay penal colonies, and the free settlement of South Australia, which was intended as a model settlement.

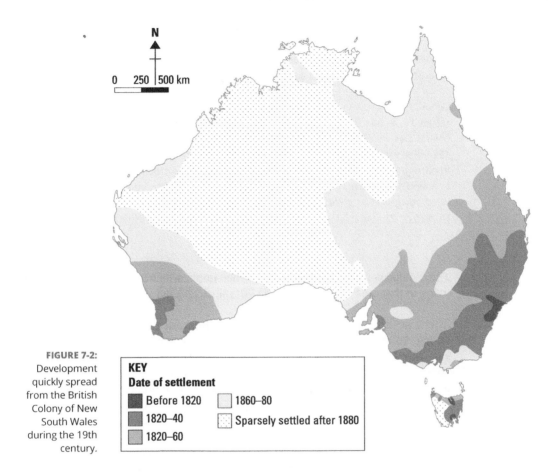

FIGURE 7-2: Development quickly spread from the British Colony of New South Wales during the 19th century.

KEY
Date of settlement

- Before 1820
- 1820–40
- 1820–60
- 1860–80
- Sparsely settled after 1880

Over the mountains

William Wentworth, Gregory Blaxland and William Lawson crossed the Blue Mountains in 1813. This step was important for the blossoming colony because this mountain range had been a barrier to colonial expansion. The land between the sea and the mountains was limited and had soon been taken up. At this time, 250,000 sheep were in the colony. Finding a way through the Blue Mountains gave access to the fertile plains to the west. In 1815, a government settlement was established as the site of the town of Bathurst, at the end of a narrow convict-built road across the mountains, from which exploration parties set out. Free settlers soon followed.

WINDRADYNE: A NOTABLE LEADER

Windradyne, also known as Saturday, was a leader of the Aboriginal resistance to white settlement in the upper Macquarie River region of the central-western area of New South Wales around Bathurst.

After a series of violent clashes between Aboriginal people and settlers that resulted in the deaths of convict stockmen and Aboriginal women and children, Governor Brisbane placed the district under martial law in August 1824.

Windradyne's involvement with incidents that had led to the death of white settlers resulted in a reward being offered for his capture — 500 acres, just over 200 hectares, of land. Despite Windradyne remaining at large, martial law was ended in December 1824. Two weeks later, in an apparent move to negotiate with Governor Brisbane, Windradyne and a large number of his people crossed the mountains into Parramatta to attend the Governor's annual feast, where he was formally pardoned by Brisbane. Windradyne was a significant figure in the resistance of the spread of white settlement. He died on 21 March 1829 as the result of wounds suffered in a tribal fight.

The expansion past the mountains also had implications for the Aboriginal people living in that area — the land of the Wiradjuri. Conflict intensified there in 1824.

After a period of guerrilla warfare, Governor Brisbane declared martial law in the region. Soldiers travelled through the area and killed any Aboriginal men they saw. At one camp, 30 Aboriginal men, women and children were killed and another 30 were forced to jump off a cliff. In revenge, a group of Wiradjuri men, including a warrior called Windradyne, attacked several pastoral properties. Military patrols responded by killing even more Aboriginal people. The intense conflict only ended when many of the Wiradjuri leaders surrendered to the Governor.

MYTH BUSTER

Europeans venturing into parts of Australia where white people hadn't been before were often said to be 'discovering' them. This term implied that this was the first time these places had been seen by people but, of course, Aboriginal people had lived in those areas for tens of thousands of years. Some memorials to European explorers now note that they were the first white visitors to arrive in a certain area, in recognition of the fact that Aboriginal people were there all along.

To Van Diemen's Land

The colony in Van Diemen's Land — to become known as Tasmania in 1856 — was established as a penal colony in 1803, when Lieutenant John Bowen landed at Risdon Cove on the Derwent River with about 50 settlers, crew, soldiers and convicts. Hobart Town was established the following year. A colony in the area was deemed desirable for several reasons, including ensuring the British claim to Australia was further secured against other colonial powers, particularly the French. The colony also provided a place for further punishment of convicts in the Sydney colony, and government officials reasoned that they could be used as free labour to assist in establishing this new colony.

Sealers had started working in the area in 1798. By 1810, the industry had overexploited the area but it had, in the meantime, ensured hostile relations with local Aboriginal people due to the practice of kidnapping Aboriginal women.

In 1804, a group of 50 peaceful Aboriginal people were murdered just outside of the colony at Risdon Cove. This set off a cycle of reprisal killings of blacks by whites and then whites by blacks. Settlers were authorised to kill Aboriginal people even if they were unarmed. Freed convicts and sealers were violent towards the Aboriginal people and they kidnapped Aboriginal women, provoking further clashes of retaliation. Some of the colonists wanted to simply kill off all of the Aboriginal people on the island. Governor George Arthur sought other attempts to control the situation but these didn't work because Aboriginal resistance was tenacious. In the end, he declared martial law, banning Aboriginal people from being in any area settled by whites.

REMEMBER

In 1830, the colony undertook an aggressive military campaign, known as the Black Line, in which more than two thousand troops swept through the whole of the island with the purpose of pushing Aboriginal people into one part of the island. The operation was unsuccessful and only two Aboriginal people were captured. It was an example of how Aboriginal people were better able to survive, navigate and hide in the landscape they had lived in for tens of thousands of years, compared with the newcomers, who had difficulty dealing with the new environment. After this failed attempt, the new governor, George Robinson, negotiated with the remaining clans to move onto Flinders Island in Bass Strait, where they would be protected from further frontier violence. They were later moved to Cape Barren Island.

Conditions on Flinders and Cape Barren Islands were tough and cruel. Often, not enough food was available and people starved to death; disease also ravaged the population. Many mourned for their traditional land and their spiritual life, and struggled with the imposition of European language, culture and religion. By 1850, few had survived. See Chapter 10 for more on Flinders Island.

MYTH BUSTER

The Tasmanian Aboriginal population, the Palawa nation, was commonly believed to have died out with the death of Truganini in 1876. This wasn't the case and the population of Aboriginal people in Tasmania today is about 16,900 — about 3.5 per cent of the total Tasmanian population. After Truganini's death, and against her wishes, her bones were displayed in a museum. A century later, the Tasmanian Aboriginal community cremated them and scattered them into the water.

Into Moreton Bay

Moreton Bay, at Redcliffe Point, lands of the Kabi people — 45 kilometres from what's now Brisbane — was established as a penal colony in 1824. Now in Queensland, at the time the colony was established it was still part of New South Wales. The Aboriginal name for Moreton Bay was Quandamooka. It was home to the Nooghie, Noonuccal and Goenpil clans.

The colony moved up the Brisbane River in 1825 to a site called Mean-jin by the Turrbul people whose land it was, now the central business district of Brisbane. Squatters began arriving from the south in the late 1830s. The first immigrant ship from England arrived in 1848, beginning a period of immigration that established the colony further.

The region, encompassing very fertile lands sought by the colonists, witnessed some violent clashes between Aboriginal people and the settlers. By the 1840s, the settlers had begun moving into the Darling Downs, which offered valuable farming lands, causing increasing conflict with Aboriginal people, the Wacca-burra and the Goonnee-burra. Aboriginal people were not only massacred, but often also poisoned, using flour laced with arsenic or other poisons that was left for Aboriginal people to consume. As the 19th century progressed, settlement spread north and west into the Hervey Bay region, and central and northern Queensland. The conflict between the colonists and Aboriginal people spread with it.

The Adelaide experiment

The colony of Adelaide, established in 1836 in South Australia, was the first in the country that wasn't begun as a penal colony. For this reason, the colonial powers hoped the settlement would be different from those with more brutal beginnings. Influenced by humanitarian movements back in London, South Australia sought to give greater protection to Aboriginal people, giving them the benefits of European civilisation and Christian religion (see the section 'Refuge at a cost: Missions and reserves', later in this chapter). Despite these good intentions, the impact of the colony was devastating on the Kaurna people and their numbers quickly dwindled. Those surviving felt limited benefit from the attempts by missionaries to look after the welfare of Aboriginal people.

Adelaide didn't become a model colony; it had the same problems as other colonies. Tensions occurred between Aboriginal people and settlers over land, and this conflict sometimes became violent. The idea of protecting Aboriginal people gave way to the perceived need to protect white settlers and their lands.

A British Select Committee examined the treatment of Indigenous people in all British colonies, but Australia came in for particular criticism. The report recommended that Protectors of Aborigines be appointed (see Chapter 9 for more on these roles). It also acknowledged that Aboriginal people had a 'plain and sacred right' to their lands.

Dealing with Frontier Conflict

Although the British believed they had taken control of the land in Australia, Aboriginal people were determined to keep it. Aboriginal people didn't accept the presence of the British and didn't take what they saw as an invasion of their land passively. They resisted vigorously — and sometimes violently. They engaged in guerrilla warfare, with small groups of Aboriginal men raiding settlers' farms, killing stock, burning buildings and killing people. And the British retaliated, forcefully.

The ferocity and duration of conflict on the frontier varied from place to place, often depending on the landscape (whether it was flat or mountainous), the speed of settlement, the number of Aboriginal people in the area and the number of colonists.

Aboriginal people were losing not only their ability to survive, but also their connection to country — their culture and their spiritual life. All of this affected their wellbeing.

A wealth of misunderstanding

Traditional food-sharing practices meant that Aboriginal people took what they needed, including cattle on their traditional hunting grounds. They didn't understand that this was considered stealing.

Even though the British now considered Aboriginal people to be under the protection of British law, this protection proved to be of little or no use on the frontier in the face of conflict. The colonial law was far better at protecting the property rights of the colonists than it was at protecting the lives of the Aboriginal people, who were struggling to retain their lands, their culture and their livelihood.

On the margins of the spreading colony, where little government or military presence existed, white settlers often felt justified in taking matters into their own hands. They didn't seem to appreciate or be concerned that their encroachment onto Aboriginal lands had taken away food and water supplies, and the ability to survive. Aboriginal people were shot and their waterholes poisoned, and they were sometimes given poisoned food. This wasn't just an economic conflict. Settlers had little, if any, understanding of Aboriginal spiritual practices. Their activities often destroyed or occupied sacred sites, and the fury this created in Aboriginal people wasn't understood either.

Many white settlers claimed they didn't believe that Aboriginal people had an attachment to the land so, therefore, they couldn't be dispossessed. Aboriginal people didn't put fences around their land. They didn't farm it (at least not according to European practices). They didn't even stay in one place. Others, however, understood that Aboriginal people had deep attachment to their lands and that the loss of their land was a key reason Aboriginal people were so actively resisting white people attempting to set up farms.

For these reasons, conflict on the frontier was inevitable. Colonial governments had no effective solutions for controlling either violence by the settlers or the violent retaliation of Aboriginal people. In this battle, Aboriginal people were at a disadvantage. They had mostly been peaceful and didn't engage in battle. Their tools were made for hunting and killing game, not people. They were no match for the firepower that the settlers had with their guns, especially with their dwindling numbers already weakened by European diseases.

REMEMBER

The exact number of people killed in frontier wars is still a matter of speculation. However, one estimate puts the total killed in frontier conflict at 20,000, with 2,000 being white settlers and the other 18,000 Aboriginal people. Debates between historians and social commentators about the number of Indigenous people killed as a result of frontier violence occurred alongside other fierce debates about the way Australian history should reflect the experiences and treatment of Indigenous people. These debates included whether Indigenous children were 'stolen' or not, and whether the assimilation policy could be considered a kind of cultural genocide or not. These debates are known as the *culture wars*, or *history wars*, and are discussed in more detail in Chapter 14. Exact numbers are difficult to quantify because most times they weren't recorded and oral histories were relied on. When they were recorded — in police reports or settlers' diaries — unofficial figures often differed from official figures. These oral histories and records were also disputed or denied by settlers as quickly as one generation later. So historians had a lot to argue about!

Official responses

By the late 1790s, the Sydney colony had spread to the Hawkesbury and Parramatta regions and this was also met with resistance from Aboriginal people.

Governor King, when he took control of the colony in 1800, initiated a policy that allowed settlers to fire on Aboriginal people. He eventually ordered that Aboriginal people gathering around Parramatta, Georges River and Prospect Hill be driven back from the settlers' areas by firing at them. This was a form of martial law and made visiting the colony a very dangerous activity for Aboriginal people.

By 1810, most of the Cumberland Plains, west of Sydney, was occupied by colonists and the Aboriginal people in the Sydney basin were completely dispossessed of their land. Along the Hawkesbury and Nepean Rivers, resistance was led by Pemulwuy and his son, Tedbury (refer to Chapter 6). Aboriginal people raided cattle and sheep stations as they were set up. They also used fire to destroy buildings and crops.

In 1815, after attacks on farms on the outskirts of the Sydney settlement, Governor Macquarie sent a party to arrest the offenders. This resulted in an attack on an Aboriginal camp at Appin, resulting in the killing of 14 Aboriginal people, none of them known to have been involved in the initial incident.

By the following year, Macquarie had established regulations to control the movement of Aboriginal people. None was to be armed within a mile of any colonial settlement and they couldn't meet in groups of more than six. He went on to issue passports or certificates to Aboriginal people who were thought to 'conduct themselves in a suitable manner' — which meant a manner acceptable to Europeans.

THE WILD WEST

The colony in Perth was set up in 1829. This is the land of the Noongar, or Nyoongar, people. Their resistance to the colonists was led by a warrior named Yagan, until he was killed in 1833. His head was cut off, preserved and sent to England. He's considered a great hero to Aboriginal people and his failure to be buried in his traditional land was a source of great distress to them and they actively sought the return of his remains. His skull was finally brought back to Australia in 1997 and in 2010 it was buried in a traditional Noongar ceremony in the Swan Valley.

Conflict in the area continued, though, with Governor Stirling leading a party down the Swan River to attack local Aboriginal clans. This conflict became known as the Battle of Pinjarra and, while official reports claim a single colonist and 14 Aboriginal people were killed, unofficial reports hold that a whole clan (possibly up to 300 people) was wiped out.

Although the colony was originally started by free settlers, it became a penal colony in 1850 and convict labour was used to help build infrastructure such as Fremantle Prison and Government House. Over 9,000 convicts were sent to the Perth colony.

The guerrilla warfare in these areas continued until 1816 and set the pattern and style of resistance that would occur across the country as Aboriginal people tried to defend their lands against the encroaching settlers.

Violence escalated against Aboriginal people in the 1830s around the colonies.

REMEMBER

The Port Phillip District Wars raged in what is now Victoria from 1830 until 1850. At the time, the area was considered part of New South Wales.

In 1838, in response to conflict on the Liverpool Plains in north-central New South Wales around present-day Tamworth, mounted police led by Major Nunn killed 60 to 70 Aboriginal people at Vinegar Hill, at a place called Slaughterhouse Creek.

On 10 June 1838, the infamous Myall Creek Massacre occurred in northern New South Wales. A group of 28 local Aboriginal people — mostly old people, women and children — were bound together and shot. They had been accused of stealing sheep but they were later discovered to be innocent. They were tied together with rope and taken to a place where they were shot, hacked to death or decapitated. Their bodies were then burned.

The station owner, William Hobbs, was away when the massacre happened but reported it to authorities when he returned. This case was unusual because the seven white station hands responsible were charged with murder. After two controversial trials, they were convicted and hanged. Many people in the colony were angered that white people could be charged and hanged for the deaths of blacks.

REMEMBER

The Myall Creek massacre was recognised by the local community who placed a memorial near the site on 10 June 2000, and both the memorial and the site were given national heritage listing on 7 June 2008.

Over a period of almost one hundred years, numerous massacres took place. Here's a list of some of the most notorious:

>> **1838:** An entire community of Aboriginal people is massacred at Long Lagoon in Queensland.

>> **1840:** At Rufus River, in New South Wales, 30 Aboriginal people are massacred.

>> **1861:** More than 170 Aboriginal people are killed at Emerald, Queensland.

>> **1868:** More than 150 Aboriginal people are killed in the Kimberley, Western Australia, for 'resisting arrest'.

>> **1870 to 1890:** More than 900 Aboriginal people of the Kalkadoon nation are killed in the Kalkadoon Wars in Queensland.

>> **1883:** A massacre of Aboriginal people takes place at the McKinley River in the Northern Territory.

>> **1916:** Nine Aboriginal men are chained together, shot and thrown off a cliff at Mowla Bluff, Western Australia.

>> **1928:** A massacre at Coniston Station in the Northern Territory lasts for several days. Official reports put the number of men, women and children killed at 31 but historians believe it was closer to 170.

An interactive map of known massacre sites has been developed based on research by the University of Newcastle Colonial Frontier Massacres Project team, led by historian Lyndell Ryan. It can be found at the website: c21ch.newcastle.edu.au/colonialmassacres/map.php.

REMEMBER

When looking at any online sources, keep in mind that dates aren't always consistent between information sources.

In the Northern Territory, conflict was no different from elsewhere, even though it occurred in the later stages of colonisation, intensifying around the 1920s and 1930s. Land was less fertile but was used for grazing cattle. When John McDouall Stuart started exploring vast areas in this part of northern Australia in the early 1860s, much conflict ensued between Aboriginal people and settlers. Administrators made futile efforts to calm the situation but matters relating to Aboriginal people were left in the hands of those seeking to take the land and establish large pastoral properties. Much of this was done through punitive expeditions and the use of *native police*, a force of Aboriginal men recruited mainly as trackers in each of the colonies. The Northern Territory force was established in 1884.

REMEMBER

The native police became a mounted police force, using their understanding of the countryside and their bush skills to assist the colonists, sometimes hunting down their own people.

CULTURAL PROTOCOLS

Massacre sites have been reconstructed using a mix of historical archive, oral history and archaeological evidence. Dates and numbers are often not exact because the killings were covered up. Talking about this history is seen by many Indigenous people as an important part of the process of truth telling about the past.

MYTH BUSTER

Not all regions of Australia succumbed to the settlers completely. In some places, such as in parts of the Kimberley and Arnhem Land, Aboriginal people stopped the frontier from spreading. Although the number of Aboriginal people killed on the frontier was far greater than colonists killed, the mere presence of Aboriginal people created great anxiety among colonists, causing some of them to abandon their farms. In the west Kimberley, the great warrior Jandamarra, a member of the Bunuba nation, led a resistance effort that stopped settlement for six years, using methods such as attacks on introduced crops and livestock. Jandamarra was shot in 1897 along with 19 other Aboriginal men who were fighting beside him.

Refuge at a cost: Missions and reserves

In some places, Aboriginal people were offered refuge on missions. Here, they could trade their physical safety for their cultural practices. They were expected to adopt European habits and language. Governments also started establishing reserves as safe havens for Aboriginal people. Although some reserve communities developed self-sufficient farms, conditions on the reserves were generally poor and the food provided was unhealthy and inadequate. Housing and health conditions added to the poor standard of living of Aboriginal people in these areas.

In other areas, Aboriginal people developed relationships with the pastoralists who now farmed their traditional land. The clans could live on the property and work in return for rations and other provisions. Chapter 8 provides more detail on Aboriginal participation in the pastoral industry.

THRELKELD: ONE MAN'S PASSION

One early missionary, Lancelot Threlkeld, was asked by the London Missionary Society (LMS) to set up a mission at Lake Macquarie, near present-day Newcastle, in about 1826. The LMS withdrew their support for the mission in 1828 but Threlkeld received private funds and a grant of land from Governor Darling on the other side of the lake to establish his mission, which was maintained until 1841.

Threlkeld's system, recognised as being very progressive, was to 'first obtain the language, then preach the gospel, then urge them from gospel motives to be industrious at the same time being a servant to them to win them to that which is right'. In fact, Threlkeld devoted much of his life to the study of the Awabakal language of the region and published a grammar of the language in 1834. His role as an interpreter was often valuable in representing Aboriginal people unable to defend themselves under white law.

The problem with Threlkeld's intent was that by the time he had learned the language, few Aboriginal people were left in the area, with the population either killed or moved on. Failure of the early missions was common.

The missions

Missionaries were active in colonies around the world and Australia was no exception. At first, these missions were aimed at improving the moral standards of the colonists but some of the early missionaries, such as Samuel Marsden, who was appointed as assistant chaplain to the Sydney colony in 1794, also intended 'to preach the Gospel to the Australian Aborigines'. The idea soon formed that Australia would become a base for missionary activity in the Pacific; 'not only the evangelisation of the Aborigines and the colonists but the nations of the south seas and beyond'. Marsden, however, put most of his work into missions in New Zealand.

Driven by the belief that Indigenous people were heathens because they didn't believe in God, the missionaries sought to take their religious beliefs to 'the natives' so they could be converted to Christianity and saved. The missionaries also believed that they could provide the benefits of their culture — including proper clothing and education — to Indigenous people. They established missions across Australia and in the Torres Strait, sometimes referred to in the Torres Strait as 'the coming of the light'. Indigenous people were often drawn to these missions out of curiosity and for protection from the violence on the frontier.

Missionaries of all denominations took their Christian missions to the south-eastern colonies, as well as to remote areas of Australia. The following list is by no means exhaustive but outlines the chronological order in which they did so:

>> **1825:** The Church Missionary Society was established in Sydney, operating the Wellington Valley Mission in New South Wales from 1830 to 1842.

>> **1836:** The first mission in Victoria was established by the Wesleyan Missionary Society at Buntingdale, near Geelong.

>> **1838:** German Lutheran missionaries set up at Zion Hill in bushland that's now the Brisbane suburb of Nundah. The mission failed to attract converts and was abandoned in 1846.

>> **1859:** The Moravian Church (evangelical Protestants also known as the Bohemian Brethren) established Ebenezer Mission at Lake Hindmarsh, Victoria; it closed in 1904.

>> **1871:** The London Missionary Society began operations on Erub (Darnley Island) in the Torres Strait.

>> **1877:** The Australian Lutheran Church and the Hermannsburg Mission Society of Germany set up the Hermannsburg Mission on the Finke River in Central Australia.

>> **1882:** A group of Jesuits established St Joseph's, at what is now the Darwin suburb of Rapid Creek, in 1882. It closed in 1899. The Jesuits were also active in the Daly River area of the Northern Territory from 1886 to 1891.

>> **1890:** Trapist monks arrived at Beagle Bay, north-west of Broome, and the Pallottine order set up at nearby Lombardina in 1910.

>> **1913:** The Seventh Day Adventist mission at Mona Mona, near Kuranda in north Queensland, began, operating until 1962.

>> **1925:** The Church of England established a mission at Oenpelli in western Arnhem Land in the Northern Territory.

>> **1935:** The Methodists began a mission at Yirrkala on the Territory's Gove Peninsula.

>> **1937:** The Presbyterian Church established a mission at Ernabella in the Musgrave Ranges just over the border in South Australia.

Dozens of missions operated throughout Australia during the 1800s and into the 1900s. Some established good relations with the Aboriginal people and afforded a degree of protection from the savagery of the frontier; some have been accused of their own brutalisation of Aboriginal people. In many cases, Aboriginal people from different nations were unhappily herded together.

Regardless of their successes or failures, today many Indigenous communities are on areas that were once missions.

BETWEEN THE CHURCH AND THE GOVERNMENT

In 1861, the Victorian colonial government set aside 3,500 acres (about 1,400 hectares) of land near Warrnambool, in western Victoria, as an Aboriginal reserve. In 1865, the Framlingham Aboriginal Reserve was established there by the Church of England as a mission station, though it soon ceded responsibility for the reserve to the Central Board Appointed to Watch Over the Interests of Aborigines.

Control of the settlement shifted between the Board and the missionaries. The government attempted to close the reserve down several times and was met with great resistance by the residents. In 1970, the land was handed over by the government in what was, along with Lake Tyers (Bung Yarnda) in Gippsland, the first Aboriginal land rights victory in Australia.

Another Aboriginal settlement that began as a mission is Hopevale in north Queensland. In 1885, a Lutheran missionary set about establishing the Elim Aboriginal Mission at

Cape Bedford, on land that had been gazetted as an Aboriginal reserve in 1881. He left the mission in 1887, passing the responsibility of managing the mission to George Schwartz, who remained at the mission, subsequently called Hope Valley, for more than 50 years. When World War II broke out, the German missionary was sent to an internment camp.

In May 1942, 254 Aboriginal people were evacuated from the mission without warning, with the majority removed to Woorabinda. The mission was taken over by the Australian Army, the RAAF, the United States Army and the Civil Construction Corps. Many people died while at Woorabinda and those who survived weren't allowed to return to the mission until 1949. A new site was established on land previously owned by the Cooktown Plantations Company, about 25 kilometres from the old mission.

The new mission site was finally gazetted as an Aboriginal reserve in September 1952. In 1955, the Hope Vale Mission Board made a complaint about the encroachment of a cattle company onto land belonging to the mission. Eventually this land was excised from the reserved land. In 1986, a deed of grant in trust was issued to the Hope Vale community for 110,000 hectares of land.

Government reserves

Governments also established reserves, with a similar intention to the missions of creating small communities of Indigenous people who could be protected but also controlled. Some communities became very politically active and campaigned to have the control of the reserve — and the ownership of the land — transferred to the Indigenous community. See Chapter 10 for details of some of these reserves and their political activism.

Although some reserves were given to their communities through land grants, many governments sold off land that had been allocated for Indigenous reserves in order to raise money.

What happened to the rest?

Often, with their traditional way of life destroyed, those Aboriginal people who didn't end up in reserves or missions lived on the edge of European settlements, begging and taking up the worst European habits, including the consumption of too much alcohol. This behaviour wasn't always viewed sympathetically. Some white people saw this degeneration of Aboriginal people as natural and inevitable because of their so-called backward and savage nature.

The population of Aboriginal people had diminished significantly by the end of the 19th century. Disease was still rampant, food supplies were scarce, water supplies polluted or taken over and conflict continued — all of which played a part in reducing the numbers. This decline in numbers also meant that cultural practices were disrupted. Beliefs and customs — and languages — were weakened. Initiation ceremonies and other rites weren't performed and oral traditions were unable to be handed down. In particular, 'right way' marriages weren't possible.

By the end of the 1800s, as Australia was moving towards becoming a nation in its own right, it was believed that Aboriginal people were a dying race.

Ignoring Prior Ownership: No Treaties

Why were no treaties made between the British and the Aboriginal people? The British engaged in treaties with indigenous people in other parts of the world — the United States, Canada and New Zealand — but no attempt was made to come to any formal agreement with Aboriginal people when their lands were being colonised, with the exception of John Batman at Port Phillip Bay (see the sidebar 'Batman's attempt at a treaty').

Given that much evidence exists that colonists conceded Aboriginal people had an attachment to their land and should rightly retain some interest in it, the question is baffling. One plausible explanation as to why no treaties were struck in Australia is that they weren't needed to secure territory.

The number of Aboriginal people was depleted across much of the country, and conflict and frontier violence occurred almost routinely. Eventually, the colonists were able to establish themselves in different parts of the country without obtaining the consent or agreement of Aboriginal people. Consent was never part of the culture of dealing with Aboriginal people in the colony.

This failure to enter into agreements meant that Australian law wouldn't recognise the laws of Aboriginal people or their governance structures and sovereignty. And it wouldn't recognise their rights to their lands under common law until 1992, though land rights legislation in some jurisdictions would give some rights to land prior to that (see Chapter 12). The issue of a treaty between Indigenous people and the Australian state remains an important part of the political agenda today. Several states, including Victoria and South Australia have undertaken contemporary treaty making processes (see Chapter 15).

BATMAN'S ATTEMPT AT A TREATY

In 1835, an ambitious pastoralist from Van Diemen's Land, John Batman, sailed to Port Phillip Bay in what is now Victoria and sought to secure good grazing land along the Yarra River. This was the land of the Wurundjeri people of the Kulin nation. He bargained with the local Aboriginal people for the land. On 6 June, he negotiated for 240,000 hectares — most of the land of the Kulin nation — but the treaty wasn't as honest as it seemed.

Aboriginal people had no notion of legal contracts, which were a foreign concept to them at the time. He thought he was negotiating with 'chiefs' when he was speaking with Elders and they weren't in a position to sell their people's land, even if they'd wanted to. In fact, the act of selling land was an unknown concept to Aboriginal people.

It was later believed that the Wurundjeri thought Batman was offering them gifts in exchange for safe passage through their lands. Some historians have also questioned whether the signatures of the Aboriginal Elders on the treaty were authentic because the markings matched some found in Batman's journals.

However, the New South Wales governor declared this private treaty to be illegal, making it clear that the government held all of the territory and only it could grant, sell or distribute land. A settlement of Europeans began in the area in what's now Melbourne, and Aboriginal people began to find their land taken and their way of life threatened. Although the colony appointed people to protect the Aboriginal people, the population declined.

over land

» **Examining the rise of the wool and cattle industries**

» **Looking at protest in the pastoral industry as part of the early land rights movement**

Chapter **8**

Land, Livestock and Loss

The colonisation of Australia by the British led to inevitable conflict over land with Aboriginal people on the mainland. Torres Strait Islanders to the north didn't yet need to be concerned about their island homes. However, Aboriginal populations around the new settlements, already substantially diminished by diseases, were pushed off their lands, preventing access to traditional food and water sources, and disrupting important cultural and spiritual connections. As the Australian wool and cattle industries were established and began to flourish, the demand for Aboriginal land increased. Aboriginal people continued to resist the encroachment onto their lands and their dispossession.

Some Aboriginal communities slowly developed relationships with the pastoralists. They worked as stockmen or domestic servants on the large properties that had been established on their traditional lands. This was an uneasy relationship. Aboriginal workers were paid in rations and allowed to live on the fringes of the properties, sometimes at least affording some protection from the frontier clashes. Over time, however, Aboriginal people became frustrated with these conditions and fought for the right to be paid proper wages and for rights to their traditional lands.

In this chapter, I look at how Australia's pastoral industries affected Aboriginal people, as well as the anomaly of Aboriginal participation in the industries, giving protection that soon turned into exploitation.

Clashing Cultures: Conflict over Land

At the heart of the conflict between Aboriginal Australians and colonists was land. Both needed it to live off. Aboriginal people believed it was rightfully theirs because they had occupied it for more than 65,000 years and had, through their traditional laws, the obligation to be the custodians of it. The British believed that they had rightfully claimed the continent of Australia under international law. They believed that their colonial laws applied and, under those laws, the colonial government was free to grant land and pastoral leases as it chose; the rights of Aboriginal people to their land were ignored. As Aboriginal people lost their lands to the spread of colonial settlements, the loss meant that not only was the livelihood of Aboriginal families, clans and communities threatened but their cultural practices and spiritual life were also under attack.

Europeans and Aboriginal people alike needed the land to survive but the British wanted to claim as much land as possible without acknowledging Aboriginal attachment or interest in their land. No attempt was made to share the land with them. (Chapter 7 examines the lack of treaties sought during the colonisation process.) As colonists cleared and fenced the land, turning it into farms for crops, sheep and cattle, the environment that supported the hunter-gatherer lifestyle of Aboriginal people disappeared. The populations of native animals were depleted and, in some cases, disappeared altogether. Farms and pastoral properties needed water to survive. Rivers, creeks and waterholes were fenced off, preventing Aboriginal people from camping around those essential sources, and this further affected their ability to survive in their traditional way.

REMEMBER

As a result of this conflict — and the disease that sometimes swept through Aboriginal communities beforehand — the population of Aboriginal people shrank drastically. Kinship systems were undermined, and traditional ceremonies and practices became harder to perform.

Aboriginal people, land grants and squatters

Although dramatically different from the landscapes of England, Australia turned out to be rich in resources and fertile land. When the colony at Sydney Cove was established and began to flourish, free men and eventually freed convicts (known as *emancipists*) became interested in farming the surrounding land. Supplies seemed plentiful and the colonial government issued land grants to settlers, military men and emancipists.

Governors had the power to make these land grants, often attaching conditions, such as that the land be cultivated and a rent paid if it was abandoned. In the early years of the colony, grants tended to be given sparingly and, by the end of Governor Macquarie's term in 1821, less than 1,000 square miles had been granted. When the Blue Mountains were crossed in 1813 (refer to Chapter 7), more fertile land became available for farming. The demand for land was so great that the colonial government had trouble keeping control over people who went out beyond the borders of the settled territory and sought to start their own farming enterprises. These men, who took land without government approval or permission, became known as *squatters*.

Squatting became a particular problem in the colonies around Australia as colonial governments seemed ill-equipped to stem the demand for land and the desire of people to go out and set up on land beyond the limits of the settlement. While the law seemed unable — and in some cases unwilling — to stop the activities of the squatters, the colonial settlements soon came to value the timber the squatters cleared from the lands. Governor Macquarie's successor, Governor Brisbane (who was governor from 1821 to 1825) dramatically increased the amount of land granted. He also made provision for land to be purchased. During his tenure, the amount of land allocated to colonists almost doubled.

As squatters and settlers occupied more and more of the fertile land, they established themselves and the spread of the colony across Aboriginal lands. But Aboriginal people didn't intend to surrender the lands they had lived off for tens of thousands of years. The colonial government tried to bring the squatters' activities under control in 1824. Regulations set out what was known as the *nineteen counties*, or the *limits of location*, shown in Figure 8-1, and it was declared that beyond these limits land couldn't be squatted on or sold. From 1833, Commissioners of Crown Lands were appointed to try to stop and manage the squatters. In 1836, Governor Bourke instituted a policy where squatters could lease their runs for a fee based on the number of sheep they had. Leasing was a more popular method of acquiring tenure over land than buying it, especially because the fees were modest.

Pastoral leases are a form of land tenure unique to Australia. The British Colonial Office created these types of leases in the 1830s to address the concern of the British colonists in Australia over the massive land grabs by squatters. The land was still owned by the government. About 45 per cent of the Northern Territory is held as pastoral leases.

Aboriginal people were never consulted about the sale of land or the granting of leases. The granting of leases sanctioned the taking of Aboriginal lands by squatters and gave them the backing of the colonial government in asserting their presence on the land over that of the Aboriginal people. Squatters would eventually become a powerful political force in the colony and lobbied strongly to make their rights over their land secure.

FIGURE 8-1:
The 19 counties
surrounding the
Sydney Cove
colony, declared
in 1824 in order
to contain initial
settlement.

REMEMBER

The term *squatter* was originally given to a person who occupied land without legal title. Later, the term came to describe people who leased large tracts of land on which to grow produce or breed sheep or cattle.

Conflict on the frontier

Away from the growing cities and rural towns, the colonists feared Aboriginal people. As squatters sought to assert their control over the land they had taken, and pastoralists took possession of their leases and land grants, conflict with Aboriginal people became inevitable. This conflict intensified due to the battle over scarce resources. Aboriginal communities and pastoralists competed for water supplies. The practices of the pastoralists put pressure on the environment and traditional foods became scarce. Squatters sometimes used violence to clear Aboriginal people off their traditional lands. Other methods, such as poisoning, were also used to remove Aboriginal populations from land wanted for farming. Waterholes were laced with poison and poisoned food was left so that Aboriginal people would consume it.

Aboriginal people resisted the encroachment onto their lands by squatters, spearing sheep and cattle — sometimes in order to eat — and burning buildings, fences and other infrastructure. In some places, such as in Arnhem Land, Aboriginal resistance stalled the spread of the frontier. In other places, conflict lasted for up to ten years. In the end, the squatters had the law and the firepower on their side. Aboriginal people, their populations depleted, drifted to the edges of towns, pastoral stations and church-run missions (refer to Chapter 7 for more on the missions).

REMEMBER

Historians such as Henry Reynolds and Ross Fitzgerald have estimated that in Queensland alone the Aboriginal population was reduced from 120,000 to 20,000, with accusations that the expansion of the pastoral industry in that state accounted for at least 10,000 direct killings.

In these circumstances and environments, Aboriginal people lost the ability to be self-sufficient and became dependent on the assistance and handouts of governments or employers. Aboriginal people were given rations of food and tobacco, sometimes even in lieu of wages for employment.

Aboriginal People and the Developing Pastoral Economy

Australia has made its wealth from its natural resources and its pastoral industries. The early colony started to generate wealth because of entrepreneurial pastoralists interested in developing strains of wool and wheat that were particularly suited to the Australian environment. Australia, with its large tracts of land, was also able to support a strong cattle industry.

Livestock was brought to Australia from the Cape of Good Hope on the First Fleet — two bulls, four cows, two stallions, four mares, a small flock of sheep and some pigs (hogs), 19 goats and various poultry. However, flocks of sheep and herds of cattle were soon introduced to areas further and further from the original colonies, along with the white settlers. They encountered Aboriginal people who had never seen farm animals — sheep, cows, horses. Confronted with these strange beasts, Aboriginal people wondered if they were devils. The white people were just as strange when they arrived. They had clothes, technology and customs that were unknown to Aboriginal people who'd had little or no contact with white people.

As Aboriginal populations were depleted in the struggle for land, Aboriginal communities had to find new ways to survive. Some formed arrangements with pastoralists where they provided a workforce in exchange for permission to live on the edges of the pastoral property, so they were still able to live on their traditional land. This created an uneasy alliance between Aboriginal people and pastoralists but was one that assisted in the growth and viability of Australia's cattle industry.

Off the sheep's back

The small flock of 44 sheep from the African Cape of Good Hope that arrived with the First Fleet in 1788 had hairy fleeces, so were better suited for food than for wool production. The sheep that survived the voyage didn't last long and seemed unsuited to the new environment. In 1794, a pastoralist, John Macarthur, discovered that a superior wool could be produced through the cross-breeding of certain types of sheep. Other colonists, particularly the Reverend Samuel Marsden, had begun experimenting with cross-breeding to improve the quality of wool but Macarthur seemed to have perfected it. In 1797, 13 Spanish merino sheep were brought from the Cape of Good Hope to the colony at Sydney Cove. Macarthur bred these sheep with his mixed breed and noticed it produced a breed with superior wool. The development of this breed — and this quality of wool — created interest and demand back in Britain. He grew his flock to over 4,000 sheep and devoted himself to the production of wool.

Aboriginal people played a major role in the development of the sheep industry in the shearing sheds, assisting the flourishing wool industry. Shearing was seasonal work, so Aboriginal labourers would travel around the countryside to where work was available.

Wool became Australia's first great export and an important part of the economy of New South Wales. In 1822 to 1823, the value of wool exports exceeded 57 million pounds. By the 1830s, the sheep industry had been established in every colony in Australia. However, the growing industry increased the demand for land in the colony. Demand for land meant further encroachment into the lands of Aboriginal people surrounding the already expanding colonies.

The rise of the cattle industry

Cattle — two bulls and four cows — were also first brought to Australia on the First Fleet (refer to Chapter 6) in 1788. They were used for transporting goods and for breeding. Some soon strayed and were found about seven years later in a herd of about 60. By 1820, cattle numbered about 54,000, with the largest herds owned by John Macarthur and Reverend Samuel Marsden (see the sidebar 'Macarthur: Just a wild colonial boy' for more about Macarthur). By 1840, more than 370,000 cattle were in Australia.

MACARTHUR: JUST A WILD COLONIAL BOY

John Macarthur was a colourful and prominent character in the Sydney colony. Born in Plymouth, Devon, in 1767, he joined the British military to fight in the American War of Independence but the war ended before his regiment set sail and it was disbanded. He then farmed near Devon and became interested in agriculture. In April 1788, he returned to the military and was assigned to the New South Wales Corps in 1789. He arrived in Sydney the following year as a lieutenant and was appointed as commandant at Parramatta. In 1793, Macarthur was granted 100 acres of land at Rose Hill, near Parramatta, and another 100 acres in 1794. He named his property Elizabeth Farm, after his wife.

Macarthur was a confrontational man, often quarrelling with neighbours, governors and his military superiors. Sometimes these quarrels ended with the fighting of a duel, one of which saw Macarthur sent back to England in 1801 to stand trial for assault. The commander of the British Army released him, however, and he resigned his commission, returning to the Sydney colony in 1805 as a private citizen. There, he concentrated on his commercial interests, including the fledgling wool export business, though not without further altercations with successive governors King and Bligh.

Macarthur also had many supporters among the New South Wales Corps, which had been using rum as currency in the small colony, a practice Bligh attempted to ban. Macarthur's trial for failure to forfeit a bond was a catalyst for the Rum Rebellion, with the New South Wales Corps siding with Macarthur against Governor Bligh and resulting in a military coup in 1808 that saw Bligh ousted. Macarthur returned to England to avoid arrest for his part in the rebellion, but was eventually allowed to return, without punishment, in 1817, and he resumed his wool business.

AGRICULTURE TAKES HOLD

Wheat was another industry that flourished in Australia, and took up vast tracts of Aboriginal land. Grain growers in Australia developed 'dry farming' to take advantage of the low rainfalls in some parts of Australia and used special methods to grow plentiful crops in arid areas. Australian wheat farmers also developed new ways of harvesting wheat, overcoming shortages of labour. They also improved the quality of the wheat. William Farrer conducted experiments to find strains of wheat that were suited to the Australian climate. He developed 33 types of wheat, including some with greater resistance to rust and other diseases.

The gold rushes and associated economic boom and population growth in the 1850s increased the demand for meat. Pastoralists moved their cattle overland as far as the Kimberley in Western Australia. In these more arid areas, the land couldn't support large numbers of cattle or sheep, so very large tracts were needed to ensure the industry could turn a profit, an aspect of the business that still holds true today.

Land was granted as pastoral leases over large tracts of land with no consultation with Aboriginal people, so white people arrived to establish their properties unannounced, sometimes with their cattle arriving before they did.

An uneasy alliance

In some places, Aboriginal populations came to live on pastoral stations. Their populations had been depleted by frontier violence and people wanted to end the conflict. They wanted to maintain their connection to their land, especially their sacred sites, and to ensure the survival of their families and communities. Aboriginal people camped on the pastoral properties that were once their traditional lands and hunting grounds. There, they provided a source of labour. Aboriginal men — and women — proved to be skilled at raising cattle; women also provided domestic labour.

From the 1830s, Aboriginal people worked a variety of jobs on pastoral properties in New South Wales, Victoria and South Australia. They became sought-after workers, especially as stockworkers and messengers. They knew the country and the climate, so were an invaluable resource to white squatters and pastoralists struggling to establish their businesses on land they weren't familiar with. Aboriginal people played a central role in the development of the cattle industry in the north and in Central Australia as well. Many stations, particularly in remote areas, only supported a few white people. Aboriginal men and women undertook all of the essential work.

Rations versus wages

By 1901, half of the pastoral workforce was Aboriginal and for the most part they were paid in rations. Although laws at the time required Aboriginal workers to be paid a wage — a third of that paid to white workers for the same jobs — this was often not done in practice and rations were still the usual way to compensate Aboriginal workers.

Aboriginal people weren't used to the food of white people. Sugar, alcohol and tobacco had a negative impact on their health and their already fragile populations.

REMEMBER

Up until the 1920s, Aboriginal people were still commonly paid only in rations of food and clothing. During the 1920s, some workers began to receive minimal wages. Legislation was passed in some states that required pastoralists to provide certain things for Aboriginal workers, such as shelter and medical needs, but this was rarely enforced. When these wages were introduced, a large proportion of the wage was placed into government trust accounts. This system was never properly explained to Aboriginal workers and they lost large amounts of money. The government used the money in these accounts to help out the pastoral industry and on other types of government expenditure. Aboriginal people who lost wages through this system are still fighting to reclaim their money today.

While the pastoral industry was structured in a way that exploited Aboriginal workers, evidence shows that Aboriginal people took great pride in their work. Employment and particular roles — such as head stockman — gave prestige and were a source of self-esteem. Aboriginal people were often gifted in training and riding horses, making them good at mustering and invaluable at droving. Even when working on pastoral properties, Aboriginal people tried to maintain their cultural practices but sometimes they had to modify them. The timing of larger ceremonial gatherings, for example, was changed. They had been held during the dry season but, in order to adapt to the cattle economy, were moved to the wet season. Pastoral bosses endorsed this as an annual holiday during the downtime on the stations. These meetings often required people to walk long distances to attend and could take up to three months.

TECHNICAL STUFF

After 1901, when the Australian Constitution came into force, the federal government took control of industrial relations matters. From this time, Aboriginal people were supposed to be paid on contracts that offered only one-third of the wages given to white men for the same work. This was later raised to two-thirds, but even then employers often paid them much less, or continued to pay them in rations.

In March 1966, Aboriginal stockworkers won the right to award wages and conditions equal to the white workers doing the same jobs, though the payments weren't required to be made until December 1968. The delay was justified on the basis that the pastoralists would need time to adjust to the change. But the victory didn't change the fortunes of Aboriginal workers the way it was hoped. Many employers simply sacked their Aboriginal workers once they were entitled to higher wages. At the same time, the pastoral industry was transforming, making use of new technology and becoming less reliant on manual labour. The Aboriginal camps on the edges of pastoral properties that had been a source of labour were no longer needed and many people were forced off the stations that had been their homes.

THE DROVER'S BOY'

The song 'The Drover's Boy' by Ted Egan was written about a time when it was illegal for white men and Aboriginal women to marry. It comes from a true story about a white drover who is forced to pass off his wife as a 'drover's boy' and the relationship between the couple:

They couldn't understand why the drover cried as they buried the drover's boy.

They couldn't understand why the drover cut a lock of the dead boy's hair.

Egan claimed he wrote the song as a tribute to Aboriginal stockwomen and the role they played in the pastoral industry. Aboriginal women doing stockwork were made to cut their hair short and flattened their breasts with scarves to conceal their identities.

Aboriginal women and pastoralists

Aboriginal women were resilient and hard workers sought out by pastoralists for their labour. They could perform stockwork as well as domestic duties and were also relied on as midwives. White women in remote areas were particularly reliant on the labour of Aboriginal women to help them to survive the arduous conditions of the Australian bush. They provided company and performed domestic tasks. In some instances, Aboriginal women workers were prevented from travelling around with their families and keeping their own children so they could continue to work and live in the homes of pastoralists. Aboriginal women were also often preferred as stockworkers, because they were able to find bush foods and knew about bush medicines. With the scarcity of white women on the frontier, white men also sought the companionship of Aboriginal women.

Relationships between white men and Aboriginal women were complex. Aboriginal women were in very vulnerable positions and the extent to which they were able to enter into consensual, equal unions with white men has been a matter of speculation among historians. Australia already had a long history of squatters forcibly taking Aboriginal women in the early days of the frontier, which had led to conflict with local Aboriginal people. Aboriginal men engaged in *payback* against white men who physically or sexually assaulted Aboriginal women, sometimes killing the perpetrators (traditionally, payback sometimes involved spearing the leg of the offender). This, in turn, sometimes led to massacres of Aboriginal people as punishment for killing a white man.

However, many unions between Aboriginal women and white men were by mutual agreement — and many children resulted from those relationships. But attitudes and laws worked against these unions. While a blind eye was turned to de facto relationships, legislation in some states prevented marriage between white men and Aboriginal women without approval from the state, creating a barrier to legal marriage.

Asserting Rights and Other Acts of Resistance

Aboriginal workers were critical to the success of the pastoral industry in Australia. They provided a pool of cheap — often unpaid — labour but, by doing so, they were allowed to stay on or near their traditional land, keeping connection to it. Inevitably, they began to protest about their poor conditions and wages, especially when compared with the conditions enjoyed by their white counterparts. Unsurprisingly, their claims also included a reassertion of their rights over the lands they had been dispossessed of.

From the 1880s, Aboriginal leaders began to ask for the right to live on the land on their own terms. Leaders in the south-east of Australia, such as William Cooper, wanted the right to own land so they could farm it and provide for their own families. Large coordinated strikes also occurred within the pastoral industry in Western Australia (the Pilbara strike) and the Northern Territory (the Wave Hill walk-off). This history of protest not only transformed the conditions of Aboriginal people working in the pastoral industry, but also paved the way for the modern land rights movement (see Chapter 12).

The petitions of William Cooper

William Cooper was a Yorta Yorta man, born in 1861, who spent most of his life in the Cummeragunja community (see Chapter 10). He helped establish the Australian Aborigines League (with Doug Nicholls, William Ferguson, Bill Onus, Margaret Tucker and others) and, as their secretary, circulated a petition seeking land rights, the right to vote and the right to have direct representation in parliament.

William Cooper was one of the most vocal advocates for Aboriginal rights, including the return of Aboriginal land. Throughout his life, Cooper and his peers had borne infringements of human rights that few other Australians have had to suffer. They were unable to earn equal wages or apply for the same level of financial support when they couldn't find employment, and were required to apply for permission to move from reserves and to marry. Cooper's vision was an Australia where these rights and freedoms weren't denied to Aboriginal people and he believed that, if the barriers to accessing the benefits and opportunities within

Australian society — such as land, employment and education — were removed, Aboriginal people were well equipped, through our own hard work and initiative, to alter their own socioeconomic circumstances.

Similar to many of his peers, Cooper had laboured on the pastoral properties that were once the traditional lands of his family, and he saw the wealth that was generated by their own productivity on those lands. Cooper wondered why it was that white people were able to engage in activities that could provide opportunities for their families but he couldn't do the same. His constant petitions and letters were aimed at making the argument that, if he and his peers could be given the same opportunity to work the land, they could break away from the position of being reliant on the state. Cooper believed that, if Aboriginal people were given this opportunity, the initial investment to set them up so they could work the land themselves would lead to long-term savings, because Aboriginal people would be self-sufficient and not reliant on perpetual government handouts. Cooper also campaigned for equal rights, described as *citizenship rights*. He and William Ferguson led the protests on Australia Day, 26 January, in 1938, the 150-year anniversary of the establishment of the colony at Sydney Cove, which became known as the *Day of Mourning*. See Chapter 10 for more on the Aboriginal campaigns for citizenship rights.

Cooper's vision of equality for Aboriginal people not only influenced his peers, but also inspired the generations of Aboriginal and Torres Strait Islander activists who followed him. The campaign and claim for citizenship rights was particularly effective in gathering support from the broader Australian community for significant constitutional change that, many people thought, would provide Indigenous people with better opportunities. See Chapter 11 for more information about the 1967 referendum.

MYTH BUSTER

On 6 December 1938, William Cooper organised the only private protest in the world against the events of Kristallnacht in Germany several weeks earlier — where 267 synagogues and 7,000 Jewish businesses were damaged or destroyed and, in the aftermath, 30,000 Jewish men were arrested and sent to concentration camps. Cooper's protest culminated with the delivery of a petition to the German Consulate in Melbourne condemning the 'cruel persecution of the Jewish people by the Nazi government of Germany'. The consulate refused to take the petition. In 2010, a memorial to Cooper was established at the Yad Vashem Holocaust Museum in Jerusalem, honouring his advocacy for the Jewish people.

The Pilbara strike

In 1942, Aboriginal law men from 23 clans in the Pilbara region of Western Australia met and, after six weeks, a consensus was reached to begin a strike on 1 May — this was not only the international day that marks the struggle of workers, but also the start of the shearing season. However, the men decided that the strike should be postponed until after World War II had ended.

In 1944, an Industrial Relations Commission refused to hear a case on the inclusion of Aboriginal workers in the federal pastoralist award. This meant that Aboriginal workers continued to have no coverage under federal or state awards. So, in 1946, 800 Aboriginal pastoral workers from 27 pastoral stations in the Pilbara region walked off the job, protesting their conditions and demanding better pay. (This strike was the first industrial action taken by Aboriginal people in Australia and lasted until 1949, making it the longest industrial strike in Australia's history.) No phones or radios were available and the Aboriginal workers couldn't read or write in English, so one of the strike organisers, Dooley Bin Bin, visited each station pretending to be a relative who was just passing through. He distributed calendars made from jam tins so the workers would know which day to strike. Other key figures in the strike were Clancy McKenna and Peter 'Kangushot' Coppin.

On 1 May 1946, the Aboriginal workers left the stations and gathered at strike camps at Twelve Mile (near Port Hedland) and Moolyella (near Marble Bar), where they stayed for the next three years, living off bush tucker and selling goats and pearl shells. For many, this was their first taste of economic independence. The strike severely affected the pastoral properties. Although the Aboriginal workers won award rates in 1949, many decided not to return to the stations.

The Wave Hill walk-off

In 1966, the federal Conciliation and Arbitration Commission handed down the decision that Aboriginal workers in the pastoral industry were entitled to wages equal to that of their white co-workers. This decision had its strongest ramifications for the industry — and its Aboriginal workers — in the Northern Territory, which was under federal jurisdiction. The Commission decided that the decision shouldn't come into effect until December 1968, to give the pastoral industry time to adjust. Aboriginal stockmen and domestic workers on Newcastle Waters station in the Northern Territory were upset by the decision to delay the implementation of equal wages. Shortly after, more than 200 people, mainly from the Gurindji nation, left Wave Hill station, owned by a group of companies controlled by the wealthy English family of Lord Vestey, who paid an annual rent to the federal government of 10 to 55 cents per square mile.

The Gurindji protestors camped on their traditional land at Wattie Creek, or Daguragu. The occupation of the camp was illegal but the place was an important spiritual site for the Gurindji and a source of water. Leaders of the walk-off included Vincent Lingiari, Mick 'Hoppy Mick' Rangiari, Lupna 'Captain Major' Giari and Pincher Manguari. Many people supported their actions, including the North Australian Workers Union, the Northern Territory Council for Aboriginal Rights and the Federal Council for the Advancement of Aborigines and Torres Strait Islanders. Many white supporters were members of unions or the Communist Party of Australia.

The Gurindji petitioned the governor-general for the return of tracts of their traditional land, about 129,500 hectares. They didn't want to leave their country and even expressed concern about the cattle that needed to be tended. Among their concerns was also the exploitation of Aboriginal women by white men. The strikes and walk-off weren't just about equal wages for work in the pastoral industry; they were also about the rights to land. They became a symbol of the Aboriginal land rights movement and a reminder that the conflict over land has never been resolved.

When the Whitlam government came to power in 1972, it promised to legislate for land rights and this gave new hope to the Gurindji. The original Wave Hill lease was surrendered and two new leases were issued in 1975 — one to Vestey and one to the Gurindji. The lease to the Gurindji covered about 330,000 hectares, more than their original petition, and included some sacred sites. On 16 August 1975, Prime Minister Gough Whitlam went to Wattie Creek and poured a handful of soil into Vincent Lingiari's hands (as seen in Figure 8-2), saying, 'I put into your hands part of the earth as a sign that this land will be the possession of you and your children forever'. Lingiari died in 1988.

REMEMBER

Australian musician Paul Kelly penned the song 'From Little Things Big Things Grow' about the Gurindji walk-off. The song has become a symbol of the reconciliation movement.

FIGURE 8-2:
Gough Whitlam pours Gurindji soil into Vincent Lingiari's hand in August 1975.

Chapter **9**

Taking the Children

Aboriginal populations were depleted dramatically as a result of the impacts of colonisation, leading to the assumption that this was a dying race. Some people believed that Aboriginal children — especially those who were 'half-caste' or light-skinned (children of Aboriginal and white parentage) — could be saved if they were assimilated into white culture and society. A key strategy in implementing the policy of assimilation was the forcible removal of Aboriginal children from their families. As Torres Strait Islanders had more contact with white settlements on the mainland, the policy affected them also, because Queensland annexed the islands in 1879 and, therefore, had jurisdiction over the Torres Strait Islanders. This chapter examines the legislation and regulations passed in all states and territories that gave governments the power to take Indigenous children from their families.

As common practice for more than 60 years, this policy affected generations of Indigenous children and their families. Indigenous children were fostered or adopted out, or placed in institutions, many suffering neglect and abuse while under the control of the state. Most white Australians were unaware of how widespread the practice of removing Indigenous children was or how badly many were treated. The generations of children removed from their families as a result of these government policies became known as the *Stolen Generations*.

This chapter also looks at the impacts of these practices on the lives of those removed from their families and on the parents who had children taken from them, which were highlighted in the report *Bringing Them Home*, published in 1997 as the result of a major inquiry. Among its key recommendations was the need for a national apology and a national compensation scheme. A national apology was delivered to the Stolen Generations in February 2008, but the issues of compensation for the impacts of removal and the recovery of stolen wages remain unresolved.

Examining the Ideology of Assimilation

From the time Sydney Cove began as a colony, the British tried to impose their own values, customs and beliefs on Aboriginal people. They assumed that their culture and worldviews were superior to those of what they believed was a savage race. From the 1850s onward, a more concerted effort was made by colonial governments to eradicate Aboriginal cultural practices. Aboriginal people were moved onto reserves, where they couldn't use their Aboriginal names, were discouraged from speaking their languages and forbidden to engage with their cultural practices. They were expected to leave their old ways behind.

Life on the reserves was heavily regulated and oppressive but Indigenous people moving to cities and towns to find work found it hard because of the racism and discrimination that was so prevalent in the broader community. Instead of being assimilated, they were often shunned or ignored, denied services and forced to live on the fringes of the community without jobs and in poverty. In towns, they were often barred from swimming pools and could only attend the cinemas at certain times and sit in certain places.

At first, the policy of removing Aboriginal children from their families was motivated by the belief that they were part of a dying race and so needed to be protected. This assumption and accepted ideas of white superiority and black inferiority, which were prevalent in the 19th and early 20th centuries, led to the development of a widespread view that Aboriginal people should be left to die out or, where possible, assimilated into the white community.

TECHNICAL STUFF

Although processes of assimilation had existed in practice long before, it became an official government policy in the 1950s. In 1951, federal Minister for the Territories Paul Hasluck was a strong advocate of the assimilation policy, believing that Aboriginal people would improve how they were treated and their living conditions if they behaved more like white people. The problem was that assimilation didn't work. Although Indigenous people were told to aspire to be white, they were never accepted as equal in a community that still considered them to be an inferior race.

COLONIAL CONTROL

Britain, similar to other colonial powers, exercised strict control over the people they colonised. British penal colonies, such as Australia, had an additional layer of regulation, discipline and control designed to constrain the convict population. This included brutal punishments, the regulation of marriage and servitude. Convicts were subjected to this behaviour and it was part of the colonial culture that people who were considered less than human could be treated that way.

REMEMBER

The notion that white races were superior to black races wasn't just an idea that related to Australia's Indigenous peoples. From the early 1900s, the White Australia immigration policy actively repatriated Chinese immigrants who had lived and worked in Australia since the gold rushes of the 1850s, and restricted migration by all non-British people until the 1940s, though its main aim was to prevent Asian and African migration. By the late 1940s, 97 per cent of the Australian population was Australian or British born. People from elsewhere, especially Asia, found making a permanent move to Australia difficult; anyone coming from abroad was expected to fit or assimilate into this culture. The policy wasn't officially abandoned until 1973. For more discussion on the White Australia policy and how it also affected Indigenous peoples' right to vote, you may want to check out *Australian Politics For Dummies* by Nick Economou and Zareh Ghazarian (Wiley Publishing Australia).

Several ideologies supported the taking of children from their families. Some held an honest belief that if Indigenous people could be 'more like white people' they would have better lives. Others thought that it was too late to change or assimilate older Indigenous people so it was best to 'focus on the children'. Many believed that actions such as removing children from their families in order to bring them up like white people were 'for their own good'.

'Making them white'

The assumption that Aboriginal people were a dying race also produced the thinking that Aboriginal people who weren't 'full-blood' should be encouraged to become assimilated into the broader society and to adopt European habits, customs, lifestyles and values. Much attention was paid to 'half-caste' and light-skinned Aboriginal children, often removing them as young as possible. Lighter skinned Aboriginal children were more likely to be considered for adoption into white families and those with darker skin more likely to be sent to institutions or to work.

The assimilation policy also targeted the marriages of 'half-caste' Aboriginal women. In some jurisdictions (such as the Northern Territory), a 'half-caste'

Aboriginal person couldn't marry anyone other than an Aboriginal or 'half-caste' without the approval of the Protector of Aborigines (a powerful position created in the late 1830s and operating in some regions of Australia). In practice, no permission was given for white or 'half-caste' males to marry 'full-blood' Aboriginal women but they were encouraged to marry 'half-caste' women. The idea behind this policy was that 'half-castes' could breed out; 'full-bloods' should be left to die out as quickly as possible, eradicating Indigenous culture. (Refer to Chapter 2 for definitions of these terms.)

'Focus on the children': Forget about the oldies

The predominant aim of forcibly removing Indigenous babies and children from their families was to absorb them into the broader community, making their cultural values and identities disappear. Adults, it was feared, were too entrenched in their Indigenous cultures so were harder to assimilate. The Chief Protector of Aborigines in Western Australia, A O Neville (see Chapter 10), stated the intentions behind the policy of removing children in a speech at a conference in Parliament House in April 1937:

. . . the native population is increasing . . . Are we going to have a population of 1,000,000 blacks in the Commonwealth or are we going to merge them into our white community and forget that there ever were any Aborigines in Australia? . . .

To achieve this end, however, we must have charge of the children at the age of six years; it is useless to wait until they are twelve or thirteen years of age. In Western Australia we have the power under the Act to take any child from its mother at any stage of its life, no matter whether the mother be legally married or not.

EARLY ATTEMPTS AT ASSIMILATION

In 1814, Governor Macquarie opened the Native Institution, a school for Aboriginal children, at Parramatta. The purpose was 'to civilise, educate and foster habits of industry and decency in the Aborigine'. When the parents of the Aboriginal children who started at the school realised that its aim was to distance them from their families and cultures, they withdrew them from the school. The school closed in 1820. In 1837, the Catholic Church began its missionary work through the establishment of schools for Aboriginal children. (Refer to Chapter 7 for more on the missionaries.)

Children were taken from their Indigenous parents so they could be brought up as white people, taught to reject their heritage and not exposed to their own cultures. Their names were changed. They weren't allowed to speak their traditional languages. Some were never told they were Indigenous or anything about the families they'd been removed from. Indigenous children were placed in institutions and schools, and trained to be labourers or domestic servants for white families and employers on their release. This path towards manual labour meant that relatively little attention was given to the level or standard of education that Indigenous children in these institutions received. The authorities had no expectation that Indigenous children would complete school or aspire to anything other than manual work.

After the 1950s, Indigenous children, especially those with lighter skin, were adopted into white families. The theory behind this was that Indigenous people with lighter skin would be more easily assimilated into the white community.

'For their own good'

Many people involved in the forced removal of Indigenous children from their families thought they were doing the right thing for the children, thinking that Indigenous culture was primitive and that Indigenous children faced harsh and unrewarding lives if they remained with their Indigenous families. These views were influenced by racist assumptions that Indigenous people were bad parents who didn't care for their children and that Indigenous women didn't have adequate maternal instincts.

Removal from Indigenous families was forcible in many cases, so parents who were capable of looking after their children and wanted to do so were cruelly denied the opportunity to care for them. They had few, if any, avenues through which to appeal to have their children returned. Some were told that their children had died when, in fact, they had been fostered or adopted to white families. Others claimed they had been made to sign adoption forms or had been misled about what they were signing.

Whatever the intentions, the reality for many Indigenous children taken away from their parents was that they didn't necessarily have better lives than if they'd stayed with their families. They were often vulnerable, exposed to physical, psychological and sexual abuse, and not given the love and affection they would've received from their natural parents, who never wanted to give them up in the first place.

Formalising the Removal Policy: Rules and Regulations

Every Australian state and territory passed legislation that regulated and formalised the policy of forcibly removing Indigenous children from their families, giving Chief Protectors or Protection Boards wideranging powers over Indigenous people. Although some early legislation required that only neglected children be removed, in practice being Indigenous was often enough. Later, all legislation allowed for the removal of Indigenous children from their families on the basis of their race alone.

The positions of Protector of Aborigines were the result of a report from the Select Committee of the House of Commons on Aborigines in 1838. The Select Committee envisaged that people in this role would learn the language of Indigenous people under their control and would watch over the Indigenous people, making sure they were not subjected to oppressive or unjust treatment and wouldn't have further encroachments on their property. While the positions were supposed to protect Indigenous people, many have suggested that the role was, in reality, one of social control. In some colonies, the positions of Protector of Aborigines were established long before being given legal status through a parliamentary Act. As the names of the Acts often indicate, the powers governments had were seen as a way of protecting Indigenous people:

>> **Victoria, *Aborigines Protection Act 1869*:** The Port Phillip Protectorate was established in 1839, employing several Protectors of Aborigines. The later Act established the Victorian Board for the Protection of Aborigines, which could remove Aboriginal children from their families and house them in dormitories.

>> **Queensland, *Aboriginal Protection and Restriction of the Sale of Opium Act 1897*:** This Act gave superintendents powers over Aboriginal people, including directing where they should live. Its inclusion with the regulation of the sale of opium highlights the way in which laws were used to specifically regulate the lives of non-white people. Opium, introduced largely by the Chinese who came to Australia to work the goldfields, was thought to be of particular danger to Indigenous people, although a large number of Europeans also used the drug and it remained freely available until 1906. Queensland established positions of Protector of Aborigines from 1898 to 1904 and again from 1963 to 1986. This legislation also applied to the Torres Strait Islands.

>> **Western Australia, *Aborigines Act 1905*:** In 1915, Western Australia created the position of Chief Protector of Aborigines, who had vast powers.

>> **New South Wales, *Aborigines Protection Act 1909*:** The first Protector of Aborigines was appointed in 1882 and the Aborigines Protection Board was

established in 1883 but changes to the legislation in 1909 allowed the board to remove Aboriginal children from their families without parental consent or court order. The board was changed to the Aborigines Welfare Board in 1940 but its powers and operations were still focused on the removal of Aboriginal children from their families.

>> **South Australia, *Aborigines Act 1911*:** South Australia had a Protector of Aborigines from 1837. The 1911 Act was similar to the powers of the Northern Territory Ordinance.

>> **Northern Territory, *Northern Territory Ordinance 1911*:** Amendments in 1918 made the Chief Protector the legal guardian of every Aboriginal and 'half-caste' person under 18 years of age. Before 1911, the Northern Territory was part of South Australia so a Protector of Aborigines had existed since 1837. Baldwin Spencer became the first Northern Territory Protector of Aborigines in 1911.

>> **Tasmania, *Infants Welfare Act 1935*:** This Act wasn't specifically for the removal of Aboriginal children but was used to implement an assimilation policy in the same way they operated in other states. In 1830, Tasmania appointed its first Protector of Aborigines, George Robinson, who later headed the Port Phillip Protectorate in Victoria.

Note: All states and territories repealed child removal legislation by 1969.

The impact on Indigenous children

A high proportion of Indigenous children removed from their families were psychologically, physically and sexually abused after being placed in state care, fostered or adopted out, or sent out to work. Aboriginal children placed in institutions were discouraged from having contact with their parents and some were told that their parents had died or had abandoned them. The institutions aimed to turn children away from their culture and force them to embrace 'white ways'. This often instilled negative feelings in children about their culture and background, making them ashamed of their Indigenous heritage. The living conditions in the institutions were harsh, with strict regimes, and children were often hungry and cold. Little affection was provided but plenty of corporal punishment. Children were whipped, beaten, placed in dark places or tied up as punishments. Psychiatrists have noted that depression, anxiety, low self-esteem, post-traumatic stress and suicide are commonplace among the Stolen Generations.

REMEMBER

Some Indigenous people who were removed under the policy don't know where they were taken from and they've been unable to locate information about their removal, or documentation has been lost or destroyed.

In New South Wales, Aboriginal girls taken from their families were placed in the Cootamundra Domestic Training Home for Aboriginal Girls; the boys were placed in the Aboriginal Boys' Training Home at Kinchela. Here's a little about each of those institutions:

>> **Cootamundra Domestic Training Home for Aboriginal Girls:** Aboriginal girls placed in this institution at Cootamundra were trained to become domestic servants in the homes of middle-class white people. The Home operated from 1911 to 1986. Girls forcibly taken from their families weren't allowed contact with their parents. Letters from family members written to the girls were often not passed on, so many wrongly believed they were unwanted, abandoned or forgotten. Evidence given to later inquiries revealed that girls were harshly punished and sometimes beaten.

>> **Kinchela Aboriginal Boys' Training Home:** The home was established in 1924 near Kempsey. It had a reputation for being poorly managed and psychologically isolating for the boys, and for not fulfilling the requirements to train its charges. In 1935, a report into the home caused the Aborigines Protection Board to 'strongly advise' the manager 'to give up intoxicating liquor entirely', particularly when in the company of the boys. The report also noted that he was 'on no account' to 'tie a boy up to a fence or tree, or anything else of that nature, to inflict punishment on him, that such instruments as lengths of hosepipe or a stockwhip must not be used in chastising a boy, no dietary punishments should be inflicted on any inmate in the Home'.

Evidence given to later inquiries documented the brutal physical punishment and sexual abuse suffered by boys placed there. Reform of the Home didn't take place until after World War II. It finally closed in 1970, by which time it had housed up to 600 boys. In 1976 the Home was converted into a drug and alcohol rehabilitation centre — 'Bennelong's Haven' — for the local Aboriginal community, only closing in 2018.

The impact on Indigenous families

Although much attention has been given to the impact on children of removal from their Indigenous families, less attention has been given to the trauma faced by parents who had children taken from them. The loss was devastating to many parents, who never recovered from the grief of having their children taken from them. Some died from their heartbreak; others succumbed to alcohol to numb their pain. Many parents fought to get their children back. They appealed to authorities or even tried legal action to have their children returned to them. Letters written to children in state care were usually not delivered and legal action was rarely successful. Families were further fractured when more than one child was removed; in many instances, all of the children were removed. Siblings who were removed were often deliberately separated from each other and grew up apart.

The removal of children over several generations meant a severe disruption to the Indigenous oral culture and much cultural knowledge was lost as a result.

Link-Up is an organisation established by the Indigenous community in New South Wales in 1980 to assist Indigenous people who were removed from their families. Link-Up assists with the process of finding a family, provides counselling services and support to family members, and facilitates reunions. It also helps to find suitable Indigenous foster care families when required and assists in finding kin or family members who can help Indigenous children being taken into state care. Similar Link-Up services now operate in Queensland, Victoria and South Australia.

Acknowledging the Stolen Generations

The policy of forcibly removing Indigenous children was devastating on those who were taken away and the families who were left behind. The resulting emotional and psychological trauma scarred people and many had difficulties overcoming their abuse. Others were angry when they found out that parents who they had been told were dead were actually alive and had fought hard to get them back but without success.

At the Going Home conference in Darwin in 1994, 600 Aboriginal people and Torres Strait Islanders from across Australia, all of whom had been removed from their families, called for an inquiry into the policy of forced child removal and its legacies. In 1995, an inquiry began, undertaking broad community consultation before delivering a report that tabled what had happened to the people who were beginning to call themselves the Stolen Generations.

Many books and movies deal with the child removal policy and its legacies. See Chapters 18 and 19 for more about Indigenous literature and movies.

The report of the inquiry into the Stolen Generations

On 11 May 1995, federal Attorney-General Michael Lavarch issued the terms of reference to the Human Rights and Equal Opportunity Commission to undertake what would become the National Inquiry into the Separation of Aboriginal and Torres Strait Islander Children from Their Families.

The terms of reference were to 'trace the past laws, practices and policies which resulted in the separation of Aboriginal and Torres Strait Islander children from their families by compulsion, duress or undue influence, and the effects of those laws, practices and policies'. The commission of inquiry was also to make recommendations on ways to redress the impacts of the policy, including consideration of compensation.

The inquiry held hearings around Australia between December 1995 and October 1996, and received 777 submissions, 69 per cent from Indigenous people. The *Bringing Them Home* report was tabled in parliament on 26 May 1997. The report estimated that between 10 per cent and 33 per cent of Indigenous children were removed from their families between 1910 and 1970. The report was careful to evaluate past actions in the light of the values and standards operating at the time but it still found that the policy of forcible removal resulted in breaches of fundamental human rights, including:

>> Abolition of parental rights by taking children and assuming custody and control over them

>> Abuses of power in the removal processes

>> Breaches of guardianship obligations by governments and 'carers'

>> Deprivation of liberty by detaining children and confining them to institutions

Children suffered many abuses in the institutions and workplaces they were sent to and sometimes in the families they were adopted into. The report detailed how these childhood traumas affected people in their adult lives, often making it hard for them to adjust to family life and parenthood. A quarter of the witnesses to the inquiry that led to the *Bringing Them Home* report who had been fostered or adopted reported physical abuse; almost one in five who had been raised in institutions reported physical abuse and one in ten reported sexual abuse. The report also documented that many Indigenous children who were sent out to work weren't paid wages. See the sidebar 'Where have all the wages gone?' for more about this issue.

The *Bringing Them Home* report documented the practice in the Torres Strait of sending children born to Torres Strait Islander mothers and non-Islander fathers to mission dormitories on islands such as Thursday Island or to mainland institutions. This practice continued up until 1970. Church representatives in the Torres Strait would notify the Department of Native Affairs of pregnancies and of any mixed parentage, and the department would arrange for girls born of those unions to be placed in the Catholic Convent dormitory on Thursday Island and for boys to be sent to mainland institutions or adopted out to Islander families.

Although many Australians knew of the practice of removing Indigenous children from their families, they were often unaware of just how widespread the practice was or how much Indigenous children who were removed suffered until the release of the *Bringing Them Home* report.

A TRAGIC CYCLE

Many Indigenous people believe that the policy of removing Indigenous children from their families still has impacts today. People who were removed under the policy and institutionalised or brought up in circumstances where they were physically, sexually or psychologically abused can find it hard to adjust to family life. Because they've never seen what good parenting is like, in some cases, parenting skills aren't learned and children are neglected. These circumstances have set up a tragic cycle in some Indigenous families, with generations growing up in state care.

In addition to this phenomenon, although laws specifically designed to remove Indigenous children from their families have been repealed, Indigenous children are still at greater risk of removal from their families. Factors found to have contributed to this include cultural bias against Indigenous modes of parenting, inadequate and inappropriate services for Indigenous families, and discriminatory treatment of Indigenous juveniles within the criminal justice system. See Chapters 21 and 22 for more on these issues.

REMEMBER

The day on which the *Bringing Them Home* report was tabled in federal parliament, 26 May, has been commemorated as *National Sorry Day* since 1998.

MYTH BUSTER

Some people have claimed that many of the Indigenous children removed from their families as part of assimilation policies were removed for their own good. Conditions in Indigenous communities could be dreadful (due to neglect by government agencies) and many Indigenous families lived in extreme poverty. However, the *Bringing Them Home* report found that Indigenous children separated from their families 'fared no better than those not separated when assessed on social indicators such as education, employment and income'. Further, it stated: 'Those removed were twice as likely to have been arrested . . . and they suffer more health problems'.

The official response

Although the Keating Labor government had commissioned the *Bringing Them Home* report (refer to the previous section), it was received by a Liberal government, that of John Howard.

The Howard government had reservations about the report. It rejected its conclusion that the removal of Indigenous children amounted to a form of genocide. It said that the number of children taken away was only one in ten and that many had been removed for their own benefit. It also questioned whether people were 'stolen' or if they could be considered a 'generation', not even acknowledging the several generations that were affected by the assimilation practices. Howard rejected two recommendations of the report very strongly — the need for a national apology to the Stolen Generations and the establishment of a compensation scheme for victims of the policies that had created them. Howard believed an apology wasn't an appropriate response to the issue. He believed strongly that a current generation shouldn't be made to feel guilty or sorry about things done by previous generations, especially if what had been done was with good intentions. Others opposed a national apology because it would 'open the floodgates' for compensation claims. Aboriginal Affairs Minister Senator John Herron said that stories of widespread removal of Indigenous children from their families were exaggerated and that, where children were taken, it was for lawful reasons.

Despite contesting the findings of the *Bringing Them Home* report and rejecting recommendations relating to a national apology and compensation scheme, the Howard government did provide funding for other services and initiatives recommended by the report. Financial support was granted for counselling services, networks to link up family members, programs to make archival material more easily available, programs to record the oral histories of people removed by the policy, and Indigenous family support and parenting services.

On 4 April 2000, the Howard government, in a submission to a Senate inquiry on compensation for children forcibly removed, stated that it was 'concerned that there is no reliable basis for what appears to be a generally accepted conclusion as to the supposed dimensions of the "stolen generation"'. It went on to add, 'At most, it might be inferred that up to 10 per cent of children were separated for a variety of reasons, both protective and otherwise, some forcibly and some not. This does not constitute a "generation" of "stolen" children. The phrase "stolen generation" is rhetorical'.

MYTH BUSTER

The *Bringing Them Home* report found that the aim of the policy of removing Indigenous children from their families was to 'breed out' Aboriginal and Torres Strait Islander peoples and their cultures. Some people believed this amounted to 'cultural genocide'. Under international law, policies and practices designed to destroy a race of people are known as *genocide* and are forbidden under the 1948 Convention on the Prevention and Punishment of the Crime of Genocide. Policies and laws can be genocidal even if they aren't motivated by hatred or animosity; people thinking the policy is for the good of the members of a particular race is irrelevant to whether the action amounts to genocide. The use of the word 'genocide' in this context, however, has caused deep debate and disagreement.

WHERE HAVE ALL THE WAGES GONE?

The practice of placing a large percentage of the wages of Indigenous workers in government trust accounts wasn't only used for Indigenous children sent out to work as domestic servants or on pastoral properties; it was widespread. Most Aboriginal workers were given some pocket money but not told where the bulk of their earnings were going, or even that they were entitled to them, and never saw them again. This meant they were effectively treated as slave labour. Not being able to access adequate wages locked Aboriginal people into a cycle of poverty.

Historians estimate that the state of Queensland alone owes around $500,000,000 to Indigenous people for these 'stolen wages'; in New South Wales, the amount is estimated to be $70,000,000. Indigenous people have made efforts to try to reclaim some of these wages in recent years but many records of the trust accounts were destroyed or lost, making it very difficult for people to prove that they had their wages stolen or to quantify the amount.

Governments have resisted claims for compensation for stolen wages and many of the claimants are old, poor and of frail health. Many have passed away while waiting for their claims to be heard. New South Wales set up an Aboriginal Trust Fund Repayment Scheme to repay stolen wages. Although it offered to pay $3,521 for every $100 owed in stolen wages, by March 2008 only 24 per cent of the 1177 claims from direct claimants had been successful. The scheme finished processing claims at the end of 2011.

In 2019, the Queensland state government settled a historic class action, agreeing to pay out $190 million. With nearly 2000 former workers registered as parties to the action, the funds will be divided between more than 11,000 Indigenous workers who had their wages stolen, or their relatives.

Unfinished Business: Reparations and Compensation

The *Bringing Them Home* report made recommendations about the appropriate reparations that could be made to the members of the Stolen Generations and their families. The report took a broad view, consistent with international law, about what these reparations should consist of, as well as making specific recommendations. These include

>> Acknowledgement of the truth and an apology, specifically that apologies should be issued to the Stolen Generations and their families

>> Guarantees that the human rights abuses wouldn't occur again, with a specific recommendation that public education about the removal policy and its impact be undertaken

>> Returning what had been lost (restitution), to the extent possible, specifically in assisting people who were removed to find their families

>> Rehabilitation, including recording oral histories of those removed

>> Compensation, with a specific recommendation to establish a national compensation fund

Only 3 of the 54 recommendations of the report have been implemented — an oral history collection at the National Library of Australia, establishing a National Sorry Day and the issuing of formal apologies by all parliaments, state and federal. However, as a result of the report, resources have been put into collecting more oral histories and towards counselling and other support services for the members of the Stolen Generations. The one area where governments have been reluctant to implement recommendations has been in the delivery of compensation packages to members of the Stolen Generations.

Saying sorry

State and territory governments were generally quick to offer apologies to the Stolen Generations:

>> **Western Australia:** Delivered 27 May 1997 by Leader of the Opposition Geoff Gallop (motion supported by Premier Richard Court)

>> **South Australia:** Delivered 28 May 1997 by Minister for Aboriginal Affairs Dean Brown

>> **Australian Capital Territory:** Delivered 17 June 1997 by Chief Minister Kate Carnell

>> **New South Wales:** Delivered 18 June 1997 by Premier Bob Carr

>> **Tasmania:** Delivered 13 August 1997 by Premier Tony Rundle

>> **Victoria:** Delivered 17 September 1997 by Premier Jeff Kennett

>> **Queensland:** Delivered 26 May 1999 by Premier Peter Beattie

>> **Northern Territory:** Delivered 24 October 2001 by Chief Minister Clare Martin

Prime Minister John Howard remained steadfast in his belief that an apology from the federal government to the Stolen Generations wasn't necessary. But, on 26

August 1999, the federal government issued a statement of 'deep and sincere regret that Indigenous Australians suffered injustices under the practices of past generations, and for the hurt and trauma that many Indigenous people continue to feel as a consequence of those actions'.

REMEMBER

This 'statement of regret' was seen by many to fall short of an apology and the issue remained a contentious matter, with many Australians urging Howard to change his mind. Actions that tried to get the government to issue an apology include:

» **26 January 1998:** Australians for Native Title and Reconciliation (ANTaR) launched the Sorry Books campaign. The books invited Australians to write something in response to the federal government's refusal to make a formal apology. Many Australians signed these books.

» **28 May 2000:** A crowd estimated to be close to 250,000 walked across Sydney Harbour Bridge to call for an apology to the Stolen Generations by the federal government and in support of reconciliation between Indigenous peoples and other Australians. The day before, Howard had once again ruled out an apology to the Stolen Generations.

» **22 November 2001:** Pope John Paul II issued a formal apology on behalf of the Vatican to the Indigenous Australians affected by the actions of any Catholic authorities in connection with the policy of removing children from their families.

» **26 May 2004:** A memorial to the Stolen Generations was established at Reconciliation Place in Canberra.

A Labor government was elected in November 2007. The party had earlier promised to make an official apology to the Stolen Generations should it win government. On 13 February 2008, Prime Minister Kevin Rudd delivered an apology from the federal government to members of the Stolen Generations on the first sitting day of the new parliament. Here's a part of that apology:

We apologise for the laws and policies of successive Parliaments and governments that have inflicted profound grief, suffering and loss on these our fellow Australians.

We apologise especially for the removal of Aboriginal and Torres Strait Islander children from their families, their communities and their country.

For the pain, suffering and hurt of these Stolen Generations, their descendants and for their families left behind, we say sorry.

And for the indignity and degradation thus inflicted on a proud people and a proud culture, we say sorry.

We the Parliament of Australia respectfully request that this apology be received in the spirit in which it is offered as part of the healing of the nation.

The day before the Prime Minister delivered the speech, Minister for Indigenous Affairs Jenny Macklin issued a statement noting that financial compensation wouldn't be paid to the Stolen Generations but reconfirmed the Rudd government's commitment to improve the lives of Indigenous people so they would match those of other Australians.

REMEMBER

In 2000, Australia appeared before the United Nations Committee on the Elimination of Racial Discrimination, which criticised the Australian government's failure to adequately respond to the recommendations of the *Bringing Them Home* report.

Seeking legal justice

Indigenous people sought compensation through the courts for the harms they suffered while in state care after having been removed from their families. Some of these cases failed because government action in taking Indigenous children was actually legal at the time or because not enough evidence existed to prove the case. Later cases have had more success. These cases have focused on the harms suffered while in state care, rather than challenging whether the removal was legal in the first place.

Kruger and others versus the Commonwealth

In 1997, the High Court of Australia heard a case brought by Aboriginal people from the Northern Territory, among them Alec Kruger, who had been removed from their families when they were young under the Northern Territory Ordinance, and a parent who lost a child under the same laws. They claimed the policy had breached their human rights, including due process before the law, equality before the law and freedom of movement. The High Court found against them on the basis that, although those rights may have been breached, they're not rights protected by Australian law, so no legal remedy is available for their infringement.

Peter Gunner and Lorna Cubillo

In 2000, Peter Gunner and Lorna Cubillo claimed they'd been wrongly taken as children. The Federal Court stressed that it wasn't denying that the Stolen Generations existed and it believed that Mr Gunner and Ms Cubillo had suffered greatly since being removed from their families but had to find, on the legal matter, that no evidence suggested that the removal from their families was done in an unlawful manner. The case was lost.

Valerie Linlow

In 2002, Valerie Linlow, a member of the Stolen Generations, received an award of compensation of $35,000 from the New South Wales Victim's Compensation Tribunal. The compensation was for sexual assault and other injuries suffered after she had been removed from her Aboriginal family by authorities and placed, at the age of 16, as a domestic servant for a white family. She said: 'It's not the money that's important to me. It is the knowledge and recognition that this happened to Aboriginal people. No-one could pay any amount for what happened to us because we lost a lot'.

Bruce Trevorrow

On 1 August 2007, Bruce Trevorrow, a member of the Stolen Generations, was awarded $525,000 by Justice Thomas Gray of the South Australian Supreme Court. The payment was to compensate for the sorrow and pain he had suffered after being taken from his mother, in 1957, at the age of 13 months while he was being treated in Adelaide Children's Hospital for gastroenteritis. Six months after he was taken, his mother wrote to the Aboriginal Protection Board asking for her son back but the board lied to her and said he was making good progress but doctors needed to keep him for treatment. Instead, he was fostered into a white family where he grew up unaware of his Aboriginality. He saw his mother again but by that time he was already troubled and unable to adjust to either culture. He found himself going in and out of prison and other institutions, had poor health, and suffered from alcoholism and depression.

The court, in its judgement, found that the circumstances in which Mr Trevorrow was removed constituted wrongful imprisonment and was a breach of the state's duty of care. It was also able to compare the problems faced by Mr Trevorrow as a result of his experiences as a child with those of his brother, who hadn't been removed. Upon hearing the judgement, Mr Trevorrow said: 'At the end of the day, you can't put a dollar value on what happened to me'. The South Australian government appealed but the decision of the court and the award of compensation were upheld in 2010. Unfortunately, Mr Trevorrow died in 2008, before the appeal was dismissed and the decision in his favour was confirmed.

The realities of litigation and compensation

Litigation is a difficult way to get justice. The claims take a long time to progress through the courts. Members of the Stolen Generations are likely to have low levels of education, few resources and poor health, including mental health issues. The combination of these circumstances makes the process long and arduous for them. For this reason, proposals have been made for a national compensation scheme that could be administered through a tribunal, which would streamline the process, make bringing a claim less expensive and be more flexible about the rules of evidence.

Federal Labor and Liberal governments continue to oppose a national compensation scheme, saying that the states, territories and churches were legally responsible and so those bodies should establish compensation measures. The federal government claims it's providing resources to community initiatives, such as counselling and the recording of oral histories, and would rather do this than pay individuals compensation. Others have countered, arguing that, even if legal responsibility does lie elsewhere, this shouldn't stop the federal government from taking leadership and establishing a national compensation framework that would be fair. People have also pointed out that the federal government did have responsibility for Aboriginal people in the Northern Territory when the policy of removing Aboriginal children was at its height, so should at least consider a compensation scheme for them.

Some states did follow with compensation schemes. In 2006, the Tasmanian government passed the *Stolen Generations of Aboriginal Children Act 2006* (Tas). It placed $5 million into the compensation scheme to be allocated to Aboriginal people who qualified. This legislation and process showed that establishing a reparations process to compensate members of the Stolen Generations was possible. New South Wales, Victoria, Western Australia and South Australia all introduced schemes for stolen wages or people who had suffered under the forced child removal policy.

On 2 April 2009, the United Nations Human Rights Committee's report on Australia recommended that the Australian government 'adopt a comprehensive national mechanism to ensure that adequate reparation, including compensation, is provided to the victims of the Stolen Generations'. Federal Attorney-General Robert McClelland advised that the Rudd government wouldn't follow that recommendation but was instead concentrating on the commitment to improve the lives of Indigenous people and to establish a 'Healing Foundation'.

The Aboriginal and Torres Strait Islander Healing Foundation was established on 30 October 2009. The foundation is an Indigenous-controlled not-for-profit organisation that funds community-based healing programs that 'seek to address the traumatic legacy of colonisation, forced removals and other past government policies'. The Healing Foundation has focused on programs to deal with trauma but has also helped to raise awareness about the concept of intergenerational trauma — the notion that, if someone has not recovered from their own trauma, they may, through their behaviour, inadvertently pass it down to their children. In this way, the impact of the child removal policy flows down to the next generation. (For more on the Healing Foundation, go to healingfoundation.org.au.)

MYTH BUSTER

The claim is often made that the child removal policy is a thing of the past, since the formal policy had ended in all states and territories by the end of the 1960s. However, the lived experiences of many living survivors of the policy show the impact is not in the past. Research highlighting the extent of intergenerational trauma among the children of the 'stolen generations' is further evidence that people are still living with the impact of the policy today.

CULTURAL PROTOCOLS

The strongest support for the members of the Stolen Generations has come from the community organisations formed by the survivors of the child removal policy. Organisations like Link-Up NSW assist people who were affected by the removal policy to find their families again (see www.linkupnsw.org.au). Organisations such as the Kinchela Boys Home Aboriginal Corporation provide support, advocacy and a sense of community for survivors of the trauma of the child removal policy (see kinchelaboyshome.org.au).

MYTH BUSTER

The Australian government has been reluctant to look at a national compensation scheme for members of the Stolen Generations. Canada, a country that practised a similar policy of forcibly removing Indigenous children from their families, announced a compensation scheme in 2005. Aboriginal children in Canada were taken from their families and placed in institutions called Residential Schools. The Canadian government allocated $1.9 billion for the compensation package. The money established an Aboriginal Healing Foundation and a Truth and Reconciliation Program but also provided for individual compensation payments — called a Common Experience Payment — of $10,000 for the first year spent in a Residential School and $3,000 for each subsequent year.

3

Indigenous Activism

Follow the struggle of Indigenous peoples, which, up until the 1960s, had a key focus on the claim to be equal with other Australians, and to be treated the same as other Australian citizens.

Examine the significant change that occurred in 1967, when a constitutional referendum gave the federal government the power to make laws for Indigenous people.

Track how Indigenous peoples continued to assert their rights through a variety of ways, particularly focusing on their rights to land.

Understand the different strategies federal governments have implemented to work with Indigenous people, including a process of reconciliation, a focus on practical reconciliation and a national apology for past wrongs.

Chapter **10**

Citizenship Rights

B y the late 1880s, colonisation had been occurring for more than a century in the south-eastern part of Australia. Aboriginal people across the country were navigating their new environment but remained steadfast in their resistance to the claims made by the British over their land and the control colonial governments sought to exert over their lives. Aboriginal resistance and political activism became more sophisticated, with Aboriginal people asserting — through letters and petitions — their claims to equal rights as citizens and their claims to land. In this chapter, I examine several examples of Aboriginal people on reserves using their newly acquired literacy skills to advocate for better conditions. Later, this advocacy led to the establishment of Indigenous organisations that provided platforms for the political reform agenda of the Indigenous communities.

The Australian Constitution came into force in 1901 but Indigenous people had been excluded from the process of drafting it, and power over the lives of Indigenous people was left with the states. The states continued an approach of 'protection', which saw the establishment of government bodies that controlled the lives of Indigenous people. Here, I also look at the ways the British legal system, and then the Australian Constitution and state laws, failed Indigenous people and denied them basic rights, placing on them controls over where they could live, who they could marry and who they could associate with. They weren't allowed to control their own incomes and were powerless to stop the removal of their children.

Indigenous people made considerable contributions during World War I and World War II, both at home and overseas. Yet, after serving their country, Indigenous people didn't return to enjoy the same rights as other Australians. In this chapter, I also take a look at how this treatment of the black diggers became a symbol of the difficulty Indigenous people faced, sparking the development of a citizenship rights movement to fight against the deep-rooted discrimination that permeated the lives of Indigenous people across the country.

Early Claims to Better Treatment

Colonial governments began moving Aboriginal people onto pockets of land for their own protection. Originally created to shield them from violence and other hardships on the frontier, Aboriginal reserves became places where government bodies exercised great control over the lives of Indigenous people. However, this 'protection' was quickly felt to reflect treatment that was different from — and lesser than — the rights of other Australians. Indigenous people began to focus on the need for recognition of their citizenship rights so they could break free from the discrimination that occurred in their lives and take control over their own destiny.

Inclusion through equal access to education, employment and the economy was seen as the key to improving the situation of Indigenous people. Aboriginal leaders emerged, such as William Cooper and Fred Maynard, who had worked on pastoral stations that they were prevented from owning. They were self-taught men and they believed that if Aboriginal people were given the same opportunities as other Australians and could make key decisions about their communities, their families and their lives, they'd be able to find their own solutions to their problems. This notion of access and opportunity underpinned the desire for citizenship rights and, alongside the claim for land and the desire for self-determination, created the key platforms in the Indigenous political agenda.

Many missionaries and humanitarians still believed that Indigenous people were inferior but, as such, the colonists had a duty to colonise and civilise them. Many also were sympathetic to the fact that Aboriginal people had been stripped of their lands through a hostile and sometimes brutal process of colonisation, and deprived of their traditional means of support. They believed the best approach for surviving Aboriginal populations was to place them on parcels of land where they could be supervised by missionaries or government officials who could 'civilise' them.

REMEMBER

From the 1830s, Aboriginal communities that had resisted the incursions onto their lands began to organise politically in a different way. The focus for their struggle was still their land — they often fought to be granted or to retain reserve lands. But Aboriginal people also campaigned to be treated fairly, and resisted the discriminatory and restrictive rules and regulations used by colonial governments and their officers to control their lives. In some places, such as Flinders Island off Tasmania and Coranderrk reserve in Victoria, they waged sophisticated campaigns to be treated fairly and to have a greater say over their own lives. This political activism and protest often focused on petitioning the British monarchy. These appeals to the Crown sought to show that the British had a responsibility to look after Aboriginal people and also showed a lack of trust in the colonial government to really 'protect' Aboriginal people or to have their best interests at heart.

Flinders Island

Aboriginal people in Van Diemen's Land — now Tasmania — bitterly resisted the colonisation of their lands by the British that began in the 1820s. Between 1831 and 1834, Aboriginal people were induced by a government representative — George Augustus Robinson — to abandon the main island and move to Flinders Island, the largest island of the Furneaux Group in Bass Strait. Here, the government promised they would enjoy sanctuary from frontier violence, and the benefits of civilisation and Christianity.

On their arrival, it became clear these promises were empty. Food was scarce and the living conditions poor. Many of the hundred or so Tasmanian survivors who were sent to Flinders Island died, and others suffered from malnutrition and disease. Life on the island was heavily regulated, with a strict regime that focused on adherence to Christian principles. Those in charge of running the island and overseeing Aboriginal people were often not very sympathetic to them.

This situation caused many of the older Aboriginal people to despair, but the younger men and women used their new literacy skills to protest against their treatment. From 1836 to 1837 they had their own newspaper — the *Flinders Island Chronicle* or *Flinders Island Weekly Chronicle*. The protest leaders used the humanitarian principles espoused by Christianity to advocate on their own behalf. They were also influenced by the anti-slavery movement that had been established by English philanthropists and evangelicals, and was gaining some support in Australia.

FIGHTING SLAVERY

The anti-slavery movement that was focused on ending the slave trade was influential among evangelical and humanitarian organisations. In Britain, the anti-slavery movement was the first large philanthropic mass movement. It influenced anti-slavery movements in other countries and sowed the seeds for other social reforms such as suffrage, the rights of women and workers' rights. It also influenced their thinking about Indigenous people. They saw Indigenous people as entitled to the same rights as white people and actively promoted the better treatment of Indigenous people in the colonies, including Australia.

Political protest on Flinders Island culminated in the mid-1840s and included a petition to Queen Victoria that claimed the colonial government had broken promises to them. The petition of 17 February 1846 pleads that its former superintendent, Dr Henry Jeanneret, not be reinstated to the island. It also gives insights into the treatment of Aboriginal people on the reserve. The petition states in part:

Our houses were let fall down & they were never cleaned but were covered in vermin & not white-washed. We were often without Clothes except a very little one & Dr. Jeanneret did not care to mind us when we were sick until we were very bad. Eleven of us died when he was here. He kept us from our Rations when he pleased & sometimes gave us Bad Rations of Tea & Tobacco. He shot some of our dogs before our eyes & sent all the other dogs of ours to an Island & when we told him that they would starve he told us they might eat each other ... We were never taught to read or to write or to sing to God by the Doctor. He taught us a little upon the Sundays & his Prisoner Servant also taught us & his Prisoner Servant also took us plenty of times to Jail by his orders.

This makes clear that the Aboriginal people of Flinders Island understood that they were entitled to be treated fairly and with dignity. Jeanneret did return to Flinders Island but the settlement was ordered to be closed in 1847 by order of the Tasmanian governor. The remaining 40 or so Aboriginal people were taken to Oyster Cove, a former convict settlement south of Hobart.

Coranderrk

Aboriginal people living in the Port Phillip District, which became the colony Victoria in 1851, had been affected by diseases, dispossession and frontier violence, all of which had caused their population to plummet to only a few thousand by the 1850s. During this period, gold rushes also added to the demand for land and pressures on the Aboriginal community. Reserves, such as the one at Coranderrk, were established for the dwindling Aboriginal population.

Coranderrk, an area of almost ten square kilometres, was gazetted as a reserve in 1863 after about 40 Wurundjeri people settled at a traditional campsite near Healesville, and appealed for its ownership. The settlement ran well for a number of years as an Aboriginal enterprise, producing wheat and hops that were sold in Melbourne. In the 1870s, the reserve was threatened with closure by the Aboriginal Protection Board. The people of the Coranderrk reserve began a sustained protest. They were also vocal and effective advocates for their own abilities to manage their affairs and were critical of the control the managers of the reserve had over their lives. Their protest was a sophisticated one. They wrote letters to the newspapers and to government ministers and sought the support of humanitarians. Their actions forced the Victorian government to hold two major inquiries — in 1877, to inquire generally into policies relating to Aboriginal people, and in 1881, to specifically inquire into conditions at Coranderrk.

When the Aborigines Protection Bill came before the Victorian Parliament in 1886, it gave the Board for the Protection of Aborigines extensive powers over the lives of Aboriginal people. The residents of Coranderrk wrote in protest to the newspapers:

We wish to ask for our wishes, that is, could we get our freedom to go away shearing and harvesting, and to come home when we wish, and also to go for the good of our health when we need it; and we aboriginals all wish and hope to have freedom, not to be bound down by the protection of the Board, as it says in the Bill, But we should be free like the white population. There is only a few blacks now remaining in Victoria. We are all dying away now, and we blacks of Aboriginal blood wish to have our freedom for all our life time, for the population is small, and the increase is slow. For why does the Board seek in these latter days more stronger authority over us aborigines than it has yet been. For there is only 21 aborigines on the station Coranderrk including men and women.

However, the 1886 legislation forced Aboriginal people of mixed descent under the age of 34 off the reserve and into the general community, on the eve of the 1890s depression. With only a handful of able-bodied people left to work the farm, Coranderrk became unviable. Almost half the land was resumed in 1893 and the reserve was ordered closed in 1924, though a handful of people refused to move and were allowed to live out their days there. In 1995, part of the reserve was handed back to the Wurundjeri Tribe Land Compensation and Cultural Heritage Council when the Indigenous Land Corporation (see Chapter 12) purchased almost one square kilometre.

Cummeragunja reserve

Maloga mission was founded on the New South Wales side of the Murray River near Echuca in 1874. Aboriginal people of the Yorta Yorta and Bangerang nations soon petitioned for their own independent reserve on their traditional lands. In this, they were supported and encouraged by Aboriginal people from the Coranderrk reserve in Victoria (refer to the previous section).

By 1881, land had been reserved about five kilometres from Maloga mission and this became the Cummeragunja reserve in 1883. But Aboriginal people began expressing their desire to own their own blocks of land and petitioned the governor in 1887 to be allowed to do so. Like the people of Coranderrk, they believed that, if they were given the opportunity to tend their own land, they would be able to provide for themselves, allowing them to be self-sufficient and no longer reliant on the government.

They also appealed to the Queen's authority. One of these men was William Cooper, who, decades later, became the leader of one of the first major Indigenous political organisations in Australia, the Australian Aborigines League, and was involved with other key political organisations such as the Aborigines Progressive Association (see the section 'Indigenous people organise', later in this chapter). Cummeragunja became famous for the activism of its residents. As well as William Cooper, Pastor Doug Nicholls also came from there. The reserve was closed by the Aborigines Protection Board in 1953 because the number of residents was low.

REMEMBER

This spirit of activism continues today. Members of the community were involved with the first native title claim lodged in Victoria, in 1994. Even though they lost the claim in 1998, the Yorta Yorta negotiated an agreement to co-manage part of the lands with the Victorian government in 2004.

British Subjects, but Not Quite . . .

Colonial governments confidently asserted that the British legal system applied over Australia and that Indigenous laws — thought to be primitive — no longer applied. In theory, Australia's Indigenous peoples became British subjects but, in practice, they were treated very differently.

REMEMBER

British law failed Indigenous people on a number of fronts. In the early years of colonisation, in some colonies, specific laws were enacted to allow settlers to shoot Aboriginal people under certain circumstances; 'protection' acts enabled the removal of children; and discrimination against Indigenous people living within the wider community was endemic, with no laws to give real protection. This section delves into a range of those circumstances.

Denying basic rights

The failure to recognise Indigenous legal systems meant that Indigenous rights to land were also ignored and no compensation was given for the loss of property. But the legal system discriminated against Indigenous people in other ways, too. They couldn't press charges or appear as witnesses. They were sometimes punished as a group for the crimes of other Indigenous people, so concepts such as due process before the law and equality before the law didn't always apply. In fact, the colonial laws that were supposed to apply equally to all British subjects targeted Indigenous people in some notable ways. Here are just a few of them:

>> **1816:** Martial law was proclaimed in New South Wales against Aboriginal people, who could be shot if they were armed or within a certain distance of colonial settlements.

>> **1824:** Tasmanian colonists were authorised to shoot Aboriginal people.

>> **1869:** A Board for the Protection of Aborigines was established in Victoria, with the power to order the removal of any child to a reformatory or industrial school.

>> **1890:** The Aborigines Protection Board in New South Wales could forcibly take children off reserves to resocialise them.

A *citizen* is someone who shares both in ruling and being ruled. The right to vote and the responsibility to obey the law are central to notions of citizenship. Today, concepts of citizenship are also linked to some fundamental human rights, such as the civil rights necessary for freedom (such as freedom of speech), political rights to take part in the political process (right to vote, right to stand for election) and social rights necessary to participate in society (right to education, right to adequate standards of living). Many of these rights weren't respected when it came to Indigenous people; hence, the protracted struggle to gain *citizenship rights*.

The 2020 High Court decision in *Love v Commonwealth; Thoms v Commonwealth* held by a majority that an Aboriginal person is not 'an alien'. Section 51(xix) gives the Federal Government the power to make laws about 'naturalization and aliens.' The case concerned men who had not been born in Australia and had not become citizens under the law but were Aboriginal. The court ruled if they could prove they were Aboriginal (had Aboriginal descent, identified as Aboriginal and were recognised by the Aboriginal community as Aboriginal), they could not be subject to a deportation order.

For their own 'protection'

All of the colonies passed laws, usually with the words 'Aborigines Protection' or 'Aborigines Welfare' in their titles, that set up specific government bodies with powers to regulate the lives of Indigenous people, particularly their children (refer to Chapter 9). These laws reduced the status of Indigenous people to *wards of the state*, placing them in a legal position where they had fewer rights than citizens. They gave these bodies almost complete control over the lives of Indigenous people:

>> **1869, Victoria:** The Aborigines Protection Act established the Victorian Board for the Protection of Aborigines.

>> **1883, New South Wales:** The Aborigines Protection Act established the Aborigines Protection Board. The 1909 Act gave additional powers to the board over the lives of Aboriginal people and their children. It was changed to the Aborigines Welfare Board in 1940.

>> **1897, Queensland:** The Aboriginal Protection and Restriction of the Sale of Opium Act gave Superintendents powers over Aboriginal people, including directing where they should live.

>> **1905, Western Australia:** The Aborigines Act created a Chief Protector of Aborigines who had vast powers over their lives.

>> **1911, Northern Territory:** The Northern Territory Ordinance gave powers to the Chief Protector. Amendments in 1918 made him the legal guardian of every Aboriginal and 'half-caste' person under 18 years of age.

>> **1911, South Australia:** The Aborigines Act expanded the powers of the Protector of Aborigines, a position South Australia had from 1836.

REMEMBER

NEVILLE'S ROLE

One of the best known people in the role of Chief Protector of Aborigines in Western Australia was A O Neville. He held the office from 1915 until 1936. He then took the position of Commissioner for Native Affairs until his retirement in 1940. He was responsible for regulations that gave the government more power over the lives of Aboriginal people, particularly children.

Consistent with views of the day, Neville's belief was that 'full-blood' Aboriginal people should be segregated. He also believed that those of mixed descent might be temporarily segregated and trained but then assimilated into white society as domestics and farm workers, eventually blending with the white population through intermarriage. He took an interest in record-keeping and frequently inspected reserves and institutions.

The Protection Boards and Chief Protectors in each state or territory had enormous powers over Indigenous people. Regulations gave them control over who could live on government-controlled land or reserves, who could work, who could marry and whether children would be removed from their families to be sent to institutions or out to work.

The realities of assimilation

Away from the reserves, Indigenous people integrated into the broader community with varying degrees of success. Some married white partners. Some worked, often for lower wages or for rations. And they didn't have full and equal rights with other Australians just because they chose to live within the broader community.

REMEMBER

Many faced discrimination in their everyday lives, through the conditions of their work, the provision of housing and the receipt of medical attention. Aboriginal people were refused rental accommodation, especially in country towns, which meant they often had to live on the outskirts, in substandard housing, sometimes in nothing more than a lean-to. Rural hospitals refused to allow Aboriginal people inside and would treat them on the verandahs. This discrimination pushed Indigenous people further to the margins of mainstream society and meant they were more likely to experience poverty and poor health.

TECHNICAL STUFF

Between 1856 and 1900, all of the states had given Aboriginal men the right to vote. However, this right was limited in Western Australia and Queensland by applying a property qualification that few could meet. South Australia (which at the time included the Northern Territory) gave women, including Indigenous women, the right to vote in 1895.

Excluding Indigenous People from the Constitution

The Australian Constitution came into effect in 1901. It was an Act of the British Parliament but established the legal system in Australia. At the time the Constitution was drafted (through a series of Constitutional Conventions in the 1880s and 1890s), the Aboriginal population had been decimated and was living on the fringes of mainstream society — on reserves, in pockets within the cities, on the edges of towns.

Several assumptions that were prominent within Australian society influenced the role and place that its Indigenous peoples were given through the document. Australian society, as in many other parts of the world that had been colonised, had a dominant culture that assumed the white races were superior to the black races, and so were natural leaders. Many people assumed that the Indigenous peoples would die out and that the kindest thing that could be done for them was to place them in areas such as reserves where they could live out their days with some dignity.

The states establish their powers

Indigenous people were excluded from being involved in the drafting of any aspects of the Constitution. Matters concerning Indigenous people would be the responsibility of the states, with the federal government having responsibility for only those Indigenous people who were living in the territories, such as the Northern Territory (see Chapter 11 for more on the referendum to change this section of the Constitution). But ideologies of white racial superiority ran more deeply in the Constitution than simply excluding Indigenous people from discussions about this document.

TECHNICAL
STUFF

The Australian Constitution established the Australian courts, including the High Court, the two houses of federal parliament — the House of Representatives (the lower house) and the Senate (the upper house) — and allocated power between the courts, the executive (the public service) and the federal parliament. It also allocated power between the federal and state governments. Any power not specifically given to the federal government in the Constitution was left with the states (known as *residual powers*). For example, industrial relations is the responsibility of the federal government; criminal law is the responsibility of the states.

From the 1850s, the Australian colonies became self-governing and most soon enabled male British subjects to vote — in South Australia from 1856, Victoria from 1857, New South Wales from 1858 and Tasmania from 1896. However, in these states, Indigenous people weren't encouraged to enrol to vote so most remained off the rolls. In 1885, Queensland specifically excluded Indigenous people from voting and Western Australia did the same in 1893. After 1901, some Commonwealth legislation did affect Indigenous people and their right to vote. For example, the federal *Electoral Act 1902* gave women the right to vote in federal elections but that right didn't extend to Indigenous women who weren't enrolled to vote in state elections. When the federal government extended the rights of Australians to the minimum wage in 1907, age and invalid pensions in 1909 and maternity benefits in 1912, these benefits weren't extended to Indigenous people. Discriminatory laws and practices were just as rife under state laws.

A legal ability to discriminate

The framers of the Australian Constitution believed that the decision-making about rights protections — which rights are recognised and the extent to which they're protected — were matters for the parliament. They looked at the French and American constitutions and discussed the inclusion of rights within the Constitution itself. They rejected this option, preferring instead to leave Australia's founding document silent on these matters. A non-discrimination clause discussed during the process of drafting the Constitution stated in part:

nor shall a state deprive any person of life, liberty, or property without due process of law, or deny to any person within its jurisdiction the equal protection of its laws.

This clause was rejected for two reasons: Entrenched rights provisions were believed to be unnecessary, and it was considered desirable to ensure that the states had the power to continue to enact laws that discriminated against people on the basis of their race.

KING BILLY DROPS BY

When Parliament House was opened in Canberra on 9 May 1927, an 80-year-old Wiradjuri man named Jimmy Clements (also called 'King Billy') had walked all the way from Brungle Mission near Tumut (about 100 kilometres as the crow flies) to see the visiting royalty — the Duke and Duchess of Kent — who were presiding over the proceedings. A policeman immediately asked him to leave on the basis he was inappropriately dressed but the crowd encouraged him to stay and a clergyman stood up and said that King Billy had a better right than any man present to a place on the steps of the House of Parliament. The following day, prominent citizens were paraded in front of the Duke and Duchess and King Billy was among them. A newspaper recorded: 'An ancient aborigine, who calls himself King Billy and who claims sovereign rights to the Federal Territory, walked slowly forward alone, and saluted the Duke and Duchess. They cheerily acknowledged his greeting'.

Some Indigenous people see King Billy's appearance at the opening of the new Parliament House in Canberra as a symbol of the assertion of Aboriginal sovereignty against the British Crown and the Australian state.

REMEMBER

The drafters of the Constitution never intended it to offer protection against racial discrimination. As a result, even today, the Australian government — and the governments of states and self-governing territories — are permitted to pass legislation that discriminates on the basis of race as long as they suspend any conflicting provisions in the Racial Discrimination Act or similar legislation. This has been done several times in recent years. (See Chapter 11 for more on the Australian Constitution and Chapter 14 for examples of governments repealing anti-discrimination legislation.)

REMEMBER

In 1936, the Torres Strait Islanders held a four-month All Island Maritime Strike to protest the poor working conditions of pearl divers, and to demand the rights to control their wages and their own affairs. As a result, in 1939, the Queensland government passed legislation that provided for elected community councils in the Torres Strait.

War Heroes: Frontier Wars and Beyond

Aboriginal people often say they fought a 'frontier war' against the British in some parts of Australia. Many protracted conflicts were referred to as wars: Hawkesbury and Nepean Wars (1790 to 1816); Black Wars in Tasmania (1803 to 1830); Port Phillip District Wars in Victoria (1830 to 1850); Kalkadoon Wars in Queensland (1870 to 1890); Western Australian Conflict (1890 to 1898).

Indigenous people have fought in all of the main wars Australia has entered since the Boer Wars (in 1880 to 1881 and 1899 to 1902), including World War I, World War II, and the Vietnam, Korean, Gulf, Iraqi and Afghanistan Wars. They have also worked as peacekeepers in places such as East Timor. Today, more than 1,000 Indigenous people are in the armed services — about 1.4 per cent of the workforce.

The black diggers

About 500 Aboriginal people and Torres Strait Islanders fought for Australia in World War I, and about 5,000 in World War II. Accurate numbers can't be assessed because many Aboriginal people didn't identify themselves as such — if they had, they may not have been allowed to join. Some pretended they were Indian or Maori. When World War I broke out in 1914, many Indigenous people who tried to enlist were rejected, though some managed to sign up. By the end of 1917, recruits were harder to find, so the military allowed for 'half-castes' to enlist, 'provided that the examining Medical Officers are satisfied that one of the parents is of European origin'.

At the start of World War II, Indigenous people were allowed to enlist. But in 1940, the Defence Committee decided that the enlistment of Indigenous people was 'neither necessary or desirable', partly because they thought white Australians would object to serving beside them. When Japan entered the war, and the need for recruits increased, restrictions were loosened and Indigenous people enlisted as soldiers or worked in the labour corps. Many of these commented that, although racial slurs and discrimination were part of their everyday life when they were civilians, once they were in the trenches, racial differences disappeared and everyone was treated equally and included in the camaraderie.

Back home, Aboriginal people contributed their labour — though they weren't paid equal wages — in the cattle industry that was feeding the soldiers and in factories, and Aboriginal women assisted in hospitals.

When Japan entered the war, the army decided that Indigenous people in the north of Australia were an important labour source, so Indigenous people were put into labour settlements. Although some struggle ensued between governments and the army about who controlled the Indigenous people in these camps, the army-run camps often had better housing and conditions than Indigenous people had been provided with before.

REMEMBER

Many Indigenous women enlisted in the women's services or worked in the war industries. In the north, they worked hard to support isolated RAAF outposts. Aboriginal poet Kath Walker (who later changed her name to Oodgeroo Noonuccal) joined the Australian Women's Army Service in 1942. She served as a signaller in Brisbane.

REMEMBER

Many local Aboriginal men in Port Hedland, Western Australia, were also members of the Volunteer Defence Corps (VDC). They operated coastal defences, anti-aircraft batteries and searchlights. They also moved people to air-raid shelters when military planes were overhead. Some received military training and ensured that people on the pastoral properties complied with blackout regulations.

In 1941, anthropologist Donald Thomson established the Northern Territory Special Reconnaissance Unit. It was an irregular army with 51 Aboriginal people, five white people and a number of Pacific and Torres Strait Islanders. They used their traditional knowledge of the bush to patrol the coastal waters and, using their fighting skills and traditional weapons, were expected to engage in a guerrilla war with the Japanese if they landed ashore. The unit was disbanded after the Japanese no longer posed a threat. The Indigenous people in the unit received no pay. They were finally compensated for lost wages in 1992 and medals were awarded to them.

Most Indigenous people enlisted in the Australian Imperial Force (AIF), a special army of volunteers for overseas service formed during both wars, but some enlisted in the other services.

The Royal Australian Air Force (RAAF)

The RAAF was less restrictive in its recruiting than the army, although, according to Australian War Memorial historians, not much is known of Indigenous aircrew. Leonard Waters was an Aboriginal man who joined the RAAF in 1942 and was, after lengthy and competitive training, selected as a pilot. He was stationed in Dutch New Guinea and then in Borneo. His squadron flew Kittyhawk fighters and Waters named his 'Black Magic'. He flew in 95 military operations. After the war, he hoped for a career in civilian flying but bureaucratic delays forced him to return to shearing. He found, as did other Indigenous people in the armed services, that civilian life in Australia didn't allow him to use the skills he had gained and used in the war.

The Royal Australian Navy (RAN)

As with the RAAF (refer to preceding section), little is known as to how many Indigenous people enlisted in the navy, but the RAN also employed Indigenous people in informal units. One notable member of the RAN was John Gribble. He had, during the war, formed a group of 36 Aboriginal men who joined him in patrolling the coast and the islands of the Northern Territory. This was a large area but the men who did this valuable work weren't enlisted. Despite promises that they would be paid for this work, they never were.

Labour units

During World War II, the army and the RAAF relied on Indigenous labour in northern Australia. They drove trucks, built construction sites, worked on the army farms and in butcheries, and handled cargo. The RAAF positioned its airfields near Aboriginal reserves so they could make use of their labour.

Indigenous people at first were employed in the war effort on much the same terms as they were employed in the pastoral industry and as domestic servants — long hours, hard labour, poor-quality food and housing, and low pay. As the war went on and the army took over control of Indigenous communities, conditions actually improved. For the first time, Indigenous people were given adequate housing, fixed working hours, proper rations and access to proper health care at army hospitals. Pay rates, however, remained low. The army attempted to raise the wages of Indigenous people, but pressure from the civilian community, particularly pastoralists, kept the rates low.

TORRES STRAIT ISLANDERS DEFENDING THE NORTH

In 1941, the Torres Strait Light Infantry Battalion was formed to defend the Torres Strait area. Other units were also created that specialised in important matters such as water transport. Although they never engaged in conflict, they patrolled an important strategic area, including areas of Japanese-controlled Dutch New Guinea. By 1944, almost every male Torres Strait Islander who was eligible had enlisted, though they were paid much less than their white counterparts. At first, wages were only a third of what was paid to their non-Indigenous counterparts, rising to two-thirds in December 1943. Other aspects of the war were particularly hard on Torres Strait Islanders. The pearl luggers, for example, that provided most of the local income were confiscated to ensure that they didn't fall into Japanese hands.

The United States Navy recruited about 20 Torres Strait Islanders as crewmen on the ships it operated around the Torres Strait Islands and Papua New Guinea. One Islander, Kamuel Abednego, was given the rank of lieutenant within the US Navy at a time when no Indigenous person served as a commissioned officer in the Australian services.

The Torres Strait Islander community is a small section of the Australian community. If the number of people in that community who made a direct contribution to the war effort in World War II is considered, it can be argued that no other community in Australia contributed as much to the war effort.

Returned soldiers and racism

On returning to Australia, Indigenous diggers found they were treated in the same discriminatory manner — and subject to the same discriminatory treatment — as they had been before they entered the armed services and fought for their country. Many didn't receive recognition for their contribution to the war and, even worse, had their names excluded from war memorials. They weren't allowed entry to the Returned Services League clubs that all the other diggers were given access to. They had no access to the veterans' benefits such as pensions. Although schemes were set up to grant land to returned soldiers, Indigenous diggers weren't eligible. In fact, Aboriginal reserve land was confiscated in order to provide land for this 'soldier settlement' scheme.

Many diggers were required to return to the reserves, where government officials regulated their lives. The Department of Veterans' Affairs provides plaques for the graves of returned soldiers. However, this wasn't done for many Indigenous diggers when they died. Some steps have been taken to rectify this neglect today. Also, over the years, other efforts have attempted to give Indigenous diggers the recognition they deserve. In 1949, the Commonwealth Electoral Act gave the vote to Indigenous people who had been or were members of the defence forces. Eventually, they were allowed membership of Returned Services League clubs and acknowledged on Anzac Day for their contribution to Australia's war effort.

CULTURAL PROTOCOLS

On ANZAC Day in 2007 — 25 April — a parade of Aboriginal people and Torres Strait Islanders, including Indigenous veterans and their families, marched through Redfern in Sydney. This was the first of what has become a yearly event to commemorate the contribution of Aboriginal and Torres Strait Islander people in the armed services. The Indigenous community celebrates the 'black diggers' with a special ceremony to show honour and respect to members of their community who made sacrifices during the war.

REMEMBER

The Australian War Memorial has significantly increased its focus on the contribution of Aboriginal and Torres Strait Islanders to the war effort, including more stories of Indigenous people through their main displays and by having a special dedicated gallery. Many community-based projects have also sought to collect the stories of Indigenous contribution to the war effort. You can check some out by going to `redfernoralhistory.org`, clicking on Organisations and selecting Coloured Diggers from the drop-down list.

Still Denied Equality

The treatment of returned veterans became a symbol of the difficult situation faced by Australia's Indigenous peoples. They were denied basic equal rights and made wards of the state for their own protection but, even when they participated fully within the broader community, they were never treated as equal. Not even military service to their country was seen as enough commitment to ensure the receipt of basic human rights.

Dispossession increases

In the interwar period, particularly in the 1930s, amendments were made to protection legislation that effectively deprived Australia's Indigenous peoples of many basic rights — where they could travel to, where they could live, who they could associate with, and whether they could own property or not — and forced savings of wages (that were often never paid). During the 1930s, powers to remove children were increased and the practice intensified. This period between the wars was also a further period of dispossession as governments began to lease or sell land that had been held as reserves for Indigenous people. In Victoria, all reserve land except for one was sold; half of the reserves in New South Wales that had existed in 1911 had been sold by 1924.

REMEMBER

No compensation was given to Indigenous people for the loss of this land or their homes. Families were often forced into worse circumstances. They had no savings and no resources, few employment opportunities and no money for rent. Many built makeshift dwellings on the edges of towns. Without decent housing — and no water or sewerage services — authorities found it easy to claim that Indigenous children were not properly cared for or neglected.

After World War II, restrictions still remained on Indigenous people and their rights. Protection boards and their legislation kept strict control over the lives of Indigenous people and the removal of Indigenous children increased.

A piece of paper to say you're white

From the 1940s, state governments gave citizenship rights to Indigenous people in certain circumstances. They had to give up their traditional ways, not associate with other Indigenous people and live among white Australians. These rights could be cancelled or suspended for bad behaviour or breaching conditions.

Citizenship Certificates (in Western Australia) or Exemption Certificates (in New South Wales and Queensland) were issued to some Indigenous people that allowed them to vote and go to hotels, and allowed their children to go to school. The certificates meant they were free from the protection laws. Legally, the certificates also meant they were no longer Indigenous. You couldn't be an Indigenous person and a citizen.

CULTURAL PROTOCOLS

Indigenous people called these certificates 'dog licences' or 'dog tags'. This name highlights the level of resentment Indigenous people had for them and the system that issued them. Of the 14,000 people eligible for the certificate in New South Wales, only 1,500 applied for one. People who did so were treated with suspicion or derision by their friends and family. However, given the difficult circumstances Indigenous people were forced to live under, some thought it was a better way to live.

Not Taking It Lying Down

The very intrusive incursions that colonial and Australian governments made into the lives of Indigenous people in the name of 'protection' were strongly resisted and objected to. Indigenous people began building their own political organisations that specifically advocated for citizenship rights, rights to land and rights to political participation, such as voting and being represented in parliament. This activism culminated in important political statements, such as the Day of Mourning held on Australia Day in 1938 on the occasion of the sesquicentenary — the 150-year anniversary — of the founding of the colony of Sydney Cove.

Indigenous people organise

Just as Indigenous people engaged in many forms of activism, they formed many organisations to assist in achieving their political goals. Some of the key ones formed prior to 1967 are listed here, along with some brief information about their founders.

The Australian Aborigines Progressive Association (AAPA)

The AAPA was established in 1924 on the north coast of New South Wales. A key figure in the organisation was well-known Indigenous rights activist Fred Maynard. The AAPA called on the government to return traditional lands, to return children and to stop the practice of removing them from their families. It particularly complained about the sexual exploitation of Aboriginal women while they were under the care of the Aborigines Protection Board after they had been removed from their families. They also petitioned to have the Protection Board dissolved.

REMEMBER

Fred Maynard was born in 1879 in Hinton, New South Wales, a member of the Wonnarua people but raised in a strict Protestant household in Maitland after his mother died. In 1914, after periods of working as a bullock driver, drover and photographer, he began working on the wharves and joined the Waterside Workers' Federation. He began speaking publicly about matters affecting Indigenous people, especially workers. He died in 1946.

The Australian Aborigines League (AAL)

The AAL was formed by William Cooper and others in 1932. It fought to end discriminatory practices against Indigenous people, and focused on gaining full citizenship rights — particularly to work and education — and an end to the Protection Board's ability to take children and to expel people from reserves. Its national campaign focused on Indigenous representation in parliament, a federal department for Indigenous affairs that would manage the state agencies and the need to include Indigenous representatives in such federal agencies.

REMEMBER

William Cooper was a great Aboriginal leader from the Yorta Yorta people, also known as the Joti-jota people, thought to have been born around 1861, who had lived on the Cummeragunja reserve. He was an articulate and literate man who engaged in a range of political activities, including writing letters and getting petitions signed. He was also a member of the Australian Workers' Union. Cooper believed that, as British citizens, Indigenous people had the right to petition King George V for better conditions and for representation in parliament. He presented the petition to the Australian government in 1937 but the government didn't forward it to the King (George VI, by this time) on the basis, it was asserted, that since it was constitutionally impossible for an Indigenous person to be a member of parliament, no point could be found in sending the petition. Cooper died in 1941. (Refer to Chapter 8 for more on Cooper.)

The Aborigines Progressive Association (APA)

The APA operated in New South Wales. Bill Ferguson and Pearl Gibbs represented the western communities and Jack Patten represented the coastal communities. It focused on ending discrimination in employment and access to social security benefits. In 1937, the APA campaigned against the Aborigines Protection Board and this led to an inquiry into the board and its practices. The board was eventually abolished and replaced with the Aborigines Welfare Board. In 1943, it elected two members — one was Bill Ferguson.

REMEMBER

William 'Bill' Ferguson was born in 1882 at Darlington Point in New South Wales. After a brief education at the Warangesda mission school, he began working in shearing sheds and later became an organiser for the Australian Workers' Union. He worked around New South Wales in a variety of jobs. He launched the APA in Dubbo in 1937 and worked with William Cooper and Jack Patten to hold the Day of Mourning protest in 1938. He sat on the Aborigines Welfare Board from 1944 to 1949, where he advocated for inquiries into the poor conditions on Aboriginal reserves. In 1949, he became vice-president of the AAL. He died in 1950.

REMEMBER

Pearl Gibbs was born in 1901 at La Perouse in Sydney. Although she had fair skin, the racial discrimination she and her family experienced caused her to strongly identify as Aboriginal. She worked at the APA in 1937 and was their secretary from 1938 to 1939. One of the few Aboriginal women speaking publicly at the time, she raised awareness about issues facing Indigenous women and children, especially about the exploitation facing young girls working as domestic servants. A member of the Union of Australian Women, she became a link between the white women's movement and the Indigenous rights movement. She became secretary of the Dubbo branch of the AAL in 1950. She worked nationally and locally at Dubbo on Indigenous issues until she died in 1983.

REMEMBER

Jack Patten was born in New South Wales in 1905 and educated on the Cummeragunja reserve. He became president of the APA in 1937. With Bill Ferguson, he co-authored material exposing the wideranging powers of — and abuse of them by — the Aborigines Protection Board, and gathered support for the Day of Mourning protest in 1938. He toured north coast reserves to speak with and engage other Indigenous people in the campaign. He enlisted to fight in World War II in 1940 and was discharged due to injury in 1942. He settled in Melbourne after the war and became involved with the AAL. He died in 1957.

A SOFTER SIDE

Other organisations developed around Australia that had a softer approach to Indigenous issues. The One People for Australia League (OPAL) was formed in 1961 in Queensland and led by Neville Bonner between 1968 and 1975. Consisting mainly of mainstream church groups, it was overtly assimilationist in its ideology and critical of overt activism, preferring to work with the Queensland government. It was suspicious of the Queensland Council for the Advancement of Aborigines and Torres Strait Islanders because it believed the council was pro-communist.

The Victorian Aborigines Advancement League

This organisation was established in Victoria in 1957 and originated as the Save the Aborigines Committee. Under the leadership of Gordon Bryant, Doris Blackburn, Stan Davey and Pastor Doug Nicholls, it grew rapidly over the next few years and had branches in suburban Melbourne and country Victoria. Other activists such as Margaret Tucker, William Onus, Eric Onus and Geraldine Briggs also became heavily involved. It moved to full Aboriginal control in the 1960s. It is the oldest Indigenous organisation in Australia still operating today (now known as the Aboriginal Advancement League).

The Federal Council for Aboriginal Advancement (FCAA) and the Federal Council for the Advancement of Aborigines and Torres Strait Islanders (FCAATSI)

The FCAA, a new national body, was created on the weekend of 15 to 16 February 1958 in Adelaide by representatives from various state organisations. In its early days, it had non-Indigenous members. Jessie Street, Faith Bandler and Joe McGuiness were among some of the prime organisers in its establishment. It became the Federal Council for the Advancement of Aborigines and Torres Strait Islanders (FCAATSI) and was instrumental in the campaigns to change the Constitution in 1967 (see Chapter 11). Under the leadership of Indigenous people such as Doug Nicholls and Kath Walker, it became an all-Indigenous body in 1973.

The 1938 Day of Mourning

On Australia Day in 1938, a group of Aboriginal people protested in front of Australia Hall after they were moved off the Sydney Town Hall steps. This small protest was the culmination of decades of activism by Indigenous communities and their leaders in the south-east of Australia, such as William Cooper, Bill Ferguson and Jack Patten, who had sought the same rights as all other Australians, especially in relation to their ability to own land and to access jobs, education and health services.

AN INTERNATIONAL MOVEMENT FOR RIGHTS

The civil rights movement for Indigenous people in Australia occurred against an international backdrop where the rights of minorities were the focus of major campaigns.

Just as the British anti-slavery movement had influenced thinking in Australia, other global rights movements in the 20th century had an impact on political movements in Australia. Events in South Africa — where a system of apartheid operated — led to strong protest in Australia and a concerted anti-apartheid campaign throughout the 1950s to the 1970s. These campaigns saw some parallel with the segregation experienced by Indigenous Australians, particularly in rural areas, and also lent support to the aspirations of Indigenous people to gain equal legal status as citizens and to be free from discrimination in their day-to-day lives.

Civil rights activism in the United States was also very influential in Australia. On 17 May 1954, the US Supreme Court, in the historic case of *Brown v Board of Education*, held that segregation — excluding black students — in public schools was unconstitutional. The following year, Rosa Parks was arrested for refusing to give up her seat for a white passenger on a bus in Alabama. The black community launched a bus boycott that lasted for more than a year and buses were finally desegregated in 1956. The ongoing political struggle of African Americans to gain equal access to all aspects of society continues to provide intellectual inspiration for Indigenous people and their supporters in Australia.

The protest was also a beginning. It was the beginning of the Indigenous rights movement and the long road to the search for equality under the legal system. The focus on citizenship rights as an important part of the campaign for Indigenous equality was a key platform in the activism of advocates such as Cooper and Maynard and it influenced future generations.

Steps Towards Equality

In the second half of the 20th century, some significant steps were taken to try to give Indigenous people the same rights as other Australians. The *Nationality and Citizenship Act 1948* (Cwlth) made Indigenous people citizens in theory because they were born in Australia. However, this didn't automatically guarantee equal rights.

In 1959, the federal Social Services Act was amended to extend age pensions and maternity benefits to Indigenous Australians. But these benefits didn't extend to

Indigenous people who were 'nomadic' or 'primitive'. Benefits were paid into trust accounts of Indigenous people who lived on reserves, but many didn't receive this money.

The Commonwealth Electoral Act was amended in 1949 and gave the vote to Indigenous people who had been or were members of the defence forces. It was further amended in 1962 to give Indigenous people the right to vote in Commonwealth elections, though it wasn't compulsory for them to enrol or to vote.

REMEMBER

The changes over time to electoral and welfare legislation didn't stop Indigenous people from being discriminated against and many felt that what was needed was a change to the Australian Constitution that would allow the federal government to make laws more specifically for the betterment of Indigenous people.

THE RIGHT TO VOTE

When the colonies began their own parliaments, from 1850, men aged over 21 were able to vote. This included Indigenous men, though they weren't encouraged to enrol, so few did. However, Queensland passed legislation in 1885 and Western Australia in 1893 that specifically denied Indigenous people the right to vote. South Australia, however, gave all adults, including women, the right to vote in 1895. This included Indigenous men and women.

At Federation, Section 41 of the Constitution seemed to decree that Indigenous people could vote in Commonwealth elections if they were allowed to vote in state elections. But, in 1902, the Commonwealth Franchise Act specifically excluded any people Indigenous to Australia, Asia, Africa or the Pacific Islands from voting, except if they were on the roll before 1901. Needless to say, this legislation created a great deal of confusion about who could and couldn't vote!

In 1949, the Commonwealth Electoral Act was amended so that people who had completed military service and those who already had the right to vote in state elections were granted the right to vote in federal elections. A step back was taken in 1957, when the federal government declared Aboriginal people in the Northern Territory were wards of the state and they were denied the vote unless they were exempted from guardianship. By 1962, the Electoral Act was amended to allow Indigenous people to enrol but it wasn't compulsory. Western Australia lifted its ban and allowed Indigenous people to vote in state elections, and Queensland followed suit in 1965. From that time, all Indigenous Australians had the same voting rights as non-Indigenous Australians in both state and federal elections.

Chapter **11**

The 1967 Referendum

In the 1960s, as a result of the culmination of activism by Indigenous people and other Australians concerned about the socioeconomic conditions of many Aboriginal people and Torres Strait Islanders, a campaign for constitutional change took place. The campaign focused on changes to the Australian Constitution that the campaigners believed would transform the circumstances of Indigenous people and bring in an era of non-discrimination.

Indigenous people and their supporters, through the Federal Council for Aboriginal Advancement (FCAA) and later the Federal Council for the Advancement of Aborigines and Torres Strait Islanders (FCAATSI), worked with churches and trade unions to gather popular support for the changes. In this chapter, I examine how their efforts culminated in the most successful referendum held in Australia.

The changes did have a lasting legacy but they didn't lead to a significant change in the circumstances of Indigenous people. The federal government has passed some legislation that has benefited Indigenous people but the constitutional change unintentionally also allowed the government to make laws that were to the detriment of Indigenous people.

The failure of the 1967 referendum to prevent discrimination against Aboriginal people sparked a more aggressive rights campaign in the 1970s and beyond. And constitutional change is still on the agenda for Indigenous people. This chapter also looks at the consequences of the referendum, including the determination to continue to push for constitutional change.

Growing Awareness of Indigenous Disadvantage

By the 1960s, Indigenous communities were marginalised from mainstream society and some people, particularly in Aboriginal reserves and communities on the mainland, were living in conditions similar to those found in the developing world. Torres Strait Islanders living in their home communities were subject to strict controls over their lives. Political campaigns such as the Freedom Ride through north-west New South Wales raised awareness among the broader community and built on earlier protests such as the 1938 Day of Mourning (refer to Chapter 10), the Pilbara strike of 1946 to 1949 and the Wave Hill walk-off, which began in 1966 and was finally resolved in 1975 (the latter two protests are detailed in Chapter 8).

As a larger number of Australians became aware of the appalling conditions in which many Aboriginal people lived, many joined the efforts to end this discrimination. The campaign to make changes to the Australian Constitution that were intended to improve the situation of Indigenous people was already well under way. The support of white Australians added significant momentum.

FAITH BANDLER: IN GOOD FAITH

Faith Bandler was born in northern New South Wales in 1919, one of eight children. Her father had been kidnapped from Ambryn, an island in what was known then as the New Hebrides (now Vanuatu), and brought to Australia, enslaved, to work on sugar plantations. This practice was known as *blackbirding*. Awareness of her father's past experience exerted a strong influence on Bandler in her later political activism, as did her own experience of racial exclusion when she was growing up. Faith, along with other activists such as Pearl Gibbs, an Aboriginal woman, established the Aboriginal–Australian Fellowship in 1956. She was also involved with the FCAA and FCAATSI, becoming the New South Wales state secretary in 1963. When the federal government decided to hold the referendum in 1967, she became the New South Wales campaign director.

She famously said, in support of including Aboriginal people in the census: 'People in Australia have to register their dogs and cattle, but we don't know how many Aborigines there are'.

FCAA and FCAATSI

The Federal Council for Aboriginal Advancement (FCAA) emerged in the 1950s as the first national representative body for Aboriginal people, though it did also include non-Indigenous members until the 1970s. In 1958, it ran a petition that called for the amendment of the Constitution. Within three months, 25,000 people had signed the petition. The Aboriginal–Australian Fellowship had run a petition campaign the year before, also calling for constitutional change. Both campaigns focused on inclusion of Indigenous people in the Australian census and giving the federal government the power to make laws for Indigenous people.

The FCAA became the Federal Council for the Advancement of Aborigines and Torres Strait Islanders (FCAATSI) in 1964 in order to include Torres Strait Islanders. It was the dominant voice on Indigenous rights until the late 1960s. The council's agenda focused on 'citizenship rights' but it also called for special rights for Indigenous peoples as well.

REMEMBER

In 1962, as a response to the political pressure the FCAA was bringing to bear, the Australian Labor Party, which was in opposition, submitted a motion seeking a referendum to include Indigenous people in the census. The Menzies government didn't, however, support the motion. From 1962 to 1964, more than 50 petitions were given to the federal government asking for changes to the Constitution. All focused on changes to include Indigenous people in the census and to give the federal government the power to make laws for Indigenous people. A large number of these petitions were the result of the work of the FCAA which, over a seven-week period in 1963, ensured that petitions were tabled in parliament every day.

KATH WALKER: POET OF THE PEOPLE

Kath Walker was a poet, activist and public speaker. She grew up on North Stradbroke Island in the 1920s, worked as a domestic servant during the Depression and joined the Australian Women's Army Service in 1941. In 1958, she joined the Queensland Council for the Advancement of Aborigines and Torres Strait Islanders, becoming its secretary in 1962.

Her first collection of poems, *We Are Going*, was published in 1964. In the 1970s and 1980s, she returned to Stradbroke Island and continued writing (see Chapter 18 for more on her literary career). She changed her name to Oodgeroo Noonuccal in recognition of her ancestors, the Noonuccal people of Stradbroke Island. She passed away in 1993.

On 1 December 1965, a group of 36 Aboriginal people protested outside of Parliament House holding placards and lobbying politicians. Among the protesters were Charles Perkins, Faith Bandler and poet Kath Walker (see the sidebars about these three people). The involvement of people such as suffragette Jessie Street saw non-Aboriginal people work alongside emerging Aboriginal leaders such as Doug Nicholls and Joe McGuiness.

The Freedom Ride

In February 1965, a group of University of Sydney students — who had formed a body called Student Action for Aborigines (SAFA) — organised a bus tour of western and coastal towns in New South Wales. Their goals on the trip were to

>> Draw public attention to the poor state of Aboriginal health, housing and education

>> Point out and hopefully lessen the social divisions in the towns and highlight the discrimination against Aboriginal people

>> Encourage and support Aboriginal people themselves to protest and fight against discrimination

CHARLES PERKINS: FIGHTING THE GOOD FIGHT

Charles Perkins was an Arrernte man born at the Alice Springs Telegraph Station Aboriginal Reserve in the Northern Territory in 1936. He was a gifted soccer player and played professionally, first in England in 1957 and then in Australia (see Chapter 20). He attended the first FCAA conference in Brisbane in 1961. Four years later, he and his fellow students embarked on the Freedom Ride.

Perkins was the first Aboriginal person to graduate with a degree from a university when he graduated with a Bachelor of Arts in May 1966. After his years of student activism, he became a distinguished administrator and public servant. In 1965, he became the manager of the Foundation for Aboriginal Affairs in Sydney and, in 1969, he moved to Canberra to begin work in the Office of Aboriginal Affairs. By 1984, Perkins was Secretary of the Department of Aboriginal Affairs, the first Aboriginal Australian to attain such a position in the bureaucracy.

Perkins remained a central figure in Indigenous affairs even after retiring from the public service. He played key roles on the boards of Aboriginal arts, sport and media organisations. He was elected to the Aboriginal and Torres Straits Islander Commission (ATSIC) in 1993 and served as Deputy Chairman in 1994 to 1995. Perkins was also a member of the Arrernte Council of Central Australia. When he passed away in October 2000, he was given a state funeral.

Inspired by protests against racial segregation in the United States, the students decided to draw attention to similar issues in Australia. The *Freedom Ride*, as it became known, was headed by Charles Perkins, an Aboriginal student in his third year of an Arts degree (see Figure 11-1 and the sidebar 'Charles Perkins: Fighting the good fight'). The group included students Jim Spigelman, who later became Chief Justice of the New South Wales Supreme Court until May 2011, and Ann Curthoys, who became a historian and wrote a book about the trip, using her diaries from the time.

FIGURE 11-1: Charles Perkins returning home after studying at Sydney University, circa 1963.

The Freedom Riders brought to the attention of people in the cities the crude and racist conditions that existed in places such as Walgett, Gulargambone, Kempsey, Bowraville, Brewarrina and Moree. It highlighted segregation in towns — showing that Aboriginal people were barred from clubs, swimming pools and cafes, and were frequently refused service in shops and hotels. They held demonstrations outside the Moree Baths, the Kempsey Baths, the Bowraville Picture Theatre and the Walgett Returned Services League. The protesters were particularly effective because they recorded their journey — and the reaction of townspeople — and this made news around the country.

In 2011, 30 high school students retraced the original route of the Freedom Ride to celebrate its importance and impact.

The Referendum Is Announced

Prime Minister Harold Holt took over from Robert Menzies in 1966. On 23 February 1967, his government decided to hold a referendum later that year. On 2 March, Holt introduced legislation for a referendum to be held on 27 May. Both the government and the opposition parties supported the referendum question. In fact, neither party even put a case for a no vote. The actual referendum question asked was:

Do you approve the proposed law for the alteration of the Constitution entitled 'An Act to alter the Constitution so as to omit certain words relating to the people of the Aboriginal race in any State so that Aboriginals are to be counted in reckoning the population'?

This question related to two sections of the Constitution and essentially covered two main issues:

>> Should Indigenous people be counted in the Australian census?

>> Should the Commonwealth government be given the power to make laws for Indigenous people?

A constitutional change in Australia can be achieved only by a referendum. The majority of people in the majority of states (known as a *double majority*) have to vote yes for the change to occur.

Australians are very reluctant to vote for changes to the Constitution. At the time of the 1967 referendum, only 5 out of 26 referendum questions put to the Australian public had been successful. Today, out of a total of 44 referendums put to Australians, only 8 have been passed. Another question asked in the 1967 referendum, relating to the make-up of parliament, was rejected by the Australian people.

Getting to 'yes': The constitutional campaign

FCAATSI (refer to the section 'FCAA and FCAATSI', earlier in this chapter) arranged for a delegation to go to Canberra in April 1967 to lobby politicians. They wanted to make sure they were working in their electorates to ensure that the general public understood the issues involved in the referendum. The churches were supportive of the 'yes' campaign. So were the trade unions. Both gave information to their members and encouraged them to vote in favour of the changes.

Underpinning the campaign for the yes vote was the belief by those advocating passionately for the changes that they would lead to better conditions for Indigenous people. Their view was that, if the federal government was enabled to legislate for Indigenous people, it would act in their best interests. Another strong argument for the changes was that they would ensure uniform laws for Indigenous people across Australia. As it stood, at the time of the referendum, laws varied greatly from state to state. Striking examples of these disparities include

>> Indigenous people could vote in state elections in all states except Western Australia and Queensland.

>> They could own property in New South Wales and South Australia but not in other states.

>> They could receive award wages in New South Wales but not in other states.

Not everyone supported all the changes. In 1965, Prime Minister Robert Menzies argued against changing the Constitution to give the federal government the power to make laws for Indigenous people because it could be divisive. He warned the change could lead to a 'separate body of industrial, social, criminal and other laws relating exclusively to Aborigines'. He was, however, supportive of the changes to include Indigenous people in the census.

One reason Indigenous people weren't counted in the Australian population was that politicians worried that their inclusion could affect the quota that decided the number of seats a state could hold in parliament. The greater the number of Indigenous people in the state, the greater the number of seats it was entitled to. Including Indigenous people in the population count gave more seats to states with larger populations and it was feared that Western Australia and Queensland could lose seats. This fear seems a historical oddity, because the white Australian population at the time of the referendum was 3.7 million and the Indigenous population estimated to be 60,000. In addition, Indigenous people weren't included in the population count by the federal government for the purposes of allocating money to the states.

Australia decides

Of the total population eligible to vote in the referendum, 90.77 per cent voted for the proposed changes. This was the biggest yes vote ever in a referendum in Australia. Table 11-1 gives the Australian Electoral Commission's breakdown of the vote by state.

TABLE 11-1

The Yes Vote by State

State	Number of votes	Percentage of eligible voters
New South Wales	1,949,038	91.46%
Victoria	1,525,026	94.68%
Queensland	748,612	89.21%
South Australia	473,440	86.26%
Western Australia	319,823	80.95%
Tasmania	167,176	90.21%
Total	**5,183,113**	**90.77%**

Source: Parliamentary Handbook of the Commonwealth of Australia, 32nd Edition.

TECHNICAL STUFF

At the time of the 1967 referendum, only people in states were able to vote in referendums. People in the Northern Territory and the Australian Capital Territory were, therefore, not eligible to vote in the referendum, including between 3,000 and 4,000 Indigenous people in the Northern Territory.

REMEMBER

Historian Marilyn Lake, in her biography of Faith Bandler, explains why the constitutional change focused in part on including Indigenous people in the census. It was thought that their inclusion would encourage Australians to think of Indigenous people as part of the Australian community and, as such, it would be a nation-building exercise, a symbolic coming together.

The referendum made two changes to the Constitution:

>> **Section 127, the census:** Before the referendum, this section of the Constitution stated:

>> *In reckoning the numbers of the people of the Commonwealth, or of a state or other part of the Commonwealth, aboriginal natives shall not be counted.*

When the population was counted, Indigenous people weren't included in the count. After the referendum, this section was repealed and is no longer part of the text of the Constitution. This change ensured that Indigenous people would be included in the census.

>> **Section 51(xxiv), the 'races power':** Before the referendum, this section of the Constitution stated:

>> *The Parliament shall, subject to this Constitution, have power to make laws for the peace, order, and good government of the Commonwealth with respect to — the people of any race, other than the aboriginal race in any State, for whom it is deemed necessary to make special laws.*

The federal government could make laws for anyone in Australia, **except** Indigenous people living in any of the Australian states; they could, however, makes laws for those living in the Northern Territory and the Australian Capital Territory. After the referendum, this section was changed to read:

>> *The Parliament shall, subject to this Constitution, have power to make laws for the peace, order, and good government of the Commonwealth with respect to — the people of any race for whom it is deemed necessary to make special laws.*

Lasting Legacies of the Referendum

The 1967 referendum had some lasting impacts on Indigenous laws and policies. The federal government has used the races power to pass legislation, such as the *Land Rights (Northern Territory) Act 1976*, that are of great benefit to Indigenous people.

In some instances, however, the federal parliament has also used the power to enact legislation that's not for the benefit of Indigenous people. Other unintended consequences of this change include additional levels of bureaucracy.

The failure of the 1967 referendum to substantially alter the circumstances of Indigenous people led to a further wave of political activism in the 1970s, including the establishment of the Aboriginal Tent Embassy in Canberra (see Chapter 12). The issue of constitutional change, therefore, remains a central part of the political reform agenda for Indigenous people.

The power to legislate

The federal government first exercised its new power to make laws for Indigenous people by passing the *Aboriginal Enterprises (Assistance) Act 1968*, to establish a fund for Aboriginal business enterprise, and the *State Grants (Aboriginal Advancement) Act 1968*, to make payments to the states. Other significant legislation that has been passed under this power includes

>> *Aboriginal Land Fund Act 1974*

>> *Aboriginal Loans Commission Act 1974*

>> *Aboriginal and Torres Strait Islanders (Queensland Discriminatory Laws) Act 1975*

>> *Aboriginal Councils and Associations Act 1976*

>> *Aboriginal Land Rights (Northern Territory) Act 1976*

>> *Aboriginal Torres Strait Islander Heritage (Interim Protection) Act 1984*

>> *Aboriginal and Torres Strait Islander Commission Act 1984*

>> *Council for Aboriginal Reconciliation Act 1991*

>> *Native Title Act 1993*

>> *Land Fund and Indigenous Land Corporation (ATSIC Amendment) Act 1995*

>> *The Northern Territory Emergency Response Act 2007*

But no protection against discrimination

Repealing legislation so that Indigenous people are denied the benefit of protection has occurred several times in recent years. For example, the federal *Racial Discrimination Act 1975* has been suspended three times — in the Hindmarsh Island Bridge dispute (see the following section and Chapter 26), the Native Title Amendment Act (see Chapter 12) and the intervention (see Chapter 14). On each of these occasions, the suspension prevented Indigenous people from getting the protection provided by that legislation, such as being able to make complaints to the Australian Human Rights Commission.

The races power

The sad truth is that laws made under the 'races power' don't have to be for the benefit of Indigenous people. Those who advocated for a yes vote in the 1967 referendum believed that the changes to this section of the Constitution, to allow the federal government to make laws for Indigenous people, would be used to make laws that would benefit Indigenous people.

However, legislation has been passed that erodes the rights of Indigenous people. For example, the *Native Title Amendment Act 1998* (Cwlth) prevented the *Racial Discrimination Act 1975* (Cwlth) from applying to certain sections of the *Native Title Act 1993* (Cwlth). So, provisions in the Racial Discrimination Act that were meant to prevent discrimination in relation to land weren't allowed to apply to native title. The practical effect was that native title could be extinguished and, when it was, Indigenous people weren't entitled to compensation for the discriminatory loss of their property rights.

TECHNICAL STUFF

Consideration as to whether the races power can be used only for the benefit of Indigenous people, as the proponents of the yes vote had intended, was given some attention by the High Court in *Kartinyeri v the Commonwealth* (the Hindmarsh Island Bridge case). In that case, Aboriginal people in South Australia were opposing the building of a bridge over their traditional territory at a place of cultural and spiritual significance. In order to stop the traditional owners from challenging the building of the bridge, the federal government repealed federal heritage protection legislation so that it didn't apply to that area. An argument was made by the Hindmarsh Island traditional owners that, when Australians voted in 1967 to give the federal government the power to make laws for Indigenous people, the intention was that those laws be for their benefit. Of the six judges who heard the case, only Justice Kirby believed that the races power didn't extend to legislation that was detrimental to or discriminated against Indigenous people. The rest of the bench found that, if the federal government had the power to make a law under that section of the Constitution, it had the power to repeal it as well.

Human rights protection

Another concept that has been tested in the High Court is that human rights aren't protected at all in Australia's Constitution. In 1997, the High Court of Australia considered the case of *Kruger v the Commonwealth*. It was the first case to be heard in the High Court of Australia that considered the legality of the formal assimilation-based policy of removing Indigenous children from their families.

In *Kruger*, the six plaintiffs included a group of people who, as children, had been removed under the Northern Territory Ordinance and a mother whose child had been taken under that same law. They claimed violation of a series of human rights, including the implied right to due process before the law, equality before the law, freedom of movement and association, and the express right to freedom of religion contained in the Constitution. They were unsuccessful on all counts, with the court finding that those rights are simply not protected within the Australian legal system. This result highlighted the general lack of rights protection in Australia's legal system, even after the changes made by the 1967 referendum.

The myths of the referendum

The focus on citizenship rights in the decades leading up to the referendum, and the rhetoric of equality for Indigenous people that was used in the 'yes' campaign, led to some perhaps inevitable misunderstandings. Several mistaken perceptions arose about what the constitutional change allowed:

MYTH BUSTER

>> **The right to vote:** A common misconception is that the referendum gave Indigenous people the right to vote. This isn't true. The right of Indigenous people to vote in federal elections was secured by changes to the Commonwealth Electoral Act in 1962.

>> **Citizenship rights:** Some people also believe that Indigenous people were granted citizenship rights in 1967. But, by 1967, Indigenous people were legally considered citizens, even if they experienced discrimination in their everyday lives.

>> **Equal rights:** Although the campaign for the yes vote highlighted the desire to extend equal rights to Indigenous people, the referendum gave no guarantee of equality. The change gave the federal government the power to make laws about Indigenous people. It made no stipulation that those laws had to ensure equality and wouldn't be discriminatory.

REMEMBER

The Australian Constitution has never protected against racial discrimination. At the time it was drafted and came into force in 1901, the writers of the Constitution intended that it be a legal system that allowed for discriminatory legislation. The first substantial legislation passed through the new Australian parliament was the immigration laws that entrenched what became known as the White Australia policy.

The unintended consequences

The 1967 referendum didn't produce a new era of equality for Indigenous people as its proponents had hoped. Instead, its most enduring, though perhaps unintended, consequence was the new relationship it created between the federal government and state and territory governments.

And, rather than being a relationship of cooperation, it is one that has seen governments of both levels try to blame the other for the failure of Indigenous policy and to shift the responsibility and the cost away from themselves. The federal government may claim that, for example, the failure to provide adequate housing is the fault of a state or territory government. In turn, the state or territory may complain that the problem is the fault — and responsibility — of the federal government. This shifting of blame from one level of government to the other is called *cost-shifting*.

Not what was hoped for . . . so what next?

The 1967 referendum wasn't responsible for improving the situation of Indigenous people the way those who campaigned for the yes vote had hoped. And, although the intention was that the federal government would use the races power only to benefit Indigenous people, this hasn't been the case.

Inevitably, constitutional reform remains part of the political agenda for Indigenous Australians and their supporters. Other ideas for constitutional reform have included

>> A preamble to the Constitution to recognise the unique position and contribution of Indigenous people

>> A non-discrimination clause, entrenching the right to be free from racial discrimination

>> Recognition of rights to prevent discriminatory legislation, such as due process before the law and equality before the law, that would make it unconstitutional to pass discriminatory legislation

>> Specific protection of Indigenous rights

>> Incorporation of the principles of the Declaration on the Rights of Indigenous Peoples

>> Removal of Section 25, which gives state governments the power to pass legislation to prevent certain people, on the basis of their race, from voting

Although the power of Section 25 has never been invoked by a state government, many people believe that such an overtly racist provision is a relic of the same ideas that created the White Australia policy and should be removed from the Australian Constitution.

Constitution reform and recognition remains on the agenda for Indigenous peoples — see Chapter 15 for more on this.

Despite the 1967 referendum not creating the even playing field or the era of non-discrimination that was hoped for, it was a high-water mark for the relationship between Indigenous and non-Indigenous people. The referendum was endorsed by just over 90 per cent of eligible voters and carried in all six states. At a time when many parts of Australia were actively practising segregation, this was an extraordinary result.

The other legacy of the referendum was that it shaped a new era of more proactive rights movements. Indigenous people quickly became disillusioned by the lack of change brought about by the referendum. They continued to face discrimination and their communities continued to suffer poor socioeconomic conditions. They rejected the notion of assimilation but, inspired by the civil rights and women's movements, embraced the idea of equal rights and equal opportunities for Indigenous people.

In this environment, a new generation of activists was born, whose protests culminated in the establishment of the Aboriginal Tent Embassy on the lawns of what is now Old Parliament House. Chapter 12 details the continuation of this struggle.

Chapter **12**

Land Rights

Reclaiming the land taken from Indigenous people has always been a central part of their political agenda. Indigenous people don't just want to reclaim their traditional land because of its cultural and spiritual significance to them; they also believe that the return of land will be the basis for self-sufficiency and economic independence.

State, territory and federal governments have had a range of responses to the claim to land rights. Some states implemented processes that allow Indigenous people to claim land. The federal government established land rights legislation in the Northern Territory. When, in 1992, the High Court found that a form of native title existed, the federal government responded with legislation that was intended to clarify the process by which Indigenous people could assert their rights over their traditional lands.

In this chapter, I track the activism of Indigenous people, from protesting against their dispossession to making the claim for land rights a central part of their political agenda. I also look at the way in which Indigenous people, when they have regained access to or control of their land, have used it as a resource for economic development or self-sufficiency.

Establishing the Modern Land Rights Movement

When Europeans first planted the British flag on what would become the city of Sydney, Aboriginal people assumed the strangers would eventually move on. That someone would want to live on land that wasn't their traditional country was incomprehensible to Aboriginal people, and they assumed that Europeans would have responsibility for their own country the way Aboriginal people had responsibilities to look after and care for theirs. When it became clear that Europeans were here to stay, and that successive colonial governments weren't particularly interested in negotiating with Indigenous people over land ownership, struggles — often violent — ensued.

Land rights have always been a central part of the political and social justice platform for Indigenous people. Dispossession and theft of traditional land was a hallmark of the colonisation process, so the fact that Indigenous political movements focus on reclaiming that land isn't surprising.

The claim for land has always been more than just a desire to reclaim soil. Being able to exercise traditional obligations to lands that Indigenous peoples have a cultural and spiritual attachment with is an imperative. Additionally, land is understood as the source of life and of sustainability.

Linking land rights and social justice

In Australia, many Indigenous leaders have understood the connection between the claim to land and its capacity to provide the basis for both economic self-sufficiency and greater independence. When Indigenous people seek to reclaim land, either through native title or land rights regimes, the purpose is to advance the goals of sustainability and self-determination as well as to reclaim land for cultural significance. (I explain the difference between land rights and native title in the section 'Comparing Land Rights with Native Title', later in this chapter.)

In 1927, Aboriginal leader Fred Maynard wrote to New South Wales Premier Jack Lang:

We respectfully solicit such easy alteration in the laws relating to the aboriginals as will make effective the following reforms and which we most sincerely assure you will enable the aboriginals of this State to prove that they are worthy of the full privileges of citizenship, viz: That all capable aboriginals shall be given in fee simple sufficient good land to maintain a family; That the family life of the aboriginal people shall be held sacred and free from invasion and that the children shall be left in the control of their parents; . . . That the control of aboriginal affairs, apart from common law rights, shall be vested in a board of management comprised of capable educated aboriginals under a chairman to be appointed by the Government.

Maynard's pleas were echoed by others over coming decades, with the fight for land justice accompanied by a broader set of claims for rights. Here are some of the notable events:

>> **1938:** Day of Mourning Protest held on 26 January 1938, calling it 150 years of 'theft and genocide'. The Australian Aborigines League stated: 'You took our land by force . . . We ask for full citizenship rights, including age pensions, maternity bonus, relief work when unemployed, and the right to a full education for our children'. (Chapter 10 has more on this protest.)

>> **1946 to 1949:** Aboriginal stock workers in the Pilbara region of Western Australia went on strike. They didn't receive cash wages and the strike was supported by many trade unions (refer to Chapter 8).

>> **1965:** Aboriginal university student Charles Perkins organised 30 white colleagues to take a bus ride through some of the most notoriously racist towns in New South Wales. The Freedom Ride attracted international publicity about the segregation of Aboriginal people from mainstream Australian life (refer to Chapter 11).

>> **1966:** The Gurindji people employed on Wave Hill Station in the Northern Territory went on strike, demanding $25 per week wages and return of some of their traditional lands. When the station manager refused, the Gurindji declared an immediate strike; 200 Aboriginal cattle workers and their families, led by Vincent Lingiari, walked off the station. Although the strike was sparked by an industrial dispute, its primary goal was repatriation of traditional land. In 1975, Prime Minister Gough Whitlam handed back 3,238 square kilometres of Wave Hill Station to the Gurindji people under leasehold title (refer to Chapter 8).

>> **1967:** Australians voted to change the Australian Constitution to allow the federal government to have the power to make laws for Indigenous people. It was assumed by the many people who campaigned for the yes vote that this would mean better treatment for Indigenous people. (Refer to Chapter 11 for a full analysis of this important milestone.)

TECHNICAL STUFF

One of the main roles of the Australian Constitution is to differentiate between the responsibilities of federal and state governments. When the Australian Constitution came into effect in 1901, it left the power to make laws in relation to Indigenous people with the states. The federal government could, however, make laws for Indigenous people living in the newly formed Australian Capital Territory and in the Northern Territory when it was created in 1911 (up to then, the Northern Territory had been part of South Australia), which were still under Commonwealth jurisdiction. The 1967 referendum altered the Constitution, giving the federal government the power to make laws in relation to all Indigenous Australians, though it shared some powers with the states. For example, state governments could pass land rights legislation to cover Indigenous people living within their borders. (See the section 'Legislating Land Rights', later in this chapter, for details.)

REMEMBER

Although the 1967 referendum gave the federal government the power to make laws for Indigenous people, it didn't result in any significant changes in their living conditions. Neither did it put an end to the discrimination that many Indigenous people experienced in their lives when seeking access to education, housing and health services. The failure of the 1967 referendum to make any real change to the lives of Indigenous people led to a change of tactics by Aboriginal activists. Inspired by the Black Panthers, a political movement of African Americans in the United States, they began the Australian Black Power Movement. One of their first actions was to set up the Aboriginal Tent Embassy.

Setting up the Tent Embassy

On 26 January 1972 (Australia Day), four Aboriginal men (Tony Coorey, Michael Anderson, Billie Craigie and Bertie Williams) set out from the Aboriginal community in Redfern, Sydney, to Parliament House, Canberra. They set up what they called the Aboriginal Tent Embassy on the lawn. Over a few months, hundreds of people — black and white — joined in the protest.

The protest began when then Prime Minister William McMahon refused to acknowledge an Indigenous right to land, saying it would 'threaten the tenure of all other Australians'. The government proposed instead to allow Indigenous people to lease land from the government, but only if it was for a project that would make money. McMahon also stated that mining would continue on Aboriginal land.

OLD MAN RIVER

Paul Robeson, a famous African-American singer, visited Australia for an eight-week period from October to December 1960 and performed 12 Australian concerts. The Australian Peace Council had invited him in 1950; soon afterwards, the United States government confiscated his passport because of his communist sympathies and loyalty to the Soviet Union. When his passport was returned in 1958, Paul Robeson went on many singing tours and advocated for a number of political causes — international peace, workers' rights, and gender and racial equality.

During his Australian visit, he sought out local Indigenous people and became interested in the issues facing Indigenous Australians. Historian Ann Curthoys described the visit as 'part of a series of significant contemporary events and changes — the growth of political activism for Aboriginal rights, the thawing of the Cold War, and the increased influence of the American Civil Rights movement and of wider processes of decolonisation in Asia and Africa on Australian understandings of racial issues'.

Coorey, Anderson, Craigie and Williams had been tutored in politics by Aboriginal activist and unionist Chicka Dixon (see the sidebar 'Onya Chicka!'). He inspired them to engage in political protest and they decided to travel to Canberra to express opposition to the McMahon government's position. Chicka Dixon also mentored other Aboriginal men who were involved with the tent embassy, including Gary Foley and Paul Coe.

The group had found a loophole in the law by discovering that camping on the Parliamentary lawn wasn't legally prohibited. The federal government had to rush through legislation to make it illegal. The police abolished the Embassy in a series of violent clashes in July 1972.

ONYA CHICKA!

Chicka Dixon was an Aboriginal activist and leader who had worked as a wharfie, builder's labourer and university lecturer. Inspired by Aboriginal activist Jack Patton, Dixon went on to become a spokesperson for the Federal Council for the Advancement of Aborigines and Torres Strait Islanders (FCAATSI). He assisted in setting up the first Aboriginal legal service and the first Aboriginal medical service in the 1970s. He was named Aboriginal of the Year in 1983. Dixon passed away in 2010 and was given a state funeral as an acknowledgement of his importance.

The Tent Embassy developed its own political agenda:

We demand:

1. *Full State rights to the Northern Territory under Aboriginal ownership and control with all titles to minerals, etc*

2. *Ownership of all other reserves and settlements throughout Australia with all titles to minerals and mining rights*

3. *The preservation of all sacred lands not included in points 1 and 2*

4. *Ownership of certain areas of certain cities with all titles to minerals and mining rights*

5. *As compensation, an initial payment of six billion dollars for all other land throughout Australia plus a percentage of the gross national income per annum*

> *—Authorised by the Aboriginal Embassy Cabinet Committee,*
> *Aboriginal Embassy Land Rights Policy, '5 Point Policy'*

The demands were designed to highlight the extent to which Aboriginal people had a sovereignty that had not been recognised when the lands they had lived on had been taken from them. They also sought to highlight the wealth that was in those lands — resources that had been taken from Aboriginal people and had made others rich, particularly through mining.

REMEMBER

The original Embassy stood for six months. It came to symbolise the political aspirations of Indigenous people and was seen as the birth of the modern land rights movement.

The Embassy was later re-established in 1992 — the 20th anniversary of its founding — and to this day still has a presence on the lawns of Old Parliament House in Canberra.

Visiting the Black Panthers

Aboriginal political activists were greatly influenced by other political movements around the world. In particular, they had a strong intellectual interest in the civil rights movement in the United States, and particularly the work of the Black Panthers (see the sidebar 'About the Black Panthers').

Aboriginal people in Australia identified with the desire to end a life of segregation and exclusion from opportunities for education, employment, adequate housing and basic health services. They also identified with the claims that racism had become institutionalised.

ABOUT THE BLACK PANTHERS

The Black Panthers was a political party active in the United States from 1966 until 1982. It had originally started in California as the Black Panther Power for Self-Defense and said its primary role was calling for the protection of black neighbourhoods from police brutality. It gained national prominence for its anti-racism campaigns and programs such as citizens' patrols and breakfast programs for children. These activities were often overshadowed by the militant-style activism of the group, especially violent tactics deployed against the police.

Aboriginal activists from Australia, particularly from Sydney's Redfern community, travelled to America to discuss their ambitions with leaders of the civil rights movement. Rights activists such as Sol Bellear and Roberta Sykes spent time travelling with the Black Panthers in the early 1970s, developing their ideas about the political movement for Indigenous people in Australia. The influence of this exchange is evidenced in the establishment of the Australian Black Power Movement and in the way that Indigenous people started to use the language of rights to express their political claims.

WHAT WAS IN THE WATER IN REDFERN?

Redfern, an inner-city suburb of Sydney, became a place where Aboriginal people lived by the 1890s. The railway yards were large employers of Aboriginal people, so men moved into the area for work and brought their families with them. By the 1920s, the suburb housed a large Aboriginal community, made up of people who had migrated there from all over New South Wales and from other states. In the 1930s, people continued to move from the country to Redfern as the Depression took its toll on jobs in the country and people moved to live with relatives in the city.

Redfern became a hotspot for political activism in the 1960s and 1970s. The first Aboriginal Legal Service, a black theatre and the first Aboriginal Medical Service were among a range of community-controlled organisations that appeared there. It was also where the four men who established the Aboriginal Tent Embassy came up with the idea (schooled in political activism by a generation who had worked on gaining equal rights for Indigenous people and were involved with the campaign for the 1967 referendum), and a battleground in the resistance of the Indigenous community to what it perceived was targeting and violence by the police.

Although just on the fringe of the city of Sydney, the Redfern community has been strong and cohesive. Today, it has a community centre where many activities take place, and family days are held on some weekends that add to the sense of community.

Comparing Land Rights with Native Title

Although native title and land rights both relate to the recognition of Indigenous peoples' rights to land, they are very different.

Land rights legislation, in the various Australian jurisdictions, was enacted in response to a broad social and political movement, which evolved from the 1960s to the 1980s to include people from a broad spectrum of society — both Indigenous and non-Indigenous people, the politically conservative and the radical. The legislation was the initiative of elected governments and a response to the political lobbying by Indigenous people and their supporters.

Native title legislation, on the other hand, had its impetus in the courts with the judicial recognition of native title in the Mabo case in 1992.

These differences are highlighted in Table 12-1, using the example of the 1983 New South Wales Land Rights Act and comparing it with the federal Native Title Act, introduced in 1993.

TABLE 12-1   Differences between Land Rights and Native Title

NSW Aboriginal Land Rights Act	Commonwealth Native Title Act
Applies only in New South Wales	Applies across all of Australia
A claim triggers government decision	A claim triggers legal proceedings
Claims are for claimable Crown lands, with:	Claims are based on:
No need to prove any traditional association with the lands	Native title rights and interests
No previous tenure of the lands required	Traditional laws, customs, practices and association with the land proven in court or accepted by all non-claimant parties (in a consent determination)
Lands are granted in freehold	A spectrum of native title rights to different parcels of land exists (some may equate to freehold and others merely to a licence)
Local Aboriginal Land Council (LALC) boundaries aren't necessarily consistent with any Aboriginal traditional boundaries	A native title group can only claim rights and interests in its traditional boundaries
Any Aboriginal person living in the LALC boundary is entitled to be a member and benefit from LALC services	Only Indigenous people who have a traditional (pre-colonisation) connection with the land can be a member of a claim group, but they don't have to live on country to benefit from any recognised rights or interests
An individual can benefit from LALC services	Native title rights and interests belong to the whole group, not just an individual or family

The political activism of Indigenous people in the 1960s to the 1980s initially focused on land rights.

Legislating Land Rights

The political activism of Aboriginal people — and support from non-Indigenous Australians for some compensation for dispossession — saw several pieces of land rights legislation passed.

TIP

Most states enacted some form of legislation, with Western Australia the notable exception, and each brought in different forms of land rights. Some states granted several parcels of land to Aboriginal people, whereas others, particularly New South Wales, established schemes that allowed Aboriginal people to continually claim land where appropriate.

Here's a summary of land rights legislation passed in Australia:

» In South Australia, although not strictly under land rights legislation, the ***Aboriginal Lands Trust Act 1966*** turned reserves into perpetual leases but didn't grant the land to Aboriginal communities. The ***Pitjantjatjara Land Rights Act 1981*** and ***Maralinga Tjarutja Land Rights Act 1984*** granted land to traditional owners of those areas.

» Victoria used legislation to grant specific land to Aboriginal communities such as Framlingham, Lake Condah and Robinvale: ***Aboriginal Lands Act 1970***, ***Aboriginal Land (Lake Condah and Framlingham Forest) Act 1987*** (Cwlth), ***Aboriginal Lands Act 1991***, ***Aboriginal Land (Manatunga Land) Act 1992***, ***Aboriginal Lands (Aborigines' Advancement League) (Watt Street, Northcote) Act 1982*** and ***Aboriginal Land (Northcote Land) Act 1989***.

» The Commonwealth passed the ***Aboriginal Land Rights (Northern Territory) Act 1976*** (Cwlth) and it granted 'scheduled' areas of land to Aboriginal land trusts. The ***Pastoral Land Act 1992*** (NT) enables parts of pastoral leasehold areas known as Community Living Areas to be claimed on the basis of 'need' and held by Aboriginal corporations.

The Commonwealth also passed the ***Aboriginal Land Grant (Jervis Bay Territory) Act 1986*** (Cwlth) that allowed for areas of land to be granted, giving ownership to the Wreck Bay Aboriginal Community Council. Jervis Bay is a Commonwealth-controlled region of southern New South Wales under the jurisdiction of the Australian Capital Territory.

» The New South Wales ***Aboriginal Land Rights Act 1983*** was passed with an acknowledgement that it was a form of compensation for dispossession. It established a state land council with a network of regional and local land councils that were able to claim and hold land. Unlike other land rights regimes, it allows for, in certain circumstances, the claim of Crown land not needed for an essential public purpose and, when granted, gives full ownership to the land council. Land can be held, developed and even sold if the land council chooses. The original Act had a provision for a fund that took money from state land taxes for a period of 15 years in order to build up a fund that would allow for the purchase of additional land and pay the administrative costs of running the land rights system.

>> Queensland granted former reserves under a special form of freehold, held in trust by community councils for their residents under *Various Amendments 1982–1988 to the Land Act 1962*. It introduced a limited land rights scheme on the basis of traditional or customary affiliation: *Aboriginal Land Act 1991* and *Torres Strait Islander Land Act 1991*.

>> Tasmania granted 12 areas under the ownership of a land council in trust for Aboriginal people: *Aboriginal Lands Act 1995*.

>> Western Australia has not passed land rights legislation.

The two key land rights regimes operating in Australia today are the Northern Territory Land Rights Act and the New South Wales Land Rights Act. Both are worth looking at in a bit more detail.

Recommending the Northern Territory Land Rights Act

Prior to becoming prime minister in 1972, Gough Whitlam had said that, if elected, he would legislate to give Indigenous people land rights because he believed that all Australians were diminished while Indigenous people were denied their rightful place in this nation. In February 1973, he appointed Justice Edward Woodward to head up an inquiry into appropriate ways to recognise Aboriginal land rights in the federal jurisdiction of the Northern Territory. In April 1974, the final report of the Woodward Aboriginal Land Rights Commission (also known as the Woodward Royal Commission) proposed land rights legislation for the Northern Territory.

Justice Woodward reported that the aims of land rights were to

>> Do justice to a people who have been deprived of their land without their consent and without compensation

>> Promote social harmony and stability within the wider Australian community by removing, as far as possible, the legitimate causes of complaint of an important minority group within that community

- >> Provide land holdings as a first essential for people who are economically depressed and who have at present no real opportunity of achieving a normal Australian standard of living

- >> Preserve, where possible, the spiritual link with his own land that gives each Aboriginal his sense of identity and that lies at the heart of his spiritual beliefs

- >> Maintain and, perhaps, improve Australia's standing among the nations of the world by demonstrably fair treatment of an ethnic minority

Justice Woodward recommended that these aims could be best achieved by

- >> Preserving and strengthening all Aboriginal interests in land and rights over land that exist today, particularly those with spiritual importance

- >> Ensuring that none of these interests or rights are further whittled away without consent, except in those cases where the national interest positively demands it — and then only on terms of just compensation

- >> Providing basic compensation in the form of land for those Aboriginal people who have been irrevocably deprived of the rights and interests that they would otherwise have inherited from their ancestors, and who have obtained no sufficient compensating benefits from white society

THE MARALINGA LEGACY

During 1955 and 1963, seven major and hundreds of minor atomic bomb tests took place at Maralinga in South Australia. This was on the land of the Anangu. They weren't consulted about the tests or warned about the effects; few steps were taken to protect them from the impact and consequences of the radiation. Traditional owners were moved off the lands and prevented from returning to them while the testing was taken place. A large number died of pneumonia after the move to colder country. After the tests, the site was contaminated with radioactive materials. A clean-up was attempted in 1967. Traditional owners — and the servicemen involved with the tests — were still suffering from illness such as cancers into the 1980s. A major inquiry, the McClelland Royal Commission, delivered a report in 1985 that examined the effects of the tests, finding that significant contamination still existed. Another clean-up was recommended, which was completed in 2000. On 18 December 2000, a section of what is now called the Maralinga Tjarutja lands was handed back to the traditional owners. After continued advocacy, the remainder of the land was returned to the Maralinga Tjarutja in 2009. They run a tourism business on the old Maralinga site and have won awards for their ranger program.

>> Further provisioning land, to the limit that the wider community can afford, in those places where it will do most good, particularly in economic terms, to the largest number of Aboriginal people

REMEMBER

Woodward said that he had taken full account of the arguments put forward by vested interests who opposed the granting of land rights. Prominent in this group were those from the mining and resources industry. Woodward insisted that mining and other development on Aboriginal land should proceed only with the consent of the Aboriginal landowners and that the right to withhold consent should only be overridden if the government of the day decided that the national interest required it.

He also proposed procedures for claiming land and for setting conditions of tenure, recommending that Aboriginal land be granted as inalienable freehold title — meaning it couldn't be acquired, sold, mortgaged or disposed of in any way — and title should be communal. He envisaged the transfer to Aboriginal ownership of government reserve lands and the hearing by an Aboriginal Land Commissioner of claims to unalienated Crown land and Aboriginal pastoral leases based on traditional affiliation.

Following the Woodward Royal Commission hearings, the Whitlam government introduced the *Aboriginal Land (Northern Territory) Bill 1975* into parliament. It proposed a system for the Northern Territory that would allow Aboriginal people to claim land on the basis of need as well as traditional affiliation. It set up land councils — the Northern Land Council and the Central Land Council — and allowed traditional owners control over mining and development on their land.

TECHNICAL
STUFF

In Australia, the federal government has control over the Northern Territory and the Australian Capital Territory, and can make legislation for them. This means the Commonwealth has more control over the territories than over the states — New South Wales, Victoria, South Australia, Tasmania, Western Australia and Queensland. Even though the Northern Territory became self-governing in 1978 and the ACT in 1988, the federal government can still exercise powers over them in a way it can't with the states.

The Whitlam government was dismissed on 11 November 1975. The Fraser government placed another Bill before the federal parliament. It was a watered-down version of the Whitlam Bill, giving less power to the land councils over their land. The Bill was passed as the *Aboriginal Land Rights (Northern Territory) Act 1976*.

Looking at the New South Wales Land Rights Act

The New South Wales *Aboriginal Land Rights Act 1983* is the most generous of all the land rights regimes established in Australia. The Act recognises dispossession and dislocation of New South Wales Aboriginal people. It was intended to provide compensation for lost lands and for Aboriginal people to establish an economic base. The beneficial intention of the New South Wales land rights regime is stated clearly in the preamble to the Act:

Land in the State of New South Wales was traditionally owned and occupied by Aborigines. Land is of spiritual, social, cultural and economic importance to Aborigines. It is fitting to acknowledge the importance which land has for Aborigines and the need of Aborigines for land. It is accepted that as a result of past Government decisions the amount of land set aside for Aborigines has been progressively reduced without compensation.

The Act set up a state land council — the New South Wales Aboriginal Land Council (NSWALC) — with regional representatives and 121 Local Aboriginal Land Councils (LALCs), all of which are governed by elected boards. As the state's peak representative body in Aboriginal affairs — and the largest elected body since the abolition of the national Aboriginal and Torres Strait Islander Commission in 2005 (see Chapters 13 and 14) — the Council had, at the beginning of 2009, an asset base of more than $2 billion in landholdings and more than $680 million in cash assets. With this asset base, it aimed to protect the interests and further the aspirations of its members and the broader Aboriginal community through social housing, scholarship schemes and community projects.

The New South Wales Land Council is empowered by legislation to

>> Buy, sell or claim land on its own behalf or on behalf of LALCs

>> Approve the terms and conditions of agreements proposed by the LALCs to allow mining or mineral exploration on Aboriginal land

>> Resolve disputes between LALCs or individuals

>> Make grants, lend money or invest money on behalf of Aboriginal people in New South Wales

>> Give advice to the New South Wales government on matters relating to Aboriginal land rights

Crown land can be claimed by NSWALC or a local council. Under the Act, claimable land includes Crown land that isn't

>> Already being lawfully used or occupied

>> Needed or likely to be needed as residential land or for an essential purpose

>> Covered by an application for native title or an approved native title determination

The minister then must grant the claim if, at the date of lodgement, the Crown land isn't excluded by any of the criteria in the preceding list. If a minister refuses a land claim with the argument the land is under one of these uses, the land council can appeal to the Land and Environment Court.

REMEMBER

Land acquired under land rights regimes in New South Wales may be used for any community purpose, including commercial enterprises and community housing. Consequently, land councils have claimed land and then built community centres or houses for the Aboriginal community. They have also bought buildings and leased them to get an income for the local Aboriginal community. Other businesses land councils are engaged in include mapping cultural sites, offering cultural tours and cultural awareness training.

Failing to Secure a National Land Rights Scheme

The push for a national land rights regime came first from Indigenous people and their supporters. A land rights scheme was also recommended by the Woodward Royal Commission (refer to the section 'Recommending the Northern Territory Land Rights Act', earlier in this chapter). The Whitlam government — which supported the concept of land rights for Indigenous people — had intended that the scheme would eventually be a national one. It started with legislation that covered only the Northern Territory but lost government before it passed.

The Fraser government passed a watered-down version of the Northern Territory Land Rights Act. A national land rights scheme remained part of the policy platform for the Australian Labor Party but, when the party returned to government under Prime Minister Bob Hawke, politics got in the way and, with pressure from mining companies, the idea was abandoned.

Here's a summary of the political history of views on Indigenous land rights:

>> The McMahon government (1971 to 1972) had said that, although it would allow Aboriginal people to lease or rent land in the Northern Territory for certain projects, it didn't support land rights for Indigenous people.

>> The Whitlam government (1972 to 1975) was committed to a land rights scheme for Indigenous people. It intended to respond to the Woodward Royal Commission, which recommended the establishment of a land rights Act. However, the Whitlam government lost office before it could implement the legislation.

>> The Fraser government (1975 to 1983) agreed to pass the legislation proposed by the Whitlam government but made many amendments to it. These included watering down the rights of traditional owners to veto mining and other activity on their land.

>> The Hawke government (1983 to 1996), with Clyde Holding as Aboriginal Affairs Minister, set up a National Land Rights Working Party to develop national land rights legislation.

The working party set up by the Hawke government established five principles for the proposed legislation for a national scheme:

>> Aboriginal control over mining on Aboriginal lands

>> Access to mining royalties

>> Compensation for lost land

>> Full legal protection of sacred sites

>> Inalienable freehold title for Aboriginal land

The original intention of these principles was that they would be a first step towards a national land rights scheme. However, in 1984, after meeting with Western Australian Labor Premier Brian Burke, Hawke shelved the proposal for a national scheme. Burke was under pressure from the mining companies to stop land rights legislation from being passed. The proposal for a national land rights regime was taken off the table in 1986. In March that year, the Hawke Government abandoned its national land rights legislation and instead amended the Northern Territory Land Rights Act to weaken it.

The failure of the federal government to deliver a national land rights scheme didn't stop some states from seeking to recognise the rights of Indigenous people to their land or to give some form of compensation for their dispossession. But this failure to produce a national land rights scheme did mean that it remained an issue for individual states as to whether or not they would legislate for land rights within their borders. It also meant that no uniformity existed among the land rights schemes that were in place.

Following the Mabo Case: A Finding for Native Title

The original failure of Australian governments to recognise Indigenous rights to land was the subject of the Gove land rights case (*Milirrpum v Nabalco*), which began in 1968 and concluded in 1971. The Yolngu people living in Yirrkala, the traditional owners of the Gove Peninsula in Arnhem Land, sought to stop a bauxite mine planned by the Nabalco Corporation by asserting traditional ownership over the land. They claimed that they had a native title right since 'time immemorial'.

Justice Richard Blackburn, a judge of the Northern Territory Supreme Court, determined that Australian common law didn't recognise native title and that the plaintiffs didn't have rights that could be recognised as property rights. He said that, even though Aboriginal people occupied Australia before the British colonised it and had systems of laws and governance, Australian law hadn't recognised these systems and had treated Australia as though it was *terra nullius* — vacant land or land without a sovereign. See Chapter 26 for more on this key legal decision.

In 1982, Torres Strait Islanders — led by Eddie 'Koiki' Mabo — from the Murray Islands (*Mer*, to the Torres Strait Islanders) began proceedings in the High Court for a declaration stating that their traditional rights to land, sea, seabeds and reefs hadn't been extinguished. A decade later, the High Court found, by a majority, that the Torres Strait Islanders who had brought the case did, in fact, hold native title to their islands. The Mabo case found that Australia wasn't unoccupied on settlement and that the Indigenous inhabitants had, and continue to have, legal rights to their traditional lands unless they have been validly extinguished by the government. The case concluded that native title existed where Indigenous people could show a continual attachment to their land and that no action had been taken by governments that extinguished their rights. Importantly, the case also overturned the doctrine of terra nullius.

REMEMBER

The legacy of the Mabo case is that it's still a trigger for Indigenous people to reclaim rights to the land and sea today. In 2010, Justice Finn of the Federal Court granted a claim over about 37,800 square kilometres of sea between Cape York Peninsula and Papua New Guinea. His finding gave the right to access, remain in and use the sea in those areas, and to take its resources — but not for commercial purposes — without excluding others from using the sea.

A native title package

As anticipated, the landmark Mabo case generated a large number of claims and the Keating government (1991 to 1996) passed the *Native Title Act 1993* (Cwlth). Michael Lavarch, the attorney-general in the Keating government, established the National Native Title Tribunal for determining claims that could be mediated or conciliated, and provided that the Federal Court would determine litigated claims. (Lavarch was also the attorney-general who commissioned an inquiry into the Stolen Generations, which lead to the *Bringing Them Home* report; read more about this in Chapter 9.)

The Native Title Act defines native title as the rights held by Indigenous people over land or water, where:

>> The rights and interests exist under traditional laws and customs

>> Indigenous people have a connection to the land

>> Those rights and interests are recognised by the common law of Australia

Native title can extend to hunting, gathering and other interests.

TECHNICAL STUFF

Legislation passed by parliament overrides common law in Australia. In practice, this means that the definition of native title in the Native Title Act overrides the definition given by the court in the Mabo case — that native title existed where Indigenous people could show a continual attachment to their land and that no government action had extinguished their rights.

In 1995, the Indigenous Land Corporation was established as the second part of the government's response to the Mabo decision. The corporation was set up to administer a fund to buy land on behalf of Indigenous people, recognising that many Aboriginal people would, due to the impact and processes of colonisation, be unable to prove that they maintained a native title interest over their traditional land in the way the law described and defined it. The government had also promised a social justice package as the third part of its response but this was never delivered.

When the Howard government was elected into office in 1996, it adopted a hostile stance towards Indigenous rights, believing that the 'pendulum had swung too far' in favour of Indigenous people. This position led to a weakening of Indigenous rights in many spheres, including native title.

REMEMBER

The Howard government immediately proposed to amend the Native Title Act to make registration of claims more difficult for traditional owners and to increase the protection of the interests of miners and pastoralists. It also reduced the right of native title holders to negotiate with respect to mining interests and limited native title claimants' rights to information and comment related to their claims, but it did provide the opportunity for traditional owners to negotiate Indigenous Land Use Agreements (ILUAs). These amendments were criticised by the United Nations Committee on the Elimination of All Forms of Racial Discrimination, who found that several amendments breached the International Convention on racial discrimination in a number of ways, including provisions with respect to the

>> Abolition and limiting of the right to negotiate

>> Expansion of pastoral interests

>> Extinguishment of native title

>> Validation of non-Indigenous interests

REMEMBER

Indigenous Land Use Agreements remain important mechanisms for traditional owners in negotiating outcomes over their lands. These negotiated outcomes are an alternative to having a determination made by a tribunal or court. An ILUA can include matters such as consent over activities on the land, protection of significant sites, compensation and agreement over the balancing of native title rights with other rights to the land. ILUAs can provide certainty to the parties.

The legacy of the Mabo case

Although the Mabo case established native title in the case brought by the people of the Murray Islands, it left open other questions that were subsequently settled by other court decisions:

>> **Wik Peoples v Queensland:** In 1996, the High Court held that native title could still exist even if other interests in the land also existed, such as a pastoral lease, as long as the exercise of native title wasn't inconsistent with that other interest. If a conflict did exist, native title would be extinguished.

>> **Yanner v Eaton:** Native title could extend, in some circumstances, to hunting and fishing rights.

>> **Commonwealth v Yarmirr:** Native title rights could extend to the sea and seabed up to and beyond the low-water mark.

>> **Western Australia v Ward:** In this 2000 case, the court held that while physical presence on land provides clear evidence of the maintaining of connection to that country, spiritual connection can be maintained when physical connection has ceased.

>> **Willis on behalf of the Pilki People v State of Western Australia:** Native title holders have the right to access and take resources from within their country for any purposes, including commercial purposes, provided it is consistent with the group's traditional system of law and custom.

>> **Griffiths v Northern Territory of Australia (The Timber Creek Compensation Case):** The Ngaliwurru and Nungali peoples were successful in 2019 in the High Court in a claim for compensation and application for the spiritual/cultural and economic loss when their access to their traditional lands was affected by actions that infringed on their native title. The High Court awarded $2.5 million in compensation, of which $1.3 million was for the spiritual/cultural loss. The case showed that where native title had been extinguished since 1975 when the Racial Discrimination Act was passed, compensation could be claimed.

REMEMBER

Over more than two decades of native title cases, an increasingly conservative High Court has taken a narrower definition of native title. These days, judges, not Indigenous people, have the largest role in defining and recognising the existence of native title.

This conservatism by courts was perhaps most famously brought home through the decision in the Yorta Yorta case in 2002. The Yorta Yorta native title claim covered Crown land and waters in parts of northern Victoria and southern New South Wales. Here, the court found that the culture of the claimants had been eroded by the history of colonisation, and taken with it the native title interests of the Yorta Yorta nation. Indigenous people across Australia came to realise the extent to which Australian courts and parliaments could recognise an Indigenous right or interest but seek to override it through narrow interpretations of facts and with a Eurocentric gaze on Indigenous history, experience, culture and life.

Examining Public Reactions to Land Claims

Some people in Australia have fiercely opposed the recognition of land rights and native title. Along with some common negative stereotypes of Indigenous people (refer to Chapters 2 and 25), here are a few of the more outlandish statements (usually a product of fear and a lack of knowledge):

>> **'It's anti-Christian':** Executive Director of Western Mining Corporation, Hugh Morgan, in 1984 described land rights as a return to paganism and as anti-Christian.

>> **'They'll take your backyard':** In Western Australia, mining and pastoral industries in 1993 mounted scare campaigns to influence their state government to oppose land rights. This included television commercials that said that land rights would mean that Australians could lose their homes. (This was incorrect, because land rights can only be claimed on Crown land, not on private property.)

>> **'Land rights are a smokescreen for a more sinister plot by Aboriginal people':** This was the view of Pauline Hanson, who was at the time, in 1998, a member of federal parliament. She said, 'There is no true honest way of connecting Aboriginal hunter-gatherer nomadic occupation with the modern understanding of land ownership, nor should we try. The endless PR campaign was never intended to raise the acceptance of Aboriginal Australians; rather, it was and is a carefully coordinated assault on the conscience of other Australians for the express purpose of producing guilt so as to extract monetary compensation'. (Hanson was re-elected to federal government in 2016, as a senator for Queensland.)

>> **'It's unAustralian':** In 1996, then leader of the Liberal Party John Howard described the right given to Aboriginal people to negotiate their native title interests as 'unAustralian'. He promised that, if elected as prime minister, he would seek to limit native title rights. He was elected and in 1998 passed amendments to the Native Title Act that limited the right to negotiate and extinguished some types of native title.

Looking At the Work Still to Be Done: Taking Back the Land

Some Australians may believe that land rights have failed because they haven't stopped the poverty facing Aboriginal and Torres Strait Islander communities today. However, the challenge that land rights and native title is yet to meet is how best to approach the return of land to Indigenous people to give Indigenous people and their communities the ability to use that resource as a source of economic development in the way they think would most benefit their communities. Chapter 22 addresses these issues.

MYTH BUSTER

LAND RIGHTS: FACT AND FICTION

Myth: Land rights mean that the homes of other Australians are at risk.

Fact: Neither land rights nor native title allow Indigenous people to make claims over the homes of other Australians.

Myth: Land rights are just Indigenous people getting something for nothing.

Fact: Native title only exists where Indigenous people can show they have an existing right to land. Land rights legislation is designed to provide compensation for rights in land that have been lost. Both acknowledge that Indigenous people had an interest in their land before it was taken off them and seek to recognise that interest.

Myth: People claim to be Indigenous now just so they can get native title.

Fact: The process of claiming native title is extensive and clear proof is needed to show a person's connection to the land and status as a traditional owner.

Chapter **13**

The Era of Reconciliation

On 10 December 1992, Prime Minister Paul Keating gave a historic speech at Redfern Park in Sydney. It was the eve of the International Year of the World's Indigenous People. This speech resulted in a shift in the debate about Australia's relationship with its Indigenous peoples and promised a commitment to the process of reconciliation, which had begun with the establishment of the Council for Aboriginal Reconciliation the previous year. Keating's speech was also a response to the decision by the High Court of Australia in the 1992 Mabo case, where the court found that Indigenous Australians have native title over their traditional land and, in some circumstances, that title survives today. The Keating government developed a strategy for dealing with the consequences of the recognition of this right.

The Council for Aboriginal Reconciliation began a series of conventions, consultations and activities to raise awareness of the issues facing Indigenous people. It also sought to identify ways to improve the socioeconomic situation of Indigenous people and the relationship between black and white Australia.

During this period, the Aboriginal and Torres Strait Islander Commission (ATSIC), a national representative body established in 1990, began to find its feet. As a body eventually elected by Indigenous Australians, it was able to put forward views on behalf of the community. The Commission was also active in articulating and advocating for the aspirations of the Indigenous community.

In this chapter, I examine the work of both the Council for Aboriginal Reconciliation and ATSIC in this exciting era, when real social change seemed within reach. I also look at the ramifications of negotiating a treaty between Indigenous and non-Indigenous Australians, one of the recommendations of the Council for Aboriginal Reconciliation.

Starting the Reconciliation Process

The Council for Aboriginal Reconciliation (CAR) was established in 1991 to develop a process to achieve reconciliation between Indigenous and non-Indigenous people. Over its lifetime, the Council consulted with Australians — black and white — and produced documents of reconciliation that contained a roadmap for the way forward.

Complementing the work of the Council were other initiatives. As a consequence of the Mabo case finding for native title, momentum gathered around several other initiatives designed to improve the socioeconomic position of Indigenous people. These included

>> The establishment of a land fund that would allow dispossessed Indigenous people to purchase land

>> A social justice package intended to identify changes across political and social institutions to improve equality for Indigenous people

>> The appointment of a Social Justice Commissioner to monitor Indigenous issues

The Council for Aboriginal Reconciliation

In 1991, the federal parliament voted unanimously to establish the Council for Aboriginal Reconciliation and a formal, nine-year reconciliation process. CAR was made up of 25 leaders drawn from Aboriginal and Torres Strait Islander communities, from the industries that had the most impact on Indigenous people, and from business and other sectors.

The legislation that established CAR — the *Council for Aboriginal Reconciliation Act 1991* — set out the rationale behind its creation. It acknowledged that many Aboriginal people and Torres Strait Islanders suffered dispossession and dispersal from their traditional lands by the British Crown and that no formal reconciliation had occurred between Indigenous people and other Australians. It went on to note that such a reconciliation being achieved by the year 2001, the centenary of

Federation, was desirable. As a part of the reconciliation process, the federal government said it would seek, in the decade ahead:

an ongoing national commitment from governments at all levels to cooperate and to coordinate with the Aboriginal and Torres Strait Islander Commission (ATSIC) to address progressively Aboriginal disadvantage and aspirations in relation to land, housing, law and justice, cultural heritage, education, employment, health, infrastructure, economic development and any other relevant matters.

The federal parliament directed CAR to undertake a range of functions, including consulting with Aboriginal peoples and Torres Strait Islanders and the wider Australian community on whether reconciliation would be advanced by a formal document or documents of reconciliation. After extensive consultation, CAR determined that such documents would have to be 'people's documents', which parliaments, organisations, institutions and people in the community could accept and commit to, and should

>> Express the Australian people's hopes and aspirations for reconciliation

>> Share responsibility with Aboriginal peoples and Torres Strait Islanders for making progress to overcome disadvantage through negotiated actions

>> Recognise that much remained to be done

>> Outline an ongoing process to enable Australians to work together towards a reconciled nation

CHAIRING THE COUNCIL

Patrick Dodson was the founding Chair of the Council for Aboriginal Reconciliation from 1991 to 1997. A Yawuru man from Broome, he has also been the Chairman of the Kimberley Institute and is the Chairman of the Lingiari Foundation. He is a former Director of the Central Land Council and the Kimberley Land Council and had been a Royal Commissioner into Aboriginal Deaths in Custody in Western Australia. In 2008, Dodson was the recipient of the Sydney Peace Prize. Since 2016, Dodson has been a member of the Australian parliament as a senator for Western Australia.

When Patrick Dodson stepped down as the Chair of the Council for Aboriginal Reconciliation in 1997, he was replaced by Evelyn Scott, an Aboriginal woman from Townsville, Queensland, who held the position until 2000, when the Council was disbanded.

National Reconciliation Week falls between 27 May and 3 June. These are both significant dates on the Indigenous calendar, with 27 May being the anniversary of the 1967 referendum and 3 June the anniversary of the decision in the Mabo case (refer to Chapters 11 and 12). The week was first celebrated in 1996 and gives Australians a chance to focus on reconciliation.

When the Council was disbanded in December 2000, having achieved what it could of its initial aims, it set up another body, Reconciliation Australia, as a non-profit, non-government foundation to continue working towards national reconciliation. See the section 'A pathway for reconciliation', later in this chapter, for more on this organisation.

Paul Keating's Redfern Park speech

Prime Minister Paul Keating gave a historic speech in Redfern Park, right in the heart of the Aboriginal community in the inner city of Sydney, on 10 December 1992. The International Year of the World's Indigenous People was to dawn in just a few weeks. The audience consisted mostly of members of the local Aboriginal community. In front of this crowd, Keating articulated his vision for the future relationship between Indigenous Australians and the rest of the nation. In this historic speech, he said:

We cannot confidently say that we have succeeded as we would like to have succeeded if we have not managed to extend opportunity and care, dignity and hope to the Indigenous people of Australia — the Aboriginal and Torres Strait Island people.

This is a fundamental test of our social goals and our national will: our ability to say to ourselves and the rest of the world that Australia is a first-rate social democracy, that we are what we should be — truly the land of the fair go and the better chance.

There is no more basic test of how seriously we mean these things.

It is a test of our self-knowledge. Of how well we know the land we live in. How well we know our history. How well we recognise the fact that, complex as our contemporary identity is, it cannot be separated from Aboriginal Australia. How well we know what Aboriginal Australians know about Australia. . . . There should be no mistake about this — our success in resolving these issues will have a significant bearing on our standing in the world. . . . I think what we need to do is open our hearts a bit. All of us.

Perhaps when we recognise what we have in common we will see the things which must be done — the practical things.

REMEMBER

In a 2007 listeners' poll conducted by ABC Radio National, Paul Keating's Redfern Park speech was voted as their third most 'unforgettable speech' behind Martin Luther King's 'I Have a Dream' speech and Jesus's 'Sermon on the Mount'.

Trying to deliver on land and social justice

The 1992 decision in the Mabo case was a high-water mark in the relationship between Indigenous and non-Indigenous Australians (refer to Chapter 12 for more on Mabo). The overturning of terra nullius marked a rejection of a legal fiction that was offensive to Aboriginal people and Torres Strait Islanders. In addition, the recognition of a form of native title was an admission by the Australian legal system that Indigenous peoples had inherent rights.

The Mabo decision became the impetus for the Keating government to negotiate the *Native Title Act 1993* and so facilitate the large number of subsequent claims to native title and establish the National Native Title Tribunal. It was also the trigger for the establishment of an Indigenous land fund and an Indigenous corporation to administer it, which were supposed to be accompanied by a social justice package.

An Indigenous land fund

Most Indigenous people weren't able to receive a direct benefit from the Mabo decision because they'd been dispossessed of their land. They, therefore, couldn't meet the test to prove their native title — which included showing a continual connection to their land — developed by the High Court. In order to address this issue, the Indigenous Land Corporation (ILC) was established, coming into effect on 1 January 1995. It had responsibility for a fund with the purpose of assisting Aboriginal peoples and Torres Strait Islanders to acquire land and to manage it.

REMEMBER

Now known as the Indigenous Land and Sea Corporation, it acquires and manages land in a way that provides Indigenous people with social, cultural and economic benefits, such as the 2010 acquisition of the Yulara resort at Uluru (refer to Chapter 3). It also prepares national and regional strategies related to the acquisition of land, and examines management and environmental issues relating to Indigenous land.

The social justice package

The third plank of the Keating government's response to the Mabo decision was supposed to be the development of further measures to remedy institutional and structural impediments to the full participation of Aboriginal peoples and Torres Strait Islanders in Australian economic, social and cultural life. In other words, they wanted to establish a social justice package. In July 1994, as a first step, a consultation process was established to develop the package. The process of delivering the package stalled when the government changed in 1996.

The Social Justice Commissioner

In December 1992, the federal parliament created the position of the Aboriginal and Torres Strait Islander Social Justice Commissioner within the Human Rights and Equal Opportunity Commission (HREOC), now the Australian Human Rights Commission. The position was a response to the findings of the Royal Commission into Aboriginal Deaths in Custody and the National Inquiry into Racist Violence. It was also a response to the extreme social and economic disadvantage faced by Indigenous Australians. The Social Justice Commissioner's role includes

» Monitoring the enjoyment and exercise of human rights for Indigenous Australians, including reviewing legislation, providing policy advice and undertaking research on Indigenous human rights issues

» Reporting and promoting an Indigenous perspective on Indigenous social justice and native title issues

» Reviewing the impact of laws and policies on Indigenous peoples

The position has an active involvement with the development of international human rights standards. Every year, the Social Justice Commissioner is required to produce a Social Justice Report and a Native Title Report that are tabled in parliament.

THE COMMISH

Mick Dodson was the first Aboriginal and Torres Strait Islander Social Justice Commissioner, serving in the position from 1993 to 1998. A member of the Yawuru people, traditional owners of the Broome area of the western Kimberley region of Western Australia, Dodson is the former Director of the National Centre for Indigenous Studies at the Australian National University and Professor of law at the ANU College of Law. At the time of writing, he is part of the ANU Emeritus Faculty, mentoring Indigenous students and providing some teaching at the ANU College of Law.

Dodson completed a Bachelor of Jurisprudence and a Bachelor of Law at Monash University and worked with the Victorian Aboriginal Legal Service from 1976 to 1981, when he became a barrister at the Victorian Bar. He joined the Northern Land Council as Senior Legal Adviser in 1984 and became Director of the Council in 1990. He was a counsel assisting the Royal Commission into Aboriginal Deaths in Custody. Subsequent Social Justice Commissioners have been Bill Jonas (1999 to 2004), Tom Calma (2004 to 2010), Mick Gooda (2010 to 2016) and June Oscar AO (2107 to present).

REMEMBER

The other important role played by the Social Justice Commissioner is an educative one that seeks to promote better understanding and respect for the rights of Aboriginal peoples and Torres Strait Islanders. During its time, the office has provided an important monitoring role, even after the budget of HREOC was drastically cut under the Howard government when it came to power in 1996. The Social Justice Commissioner remains a prominent and respected voice on the national stage, providing critique of policy directions and advice on Indigenous issues.

Establishing the Aboriginal and Torres Strait Islander Commission

In 1987, the Hawke government announced it would establish the Aboriginal and Torres Strait Islander Commission (ATSIC), a body that would combine both representative and executive roles, through a system of regional councils and a national board elected by Indigenous people. Following an extensive consultation process on its ATSIC proposal, the ATSIC legislation was originally introduced into the parliament in August 1988. This bill was withdrawn and revised legislation — featuring considerably stronger public accountability mechanisms — brought into the parliament in May 1989.

But not everyone supported the creation of a body to represent Indigenous peoples. The John Howard–led opposition vehemently opposed the concept of ATSIC because it believed that it gave Indigenous peoples 'separate' status. Mr Howard expressed his opposition to ATSIC:

I take the opportunity of saying again that if the Government wants to divide Australian against Australian, if it wants to create a black nation within the Australian nation, it should go ahead with its Aboriginal and Torres Strait Islander Commission (ATSIC) legislation . . . The ATSIC legislation strikes at the heart of the unity of the Australian people. In the name of righting the wrongs done against Aboriginal people, the legislation adopts the misguided notion of believing that if one creates a parliament within the Australian community for Aboriginal people, one will solve and meet all of those problems.

The *Aboriginal and Torres Strait Islander Commission Act 1989* was eventually passed by the parliament in November 1989. ATSIC began operating in March 1990.

More than 90 amendments were made to the ATSIC legislation, making it the second most amended piece of legislation to have passed through the Australian parliament. The native title legislation was the most amended.

Defining the aims of ATSIC

The legislative objectives of ATSIC, combining both representative and executive roles as set out in the ATSIC Act, were to

>> Ensure coordination of Commonwealth, state, territory and local government policy affecting Indigenous peoples

>> Ensure maximum participation of Aboriginal peoples and Torres Strait Islanders in government policy formulation and implementation

>> Further Indigenous economic, social and cultural development

>> Promote Indigenous self-management and self-sufficiency

To meet these objectives, ATSIC was given the power to

>> Advise the minister and provide advice when requested

>> Collect and publish statistical material

>> Develop policy proposals

>> Formulate and implement programs, and monitor their effectiveness

>> Protect cultural material and information

The objectives and functions, when taken together, established a framework of responsibilities that conferred to ATSIC the primary role of advising the federal government on any matters relating to Aboriginal peoples and Torres Strait Islanders. They also gave ATSIC the oversight of all government effort in policy development relating to the provision of services to Aboriginal peoples and Torres Strait Islanders. This level of responsibility appeared to give genuine power to Indigenous people over the management of, and decision-making in, Indigenous affairs. However, the combination of these roles produced tension: ATSIC was to be accountable to the federal government in its service delivery and monitoring role, and at the same time its elected arm was to be accountable to its Indigenous constituency.

ATSIC's original structure consisted of two parts — a representative arm, and an administrative arm. The representative structure comprised 35 elected ATSIC Regional Councils. They were clustered into 16 zones, each of which elected a full-time commissioner to sit on the ATSIC board. Another commissioner was elected from the Torres Strait, which comprised its own zone. Up until 1999, the federal government appointed the chair of ATSIC. After that, the commissioners elected the chair. ATSIC's administrative arm consisted of several hundred Commonwealth public servants (at its peak, 48 per cent of them Indigenous), and headed by a chief executive officer appointed by the minister. The role of the administrative arm was to support ATSIC's elected representatives and administer the various programs it ran.

In April 2003, then Minister for Indigenous Affairs Philip Ruddock announced the establishment of a new agency, Aboriginal and Torres Strait Islander Services (ATSIS), to administer ATSIC's programs and make decisions about grants and other funding to Indigenous organisations. Although Ruddock emphasised at the time that the establishment of ATSIS didn't represent a move towards 'mainstreaming' of ATSIC's programs, it effectively removed direct control of ATSIC's budget and its programs away from ATSIC's elected representatives. See Chapter 14 for more about ATSIC.

REMEMBER

Up to 85 per cent of ATSIC's budget (around $1.3 billion in the 2003–2004 budget year, its last year of operation) was quarantined for its main programs — the Community Development Employment Projects (CDEP) scheme and the Community Housing and Infrastructure Program (CHIP). The remaining money was spent on a range of programs, including those geared towards the preservation and promotion of Indigenous culture and heritage, and the advancement of Indigenous rights and equity. It often footed the bill for services and programs that should have been delivered by state or territory governments and/or the federal government.

IN THE CHAIR

Lowitja O'Donoghue was the first chairperson of ATSIC. She was appointed to the position by the Hawke government and held the position from 1990 to 1996. Gatjil Djerrkura was appointed to the chair from 1996 to 2000. From that time, the ATSIC commissioners, who had been elected by Aboriginal people and Torres Strait Islanders, chose the chair. Geoff Clark held the position from 2000 to 2004. For a period when Geoff Clark stepped down from the position between 2003 and 2004, Lionel Quartermaine acted in the chair's position until ATSIC was abolished.

Recognition, rights and reform

When the Keating government announced it was going to formulate a social justice package in 1994, it began a consultation process to assist with mapping out what such a package may look like.

ATSIC, the national representative body for Indigenous people, undertook its own consultation process among Aboriginal peoples and Torres Strait Islanders around the country. ATSIC consulted widely, asking Indigenous people about the key issues that affected them and what they thought needed to change to improve their socioeconomic position. It was the largest survey of this kind undertaken in Australia to date. *Recognition, Rights and Reform: A Report to Government on Native Title Social Justice Measures* was published in 1995. The report provided a roadmap from Indigenous Australia about what the people thought the key issues were, and it remains an important documentation of the political aspirations of Indigenous communities.

THREE CHEERS FOR AUNTY PAT!

From 1994 to 1998, Patricia Turner was the chief executive officer of ATSIC. Patricia is an Arrernte woman who was born and raised in Alice Springs, Northern Territory. She earned a master's degree in public administration at the University of Canberra. She was always determined to get a good education and went on to become one of the most senior Indigenous people in the federal public service. She had responsibility for some 1,200 staff throughout the country and the proper administration of ATSIC's budget and programs.

Turner went on to work in senior positions in Centrelink and the Department of Health, and later became the inaugural CEO of the National Indigenous Television (NITV), overseeing the launch and establishment of the service. In 2010, she won the Deadly Award for Leader of the Year. (The Deadly Awards are Indigenous community awards for arts, sport and community contribution.)

The current CEO of the National Aboriginal Community Controlled Health Organisation (NACCHO), Turner has led the Council of Indigenous Peaks and been a key person at the table in negotiating the Partnership and Close the Gap Outcomes and Priority Reforms (see Chapter 21 for more on Closing the Gap reforms and NACCHO). An extraordinary career; an extraordinary woman!

Recognition of the fundamental rights and entitlements of Indigenous people was a central aspect of the proposals in *Recognition, Rights and Reform*. The report noted that the ability to exercise and enjoy those rights — the normal citizenship rights or equality rights that should be shared by all Australians, and the distinctive rights of Indigenous peoples — was critical to the achievement of social justice for Aboriginal peoples and Torres Strait Islanders. It identified two key areas where rights could be protected and made proposals in relation to each of them; namely:

>> **Citizenship and equality rights:** These are the rights that should be enjoyed by all Australians but that, for Indigenous people, are often denied. Particular issues were identified as

  ● The enormous level of unmet need in Aboriginal communities and Torres Strait Islander communities for basic service delivery, such as housing and infrastructure, resulting from the failure of governments to provide adequate funding and ensure delivery of those services

  ● Equity of access by Aboriginal people and Torres Strait Islanders to mainstream services from all levels of government

  ● An adequate and fair range of service delivery for remote and predominantly Aboriginal and Torres Strait Islander communities

>> **Indigenous rights:** Some rights are identified as being specific to Indigenous peoples, with a view that the recognition of and support for self-determination is fundamental. Further work required was identified in the areas of

  ● Autonomy rights, which focus on the right of Indigenous peoples to determine the way in which they live and control their social, economic and political systems

  ● Identity rights, which relate to the right to exist as distinct peoples with distinct cultures

  ● Territory and resource rights, which encompass such things as land entitlement, the right to the resources of that land and the use of those resources

Recognition, Rights and Reform put forward a broad range of recommendations that covered several key areas, outlined in Table 13-1.

Other major proposals canvassed by the *Recognition, Rights and Reform* report were major institutional and structural change (including constitutional reform and recognition), regional self-government and regional agreements, and the negotiation of a treaty or similar document.

TABLE 13-1   Recognition, Rights and Reform: Recommendations

Key Area	Strategies to Achieve These Aims
The rights of Aboriginal peoples and Torres Strait Islanders as citizens	Reinforcing access and equity provisions through legislation to ensure Indigenous people can better access their citizenship entitlements
	Increasing commitment to supporting international instruments that reinforce Indigenous rights
	Supporting measures to define, recognise and extend Indigenous rights, including new initiatives in areas such as communal title and assertion of coextensive rights
The recognition of the special status and rights of Indigenous Australians and the achievement of greater self-determination for Aboriginal peoples and Torres Strait Islanders	Promoting and advancing the constitutional reform agenda
	Supporting Indigenous representation in parliament, with interim arrangements for speaking rights by the ATSIC chairperson
	Developing processes to start work on compensation issues
	Promoting regional agreements as a means of settling social justice issues on a regional basis, commencing with pilot studies
	Recognising a self-government option for Indigenous peoples within the framework of self-determination
	Supporting initial work to develop a framework for a treaty and negotiation arrangements
	Giving legislative recognition to the Aboriginal and Torres Strait Islander flags
	Increasing support for public awareness initiatives
Ensuring that Indigenous Australians are able to exercise their rights and share equitably in the provision of government programs and services	Educating about rights and available remedies
	Reforming public service decision-making
	Providing more equitable budget allocations
The protection of the cultural integrity and heritage of Indigenous Australians	Supporting legislative reforms to strengthen heritage protection legislation and protect Indigenous rights to cultural property
	Providing for greater involvement in environmental decision-making
	Implementing the report of the Law Reform Commission on Aboriginal customary law
	Supporting the extension of language programs and broadcasting initiatives
Measures to increase Aboriginal and Torres Strait Islander participation in Australia's economic life	Fostering closer links with industry
	Accessing Community Development and Employment Projects (CDEP), a work-for-welfare scheme in communities where no jobs are available
	Implementing business training proposals
	Fostering regional economic development
	Further developing strategic business opportunities and resources for a stake in industry

The report recommended that the social justice package should be targeted for implementation by 2001, when the Council for Aboriginal Reconciliation was to report on its progress. However, the election of the Howard government in 1996 meant that no social justice package was implemented.

The Unfinished Business of Reconciliation

After a very extensive public consultation process, the Council for Aboriginal Reconciliation (CAR) drew up two documents of reconciliation — the *Australian Declaration towards Reconciliation* and the *Roadmap for Reconciliation*. It presented these documents at Corroboree 2000 on 27 May 2000. The following day, more than 300,000 people walked across the Sydney Harbour Bridge to show their support for the reconciliation process (see Figure 13-1).

FIGURE 13-1: More than 300,000 people walked across the Sydney Harbour Bridge during the Walk for Reconciliation in 2000.

The *Australian Declaration towards Reconciliation* states:

We, the peoples of Australia, of many origins as we are, make a commitment to go on together in a spirit of reconciliation.

We value the unique status of Aboriginal and Torres Strait Islander peoples as the original owners and custodians of lands and waters.

We recognise this land and its waters were settled as colonies without treaty or consent.

Reaffirming the human rights of all Australians, we respect and recognise continuing customary laws, beliefs and traditions.

Through understanding the spiritual relationship between the land and its first peoples, we share our future and live in harmony.

Our nation must have the courage to own the truth, to heal the wounds of its past so that we can move on together at peace with ourselves.

Reconciliation must live in the hearts and minds of all Australians. Many steps have been taken, many steps remain as we learn our shared histories.

As we walk the journey of healing, one part of the nation apologises and expresses its sorrow and sincere regret for the injustices of the past, so the other part accepts the apologies and forgives.

We desire a future where all Australians enjoy their rights, accept their responsibilities, and have the opportunity to achieve their full potential.

And so, we pledge ourselves to stop injustice, overcome disadvantage, and respect that Aboriginal and Torres Strait Islander peoples have the right to self-determination within the life of the nation.

Our hope is for a united Australia that respects this land of ours, values the Aboriginal and Torres Strait Islander heritage, and provides justice and equity for all.

A pathway for reconciliation

To support the *Australian Declaration towards Reconciliation*, CAR developed four key strategies that made up the *Roadmap for Reconciliation*:

>> **The National Strategy to Sustain the Reconciliation Process:** This strategy focused on engaging all levels of government, the private sector, and community and voluntary organisations to publicly support the ongoing reconciliation process, provide resources and increasingly involve Aboriginal people and

Torres Strait Islanders in their work. It recommended the establishment of Reconciliation Australia, a non-government body, to maintain a national leadership focus for reconciliation, report on progress, provide information and raise funds to promote and support reconciliation activities. It further highlighted the importance of concentrating on education about reconciliation.

>> **The National Strategy to Promote Recognition of Aboriginal and Torres Strait Islander Rights:** This strategy proposed a number of actions, including some constitutional and legislative processes, to assist the progressive resolution of outstanding issues for the recognition and enjoyment of Aboriginal and Torres Strait Islander rights. It included recommending the establishment of legislative processes to deal with the 'unfinished business' of reconciliation, allowing for negotiated outcomes on matters such as Indigenous rights, self-determination within the life of the nation and constitutional reform.

>> **The National Strategy to Overcome Disadvantage:** The aim of this strategy was to create a society where Aboriginal people and Torres Strait Islanders enjoy a similar standard of living to that of other Australians, without losing their cultural identity. It focused on education, employment, health, housing, law and justice.

>> **The National Strategy for Economic Independence:** This strategy focused on pathways to economic independence, looking at the importance of education and skills development, economic participation through access to jobs and resources, and effective business practices.

TECHNICAL STUFF

REMOVING A DISCRIMINATORY RELIC

Section 25 of the Australian Constitution says that if a state disqualifies people, on the basis of their race, from voting in elections, those people won't be counted in the population of that state for the purposes of determining how many House of Representatives seats that state can have. This provision particularly affected Western Australia and Queensland until those states lifted their bans on Indigenous people voting, in 1962 and 1965 respectively.

Since the 1967 referendum, however, Indigenous people were included in the census, so the provision is a historical relic but, as it makes reference to a practice that was overtly discriminatory, many people feel that it should be removed from the Constitution.

In its final report, CAR also made six key recommendations:

>> Governments implement and monitor a national framework to overcome Indigenous disadvantage, through setting performance benchmarks agreed in partnership with Indigenous peoples and communities, and public reporting

>> All parliaments and local governments pass formal motions of support for the **Australian Declaration towards Reconciliation** and the **Roadmap for Reconciliation**, enshrine their basic principles in legislation and determine how to implement their key recommendations

>> The federal parliament prepare legislation for a referendum that seeks to

- Recognise Aboriginal peoples and Torres Strait Islanders as the first peoples of Australia in a new preamble to the Constitution

- Remove Section 25 of the Constitution and introduce a new section making it unlawful to adversely discriminate against any people on the grounds of race (see the sidebar 'Removing a discriminatory relic' for an explanation of this aspect of the Constitution)

>> All levels of government, non-government, business, peak bodies, communities and individuals commit themselves to continuing the reconciliation process and sustaining it by

- Affirming the **Australian Declaration towards Reconciliation** and actioning the **Roadmap for Reconciliation**

- Providing resources for reconciliation activities and involving Indigenous people in their work

- Undertaking educational and public awareness activities to help improve understanding and relations between Indigenous peoples and the wider community

- Supporting Reconciliation Australia, which was established to maintain a national leadership focus for reconciliation, report on progress, provide information and raise funds to promote and support reconciliation

>> Each government and parliament:

- Recognise that this land and its waters were settled as colonies without treaty or consent and that, to advance reconciliation, it would be most desirable if agreements or treaties were in place

- Negotiate a process through which an agreement or a treaty might be achieved that protects the political, legal, cultural and economic position of Aboriginal peoples and Torres Strait Islanders

>> The federal parliament enact legislation to put in place a process that would unite all Australians by way of an agreement, or treaty, through which unresolved issues of reconciliation can be resolved

THE FAILURE TO RESPOND

On 15 May 2002, the then Social Justice Commissioner, Dr William Jonas, gave a speech in which he noted that the federal government had failed to respond adequately or comprehensively to the Council for Aboriginal Reconciliation's recommendations. He said, 'They have quite deliberately sought to shut down debate and avoid any engagement about them by stating that they are committed to practical reconciliation'.

He added that the government had responded to only one of the six recommendations of the final report — through the limited focus of the framework established by the Council of Australian Governments (COAG) for addressing disadvantage — but they ignored the broader agenda for reconciliation, which recognised the necessary interrelatedness of symbolic and practical measures to Indigenous peoples' self-determination.

Not one of these recommendations was taken up. An earlier referendum to add a preamble to the Constitution, largely authored by John Howard, was defeated in 1999, failing to achieve a majority in any of the six states.

REMEMBER

CAR's final report included a draft Reconciliation Bill 2001. Aboriginal Senator Aden Ridgeway, a member of the Australian Democrats, introduced it to parliament as a private member's bill but it was never passed.

REMEMBER

In 2000, when the work of the Council for Aboriginal Reconciliation was completed, Reconciliation Australia was established. A private foundation, it remains one of the leading organisations promoting reconciliation between Indigenous and non-Indigenous Australians.

HISTORICAL ATTEMPTS AT A TREATY

In 1837, Saxe Bannister, the first attorney-general of New South Wales, promoted the idea of a treaty with Aboriginal people in a submission to the Select Committee of the House of Commons on Aborigines. He wasn't the only one who thought it was a good idea. The former governor of Tasmania, Governor Arthur, also advocated for entering into treaties with Aboriginal people.

In 1885, John Batman negotiated a treaty with the Kulin people. It was later declared invalid, because only the Crown, not a private individual, could enter into a treaty with Aboriginal people. The Kulin people also disputed the content of the treaty, saying that it didn't reflect what they understood they were agreeing to.

'We call for a treaty'

The call for a treaty between Indigenous people and other Australians wasn't new. The Aboriginal leadership had been discussing the need for a treaty for over two decades. The Council for Aboriginal Reconciliation, with its recommendations (refer to preceding section), put it firmly back on the agenda. As did ATSIC when it launched the campaign 'Treaty: Let's Get It Right'.

TECHNICAL
STUFF

A *treaty* is a settlement or agreement arrived at by 'treating', or negotiating, between two parties who seek to have their relationship formalised. It gives rise to binding obligations between the parties. The word 'treaty' covers a range of ideas and concepts, including a contract or compact, a covenant, an agreement, a settlement, or international arrangements between nation states.

In 1979, a group of non-Indigenous Australians set up the Aboriginal Treaty Committee, which operated for five years. In 1983, the Senate Standing Committee on Constitutional and Legal Affairs issued a report, *Two Hundred Years Later*, that rejected a treaty with Indigenous people because, it argued, Aboriginal peoples and Torres Strait Islanders weren't sovereign entities and so didn't have the capacity to enter into a treaty with the Commonwealth. It argued instead for a 'compact' that could eventually be inserted into the Constitution.

A statement of Indigenous aspirations was handed to Prime Minister Bob Hawke at the Barunga Festival in the Northern Territory in 1988 (see the sidebar 'The Barunga Statement'). Hawke said he would like to see a treaty negotiated with Indigenous people by 1990. The Council for Aboriginal Reconciliation, in its final report, delivered in 2000, recommended that a treaty process be established. By this time, ATSIC had also started a campaign for a treaty. Prime Minister John Howard rejected the idea of a treaty, saying he thought it was divisive, and the momentum and political will for such an agreement was lost — at least for the time being.

MYTH
BUSTER

Although some people have argued that a treaty can't be entered into with Indigenous people because they aren't sovereign, this isn't true. First, Indigenous people claim they are a sovereign people. Second, examples can be found in other countries — namely, the United States and Canada — where treaties have been entered into with Indigenous people.

TECHNICAL
STUFF

The terms *compact* and *Makarrata* have been used to describe a *treaty*. All these words describe an agreement between Indigenous and non-Indigenous people but, as the concept of a treaty is often criticised as divisive and more often describes agreements between countries rather than within countries between different parts of the population, some people believe using another word to describe the concept is a better strategy.

NUGGET COOMBS: THE LISTENER

H C 'Nugget' Coombs was an economist and highly respected public servant who had retired in 1968 as governor of the Reserve Bank. In retirement, he was actively involved with Indigenous people and became chairman of the Australian Council for Aboriginal Affairs, set up in 1968 in the wake of the 1967 referendum.

Coombs had earlier shown his interest in the rights of Indigenous people when he became aware that the image on the $1 note circulating at the time he was governor of the Reserve Bank had been used without the approval of the Aboriginal artist, David Malangi Daymirringu. Coombs rectified this by giving attribution on the note to the artist and travelling to Darwin to present Malangi with an especially struck medallion, a cheque for $1,000 and some fishing equipment.

A close adviser to Gough Whitlam, he was largely responsible for Labor's policy on Aboriginal affairs, particularly its commitment to Aboriginal land rights. He was renowned for 'actively listening' to Indigenous people. He died in 1997.

THE BARUNGA STATEMENT

The Barunga Statement, handed to Prime Minister Bob Hawke at the Barunga Festival in 1988 (see Chapter 20 for more on this festival), is actually a piece of art, with the text set inside a group of ancestral Aboriginal designs, or deeds, by eight Aboriginal artists from the Northern Territory. The paintings symbolise how the clan groups got together to formulate the wording of the statement, representing the rights of all Aboriginal people of Australia.

Why a treaty?

Several arguments have been put forward as to why a treaty should be negotiated between Indigenous and non-Indigenous Australians. One argument, in particular, is that a treaty could recognise and protect Indigenous rights and make up for the exclusion of Aboriginal peoples and Torres Strait Islanders from the nation-building process of drafting the Constitution. A treaty is also seen as a way of recognising the unique status of Aboriginal peoples and Torres Strait Islanders as first peoples and the distinctive rights and special status based on prior occupation that flow from that.

Another argument is that a treaty would deliver many important benefits, including a framework for settling relationships between Indigenous peoples and governments at local, state, territory and federal levels. Legal recognition, including constitutional recognition, that Aboriginal peoples and Torres Strait Islanders have inherent rights that must inform all processes of governments in Australia could also be given through a treaty, as well as improved services, such as health, housing, education and employment, in accordance with the legitimate aspirations of Indigenous peoples.

What would a treaty look like?

A treaty under Australian law could take many forms. It could be an agreement under international law in the form of a treaty, an agreement that's supported by the Constitution, an agreement that's supported by legislation or a simple agreement that's not legally binding. An agreement under international law would be most difficult to pursue because Indigenous people aren't recognised as a separate state under international law. An agreement that had no legal status would be merely symbolic and, therefore, of little use in terms of substantially changing the relationship between Indigenous and non-Indigenous Australians.

The more likely options for such an agreement would be as part of the Constitution or as legislation. Inclusion in the Constitution would give a treaty the greatest protection but would need a referendum in order to implement. As an example, Section 35 of the Canadian Constitution provides for the protection of rights, stating: 'The existing Aboriginal and treaty rights of the Aboriginal peoples of Canada are hereby recognised and affirmed'.

A treaty in legislative form could be passed by any federal parliament with the will to do so but would, as a piece of legislation, be vulnerable to being overruled by subsequent legislation. The parliament has the power to legislate for a treaty under the races power, which was one of the sections of the Constitution changed at the 1967 referendum (refer to Chapter 11). The content of a treaty can be as broad or narrow as the parties agree. In the context of a treaty between Indigenous and non-Indigenous Australians, specific areas that might be covered include

>> Access to education, training and employment opportunities

>> Benefits from resource development, and economic and social development

>> Control, ownership and management of land, waters and resources

>> Prohibition of racial discrimination

>> Protection of laws, cultures and languages

>> Recognition of the rights of equality and ways in which self-determination can be exercised

A treaty could provide, among other things, a symbolic recognition of sovereignty and prior occupation, a redefinition and restructuring of the relationship that Indigenous peoples have with Australia, the granting of better rights protection and the basis for regional self-government. A national treaty could also be a standard-setting document that allows for local or regional treaties containing fundamental, bottom-line principles. At the same time, a treaty could provide mechanisms for local and regional decision-making processes.

While a treaty never stopped being part of the national Indigenous political agenda, it has come back to the centre of national conversations through the Uluru Statement from the Heart. For more on the Uluru Statement, see Chapter 15.

First steps?

A few steps have been taken at the state and territory level to develop a treaty process:

>> **Victoria** has the most advanced state-based treaty process. The Victorian Treaty Advancement Commission and statewide consultations began in 2016. As a result, a representative body, the First People's Assembly of Victoria, was established to continue the treaty process. You can find out more at www.firstpeoplesvic.org/about.

>> **Queensland** took the first steps to a treaty process in 2019 and an Eminent Panel of experts delivered a report in 2020 that recommended a pathway to a treaty. The Queensland Government announced that it would establish a Treaty Advancement Committee to assist with the implement the recommendations of the Eminent Panel's report — see www.datsip.qld.gov.au/programs-initiatives/tracks-treaty/path-treaty for more information.

>> **South Australia** began a treaty process in 2016 but it stalled with a change of government in 2018 and the role of Treaty Commissioner ended in July 2018. Before it ended, an historic Buthera Agreement was signed with the Narungga nation that was a first step towards a treaty.

>> **Northern Territory** made a commitment to a treaty process in 2016 and agreed to a treaty process in 2018. A Treaty Commissioner was appointed in 2019 to head the Northern Territory Treaty Commission — see treatynt.com.au/home.

These state- and territory-based treaty processes have shown that steps can be taken for entering treaties with Aboriginal and Torres Strait Islander peoples, even if it is not part of the national agenda. Importantly, these processes show that treaty-making can be done.

DITCHING TERRA NULLIUS

Aboriginal leader Galarrwuy Yunupingu made the following statement about a treaty in 1987:

> A treaty which is recognised by international convention must state that Aboriginal people are the indigenous sovereign owners of Australia and adjacent islands since before 1770 and as such have rights and treaty rights; their sovereignty was never ceded, and the doctrine of terra nullius cannot be supported in international law as the legal basis for European occupation of, and acquisition of sovereignty over, our land.

IN THIS CHAPTER

» Winding back the clock on reconciliation and Indigenous rights

» Checking Australia's human rights record

» Dismantling ATSIC, the national representative body

» Replacing ATSIC with a new administration and a hand-picked advisory group

» Establishing 'mutual obligation' and 'shared responsibility'

» Declaring an emergency and an intervention after decades of neglect

Chapter **14**

Practical Reconciliation

The election of John Howard's government in 1996 marked a significant change in the direction of Indigenous affairs in Australia. Howard was of the view that the pendulum had swung too far in favour of Indigenous rights. He also took a different view on the way in which Australian history should treat the experiences of Indigenous Australians.

These arguments led to a shift in policy approaches, with a return to a focus on mainstreaming. They also led to a clash between historians and public commentators about how Australian history should be told. In this chapter, I look at how Howard's views were representative of a sector of the Australian community but not universal, evidenced by the number who participated in bridge walks to show support for reconciliation.

I also examine one of the key changes to the policy landscape during the Howard era — the abolition of the Indigenous national representative body, the Aboriginal and Torres Strait Islander Commission (ATSIC) and its replacement with an appointed advisory body. With the return to the mainstreaming of Indigenous policies and services, some new ideologies emerged about the delivery of services to Indigenous communities. The language of 'mutual obligation' and 'shared responsibility' entered the political landscape. And, just as this new policy approach seemed to be failing, a report into levels of child abuse in the Northern Territory sparked a new era of intervention and hardline policy. Here, I note the arguments for and against the intervention.

'The Pendulum Has Swung Too Far'

John Howard became Prime Minister of Australia in 1996. In the campaign leading up to his election, he made several speeches that indicated he had a very different view of Australian history than the vision his predecessor, Paul Keating, articulated in his Redfern Park speech (refer to Chapter 13). In a speech given to the Longreach community in Queensland, Howard made the following comments about native title:

Although I was born in Sydney and I lived all my life in the urban parts of Australia, I have always had an immense affection for the bush. I say that because in all of my political life no charge would offend me more than the suggestion that what I've done and what I've believed in has not taken proper account of the concerns of the Australian bush.

REMEMBER

This approach gives a key insight into Howard's view of Australia. Here, Howard isn't using 'the bush' to refer to pristine forests or Aboriginal communities but the non-Indigenous landholders who work the country, made clear later in the speech (read on). He embraces the 'white-settler-conquering-the-land' story that emphasises the taming of the country. Although this is one side of the Australian story, it's not one that sits comfortably alongside stories of ill-treatment of Indigenous people and their dispossession. In the same speech, Howard talked about Indigenous rights, particularly the right to negotiate in native title cases, which had been recognised by the High Court. These comments showed that he thought native title, as it stood, gave too much to Indigenous people:

... under the guarantees that will be contained in this [amending] legislation, the right to negotiate, that stupid property right that was given to native title claimants alone, unlike other title holders in Australia ... that native title right will be completely abolished and removed for all time ... We knew the right to negotiate was a licence for people to come from nowhere and make a

claim on your property and then say until you pay me out, we're not going to allow you to do anything with your property. Well, let me say I regard that as repugnant, and I regard that as un-Australian . . . You won't have to put up with that anymore.

Howard was always clear that he thought the pendulum had swung too far and, as a result, was committed to changing the playing field. Howard's tone continued after he achieved the prime ministership. At the 1997 Reconciliation Convention, he delivered an address but, by that time, his antagonism towards the rights focus of reconciliation was apparent, and his failure to apologise to the members of the Stolen Generations was seen as a symbol of his disregard for the key elements of the reconciliation process. Delegates at the convention stood and turned their backs on him as a silent (and powerful) protest against his derailing of the reconciliation process.

When the Council for Aboriginal Reconciliation (refer to Chapter 13) released its final report and documents of reconciliation, Howard announced that his government rejected the recommendation of a treaty, preferring instead to concentrate on what he called 'practical reconciliation'.

'Practical reconciliation' explained

Practical reconciliation was described as a policy where government funding would target the areas of core disadvantage — health, education, housing and employment. The subtext to this was that, while the focus was on these 'practical' issues, Indigenous rights wouldn't be the focus. Although better targeting of key problem areas of socioeconomic disadvantage was needed, what wasn't clear was how this was going to be done when analysis of budget figures showed huge shortfalls in what was needed. In 2007, for example, the underfunding of Indigenous health needs was estimated at about $460 million.

Critics of the approach also said that saying you either focus on 'practical' issues or bigger picture issues created a false dichotomy, when focusing on both at the same time is quite possible. When the policy of practical reconciliation failed to perceivably shift the disadvantage of many Indigenous people and their communities, a new explanation started to filter into the political dialogue. Increasingly, governments, exasperated by failing to improve health, education, employment and housing outcomes, decided to blame Indigenous people for the failures, rather than review their policies or spending patterns. Indigenous people were accused of wallowing in a culture of dependency and victimhood and of becoming welfare-dependent.

Past government policies such as child removal practices had contributed to the socioeconomic inequalities and systemic racism experienced in Indigenous communities and families today. But this had been compounded by the failure of governments to provide adequate services and infrastructure in many communities, so from the start many people questioned what was gained by blaming the victim. Large sectors of the Indigenous community were poor and unemployed or suffered from health problems, so were on welfare. Governments wanted to see this dependency broken. Indigenous communities wanted to see it broken too. But the challenge became: How?

Winding back Indigenous rights

John Howard had said he would make changes to the native title regime if he was elected, and he did that by passing amendments to the *Native Title Act 1993*. These included the removal of the right to negotiate pastoral leases on traditional land. Procedural changes were also made, including a higher test for registration that meant that claims were harder to make. One positive change for native title holders in the new legislation was that provision was made for voluntary Indigenous Land Use Agreements (ILUAs) between parties. These binding agreements covered the use of the land and how competing interests in it would be balanced.

The history wars, or culture wars

All countries have competing stories about their histories. Australia is no different. The visions of the successive prime ministers, Paul Keating (1991 to 1996) and John Howard (1996 to 2007), represented opposite views on how Australia's national story should be told. Keating's view was that the story that needed to be told was about the dispossession and mistreatment of Indigenous people, evident in his Redfern Park speech (refer to Chapter 13). Howard thought that Australians shouldn't be made to feel guilty about their past by dwelling on the negatives but should instead be encouraged to celebrate the achievements.

For Howard, Keating's negative view was like a 'black armband' version of history — one of shame and guilt. For Keating, Howard's view was like a 'white blindfold' version, wilfully overlooking the mistakes and tragedies of the past that needed to be acknowledged. As Howard sought to reassert his view of the way the national story should be told during his time as leader, conflict between the two visions raged in newspapers and in academia.

Historians, in particular, got involved. Henry Reynolds had become one of the leading historians on Indigenous frontier history with his influential books, including *The Other Side of the Frontier: Aboriginal Resistance to the European Invasion of Australia* (1981) and *Frontier: Aborigines, Settlers and Land* (1987). His writings came under particular attack as being an embodiment of 'black armband' history. His biggest critic was Keith Windschuttle, who, in his 2002 book *The Fabrication of Australian History: Volume 1, Van Diemen's Land 1803–1847*, challenged the assumptions Reynolds had made about the level of violence on the frontier. In particular, Windschuttle challenged assertions about the number of massacres and the number of Aboriginal people killed. Reynolds and other historians replied that Windschuttle's assumptions were also speculative.

At the same time as these debates about frontier violence and the number of Indigenous people killed were taking place, known as the *history wars*, or the *culture wars*, the response to the *Bringing Them Home* report, published in 1997 (refer to Chapter 9) was also generating discussion about the way history was told. The official government response to the report was to question the authors' use of the term *genocide* and to challenge the case studies documented in the report by countering that many children were taken away for their own good and with the best of intentions.

REMEMBER

While historians, politicians and public commentators argued about numbers on the frontier and whether the removal of children was a form of cultural genocide or not, Indigenous people remained relatively detached from these debates. Some Aboriginal historians, such as John Maynard, Tony Birch and Gary Foley, engaged in public forums and discussions. But for many Indigenous people, these debates were irrelevant. They had strong oral histories and their own experiences were unchanged by the debates occurring in universities and in the media. This caused many Indigenous people to conclude that the history wars and culture wars weren't about Aboriginal history but about the story that non-Indigenous Australians wanted to tell about their history.

REMEMBER

The Howard government treated the ideological struggle over the story told about Australia's history very seriously. It didn't just engage in these debates in the abstract. In making appointments to key Australian cultural institutions such as the Australian Broadcasting Corporation and the National Museum of Australia, it took care to make sure its nominees shared the government's view. Cleverly, perhaps, these appointments ensured that this view of history would be promoted and shape public institutions long after the Howard government was no longer in office.

A walk across the bridge

Prime Minister Howard appealed to a sector of the Australian community who were suspicious of the rights of Indigenous people being protected and thought too much recognition of the wrongs done to them was bad for the country. However, he didn't speak for all Australians. In 2000, when the Council for Aboriginal Reconciliation handed over the documents it had been working on for the previous nine years, they anticipated that the federal government would reject some of their recommendations. In particular, it was clear that the Howard government wouldn't support a treaty with Australia's Indigenous peoples.

Also clear was that the Howard government wouldn't support an apology to the Stolen Generations as a step towards reconciliation. This was not only part of the recommendations of the Council for Aboriginal Reconciliation, but also a recommendation in the *Bringing Them Home* report of the inquiry into the Indigenous child removal policy and its implications. Commissioned by the previous Keating government, the report was delivered to the Howard government and it rejected many of the inquiry's findings and conclusions. (Refer to Chapter 9 for detail on the report.)

On 28 May 2000, the day after the Council for Aboriginal Reconciliation handed over its final documentation to Prime Minister Howard, more than 300,000 people walked across Sydney Harbour Bridge as a symbol of support for the reconciliation movement. Australians from diverse backgrounds participated in the event in Sydney and similar events that followed.

REMEMBER

Large numbers of Australians walked over bridges and streets in Sydney, Brisbane, Adelaide, Canberra, Melbourne and Perth, as well as in towns all over Australia. More than 300,000 people walked across the Sydney Harbour Bridge; 60,000 walked across the William Jolly Bridge in Brisbane; and 55,000 walked over King William Street Bridge in Adelaide. Several thousand walked across the Commonwealth Bridge in Canberra (in the snow!); and another 300,000 walked the streets of Melbourne and Perth later that year in events designed to show support for the reconciliation movement.

This show of popular support for reconciliation was symbolic of the rift that was developing between the federal government's official view and the views of many other sectors of the Australian community regarding Indigenous people, their rights and their place in the country's national story.

A Human Rights Scorecard

In 2000, four years into John Howard's prime ministership, the United Nations Committee on the Elimination of All Forms of Racial Discrimination handed down a report on Australia's performance under the convention that it oversees. The report found that Australia was breaching its obligations in several ways, including

- >> The absence of any entrenched law guaranteeing against racial discrimination

- >> The provisions of the **Native Title Amendment Act 1998** (Cwlth) that extinguished native title and took away other rights from native title holders

- >> The failure to apologise to the Stolen Generations

- >> The refusal to interfere to change mandatory sentencing laws in states and territories that were having a negative and disproportionate impact on Indigenous young people

In response to the report, the Howard government claimed that the United Nations couldn't tell it what to do and that it should remember that Australia had a better human rights record than other countries — such as China.

The Abolition of ATSIC

In November 2003, the federal government announced a review that would 'examine and make recommendations to government on how Aboriginal and Torres Strait Islander people can in the future be best represented in the process of the development of Commonwealth policies and programs to assist them'. This review was also to 'consider the current roles and functions of ATSIC'. The review delivered its report, *In the Hands of the Region: A New ATSIC*, to the federal government in November 2003. It recommended against abolishing ATSIC but wanted fundamental structural changes, including

- >> An overhaul of ATSIC's representative structure, in order to strengthen the relationship between Indigenous communities and the national board

- >> A strengthening of, and increased emphasis on, regional planning processes

- >> A permanent delineation of the roles of ATSIC's elected representatives and its administrative arm

Despite the recommendation that the body be reformed, Prime Minister Howard and Minister for Indigenous Affairs Senator Amanda Vanstone announced the government's intention to abolish ATSIC on 15 April 2004. The Australian Labor Party had announced a few weeks earlier that it would do likewise if elected to government later that year. The national body would be abolished immediately legislation could be passed and the regional councils the following year.

In making the announcement to abolish ATSIC, Prime Minister Howard said, 'We believe very strongly that the experiment in separate representation, elected representation, for Indigenous people has been a failure'. He made it clear that ATSIC wouldn't be replaced by another form of representative body. Instead, he announced, his government would appoint a group of Indigenous people to advise it. Many observers believed it inevitable that Howard would move to abolish a body whose creation he had opposed as divisive when the legislation to establish it was first put before parliament. (Refer to Chapter 13 for more on the establishment of ATSIC.)

Prime Minister Howard's claim that ATSIC was a 'failed experiment' was often repeated. The claim was extended to assert that ATSIC was a 'failed experiment' in self-determination. But that assertion may not be a fair assessment for two reasons.

First, ATSIC wasn't the overwhelming failure that the Howard government asserted. Probably closer to the truth was that the Howard government saw a representative body as divisive rather than that it was concerned that body was failing. Objectively, plenty of evidence of ATSIC's successes existed. Second, although ATSIC may have been implemented as part of what the government of the day called 'a policy of self-determination', the policy in practice wasn't really focused on fostering self-determination in the way the term is used under international law (see the sidebar 'Self-determination and international law').

REMEMBER

ATSIC was in many ways a quite innovative representative body. It sought to accommodate an elected body within a federal government agency. Its strengths included its ability to give a national Indigenous perspective on a range of key issues, from native title to human rights, positions that often challenged the government's own view. It also had an interface with the federal bureaucracy that previous elected bodies didn't have and it had a large budget that allowed it to exert more influence than a body that simply had an advisory role. ATSIC's regional representative structure and the planning processes it engaged in gave it the ability to identify the specific needs of diverse Aboriginal and Torres Strait Islander communities in consultation with the people who lived there.

ATSIC also suffered some problems, however. The legislation that established ATSIC's structure failed to clearly explain how all of the complex relationships within the organisation would work. The relationship between the board and the regional councils wasn't articulated and the relationships between the CEO of ATSIC and the minister, and between the CEO and the chair of ATSIC had little clarity. The legislation also failed to provide ATSIC with an interface with state governments, which have responsibility for so much of the Indigenous portfolio.

SELF-DETERMINATION AND INTERNATIONAL LAW

Self-determination is a complex idea under international law but it has been defined in relation to Indigenous people in the Declaration on the Rights of Indigenous Peoples. Article 3 of the declaration states: 'Indigenous people have the right to self-determination. By virtue of that right they freely determine their political status and freely pursue their economic, social and cultural development'.

Expanding on what the right to self-determination means in practice for Indigenous peoples, Article 4 states: 'Indigenous people, in exercising their right to self-determination, have the right to autonomy or self-government in matters relating to their internal and local affairs, as well as ways and means for financing their autonomous functions'.

(For more information about the Declaration on the Rights of Indigenous Peoples and the development of the idea of self-determination under international law, see Chapter 15.)

ATSIC spent most of its time administering Community Development Employment Projects (CDEP) — a 'work-for-the-dole' scheme — and the Community Housing and Infrastructure Program (CHIP) at the expense of developing policy in other areas (refer to Chapter 13). And some of the key functions the body had been given, such as monitoring the effectiveness of programs for Aboriginal people and Torres Strait Islanders, had been under-resourced.

Perhaps the biggest weakness ATSIC had was the public's perception of it. ATSIC was portrayed as being responsible for every Indigenous issue and for funding every Indigenous program. The fact that it didn't have fiscal responsibility for the areas of health and education, and was only a supplementary funding provider on issues such as domestic violence, languages, heritage protection and housing wasn't widely appreciated. A large percentage of the ATSIC budget was, in fact, quarantined for programs such as CDEP and CHIP. These misconceptions directed attention away from the government departments (federal as well as state and territory) that did have responsibility for Indigenous policy and service delivery.

These public misconceptions were compounded when serious criminal allegations were made against ATSIC board members, including the chair (who was accused of sexual assault, though the criminal charges were never proven) and the deputy chair (who was accused of financial impropriety, again unproven). The presence of ATSIC board members who were subject to continuing allegations and questioning undermined the credibility of the institution — even though the allegations were never proven — and made the institution vulnerable to attack from people who opposed it. ATSIC's position was exacerbated by misinformation about the organisation and its responsibilities, which was prevalent in media and political comment. These attacks not only accused ATSIC of ineptitude in relation to policy-making and program delivery, but also criticised its governance processes.

ATSIC never had responsibility for Indigenous education and for most of its life had no fiscal responsibility for Indigenous health. In other words, a large part of the responsibility for policy development and service delivery remained with federal and state governments. But this didn't stop most of the blame for poor socioeconomic statistics and failure of policies and programs falling at ATSIC's feet. However, the fact that it was never clearly able to articulate its successes gave ammunition to its critics, who claimed that it was a 'failed experiment'.

REMEMBER

When ATSIC was abolished, one of the biggest gaps left by its demise was in the role previously filled by the ATSIC regional councils. These were also elected bodies but, given that they were regionally focused, were well placed to look at particular needs and priorities in their areas. Understandably, they had a stronger relationship with local communities than the national body did. Importantly, they also provided a place where governments could go to consult with and work with local Indigenous communities. When the system was abolished, it was harder for local, state and territory, and federal governments to know who they should talk to when they wanted to do business with local Indigenous communities.

After ATSIC

With the abolition of ATSIC in 2004, the responsibility for programs formerly managed by ATSIC and then ATSIS (Aboriginal and Torres Strait Islander Services, an agency set up in 2003 to administer ATSIC programs) was transferred to mainstream Commonwealth departments and agencies.

The Office of Indigenous Policy Coordination (OIPC) was created in 2004 within the Department of Immigration and Multicultural and Indigenous Affairs to coordinate services and programs, and take over the responsibilities of ATSIS. A network of 22 Indigenous coordination centres (ICCs), coordinated by the OIPC and staffed by government agencies, replaced existing ATSIC–ATSIS offices. The fundamental impact of this move was to mainstream Indigenous policy-making and service delivery, contrary to the stated intent at the time ATSIS was set up (refer to Chapter 13).

Ironically, the decision to abolish the national and regional representative bodies coincided with a new approach to Indigenous affairs by the government, which sought to negotiate more with Indigenous communities. (See the section 'Shared Responsibility and Mutual Obligation' later in this chapter.)

REMEMBER

ATSIC had been able to attract a large number of Indigenous people into its workforce. Understandably, Indigenous people were interested in working for an organisation that was focused on the needs of Indigenous people. At its peak, Indigenous people made up 48 per cent of its workforce. When ATSIC was abolished, many Indigenous employees left the public service to work in other areas. Today, Indigenous people make up only 2 per cent of the federal public service. This loss of employees has been noted as symbolising a loss of corporate knowledge from within the federal bureaucracy.

The issue of representation remains on the national agenda. A key plank in the Uluru Statement from the Heart is a voice to parliament. For more on the Uluru Statement, see Chapter 15.

A new administration

The changes to the administrative arrangements required in order to abolish ATSIC were driven by two ideologies:

>> The elimination of Indigenous representation from effective participation in government policy and program delivery

>> The transfer of Indigenous-specific programs to mainstream agencies

The strength of the new administrative arrangements, it was argued, was its attempt to better coordinate agencies that have responsibility for service provision to and policy development for Indigenous communities. However, several major problems with the new administrative arrangements were immediately identified:

>> Changes to the administration of Indigenous affairs at the national level were done swiftly, without vision, planning or consultation. The development of the new regime was ad hoc, reactionary and without solid evidentiary foundation. No evidence existed that the assumptions underpinning the new arrangements were workable.

>> The removal of regional councils took away a key level of representative Indigenous governance.

>> The new arrangements focused more on service delivery than policy development.

>> Little consultation was conducted with Indigenous peoples about the new arrangements.

>> The transfer of staff from ATSIS to other agencies resulted in a loss of corporate knowledge that wouldn't be replaced. The public service lost most of its senior Indigenous bureaucrats as part of the transfer. The five senior staff at the Office of Indigenous Policy Coordination were non-Indigenous.

The National Indigenous Council

The government established the National Indigenous Council to replace the elected arm of ATSIC. It operated from November 2004 to December 2007. The government made clear when it set up the Council that it wasn't a replacement for ATSIC and it wasn't a representative body. Council members were appointed by the federal government.

ELECTED VERSUS APPOINTED BODIES

The replacement of ATSIC with an appointed body raised several issues about the principles of representation. Appointed bodies are nothing new in the Indigenous arena; most Indigenous bodies have them, including the Indigenous Land Corporation (ILC), Indigenous Business Australia (IBA) and Aboriginal Hostels.

The replacement of elected representatives at the national level by a group of hand-picked appointees fundamentally changed the nature of the advice given. The appointed positions didn't have the legitimacy of being able to put forward views on behalf of Indigenous peoples and weren't accountable to them in the way that the elected representatives were. Appointed representatives have no responsibility to represent broader Indigenous interests. They are appointed as individuals, often with specific expertise, and act in that capacity.

The new body was advisory only. It had no capacity to ensure that its advice was followed. In particular, the appointed body had no leverage with the bureaucracy. It was abolished when the Rudd government was elected.

The new body was tasked with providing advice on Indigenous affairs to the government. It consisted of 14 appointed members and was chaired by Sue Gordon, an Aboriginal magistrate from Western Australia. Members included former ALP president Warren Mundine, consultant Wesley Aird, investment banker Joe Proctor, educator Mary Ann Bin-Sallik, Australian Rules footballer Adam Goodes, rugby league footballer Dean Widders and lawyer Tammy Williams. Gordon, Mundine and Aird were strong supporters of the Northern Territory intervention when it was rolled out by the government, and had given evidence to support it at the Senate inquiry before the legislation came into effect. (See the section 'Emergency! Emergency! The Northern Territory Intervention' later in this chapter.) Although the federal government claimed this new body wasn't designed to replace ATSIC, it became the primary Indigenous advisory body to the government.

Shared Responsibility and Mutual Obligation

The concepts of *shared responsibility* and *mutual obligation* started entering the political conversation around Indigenous policy in 2004. Indigenous leader Noel Pearson (see the sidebar 'Noel Pearson: A strong advocate') advocated the need for Indigenous people to share responsibility with government for fixing problems in Indigenous communities, arguing that each side had a mutual obligation.

The federal government claimed it was adopting Pearson's ideas when it developed a new way of doing business with Indigenous communities — *Shared Responsibility Agreements*, based around the concept that, to receive services, individuals and communities had to agree to certain behavioural standards. Pearson himself had never advocated for formal agreements of this type but the National Indigenous Council had endorsed their use.

The implementation of these policy concepts was through an agreement process, to be negotiated between Indigenous communities and governments, that linked the provision of services with behavioural reforms.

From the start, the agreements encountered problems. The recent abolition of ATSIC created difficulties for governments in identifying who they should negotiate with. People asked why Indigenous communities had to sign up to these agreements to receive services that other Australians received without any such agreement. And concern was expressed about the wisdom of linking essential services to behavioural change.

WASH YOUR HANDS!

One of the most famous examples of a Shared Responsibility Agreement was signed with the community of Mulan in the Kimberley region of Western Australia. The agreement stated that the government would provide a petrol bowser to the community in exchange for an undertaking that the people would wash children's faces and hands. Why these two things were linked was queried. The agreement was also questioned when, a year after signing the agreement, the government hadn't delivered the bowsers.

In fact, a successful hygiene program had already been started and implemented by the community — without any government incentive. The government had simply linked the provision of the bowsers to the Shared Responsibility Agreement so it would look as if the agreement had been successful in improving the community's behaviour.

Critics claimed this was unfair to the community, which had tackled the issue of hygiene itself, but was then portrayed as needing an incentive to undertake simple hygiene measures.

Eventually, the federal government quietly moved away from Shared Responsibility Agreements as a key aspect of its policy approach. A Commonwealth Grants Commission report in 2001 summed up the problems with mainstreaming as an approach to Indigenous service delivery and policy-making. These problems included evidence that

>> Indigenous people access mainstream services at much lower rates than non-Indigenous people do.

>> People living in remote areas have problems accessing mainstream services.

>> Indigenous people encounter many barriers when accessing government services, including the design of programs, their funding, the way they are presented to the public and the cost to the public of using them.

The report concluded that 'mainstream services do not meet the needs of Indigenous people to the same extent that they meet the needs of non-Indigenous people'.

Emergency! Emergency! The Northern Territory Intervention

In August 2006, the Northern Territory government commissioned an investigation into allegations of serious sexual abuse of Aboriginal children. On 15 June 2007, the report, *Little Children are Sacred*, was delivered to the government. The report had found that abuse and neglect were widespread, and also identified a range of factors as the underlying causes of disadvantage.

Less than two weeks later, on 23 June 2007, the Howard federal government announced that, prompted by the failure of the Northern Territory government to have acted earlier to prevent this crisis, it would intervene. The cluster of policies it adopted was called the Northern Territory Emergency Response (NTER), though the program itself continues to be known as *the intervention*.

REMEMBER

The *Little Children are Sacred* report, which was the catalyst for the Northern Territory intervention, had found that a majority of the people who abused Aboriginal children were non-Indigenous. It also said, as its first recommendation, that solutions to the issues facing Indigenous people, such as sexual abuse of children, violence against women and poverty, need to be addressed in partnership with Indigenous people and their communities.

The NTER was designed in a 48-hour period by bureaucrats in Canberra. The legislation — over 600 pages of it — came before the federal parliament with only a day-long inquiry and was passed by both the coalition government and the Labor opposition.

Key aspects of the Northern Territory Emergency Response

The Northern Territory Emergency Response identified 73 Aboriginal communities — they became known as 'prescribed areas' — in the Northern Territory that were to be subject to the intervention.

Key elements of this intervention included

>> The removal of the permit system that allowed Aboriginal people to control who came onto their lands

>> The abolition of the CDEP scheme, moving people who had been employed under the scheme onto welfare payments

>> The quarantining of 50 per cent of all welfare payments received by people living in the prescribed areas

>> The suspension of the operation of the Racial Discrimination Act, the anti-discrimination legislation in the Northern Territory and the right of appeals to the Social Security Appeals Tribunal

>> The requirement that Aboriginal-controlled land be leased back to the government in order to obtain basic services such as housing

>> The power to compulsorily acquire Aboriginal land and property

>> Mandatory health checks for Aboriginal children

>> The allocation of more police in Aboriginal communities

>> The appointment of government business managers to prescribed areas

>> Alcohol bans and restrictions in remote communities

>> A ban on pornography in Aboriginal communities

Objection!

Many Indigenous people objected to the Northern Territory Emergency Response, expressing concerns that the measures being imposed wouldn't address the underlying causes of disadvantage or stop child abuse and neglect. The top-down approach taken by the government in Canberra also caused concern that expertise on the ground about what worked in the Northern Territory was being overlooked. More specifically, concern was expressed about almost all of the key aspects of the intervention.

Removal of the permit system

The permit system, where visitors had to acquire a permit from the relevant land council or from the specific community, allowed Aboriginal people to control who came onto their lands. The Northern Territory police expressed concern that abolishing the permit system would mean more people could come and go from Aboriginal communities without monitoring.

Abolition of CDEP

Abolishing the CDEP scheme — a 'work-for-the-dole' program — meant that many services, from garbage collection to the provision of teachers' aides, and other projects such as community gardens were abandoned. According to the employment minister at the time, Joe Hockey, the government's intention in dismantling the scheme was to move people off welfare and into 'real' employment. However, pushing people who were employed by CDEP schemes onto welfare payments created concern over increasing welfare dependence.

HANDING OVER THE LAND IN ALICE SPRINGS

The Tangentyere Council, which supports the town camp communities in and around Alice Springs, initially rejected a Labor federal government proposal to spend $125 million on upgrades and repairs to its houses and community infrastructure in exchange for a 40-year lease to the government over its land. (Labor won government in 2007 and continued the intervention, with some amendments to the original legislation — see Chapter 15 for more on this.)

The Council opposed the agreement on the basis that non-Indigenous social housing providers aren't required to give the government a lease over their stock in order to get money for new houses or for infrastructure repairs. The Council also said it didn't trust the government to deliver housing maintenance to the community more efficiently than the Council did.

When federal minister Jenny Macklin said she would use the power to compulsorily acquire the land with a lease, the Council gave in on the basis that it was better to have an imposed lease of 40 years than to risk losing its land altogether, even though it would have preferred not to enter the lease at all.

Quarantining of welfare payments

The quarantined welfare payments were administered on a 'BasicsCard' that could only be used at certain shops.

REMEMBER

When income quarantining was introduced, it had several problems. Some cards didn't work, so people were left without food. People couldn't tell how much was left on their card and often found themselves lining up for groceries they couldn't afford and being forced to put some back. Stores started separate queues for people on the BasicsCard, causing people to complain that they were being segregated and stigmatised. People on the cards couldn't travel interstate because their cards wouldn't work there. The card system was difficult, and administratively time-consuming and complicated.

Denial of complaints mechanisms

The suspension of the Racial Discrimination Act, anti-discrimination legislation and the right to address the Social Security Appeals Tribunal meant no mechanism was available for people who were on quarantined welfare payments to complain that their payments were administered wrongly or unfairly. The government could, therefore, not adequately review the impacts of this aggressive new policy.

Land lease-backs

The requirement that Aboriginal-controlled land be leased back to the government in order to obtain basic services such as housing was a condition that didn't apply to non-Indigenous social housing, making the requirement racially discriminatory.

Compulsory acquisition of land and property

The power to compulsorily acquire Aboriginal land and property meant that Indigenous communities had no bargaining power about the conditions being imposed on them. Some leases included conditions that would put the land under the control of the government. If they resisted signing those leases, the land was taken forcibly from them with a compulsory lease.

Mandatory health checks

The mandatory health checks given to Aboriginal children were administered by fly-in, fly-out doctors. Aboriginal medical services in the Northern Territory pointed out that they screened more children than the fly-in, fly-out services because they'd built a relationship with local Aboriginal families. Another observation was that those children who were at greatest risk (the ones the intervention was aimed at helping) weren't being taken to see the fly-in, fly-out doctors.

Increased police presence

Many communities welcomed the increased police presence because it was something they'd been asking about for a long time. However, the increase in police led to an increase in the arrest and conviction rates for driving offences. The Australian Federal Police began concluding, in the first six months of the intervention, that no organised paedophile rings were operating in Aboriginal communities in the Northern Territory.

REMEMBER

More than a decade on from the introduction of the NTER, assessing the effectiveness of the policies has been possible. Studies have shown school attendance rates didn't rise, youth suicides increased, and the number of Indigenous people incarcerated has risen. For more information on the policy failure of the NTER, see Chapter 15.

Government administrators

The appointment of government business managers was seen as a return to the days of the mission managers, and communities were suspicious. These managers were usually from outside of the community and struggled to build relationships with the communities. Adding to the tension, some of the only infrastructure that flowed into communities as a result of the NTER was the building of the general business managers' houses.

Alcohol restrictions

The imposition of alcohol bans was a complex matter. Many Aboriginal communities in the prescribed areas were already dry communities because that's what they wanted. Alcohol bans were seen as being problematic when imposed on a community and concern — and evidence — existed that the bans did nothing to alleviate alcohol consumption but simply moved drinkers from one place to another.

BROKEN PROMISES

The community of Ampilatwatja, north of Alice Springs, was a prescribed area. The people had signed their community-controlled land over to the government with the promise of new housing, but no new houses were built and the old ones weren't repaired. The infrastructure became so poor that sewage started to run through the town.

In protest, many of the Aboriginal community members walked out of the town and set up another camp just outside the boundary of the prescribed area. They also, with the help of several trade unions, built a house on their new site to show they could build one faster than the government could.

Achieving child protection

Critics also pointed out that, for a national emergency targeted at the protection of children, seeing how some of the measures would achieve that goal was difficult and that the words 'child' or 'children' didn't appear once in the legislation.

TECHNICAL STUFF

Northern Territory creep was a phrase used to describe Aboriginal people who moved from their smaller communities when they fell under the control of the intervention to larger centres and cities such as Mount Isa, Alice Springs and Darwin, driving up the number of homeless people.

ARGUMENTS FOR AND AGAINST THE INTERVENTION

The value of the intervention continues to be hotly debated by Indigenous and non-Indigenous people alike. Here are some of the arguments, for and against:

Key arguments for the intervention

- 'The state of Aboriginal communities is a national emergency that needs to be addressed.'

- 'Governments have failed and they need to act.'

- 'At least they're finally doing something.'

Key arguments against the intervention

- 'The measures don't address the underlying causes of disadvantage.'

- 'Change will only come if you work with communities, not impose measures from the top down.'

- 'Some of the measures are experimental, with no evidence they'll work.'

Chapter **15**

From Apology to Uluru

The federal election of November 2007, when John Howard's Liberal government was voted out and Kevin Rudd's Labor government was voted in, signalled an end to an era in which progress on reconciliation had stalled. Rudd said that, on election, he would acknowledge the Stolen Generations and deliver the apology that Howard didn't think was necessary. Rudd's government also undertook another important symbolic gesture — it would endorse the Declaration on the Rights of Indigenous Peoples, an international human rights instrument that set a benchmark for the protection of Indigenous rights.

In this chapter, I examine these positive steps but also look into the way the Rudd government continued with many aspects of the Northern Territory Emergency Response, even when reviews recommended that some of these policies be modified. When Julia Gillard took over as leader of the Labor government in 2010, very little changed. With few human rights benchmarks within Australia, international instruments such as the Declaration on the Rights of Indigenous People must provide a guide to appropriate human rights standards.

The ongoing policy environment hasn't meant that Indigenous people aren't still focused on big-picture issues such as a treaty, a new representative body or constitutional reform. This chapter looks at how Indigenous people are facing these issues into the future.

A New Government — A New Era?

Prime Minister John Howard's firm belief that an apology to the Stolen Generations was unnecessary (refer to Chapter 9) became a symbol for his views on Indigenous peoples and their rights, as well as an example of his beliefs about Australian history and reconciliation.

When Kevin Rudd became prime minister, he was quick to show that he had a different view about the importance of symbolic gestures such as an apology. Not only did he deliver a national apology, but his government also endorsed the Declaration on the Rights of Indigenous People.

The apology

Kevin Rudd had said he would deliver the long-awaited apology to the Stolen Generations on the first sitting day of the new parliament. And he was true to his word. On 13 February 2008, Rudd tabled an apology to Indigenous people, particularly the Stolen Generations and their families. The apology was broadcast across Australia and played in public spaces such as Martin Place in Sydney and Federation Square in Melbourne. Interestingly, some polls showed that, before the apology, a third to a half of Australians supported the idea. After the apology was delivered, polls showed that two-thirds of Australians thought it had been a good thing for the country. For more information about the call for a national apology, refer to Chapter 9.

REMEMBER

When the apology was delivered to the Stolen Generations, the federal government made clear that it wouldn't broach the issue of compensation for those people who were removed from their families and suffered harm while under the care of the state.

REMEMBER

In 2009, Prime Minister Rudd, launching a book by author Thomas Keneally, said that he thought it was time that Australia moved on from the 'history wars' (refer to Chapter 14). He said that we should celebrate 'reformers, renegades and revolutionaries, thus neglecting or even deriding the great stories of our explorers, of our pioneers and of our entrepreneurs'. He believed that we should also no longer refuse to confront hard truths about our history as if all our forebears were without blemish. He said, 'In a liberal democratic society, we can agree that events happened while we agree to differ in how we interpret them'. The issue of whether Indigenous children had been 'stolen' and whether they were removed 'for their own good' were issues that were argued over as part of these history wars.

CULTURAL PROTOCOLS

The anniversary of the National Apology is often acknowledged as 13 February. National Sorry Day or the National Day of Healing is 26 May, and this is a day to remember and reflect on the past injustices as a part of the on-going process of reconciliation. This day was first observed in 1998, a year after the *Bringing them Home* report was tabled in Parliament.

The Declaration on the Rights of Indigenous Peoples

The Declaration on the Rights of Indigenous Peoples was adopted by the United Nations General Assembly on 13 September 2007. Australia was one of four countries that voted against its adoption. That position changed when the Rudd government endorsed the declaration on 3 April 2009. However, the government gave no indication as to *how* it would implement the principles contained within the document.

The declaration is the most comprehensive statement of the rights of Indigenous peoples ever developed, giving prominence to collective rights to a degree unprecedented in international human rights law. The adoption of this instrument is the clearest indication yet that the international community is committing itself to protecting the individual and collective rights of Indigenous peoples.

REMEMBER

The four countries that voted against the Declaration on the Rights of Indigenous People in the General Assembly of the United Nations in 2007 were Australia, Canada, New Zealand and the United States. Because these countries didn't sign the declaration on that day, they can't become signatories. They can, as Australia has done, endorse the declaration.

Some of the central principles contained in the declaration concern non-discrimination and fundamental rights, self-determination (including autonomy and participation rights), cultural integrity, rights to lands, territories and natural resources, and other rights relating to socioeconomic welfare. Applying these principles, however, is not always straightforward.

Self-determination

One of the key principles in the declaration, for which Indigenous peoples consistently fought, is Article 3, which deals with the collective right to self-determination. Self-determination is found in both of the major international human rights covenants — the International Covenant on Civil and Political Rights and the International Covenant on Economic, Social and Cultural Rights — and the declaration mirrors their language. Article 3 of the declaration adopts this language and applies it specifically to Indigenous peoples.

The difference between a *covenant* and a *declaration* under international law is that covenants are said to create standards that are binding on signatories. Declarations are considered to be aspirational documents only.

Substantial disagreement exists at the international level over what self-determination requires in any particular context, and especially over how the right to self-determination interacts with another fundamental principle, state sovereignty, as expressed through the protection of a state's territorial integrity and its political unity.

Article 46(1) now provides that nothing in the declaration may be 'construed as authorizing or encouraging any action which would dismember or impair, totally or in part, the territorial integrity or political unity of sovereign and independent States'. On one hand, the declaration as adopted by the General Assembly imposes constraints on self-determination; on the other, it simply replicates existing tensions in international law, leaving potential conflicts between the principle of self-determination and that of state sovereignty to be addressed on a case-by-case basis. Just how Article 46 will interact with the main provisions on lands and resources (Article 26) and on existing treaty rights (Article 37), which were left untouched, remains to be seen.

In a nutshell, the difficulty of this aspect of the declaration is that, although it recognises the right to self-determination, this right can't override the rights of a state or sovereign nation.

Autonomy

Article 4 states that Indigenous peoples have 'the right to autonomy or self-government in matters relating to their internal and local affairs, as well as ways and means for financing their autonomous functions'. Although Indigenous peoples 'have the right to maintain and strengthen their distinct political, legal, economic, social and cultural institutions', they also retain 'their right to participate fully, if they so choose, in the political, economic, social and cultural life of the State'.

With respect to participation, Indigenous peoples have the right to participate in decision-making in matters that would affect their rights, through their chosen representatives (Article 18). More specifically, law-makers and policy-makers are required to consult, in good faith, with Indigenous peoples with the aim of obtaining their 'free, prior and informed consent before adopting and implementing legislative or administrative measures that may affect them' (Article 19). In particular, Indigenous peoples are entitled to be 'actively involved in developing and determining health, housing and other economic and social programmes affecting them and, as far as possible, to administer such programmes through their own institutions' (Article 23). According to Article 33(2), Indigenous peoples are entitled to 'determine the structures and to select the membership of their institutions in accordance with their own procedures'.

The combined effect of these principles of autonomy is that

>> Governments must consult with Indigenous people on policies, laws and programs that affect them, and obtain consent before implementing them.

>> Indigenous people should be actively involved in developing programs that affect them and should, if possible, administer those programs through their own institutions and representatives.

>> The structure and membership of Indigenous institutions should be decided by Indigenous people.

>> Indigenous people should have access to ways of financing these autonomous functions.

>> Indigenous people should retain their right to participate in mainstream political, economic and cultural institutions.

Fundamental rights and principles

The rights recognised in the declaration are intended to constitute a minimum standard for the 'survival, dignity and well-being' of Indigenous peoples (Article 43). Further, nothing in the declaration may be construed as diminishing the rights Indigenous peoples already have now or may acquire in the future (Article 45). Article 46 provides that the declaration must be read in accordance with the principles of justice, democracy, respect for human rights, equality and non-discrimination, as well as the principles contained in the UN Charter. However, any limitations placed on the exercise of declaration rights as a result must be 'strictly necessary' for securing respect for the rights and freedoms of others and for meeting the 'most compelling requirements of a democratic society'.

States are required, in consultation with Indigenous peoples, to take appropriate measures (including national legislation) to achieve the goals of the declaration, and to provide Indigenous peoples with access to financial and technical assistance for the enjoyment of the rights contained in it (Articles 38 to 39).

REMEMBER

Basically, these principles outline the recognition that the declaration intends to provide for fundamental rights and principles, which can only be limited by the situation where the rights themselves contravene the rights of others. Further, they require governments to ensure that Indigenous people have access to financial and technical assistance to carry out the functions outlined in the declaration.

Controlling Lives: The Intervention Continues

The Rudd government was very different from the Howard government in the way it embraced symbolic gestures such as the apology and the endorsement of the Declaration on the Rights of Indigenous People. On the ground, however, many policies remained the same, even though the government changed.

The Howard government's policies that surrounded the Northern Territory Emergency Response (the intervention) are a particular case in point. Key policies implemented as part of the intervention that the new government favoured were income management, where 50 per cent of welfare payments to Indigenous people were quarantined, and the requirement that Indigenous people lease their land back to the government before they could access housing and infrastructure funding. Refer to Chapter 14 for detail on these and other aspects of the intervention.

REMEMBER

The Northern Territory Emergency Response was introduced in the lead-up to the 2007 election. The Howard government had no time to evaluate the effectiveness of the intervention before it was voted out. The incoming Rudd government promised a review and, when that was finally undertaken, it recommended changes to the key policies of the intervention and expressed concerns about its impact on the lives of the Indigenous people affected by it. It implemented the Stronger Futures legislation in 2013 and, while claiming that it repealed the NTER in full, that is not correct. While it did reinstate the operation of the Racial Discrimination Act, it kept in place the controversial aspects of welfare reform that quarantined income and linked school attendance with welfare payments.

Evaluating the Northern Territory intervention

One of the key purposes of the intervention was to respond to the *Little Children are Sacred* report, which found widespread child sexual abuse, neglect and a range of factors underlying disadvantage within Northern Territory communities. Less than two weeks after the tabling of the report, in June 2007, the Howard government announced the intervention. Six months after its implementation, no new charges had been laid for child sexual abuse, no new community-based programs had been established and the administration of the BasicsCard, which underpins the policy of income management, had cost $88 million.

A year after the Rudd government came to power, it commissioned the Northern Territory Emergency Response Review. Chaired by former Kimberley Land Council chairman Peter Yu, the review committee delivered its findings and recommendations on 13 October 2008. Principal among its recommendations was that the policy of compulsory income management be abandoned. It said that a place for targeted income management existed but it shouldn't be applied to people in a blanket way and it shouldn't be restricted to the Indigenous community. The review concluded that many Indigenous people had found the policies 'punitive, coercive and racist'. Despite the recommendations of the review, the government decided to keep the intervention policies unchanged.

The federal government said it supported most of the recommendations of the review, including better resourcing of legal services, additional policing, and additional resources for education and child protection. It didn't agree to abolish compulsory income management. It did, however, agree that management should be subject to external review.

REMEMBER

Two years after the Northern Territory Emergency Response had been introduced, anaemia rates in children were up, malnutrition rates in the Indigenous community had risen, Indigenous community-owned housing was transferred to the Northern Territory and rents had gone up. At the same time, complaints that houses weren't being maintained were widespread, the number of Indigenous people being charged with driving offences increased, school attendance rates for Indigenous children were slightly lower, no houses had been built under the $600 million housing program (though some were built later), violent offences were up, substance abuse had increased and suicide rates had increased. The coalition, now in opposition, asserted that the intervention was failing because the current government hadn't implemented it properly and should have made the measures tougher.

Ten years after the NTER, its impact was assessed further by Dr Paddy Gibson. He found the following:

>> Rates of Aboriginal children being removed from their families had increased.

>> School attendance rates had not improved.

>> Suicide and self-harm had increased.

>> Houses were still overcrowded.

>> Income quarantining made life harder for families and was discriminatory.

>> Unemployment had increased.

>> Rates of family violence had not increased.

>> The number of Aboriginal people in custody had increased significantly.

In 2016, a Royal Commission into the Protection and Detention of Children in the Northern Territory was held after images of children being abused in the Don Dale Youth Detention Centre became public. It delivered its report in 2017 and made several findings including that youth detention centres were not fit for accommodating, let alone rehabilitating, children and young people. It confirmed children were subject to verbal abuse, physical control and humiliation. A large number of children in juvenile detention were in out-of-home care and the Royal Commission also found that the Northern Territory Government failed to comply with the statutory requirements that all children in out-of-home care have care plans.

International criticism

In August 2010, a report of the Committee on the Elimination of Racial Discrimination raised concerns about Australia's policies regarding Indigenous people. While acknowledging the apology, the signing of the Declaration on the Rights of Indigenous People and the commitment to 'closing the gap' (a reference to the wide difference in many socioeconomic, health and educational factors between Indigenous people and mainstream Australia), it also noted that these were only first steps towards genuine reconciliation and reparation. Its main criticisms were focused on the Northern Territory Emergency Response. Compulsory income management was seen as discriminatory and ineffective. Compulsory leasing back of land was also targeted. And the committee raised concerns about the over-representation of Indigenous people in the criminal justice system.

In September that year, the United Nations Human Rights Committee issued a report that identified aspects of the Northern Territory Emergency Response, particularly mandatory income management and compulsory leasing, as policies that breached Australia's obligations under international human rights instruments. That same year, the Special Rapporteur on the rights of indigenous peoples, S James Anaya, visited Australia. After visiting the Northern Territory and other parts of Australia, he made similar observations about the negative impact of the measures in the Northern Territory and recommended that the government remove the 'overtly' racially discriminatory aspects of the intervention. He said that proof that some aspects of the intervention were working — grog bans and pornography bans — was 'ambiguous at best', whereas the hardship being caused by compulsory income management was clearly evident.

As a response to the criticism from international human rights monitoring, the Rudd government announced it would make sure that the policies were compliant with the principles of the Racial Discrimination Act. The government changed the policy of income management so it could be applied in non-Indigenous communities — making it no longer racially discriminatory. However, the majority of people who were subjected to this arrangement were Indigenous. Other aspects of the policy approach — such as compulsory leasing — were argued to be 'special measures' and, therefore, exceptions to the Racial Discrimination Act. Indigenous people subjected to the policies pointed out that, despite the government's claims, the change was only technical and the way that these policies are applied to them hadn't changed. Others have pointed out that the spirit of the Racial Discrimination Act, which is supposed to prevent people from being subjected to racial discrimination, has not been respected.

REMEMBER

Although policies such as compulsory income management were part of the Northern Territory Emergency Response, they were rolled out into other Indigenous communities around Australia. The arrangement now can apply to both black and white Australians but still the majority of people subject to the policy are Indigenous. Similarly, the requirement that land be leased back before housing money could be accessed was also rolled out into Indigenous communities around the country.

Finding a National Voice

A new national representative body — the National Congress of Australia's First Peoples — was announced in November 2009, supported by the Rudd and Gillard governments. This body was the first nationally elected representative body for Indigenous people since the demise of ATSIC (the Aboriginal and Torres Strait Islander Commission) in 2004. Refer to Chapters 13 and 14 for more on ATSIC. However, it would go on to suffer a similar fate.

In 2017, after a series of processes discussing constitutional recognition, the Uluru Statement from the Heart was delivered and set a pathway forward for Voice, Truth and Treaty.

Finally, while breaches of human rights and few internal protections of the rights of Indigenous people (refer to preceding section) continue, international human rights benchmarks still play an active role in the debates around whether current policy approaches in Indigenous affairs are equitable, effective and fair.

Another representative body

When the Rudd government was elected in 2007, it had a policy to establish a new representative body for Indigenous people. In December that year, the terms of the appointees to the National Indigenous Council, which had effectively replaced ATSIC, came to an end and new Minister for Indigenous Affairs Jenny Macklin didn't renew their appointments.

The Rudd government indicated that the new body wouldn't be another ATSIC and it would, at the first opportunity, consult with Aboriginal people and Torres Strait Islanders about what such a body should look like. The government was lucky that Aboriginal people and Torres Strait Islanders had already done quite a bit of work on what they would like a new representative body to look like.

REMEMBER

After ATSIC was abolished in 2004, a large national meeting was held in Adelaide to begin an informal consultation process among Aboriginal peoples and Torres Strait Islanders about the kind of replacement body they wanted. Eventually, the Australian Human Rights Commission, through its Social Justice Commissioner, took over this process, leading to the recommendation of the establishment of the National Congress of Australia's First Peoples. Throughout the consultation process for the new representative body, two factors seemed of particular importance in building a new body. First, that, unlike ATSIC, which was focused on service delivery, the new organisation should have the primary roles of developing policies and monitoring government performance. Second, that the new representative body should be independent of government so that, unlike ATSIC, it couldn't be abolished by the government at a whim.

Not surprisingly, a new model emerged that included a process of electing representatives. It developed an ethics council as a mechanism to monitor behaviour and manage conflicts of interest. Of the 120 delegates that would make up the National Congress of Australia's First Peoples, half had to be women. Representatives would be elected through three chambers, 40 coming from each — national Aboriginal and Torres Strait Islander peak bodies and organisations, all other Aboriginal and Torres Strait Islander organisations, and all Aboriginal people and Torres Strait Islanders 18 years and over.

The National Congress of Australia's First Peoples was founded in 2010 and had its first elections in 2011. The new body was established as a company — but one that was reliant on ongoing federal government funding.

REMEMBER

The original model put forward proposed that the Congress be given a large one-off grant that would then allow it to operate on the interest earned by that money, limiting its reliance on government resources. This aspect of the model wasn't followed and it remained reliant on government funding. That ended in 2019 and the national representative body went into voluntary administration and closed.

Constitutional change

The 2010 election saw the issue of constitutional recognition put back on the table, and it was considered in a number of different ways, including the following:

- **An Expert Panel:** An Expert Panel on Constitutional Recognition of Indigenous Australians was established in 2011. It recommended that section 25 (which gives state governments the power to pass legislation to prevent certain people, on the basis of their race, from voting) and section 51 (xxvi) (the 'races power') be repealed. The panel instead proposed a new provision that would recognise Aboriginal and Torres Strait Islander peoples and give the federal government the power to make laws for Indigenous people consistent with that recognition. It also recommended insertion of a provision that prohibited racial discrimination and a provision that recognised Indigenous languages. To make these changes, the panel recommended a single referendum question and that the referendum only proceed when it had the support of all major political parties and a majority of state governments. It also recommended the funding of a public information campaign.

- **A Joint Select Committee:** The Joint Select Committee on Constitutional Recognition of Aboriginal and Torres Strait Islander Peoples was established in federal parliament in 2013, with its report handed down in 2015. This report recommended that a referendum on constitutional recognition be held when it has the highest chance of success. It also recommended the repeal of sections 25 and 51 (xxvi), and that a new section retain the ability for the federal government to make laws for the benefit of Aboriginal and Torres Strait Islander peoples and recognise Aboriginal and Torres Strait Islander peoples in the constitution. It also recommended a prohibition on racial discrimination.

- **Recognise:** A new movement to facilitate constitutional change that would include Aboriginal and Torres Strait Islander peoples in the constitution found momentum from 2012, when the Recognise campaign was launched. Auspiced by Reconciliation Australia, the campaign ran to 2017, and focused on gaining acceptance for the general proposition that Aboriginal and Torres Strait Islander peoples should be included in the constitution, though it didn't put forward a specific model. During that time, a poll conducted by the ABC showed that 72 per cent of Australians surveyed supported a change that recognised Indigenous people and their culture.

- **A Referendum Council:** Building on the work of the Expert Panel and the Joint Select Committee, the Referendum Council was established in 2015, and delivered its report in 2017. The Council recommended a referendum to include a representative body in the Constitution that gives Aboriginal and Torres Strait Islanders a voice to the Commonwealth Parliament. This would also recognise Aboriginal and Torres Strait Islander peoples as Australia's first peoples. It also recommended a Declaration of Recognition be enacted by legislation and passed by all Australian Parliaments.

The Joint Select Committee on Constitutional Recognition of Aboriginal and Torres Strait Islander Peoples delivered a further report in 2018 that provided several recommendations about an Indigenous voice to parliament, including suggesting further considerations about its form and constitutional recognition.

TECHNICAL STUFF

A question of whether to insert a preamble into the Constitution was put to the Australian people in 1999. The proposed preamble included phrases such as 'honouring Aborigines and Torres Strait Islanders, the nation's first people, for their deep kinship with their lands and for their ancient and continuing cultures which enrich the life of our country' along with 'recognising the nation-building contribution of generations of immigrants'. However, 39.34 per cent of Australians voted yes to the change, with 60.66 per cent voting no.

REMEMBER

The preamble to the South African Constitution includes phrases such as, 'We, the people of South Africa, recognize the injustices of our past; honour those who suffered for justice and freedom in our land'. It also talks about healing the 'divisions of the past' and establishing 'a society based on democratic values, social justice and fundamental human rights'. Section 35 of the *Canadian Constitution Act 1982* provides for constitutional protection of 'aboriginal and treaty rights'.

The aspiration for constitutional change remains on the agenda; however, focus moved from constitutional recognition to the Uluru Statement from the Heart when it was released in 2017. This Statement calls for a 'voice to parliament' to be enshrined in the Constitution as a priority.

The Uluru Statement

In 2017, a meeting of 250 Aboriginal and Torres Strait Islanders met and released a 'statement from the heart' that, among other things, set a roadmap forward that includes

>> A First Nations Voice enshrined in the Constitution

>> A Makarrata Commission to supervise a process of agreement making and truth telling about Australia's history

The Statement reads:

We, gathered at the 2017 National Constitutional Convention, coming from all points of the southern sky, make this statement from the heart: Our Aboriginal and Torres Strait Islander tribes were the first sovereign Nations of the Australian continent and its adjacent islands, and possessed it under our own laws and customs. This our ancestors did, according to the reckoning of our culture, from the Creation, according to the common law from 'time immemorial', and according to science more than 60,000 years ago.

This sovereignty is a spiritual notion: the ancestral tie between the land, or 'mother nature', and the Aboriginal and Torres Strait Islander peoples who were born therefrom, remain attached thereto, and must one day return thither to be united with our ancestors. This link is the basis of the ownership of the soil, or better, of sovereignty. It has never been ceded or extinguished, and co-exists with the sovereignty of the Crown.

How could it be otherwise? That peoples possessed a land for sixty millennia and this sacred link disappears from world history in merely the last two hundred years?

With substantive constitutional change and structural reform, we believe this ancient sovereignty can shine through as a fuller expression of Australia's nationhood.

Proportionally, we are the most incarcerated people on the planet. We are not an innately criminal people. Our children are aliened from their families at unprecedented rates. This cannot be because we have no love for them. And our youth languish in detention in obscene numbers. They should be our hope for the future.

These dimensions of our crisis tell plainly the structural nature of our problem. This is the torment of our powerlessness.

We seek constitutional reforms to empower our people and take a rightful place in our own country. When we have power over our destiny our children will flourish. They will walk in two worlds and their culture will be a gift to their country.

We call for the establishment of a First Nations Voice enshrined in the Constitution.

Makarrata is the culmination of our agenda: the coming together after a struggle. It captures our aspirations for a fair and truthful relationship with the people of Australia and a better future for our children based on justice and self-determination.

We seek a Makarrata Commission to supervise a process of agreement-making between governments and First Nations and truth-telling about our history.

In 1967 we were counted, in 2017 we seek to be heard. We leave base camp and start our trek across this vast country. We invite you to walk with us in a movement of the Australian people for a better future.

In short: Voice, Treaty, Truth.

REMEMBER

The Uluru Statement from the Heart pulls together several strands of the long-standing Indigenous reform agenda: a representative voice (refer to Chapter 14), constitutional recognition (refer to Chapter 11), treaty, (refer to Chapter 13) and a truth telling about Australian history.

In response to the statement, Prime Minister Malcolm Turnbull confirmed that his cabinet rejected the idea of an Indigenous voice to Parliament as proposed by the Uluru statement, saying it wasn't 'desirable or capable of winning acceptance at referendum'. Turnbull argued it would be seen as 'a third chamber of parliament'.

In 2020, Minister for Indigenous Australians Ken Wyatt began a co-design process that engaged Indigenous experts in coming up with a model that could give advice to government. It was not intended to be put into the Constitution but, whatever the model decided upon, would be established through legislation.

International benchmarks

Australia is the only Commonwealth country that hasn't modernised its legal system to include a bill or charter of rights, so is greatly dependent on international human rights standards as a guide for the protection of human rights domestically. Without a framework that can provide a mechanism to scrutinise government policy and its impact on the human rights of its citizens, the Australian government has no internal human rights benchmark that makes it accountable for its actions. Both the International Labour Organization (ILO) and the United Nations have developed international human rights instruments that have been useful for Indigenous peoples as a standard against which to judge government action.

The International Labour Organization

ILO Convention No. 107 of 1957 (ILO 107) was the first contemporary international human rights document that recognised Indigenous peoples as having distinct issues of international concern. Concerns were expressed, however, about its assimilationist approach (the document didn't recognise rights to self-determination, autonomy or self-government), which made Indigenous people wary of it. On the other hand, its recognition of the rights of Indigenous people to lands made governments wary of the document.

Concern over the ideology of assimilation underpinning ILO 107 led to revision of the document and the introduction of ILO Convention No. 169 of 1989 (ILO 169). Even though ILO 169 moved away from the ideology of assimilation, the convention still refused to recognise the right to self-determination. It did, however, recognise other rights, such as

>> Non-discrimination and freedom from oppression

>> Ownership of the land that Indigenous peoples traditionally occupied

>> Protection of social, cultural, religious and spiritual values and practices

>> Protection of the institutions of Indigenous peoples

>> The ability to participate freely in the dominant culture of the state

The United Nations

The United Nations was established after World War II and developed several key international human rights instruments. These include

>> The Convention against Torture (CAT)

>> The Convention for the Elimination of All Forms of Racial Discrimination (CERD)

>> The Convention on the Elimination of All Forms of Discrimination against Women (CEDAW)

>> The Convention on the Prevention and Punishment of the Crime of Genocide

>> The International Covenant on Civil and Political Rights (ICCPR)

>> The International Covenant on Economic, Social and Cultural Rights (ICESCR)

>> The Universal Declaration on Human Rights

Several forums also deal specifically with Indigenous issues within the United Nations system:

>> The Expert Mechanism on the Rights of Indigenous People

>> The Permanent Forum on Indigenous Issues (established by the Economic and Social Council on 28 July 2000)

>> The Special Rapporteur on the rights of Indigenous peoples (first appointed in 2001)

Indigenous people can fit their grievances within the framework of these conventions and covenants. In some cases, they can petition as individuals; in some, they can seek to have an international non-government organisation represent their case in the international arena; and in other cases, they need to have another state press their claims for them. Reports can be submitted to the Human Rights Committee and the Committee for the Elimination of All Forms of Racial Discrimination. These reports can counter the reports submitted by states under the reporting requirements. The committees can then confront states about alleged human rights violations.

The provisions of many international instruments aren't yet interpreted in a way that ensures strong protection of the rights of Indigenous peoples. However, Indigenous groups are actively working within the institutions of the United Nations to ensure their presence is noted and their political agendas are taken into account in policy formation whenever possible.

REMEMBER

In 1994, the United Nations General Assembly launched the International Decade of the World's Indigenous Peoples (1995 to 2004) to increase the United Nations' commitment to promoting and protecting the rights of Indigenous peoples world-wide. A second International Decade of the World's Indigenous People (2005 to 2015) was then proclaimed by the General Assembly. Its goal was to further strengthen 'international cooperation for the solution of problems faced by Indigenous people in such areas as culture, education, health, human rights, the environment and social and economic development, by means of action-oriented programmes and specific projects, increased technical assistance and relevant standard setting activities'.

TECHNICAL STUFF

How does international law become part of the law of Australia? Norms established under international protocols can filter into the domestic law of member states such as Australia in several ways:

>> Obligations under international conventions can lead to substantive legislative changes and institutional developments within ratifying states. Australia's obligations under the Convention on the Elimination of All Forms of Racial Discrimination provided the basis for the government to pass the *Racial Discrimination Act 1975* (Cwlth).

>> The federal government can make laws in relation to any of the heads of powers set out in Section 51 of the Australian Constitution. Section 51(29) states that the government has the power to 'make laws for the peace, order, and good government of the Commonwealth with respect to . . . external affairs'. The High Court has found that an obligation under a treaty falls within that section.

>> Standards that have developed under international law can be used to interpret laws in Australia. In the 1995 case of *Minister for Immigration and Ethnic Affairs v Teoh*, the High Court found that the international customary norm of 'the protection of the child' should be invoked by the court to give guidance on the interpretation of Australia's domestic law.

4

Contemporary Indigenous Cultures

Get to know how contemporary expressions of Aboriginal and Torres Strait Islander cultures don't just keep Indigenous communities vibrant and strong but also make a significant contribution to Australian cultural life.

Examine Indigenous peoples' traditional and contemporary expression of culture through fine art, music and dance.

Understand how Indigenous storytelling traditions have been retained through poetry, books, films and broadcasting.

Look at the contribution of Indigenous people to many different forms of sport in Australia, often displaying exceptional skill.

IN THIS CHAPTER

» Recognising the spirituality and symbolism of Indigenous art

» Exploring the distinctive styles of Indigenous art and crafts

» Diving into the art of the Torres Strait

» Taking stock of urban art and photography

» Promoting Indigenous art to the world

» Protecting Indigenous artists and their art

Chapter **16**

More than Rocks and Dots: Indigenous Art

For Australia's Indigenous peoples, art is a living and evolving tradition. Its continued practice is vital to the identity and cultural survival of Indigenous communities the length and breadth of the country. The oldest Aboriginal art that survives are the rock paintings seen across the country in rock shelters, especially in northern Australia. From the early 20th century, artists began transferring traditional artistic practices. The images that were painted on bark shelters, the symbols painted on the body and patterns made in the sand during ceremonies began to be transferred to bark, canvas, textiles and pottery, and new artforms evolved.

In this chapter, I examine the distinctive types of Indigenous art that have emerged, reflective of the diversity of Indigenous cultures — bark painting in Arnhem Land, the designs of the Tiwi Islands, the iconic dot style of the Central and Western Deserts, and sculptural forms in the Torres Strait. I also note some of the revered artists whose names have become synonymous with Australia's

Indigenous art and look into the confronting, highly political art from urban areas, strongly linked to traditional country, values and practices.

Over recent years, Aboriginal and Torres Strait Islander art has moved from being treated as cultural artefacts to become coveted artworks — and big business. As the commercial value of Indigenous art has risen, instances of art fraud have also increased. Here, I also look at the increasing efforts by Indigenous people to protect their rights to artwork.

Understanding the Role of Art in Indigenous Cultures

Indigenous art has become an important means of creative expression and economic self-sufficiency but it's also appreciated as a way of communicating with non-Indigenous people about things of importance — sovereignty, self-determination and land rights.

Aboriginal art and that of the Torres Strait Islands contains symbols as a record of Indigenous experience and history. Its very existence is a political statement. Although Indigenous art seems strikingly beautiful, vibrant and aesthetically pleasing (and it is), it also has strong spiritual as well as political messages.

Connecting to the spirit through art

Art is intimately connected to the spiritual realm, playing a crucial role in the religious life of Indigenous peoples. Works of art depicting the actions of ancestors, and the right to produce their designs, are inherited by birth or initiation and are, still today, produced in ritualistic contexts.

Such ceremonies are often an amalgamation of song, dance, sculpture and painting. Each component is an aspect of the actions of ancestors and the fulfilment of religious obligation, often comprising only a small part of a much larger ceremony. Performance of the rites was integral to meeting obligations to the ancestors and the land. The right to produce a story, an image or clan symbols belonged to the group, and were handed down and reproduced faithfully. (See the following section for more information about the cultural protocols surrounding Indigenous art.)

REMEMBER

The reproduction of artwork (including the patterns, artefacts and symbols), is part of the performance of the cultural obligation. Producing the art allows the painter to keep a connection with the ancestors in the spirit world.

To read more about what the patterns and symbols mean, see the section 'Reading between the dots: Knowing what the symbols mean', later in this chapter.

TIP

Using art to inform

In the past, the process of creating art was a communal activity and a way of communicating with and honouring ancestors. The creative result was often discarded or destroyed; made with non-permanent mediums — such as sand, in the case of the original dot paintings — the end products weren't kept for aesthetics or valued as property.

The process of creating an artwork is often educational, instructing others how to proceed in a ceremony, or teaching them laws, obligations, duties and rights. People aren't allowed to appropriate or paint the wrong way, and strict rules and protocols remain for reproduction. Artworks produced in this way and for these purposes weren't produced for aesthetic value. They weren't for the general public and certainly not for the collector of fine art.

**CULTURAL
PROTOCOLS**

Under traditional Aboriginal practice, knowledge of the content of the painting or sculpture, the creation of the painting or sculpture, and even viewing of an artwork, are carefully guarded and controlled by those who are the proper recipients of the knowledge, rights and obligations. Unauthorised reproduction is a serious breach of law and is even today met with reproach and punishment. Other people of different kinship groups within the same language group, as well as members of other Aboriginal groups who don't have rights to a particular Dreaming, aren't allowed paint, create or otherwise represent the specific combination of images associated with that Dreaming.

Aboriginal paintings are often maps of traditional land. Some artworks can be read as a topographic map where features of the landscape are symbolically represented. However, proportions may be skewed and distances may not be to scale, with no conventional compass orientation. Sometimes, these artworks map spiritual significance rather than landscape features.

Painting can also reflect the relationship with the sky. Aboriginal and Torres Strait Islanders were astronomers, studying the movement of the skies, using them for navigation and tracking the seasons. Cultural stories about the sky are an inspiration for artists.

TIP

If you are flying over large parts of the Australian country, look out the window and see how the land below looks like Aboriginal paintings. It is a great reminder of how well Aboriginal artists know their country and how much their paintings reflect the topography of their land.

As art evidences connection to land, including responsibility, Indigenous peoples view artworks as akin to legal documents — a chain of title. These 'legal rights' are traced back to the Dreaming. They reflect stories and obligations that define the relationship with the land.

Reading between the dots: Knowing what the symbols mean

An artwork may have multiple perspectives: Trees may be viewed vertically on the same painting that shows waterholes from an aerial view, or several geographic locations may be contained in the painting. Often, a different spatial conception is evident; the same painting can show people both from above and face on.

Pictorial symbols can carry a multitude of meanings. Much art is representational, employing symbols, dots, aerial views and x-ray (internal) views to tell of events and journeys. In most places, figures and geometric symbols work together to create representations.

In the Central and Western Deserts, each design has a particular meaning, and symbols (such as the following) are used to tell stories:

>> A half-circle like a crescent moon could represent a person, and several clustered around a circle could indicate people meeting.

>> A series of concentric circles might denote a campsite or a waterhole.

>> Concentric circles linked by lines could mean waterholes connected by running water.

Aboriginal artworks may also map kin or communal relationships, just as they map landscape, expressing the relationships between land and people. Clans have their own particular markings (highlighting both connectedness and difference) and paintings show the clan links.

Because Aboriginal and Torres Strait Islander art is so connected to culture and cultural stories, artworks are often accompanied by an artist's statement that will allow you to better appreciate the deeper meanings of the work.

NGURRARA: THE GREAT SANDY DESERT PAINTING

The *Ngurrara Canvas* is an example of how painting is an exercise of legal obligations and rights, a legal narrative. The canvas is the largest example of Western Desert art, painted by over 60 artists from the southern Kimberley region at Pirnini, an area at the northern edge of the Great Sandy Desert.

It makes sense that *Ngurrara* means home, the place that people have attachment to. In 1997, the canvas was presented to the National Native Title Tribunal as evidence of ancestral, social, economic and personal connections to land. The *Ngurrara Canvas*, by bringing an embodiment of Aboriginal law to the court for consideration by the dominant legal system, communicated across the cultural divide. The Ngurrara native title determination was the largest claim in the Kimberley region and recognised exclusive possession native title over about 76,000 square kilometres of land. The determination was also handed down at Pirnini, where the *Ngurrara Canvas* had been painted. The canvas has been exhibited in galleries around Australia, including the National Museum of Australia, and is shown in the following figure being unrolled for a temporary exhibition at the South Australian Museum.

The canvas is colossal, measuring eight by ten metres. It is made of ten colourful harmonised patchworks, each denoting a different story, a different place, a different piece of evidence of connection and attachment to land. The waterholes, trees, salt lakes and people are visible. It shows the path of serpents and ancestors, and tells a panoramic story of ceremonies being performed, creation stories, of spirits, and even of snoring fathers.

Considering Indigenous Art around Australia

Indigenous artists have always been inspired by the world around them and the culture they know. Using the environment, they created artworks of deep spiritual importance with the materials that were most readily available to them. The earliest remaining art — in the Pilbara and dating from around 40,000 years ago — is rock art painted on the walls of shelters. Paintings were also created on the bark that was used to build shelters.

Recognising rock art

Rock art has left an enduring legacy that has survived the passage of time — existing rock art and ochre fragments prove human existence in Australia for over 65,000 years (refer to Chapter 2 for more on archaeological finds). Rock art provides insights into how people lived and how they saw their world. One piece of rock art could be linked in meaning to other pieces in the area, and this art often appears at places that were significant meeting places.

Artists made different types of rock art:

>> Figures were carved into sandstone. These carvings were re-carved on the rock over time, which is what ensured survival of the artwork over so many thousands of years.

>> Ochre was used to paint on the rock surface. Art was created as paintings or by using stencils. In stencil art, a hand was placed on the rock and ochre was sprayed from the mouth leaving an outline of the hand on the rock surface. The ochre created a chemical reaction with the rock, sinking into it. These were usually made on rock surfaces protected from the elements — in caves or overhangs. Examples of these ochre paintings still exist in south-eastern Australia and in central Queensland, as well as the better known sites in Arnhem Land in the Northern Territory and the Kimberley in the north of Western Australia.

Today in Australia, evidence of rock art exists across the country in urban areas — around Sydney Harbour and at Bondi and Kuring-gai National Park in Sydney — rural areas, and remote areas, including in Western Australia, the site of the oldest evidence of rock art at Carpenter's Gap, near Windjana National Park in the Kimberley, and the oldest surviving paintings on the Burrup Peninsula.

Unfortunately, however, many sites have been destroyed through the development of urban centres, mining activities, vandalism and graffiti, and by environmental pollution. Governments continue to give approval for the destruction of sites. Wrongful destruction of sites gives rise to a fine but this is little compensation to the communities, who could never put a price on the spiritual and cultural significance of rock art sites.

CULTURAL PROTOCOLS

In the Kimberley, one of the most frequently painted images, especially in rock art, is that of the Wandjina, a creation being of great spiritual significance. These figures have large circular faces, though no mouth, and a headdress.

REMEMBER

Some early European visitors to Aboriginal communities didn't believe that Aboriginal people could have made the rock art the Europeans had seen. The paintings were thought too sophisticated to have been done by people who (some) Europeans considered 'savage' and 'primitive'.

REMEMBER

In 2020, mining company Rio Tinto was subject to intense criticism after it destroyed a significant site of rock art in the Pilbara. The caves contained engraved rock art and evidence of human habitation dating back 47,000 years in one and 60,000 years in another. The company explained the act of destruction as a 'misunderstanding' but public outcry over the incident led to the CEO and two other senior executives of the mining company resigning.

Looking at bark painting

Traditionally, painting was done on the bark used to build shelters. Today, bark is used as a canvas. The bark is cut from the stringybark tree (a type of eucalyptus) immediately after the wet season, when it's still moist. The bark has to be in good condition — free from splits and knots and not eaten by termites. Bark is cut off in rectangular pieces and then flattened.

TECHNICAL STUFF

The bark is prepared by placing a wet sheet on the heat of hot coals (without directly touching them) and then pressing it flat, with the rough side, not the side to be painted, having contact with the heat. This process also removes the moisture from the bark. Weights are then placed on the bark for several days to flatten it further. To prevent the bark from warping, sticks are tied to the ends of the bark with string.

Bark painting uses four basic colours that come from the soils — red, yellow, white and black. These colours are occasionally mixed to produce grey, orange or pink. The red and yellow come from iron oxide ochres, white comes from gypsum, and black from charcoal or manganese ore. The pigments were traditionally mixed with water and fixed with the resins from trees. Today, artists also paint with acrylics.

Bark painting has been practised in parts of Australia for thousands of years:

» In south-eastern Australia, paintings were often done on shelters made with bark. In these areas, figures were either scratched into bark that had been blackened by smoke, or were drawn in charcoal.

» In the Kimberley region, painting on bark was of the same artistic style as the rock art, including images of the Wandjina, and often quite distinctive, using bold blocks of colour. Artists of the Kimberley now sometimes paint on boards rather than bark.

» In the Arnhem Land region, bark paintings depicted the same patterns used on important ceremonial objects, and could represent landscapes and their important features, ancestors or creation spirits. In western Arnhem Land, a distinctive x-ray style was popular, showing the internal organs and workings of animals that represented creation spirits. Bark paintings from central and eastern Arnhem Land mirrored the patterns that were used in ceremonial body painting.

» In the Tiwi Islands, a cross-hatching style was popular. Different patterns and designs had different meanings, most often identifying particular clans.

» Bark paintings from Groote Eylandt (an island in the Gulf of Carpentaria) also have a distinctive style, with figures painted against a black background.

Macassan sailors visited northern parts of Australia and the artwork from those areas reflects these exchanges, with bark paintings that show the Macassan boats. Interesting stylistic similarities exist between the art of the Macassans and of the Groote Eylandters.

REMEMBER

From the early 20th century, Indigenous people, particularly in the Arnhem Land region, started using pieces of bark as a canvas, replicating the same designs they previously used on the bark shelters. By the 1930s, bark paintings were being offered for sale by Indigenous artists.

Today, bark painting is an important industry, particularly for artists from the Kimberley, among the Tiwi and in Arnhem Land.

REMEMBER

Here are a number of internationally renowned artists who paint on bark:

» **Wandjuk Marika** was a senior leader of his clan in the Yolngu community. Not only a talented artist, he was also active in protecting and promoting Indigenous art. He was a founding member of the Aboriginal Arts Board and went on to become its chair. He was awarded an OBE in 1979 for his contribution to Aboriginal arts in Australia. He passed away in 1987.

- ≫ **Narritjin Maymuru** was a Yolngu artist and a dancer who, in the 1960s, became one of the most prolific Indigenous artists, and his highly symbolic work came to international attention. He saw his painting as an important way of keeping the Yolngu culture vibrant and alive. He died in 1982.

- ≫ **John Mawurndjul** is an artist from the Kuninjku nation of western Arnhem Land, and he is well known for his bark painting. He employs a style of intricate cross-hatching that is then filled in; this particular style is called *rarrk*. His work has been shown around the world, including at the Hermitage Museum in St Petersburg, Russia. His work is represented in major collections in Australia, including Sydney's Museum of Contemporary Art and the National Gallery of Australia in Canberra.

- ≫ **Lofty Bardayal Nadjamerrek** was taught to paint by his father, who instructed him in rock art. Also from western Arnhem Land, he transferred those designs to both paper and bark. Some of his work uses traditional cross-hatching but he also expanded his artistic style. A major exhibition of his work was held at the Museum of Contemporary Art, Sydney, in 2011. He passed away in 2009.

Dot, dot, dot . . . art

Central and Western Desert art is known best for its use of dots in paintings. They can be used to express many things, from the night sky to the landscape. (Refer to the section 'Reading between the dots: Knowing what the symbols mean' for more information about the symbolism of these paintings.)

In the 1970s, Aboriginal artist Johnny Warangkula used dots to create the background for his paintings. The effects were so stunning that others soon followed. Artists could obscure the symbolism in their painting so that it could be hidden from people who weren't initiated and so dots were used as a way of hiding the true meanings of paintings. Artists from Papunya, then Yuendumu and other Central Desert communities also started to paint in this style.

From this important development in Indigenous art came a huge change in Indigenous economic advancement: Indigenous people began to set up their own companies to protect their artwork. One of the first Indigenous communities to set up their own art company was Papunya, a settlement about 240 kilometres northwest of Alice Springs created to accommodate the Pintupi and Luritja people.

In 1971, school teacher Geoffrey Bardon encouraged some of the men of the community to paint on a school wall and this sparked an interest in painting across the community. The style of art from the school was inspired by the patterns and symbols used in body painting and sand painting, which was a central part of their ceremonies, though the artists have always been careful to remove the sacred symbols from their public art. The art from this group is highly coveted and includes artists such as Clifford Possum Tjapaltjarri and Johnny Warangkula Tjuppurulla. (Although started by men, women artists in Papunya also came to prominence in the 1980s.)

In 1972, the artists formed their own company, the Papunya Tula Artists, to help promote the sale of their work. The idea behind establishing the company was to promote the work of the artists, to ensure that financial benefits flowed to the artists from the sale of their work and they weren't ripped off. The company also ensures that cultural heritage is kept strong through the promotion of creating art. The group company is now owned by the Aboriginal people of the area and represents about 120 artists.

The arrangement became an inspiration to other communities of artists who then started their own collectives, especially in the Central and Western Deserts, with artists engaging more with the production of art as a creative outlet but also as a possibility for sale and income. Many Aboriginal communities and outstations have now been formed — such as Utopia and Hermannsburg in the Northern Territory, Ernabella in South Australia and Warmun (Turkey Creek) in Western Australia — with a group of actively working artists. Forming these groups is seen as an important cultural practice and a means of economic support for the community. Many of these communities have joined artists' collectives to ensure that they receive the appropriate royalties for their work.

Here are some of the best known artists of the dot style:

>> **Paddy Bedford** was born in the East Kimberly in 1922 and experienced the harsh racism of the times. He worked as a stockman for rations and was laid off when the law changed in 1969 requiring wages to be paid. Familiar with traditional body painting, he began painting on canvas in 1998 and became one of Australia's most respected artists. He was the subject of a retrospective at the Museum of Contemporary Art that opened in 2006. Bedford died in 2007.

>> **Emily Kngwarreye** was born in 1910 and, in the 1990s, became one of Australia's most successful and accomplished painters. She was a skilled artist who painted landscapes and other themes inspired by nature, such as the cycle of the seasons and the patterns of seeds, on large canvases. She lived in Utopia (an Aboriginal community in the Northern Territory) and in 1977 became a founding member of the Utopia Women's Batik Group, who made their art collectively with no individual artist being singled out. The techniques and skills that Kngwarreye developed while producing batik shaped her style and technique when she moved to painting on canvas. As her work became

more popular, she continued to distribute her income across her large extended family. Kngwarreye passed away in 1996.

» **Rover Thomas** was born in 1926 in the Great Sandy Desert in Western Australia. His family moved to the Kimberley when he was a child and as he grew into adulthood he began working as a stockman. He later moved to Warmun (Turkey Creek). His uncle, Paddy Jaminji, had painted storyboards used for a ceremony — the Krill Krill (see Chapter 17). These boards inspired Thomas to paint and he developed his own unique style. He became active, along with fellow artist Trevor Nickolls, at continuing and evolving the Krill Krill ceremony, which is primarily music and dance. Thomas won art prizes for his pieces and his work was shown in galleries around the world. He had a solo exhibition in 1994 at the National Gallery of Australia. Thomas died in 1998.

» **Clifford Possum Tjapaltjarri** was one of Australia's most influential Indigenous artists. He was born in 1933 at Napperby Station, north-west of Alice Springs, on his traditional country, the land of the Anmatyerre people. With no formal education, he grew up in the bush and worked as a stockman. Already known as a talented woodcarver when he started painting in the 1970s, he emerged as one of the most gifted artists of his community of Papunya with his large and complex paintings. He was chair of the Papunya Tula Artists — the community artists' collective — from the late 1970s until the mid-1980s. In 2004, one of his pieces, *Warlugulong*, sold at an auction by Sotheby's for $2.4 million; he had originally sold it for $1,200. He passed away in 2002.

» **Johnny Warangkula Tjuppurrulla** was born in the mid-1920s, of the Luritja and Pintupi people in the Papunya area. He was raised traditionally, never receiving European education. He emerged as a leading artist in the Papunya movement in the 1980s. He developed a distinctive style where he used several layers of dots in his works — a technique known as *over-dotting* — and this created powerful optical illusions. In 1997, his painting, *Water Dreaming at Kalpinypa* was sold at Sotheby's for $206,000. He had received just $150 for it when he sold it 25 years earlier.

Appreciating Indigenous crafts

Skilled Aboriginal and Torres Strait Islander craftspeople have made objects for everyday use that are also of great artistic merit. From woven bags to carved spears, great skill was needed to make these artefacts.

Today, the artefacts are collected, not just as cultural curiosities, but because they are aesthetically beautiful. Aboriginal artists now engage in the creation of objects, such as woven bags and possum coats, specifically to create a work of art, with little intention that the piece will be put to practical use. Similarly, objects that once may have had spiritual significance — such as the morning star poles used in funerals (see the sidebar 'Morning star poles'), and the elaborate headdresses used in ceremonies in the Torres Strait (see the following section) — are now made as art pieces for display and sale.

Indigenous people have expanded their arts and crafts practices into areas such as fabric design and batik, rug making, pottery, jewellery design and making, possum cloak making and papermaking.

TECHNICAL STUFF

String bags are made by techniques using knots, loops and twists. Basket making also employs a variety of techniques; some are made with a weaving technique and others with a coil technique. In one method, the youngest branches of leaves of a palm tree are stripped of their prickly edges by hand, stripped into several fibres then left to dry. They are then decorated with ochres or bush dyes or left with their natural colour before being used for weaving.

MORNING STAR POLES

Morning star poles were used in mortuary ceremonies but today are also made as beautiful works of art. The poles are painted and decorated with objects such as feathers and shells. They are works of art in themselves but are often displayed standing in groups, like soldiers, as shown in the accompanying figure.

REMEMBER

Elizabeth Djuttara was a notable weaver from Arnhem Land, born near Ramingining in 1942. She won the Victoria Health National Craft Award for a richly coloured woven floor pandanus mat in 1992.

REMEMBER

The Tjanpi Desert Weavers is a social enterprise of the Ngaanyatjarra Pitjant-jatjara Yankunytjatjara (NPY) Women's Council representing women of the of the Central and Western desert. They also produce beginner's kits so you can learn how to weave see tjanpi.com.au for more information.

Examining Torres Strait Islander Art

The Torres Strait Islanders were active traders with the people of Cape York Peninsula and other islands off the mainland of New Guinea. Not surprisingly then, their culture — and art — is influenced by both its Melanesian and Australian neighbours. Torres Strait Islander art, as with its music and dance, pays strong tribute to the sea (which provides so much of the peoples' livelihood) as well as to the seasons, rain and the distinctive winds.

A lot of the materials used in Torres Strait Islander art also come from the sea. Turtle shells and pearl shells are highly prized and used to beautiful effect; shells and bones are also used in making ceremonial objects, jewellery and art. Wood, hair and fibre string were also used in making art and other objects.

Torres Strait Islander art was recognised early on for its uniqueness, beauty and craftsmanship. The Spanish explorer after whom the island chain got its European name (Luis de Torres) observed in his journals the beauty of the turtle shell masks worn in ceremonies.

Contemporary Torres Strait Islander art has stayed very faithful to its traditions, using traditional materials and inspired by cultural stories, totemic systems and ceremonies. However, some artists have experimented with evolving art practices in the Torres Strait.

REMEMBER

As do all other Indigenous artists, the Torres Strait Islander artists also produce artworks that speak to their political situation (see the section 'Pulling no political punches' for more about Indigenous political art). The 1991 legal case that found that Indigenous people have native title over their traditional land in certain circumstances — referred to as the Mabo case (refer to Chapter 12) — was over land in the Torres Strait. Torres Strait Islander artists, such as Ellen Jose, have taken up the theme of native title and the implication of the Mabo case in their work.

Today, a new generation of Torres Strait Islander artists are continuing the tradition of creating art pieces inspired by traditional dress and ceremony, and the Torres Strait Islanders' view of the world, their spiritual life and totemic systems and their relationship with the sea. But they have also gone into new territory, using non-traditional materials, and some Torres Strait Islander artists (for example, Alik Tipoti and Brian Robinson) have tried their hand at printmaking.

Some notable Torres Strait Islander artists include:

>> **Destiny Deacon** is a photographer and artist. Her experimental photography and video work contrasts European culture against Aboriginal and Torres Strait Islander identity and experience. She introduced the word 'blak' as a term to refer to contemporary art history and culture.

>> **Ellen Jose** was an artist who was a painter, printmaker, photographer and sculptor. She explored issues of identity, the impact of colonisation and the resilience of her people. She was interested in the way tradition blends with the modern world. Her work appears in major galleries around Australia.

>> **Dennis Nona** began his career as a traditional woodcarver. Nona then used his skills to create linocuts, etchings and sculptures that depict important stories and legends of the Torres Strait. His work appears in major galleries around Australia and he's regarded as one of the most important artists of the Torres Strait.

>> **George Nona** is a craftsman specialising in headdresses (Dhoeri). Nona uses natural materials such as seeds, feathers, bones and shells to make headdresses that are pieces of art. Nona constructs each piece based on advice and knowledge from Elders and from archival records and photographs. Some of his pieces are in the National Museum and the National Gallery of Australia.

>> **Ken Thaiday** was born on Darnley Island in the Torres Strait. He began to paint while he attended ceremonies with his father, who was himself an important dancer in their community. Thaiday also performed as a dancer and he made the masks that were used in the performances. From here, he began to make them as standalone pieces of art, experimenting with different shapes and materials to create sculptures truly inspired by his Torres Strait Islander heritage. The masks are works of art more like sculpture than headdresses.

REMEMBER

Torres Strait Islanders have made ghost nets, sculptures made from discarded fishing nets and other artificial materials that are polluting the seas. Their sculptures, made from this recycled material, reflect the importance of our relationship to the oceans and the need to keep them pollution free.

Contemplating Urban Indigenous Art

Urban Indigenous art emerged as a strong art movement in the 1960s and 1970s, including contemporary artforms such as installation pieces and photography as well as painting and sculpture. It reflected the strong politics and the political struggles that Indigenous communities were engaged in at the time. (For more information about these issues, refer to Chapters 10, 11 and 12.) Modern Indigenous art is largely related to the important social and political issues facing Indigenous people today.

Pulling no political punches

Many urban artists have engaged in a range of mediums, including acrylic, oils and sculptural forms. Artists such as Gordon Bennett, Harry Wedge, Richard Bell, Gordon Syron, Gordon Hookey and Blak Douglas (Adam Hill) have incorporated strong imagery into their paintings that make comments about racism in Australian society and the legacy of colonisation. Artists such as Destiny Deacon, Brenda L Croft, Judy Watson, Bronwyn Bancroft and Fiona Foley explore issues of contemporary Indigenous identity and particularly, as women artists, the intersectionality of race and gender politics.

REMEMBER

In 1987, a group of Aboriginal urban artists formed the Boomalli Aboriginal Artists Co-operative (*Boomalli* means 'to make a mark' or 'to strike' in three prominent New South Wales languages: Bandjalung, Gamilaraay and Wiradjuri). These artists were Bronwyn Bancroft, Euphemia Bostock, Brenda L Croft, Fiona Foley, Fernanda Martins, Arone Raymond Meeks, Tracey Moffatt, Avril Quaill, Michael Riley and Jeffrey Samuels. The cooperative provided a supportive and creative environment for artists, as well as an exhibition space. Several (such as Tracey Moffatt, Michael Riley, Fiona Foley and Bronwyn Bancroft) went on to enjoy international success. Brenda L Croft, who has also become a curator and academic, still practises her art, using it to explore Aboriginal family life, especially the connection between mother and child that was once so derided by the policy of removing Indigenous children. Funding cuts have threatened the gallery but it continues to survive.

Here are some provocative urban artists:

>> **Vernon Ah Kee** is known for his bold artistic statements, sometimes using text, exploring contemporary issues such as deaths in custody and challenging the historical treatment of Aboriginal people. His vibrant, painted surfboards are further evidence of his broad range and intellectual and creative strength.

- **Tony Albert** is an artist who uses eclectic mediums to explore issues of identity, racism and Indigenous experience. In 2014 he won both the Basil Sellers Art Prize and the Telstra National Aboriginal and Torres Strait Islander Art Prize. His large sculpture *Yininmadyemi Thou didst let fall*, based on his grandfather's experience in the war, is prominent in Sydney's Hyde Park and is a homage to the black diggers.

- **Bronwyn Bancroft** is an accomplished Bundjalung artist and illustrator who started her career as a fashion designer. She was a founding member of the Boomalli Aboriginal Artists Co-operative and has been a key driver in making sure the gallery has remained open during difficult financial periods. Bancroft's work uses rich contrasts of colours and intricate symbols that are eye-catching yet also deeply meaningful. A range of themes, from concepts of Indigenous identity to contemporary health issues, has inspired her artworks, and she has also illustrated over 20 children's picture books.

- **Richard Bell** won the Telstra Aboriginal Art Prize in 2003. His work is focused on challenging colonial stereotypes. He also challenges the prejudices of the mainstream art world, setting up his own event at the 2019 Venice Biennale. His solo show at the Tate Modern was the first solo exhibition of an Indigenous artist to be held there.

- **Gordon Bennett** is an Aboriginal artist who works in vibrant styles. He makes bold statements about the place of Indigenous people in Australian society and the historical treatment of Indigenous peoples. His work has been compared with Jackson Pollock and has included artistic responses to artists such as Jean-Michel Basquiat (an American multimedia artist).

- **Daniel Boyd** reinterprets colonial narratives in ways that also speak to the ongoing contemporary legacy. He uses a unique and creative reinterpretation of dot-focused art to reclaim the archive and to create visually stunning video pieces. His *Captain No Beard* shows Cook with a parrot and eye patch.

- **Karla Dickens** is a Wiradjuri artist who works in installations and multimedia to make powerful statements about her identity, gender and sexuality. She explores the historical impacts of colonisation and dissects contemporary experiences and perspectives.

- **Blak Douglas (Adam Hill)** is an accomplished painter whose style is influenced by his background as a graphic designer. He has staged over 25 solo shows and his distinctive work is often used on posters and book covers. Hill is known for his use of stylised landscapes in which he uses symbols that critique the dominance of white culture in Australia. He is also known for his cheeky installations and plays on words. For example, in one installation he used stolen milk crates to spell out the word 'Stolen', a reference to the Stolen Generations (refer to Chapter 9).

- **Fiona Foley** is a Badtjala artist who uses a variety of mediums (such as photography, painting, sculpture and installation) in her creative practice. She makes sharp critiques in her work about identity, dispossession, historical narrative and racism. Her works range from self-portraits representing colonial photographs of Indigenous women to installations of clan-style outfits in vibrant African designs.

- **Jonathan Jones** is a Wiradjuri artist who integrates traditional cultural practices and knowledges into his art. He often incorporates language into a soundscape for his installations. His ambitious installation in 2016, *barrangal dyara (skin and bones)*, and part of the Kaldor Public Art Project, saw him use ceramic shields to recreate the outline of the Garden Palace which, when it burnt down in 1882, saw the destruction of a large number of important Aboriginal artefacts.

- **Lin Onus** was a Wiradjuri artist whose works included sculptures of animals such as dingoes and bats. In one famous piece, now held by Art Gallery NSW, painted wooden fruit bats hang on a Hills Hoist, like washing on a line. Round droppings on the ground below complete the installation. Onus was very active in Aboriginal rights issues, particularly on the campaign for a yes vote in the 1967 referendum, and he was a founder of the Aboriginal Advancement League in Victoria.

- **Gordon Syron** is a Biripi man, born on the mid-north coast of New South Wales in the town of Minimbah. He was an amateur boxer and an electrical tradesman who was given a life sentence in 1972 for the murder of a white man in a dispute over his family's land. He started painting in prison and was released in 1982. Syron is famous for his vibrant landscapes of colourful wildflowers, a testament to what his traditional country looked like before it was mined. His other famous work, ***Judgement by His Peers***, painted while Syron was in prison, shows a white defendant in a courtroom where the judge and jury are all Aboriginal.

- **Judy Watson** has had her work described as contemplative, original and seductive that works to expose suppressed histories. She uses bold colour that is strongly connected to place and history. She works across print making, painting, video and installation. Her sculpture *Fire and Water* is in Reconciliation Place in Canberra.

- **Jason Wing** is a talented emerging artist who has a graphic design background. He heavily employs stencilling, a method used in traditional rock art painting. Of Aboriginal–Chinese heritage, he explores issues of dual identity in his work. He often paints on metal and also places his stencil art around urban landscapes. His work looks at the social problems facing Indigenous Australians; one installation had a bed of nails made up of syringes as an evocation of the problems of substance abuse in the community.

REMEMBER

proppaNOW is an important Queensland-based art collective established in 2003 that includes Richard Bell, Gordon Hookey, Karla Dickens and Vernon Ah Kee.

TIP

Two excellent TV series about Aboriginal and Torres Strait Islander art were *Colour Theory with Richard Bell* (screened on NITV and SBS between 2013 and 2017) and *Art + Soul* (screened on ABC between 2010 and 2014) hosted by Hettie Perkins. While no longer readily available, these are definitely worth checking out if you see past episodes.

Finding out more about Indigenous photographers

For a long time, Aboriginal people and Torres Strait Islanders were the subjects of photographs. Among the earliest are the posed 'ethnographic' photos of Aboriginal people from around 1847, the same time that the medium made its way to Australia.

In the earliest photographs, Aboriginal people were positioned in dioramas with props such as boomerangs, spears and possum coats. This staging was often done with little regard for cultural correctness of the artefacts to the area they were supposed to represent. The results are a haunted, hunted look, understandable from subjects that were viewed with curiosity, as relics of a disappearing world. The studio portraits of family groups with bark shelters and cultural clothing and artefacts, and the portraits of men in their possum or kangaroo coats and women bare-chested, facing the camera directly, show an attempt to catalogue a people and culture that were assumed to be inferior to that of the colonisers.

REMEMBER

Some Aboriginal people didn't like having their photograph taken when they first came into contact with Europeans because they feared that the photograph would cause their souls to be taken away.

Today, a growing number of Indigenous artists are on the other side of the camera; unsurprisingly, many Indigenous photographers are interested in imagery that reshapes and challenges concepts of identity.

The photographs of Aboriginal people changed profoundly with the images of protest from the 1960s and 1970s. Indigenous people started to get more involved with photography. They started taking their own photographs of important events. Mervyn Bishop's photograph of Prime Minister Gough Whitlam pouring sand into the hands of Vincent Lingiari at the ceremony to mark the handing back of his traditional land in 1975 is one such moment. (You can see an image of this event in Chapter 8.)

By the 1980s, Aboriginal photography had come into its own, contributing to the powerful counter-narrative about Australia's history. In September 1986, the first exhibition of photographic works exclusively by Aboriginal people and Torres Strait Islanders was opened in the Aboriginal Artists Gallery in Sydney. The show included over 60 photographs from Indigenous photographers (including Mervyn Bishop, Brenda L Croft, Tracey Moffatt and Michael Riley), and the collection symbolised the emergence of Indigenous photography as a creative and political force.

Here's a snapshot of some well-known Indigenous artists using photography as a part of their artistic practice:

>> **Mervyn Bishop** was born in Brewarrina and worked as a photojournalist for *The Sydney Morning Herald* in the 1960s before leaving in 1974 to work as a photographer for the Department of Aboriginal Affairs. He left the department in 1978 to become a freelancer and also began teaching.

>> **Brenda Croft** is a photographer and digital artist whose work spans from portraiture and landscape through to multimedia collages that integrate text and image. Her work strongly critiques colonisation and attempts to control identity, and celebrates the vibrancy of Aboriginal community and family. Born in 1964, she is the daughter of artist Joe Croft and a founding member of the Boomali Aboriginal artists collective. She has also worked as a curator, educator, writer and academic.

>> **Ricky Maynard** is a Tasmanian Aboriginal man who provides commentaries about contemporary Indigenous life through his photographs. He has documented the Tasmanian landscape, the people and their way of life. He has also taken photographs of Aboriginal inmates, street scenes and other slices of life, including portraits of Wik Elders from northern Queensland. He worked as a stills photographer on the 2002 Phillip Noyce movie *Rabbit Proof Fence* (see Chapter 19), and had a major solo show at Sydney's Museum of Contemporary Art in 2009, *Portraits of a Distant Land*, which later toured the country.

>> **Tracey Moffatt** is an artist who takes photographs of highly stylised and posed panoramas. Her recent work retains its surreal quality; her 2004 *Adventure* series is a set of images of what appear to be overacted scenes from a soap opera set on a tropical island, populated by doctors, nurses and pilots. However, Moffatt has refused to be categorised as a photographer and she does delve deeply into other mediums, such as film (her films are described in Chapter 19).

>> **Michael Riley** was an important visual artist. He used photography and film throughout his life. He had a large and diverse body of work, from striking portraits of dancers to objects floating through the air and scenes depicting religious experiences. Born in Dubbo in 1960, he died in 2004 at the age of just 44.

Moving in the Mainstream: Indigenous Art as a Means to an Economic End

Before the 1940s, Indigenous art — rock paintings and the x-ray style bark paintings with their cross-hatching — were seen as cultural artefacts, not art. Museum collections gathered these items, considered to be the relics of a 'stone age' people, objects from 'past worlds'.

REMEMBER

Some anthropologists, such as A P Elkin, believed that collecting Indigenous art would establish respect and compassion for Indigenous people. Nicholas Thomas observed that Elkin thought 'the prestige the art acquired would bolster indigenous pride in a fairly paternalistic way: it would be something that "we" could do for "them"'.

Indigenous people were encouraged on missions, such as those in the Warburton Ranges and at Ernabella, to produce wood carvings for sale to the mission shops in the cities. In this way, missions promoted the production of Indigenous art to facilitate economic self-sufficiency and develop a Protestant work ethic. Missionaries traded these pieces as curios for collectors, and this enterprise saw the development of paintings and sculptures that were produced outside of the ritual creation process. Ironically, these pieces often referred to the very religious, ceremonial and cultural events and beliefs that the missionaries were trying to eliminate. Such artworks may have had 'traditional' stories as their base but still very much reflected the current experiences and issues in the artists' lives, including their connection to land.

For example, the Aboriginal mission at Hermannsburg, located 125 kilometres west of Alice Springs, has been a major producer of Indigenous art for many years. Founded in 1877 by Lutheran missionaries, Hermannsburg is the traditional land of the Western Arrernte people. The mission gave rise to one of the first distinctive Aboriginal art movements, identified by the deep watercolours used to paint outback landscapes of the Western Arrernte's traditional country, including the West MacDonnell Ranges, in a European style. The community has continued with its artistic tradition even though that has changed over the years. Today, the area is best known for its pottery, mostly made by Aboriginal women. Hermannsburg also produced one of Australia's best known artists: Albert Namatjira.

Albert Namatjira was the first Indigenous painter to achieve national and international success. He painted rich, colourful landscapes of his home country — over 2,000 paintings during his lifetime — and his work had a European aesthetic. Namatjira was an Arrernte man, born in 1902 at the Hermannsburg Lutheran Mission. He learned to paint in 1936 when he was a guide for Australian painter Rex Batterbee. Fans of his work included Queen Elizabeth II, whom he met in

1954. His fame meant that he was the first Aboriginal person to be exempted from the legislation that made Aboriginal people wards of the state in the Northern Territory, giving him the right to vote. He became an Elder of his clan and supported many of his extended family but lost his money and eventually lived in a camp. He was imprisoned for two months for providing alcohol to Aboriginal people, and was never the same after his experience in prison. He died in 1959.

Commissions by ethnographers, anthropologists and collectors also saw a transformation of Indigenous art. For example, bark paintings, once found only on the interiors of shelters, developed as a way of cross-cultural communication, facilitated by bark paintings' resemblance of the rectangular works of the European art tradition.

REMEMBER

Indigenous art expert Wally Caruna relates how in Yuendumu in 1984 a group of older women switched from decorating objects such as carrying dishes and digging sticks for sale to painting small canvasses in order to raise money for a vehicle that would allow them better and easier access to their often-distant ceremonial grounds. His anecdote highlights the underlying economic incentive that boosted the creation of Aboriginal art.

Indigenous art evolved from the 1950s in the following ways:

>> **1950s:** Art galleries, such as the Art Gallery of New South Wales, began to collect Indigenous art for their major collections and it was no longer seen as just something for museums.

>> **1960s:** Indigenous art began to be given widespread mainstream recognition. The recognition of Indigenous art as aesthetic, not simply cultural artefacts, meant Europeans reconceptualised ethnographic objects into art. Aboriginal people were encouraged to put their fragile and non-lasting artwork into permanent forms — such as on canvas, board and bark (where it was not traditionally done) — and use watercolours and acrylics.

REMEMBER

This mirrored the process of changing the mediums for Aboriginal artists — turning sand paintings into acrylic paintings, placing body paint onto canvas and the classification of functional pieces (such as baskets, boomerangs, shields) as sculpture. These new mediums were an extension of the traditional motifs, symbols and representations, and remained fundamentally and intrinsically Indigenous. Indigenous artists were producing and selling a whole new genre of art that was specially created to communicate with the outside world.

>> **Late 1970s and early 1980s:** Other Australian art galleries followed the early example set by the Art Gallery of New South Wales in the 1950s (although it did not make a major purchase for 30 years after its initial acquisition of Aboriginal art). It was around this time that the Aboriginal Arts Board was established (see the sidebar 'The Aboriginal Arts Board comes to life').

Corporations and public bodies also began to acquire Indigenous art for the walls of their offices and in their advertising, especially to highlight their Australian identity. By the mid-1980s, art galleries were scrambling to develop collections of Indigenous art.

>> **1990s:** Aboriginal art had become big business, sought by collectors and collecting institutions internationally — and continues to be so today.

REMEMBER

In 2013, the Musee du Quai Branly in Paris put an enlarged version of an artwork by Indigenous artist Lena Nyadbi on their roof so it would be seen by millions of people a year from the Eiffel Tower, a symbol that Indigenous art was well and truly making its mark on the art world internationally.

As Indigenous artists became more prominent, the number of Indigenous curators at major galleries also grew (just as Aboriginal people and Torres Strait Islanders are increasingly represented in a cross-section of Australian professional life). Here are some of these curators and the galleries they have variously worked in:

>> Brenda Croft at the Art Gallery of Western Australia and the National Gallery of Australia

>> Djon Mundine at the Art Gallery of New South Wales, the Museum of Contemporary Art, the National Museum of Australia and the Queensland Art Gallery

>> Keith Munro at the Museum of Contemporary Art

>> Margo Neale at Art Gallery NSW, the Queensland Art Gallery and the National Museum of Australia

>> Hetti Perkins at the Art Gallery of New South Wales

>> James Wilson Miller at the Powerhouse Museum

REMEMBER

In 2020, Wiradjuri artist Brook Andrew became the first Indigenous person appointed to be Artistic Director of the Biennale of Sydney.

REMEMBER

The first Indigenous artist to win the prestigious Archibald Prize was Vincent Namatjira, who won for his portrait of footballer Adam Goodes in 2020. That same year, actor and writer Meyne Wyatt became the first Indigenous person to win the Archibald's Packing Room Prize with a self-portrait, the first painting he'd done in over ten years.

TIP

Most Australian art galleries have an Indigenous collection or gallery. These are usually accompanied by talks programs so you can find out more about the artworks.

Revealing Indigenous Art Fraud

Big money has been made from the sale of Indigenous art and, disappointingly but perhaps not surprisingly, an illegal business has developed in its sale.

CULTURAL PROTOCOLS

Some art is sold as having been painted by Indigenous artists when it's not. This not only cheats the buyer, but also causes offence to Indigenous people. Also, non-Indigenous artists using sacred Indigenous symbols can cause offence to the Indigenous people whose cultural heritage has been appropriated.

In other instances, the work of Indigenous artists has been appropriated and used without the artists' consent. Some reports state that over $500 million of Indigenous art fraud takes place internationally every year, and 20 per cent of Aboriginal art in Western Australia is fake.

Here's a look at some notorious cases of Indigenous art fraud:

>> David Malangi was a Yolngu man, head of the Manarrngu clan and an established artist who painted on bark. In 1966, when Australia converted to decimal currency, one of his designs was used on the $1 note. This was done without his knowledge. The then Governor of the Reserve Bank, Dr H C

Coombs, the following year ensured that Malangi was given financial compensation and also a specially made medal. (You can read more about Coombs in Chapter 13.)

» The 1991 case of ***Yumbulul v Reserve Bank of Australia*** concerned the reproduction of a morning star pole on the bicentennial $10 note. The object was important in the plaintiff's cultural ceremonies and the right to create the poles governed by Aboriginal laws. The plaintiff claimed that, had he known the full nature of the agreement with the Reserve Bank of Australia, he wouldn't have consented to it. The Court found that the plaintiff had mistakenly believed that the licence to the Reserve Bank would impose limitations similar to those under customary law.

» In the 1998 case of ***Bulan Bulan v R & T Textiles***, the argument was about original artworks created by the plaintiffs being reproduced on carpets and sold without the artist's permission or knowledge. The artworks showed traditional imagery from the artist's clan group. The carpet importers argued that copyright didn't exist in the artworks because the works drew from pre-existing traditional designs and didn't meet the originality and authorship requirements of the ***Copyright Act 1968*** (Cwlth). The Federal Court disagreed and found that, if a design has intricate detail and complexity reflecting great skill and originality, the design therefore satisfies the originality requirements in the law, despite the fact that it may have followed a pre-existing design.

A greater awareness of the fraudulent activities surrounding Indigenous art has led to attempts to protect the work of Indigenous artists and Indigenous art styles. Here's some information about such attempts:

CULTURAL PROTOCOLS

» The Australia Council has produced protocols for working with Indigenous artists and their art that are aimed at improving the respect for both. These include respect, Indigenous control, using the principles of communication, consultation and consent, ensuring proper attribution and copyright protection, and proper returns and royalties. You can find the protocols on their website (www.australiacouncil.gov.au/aboriginal-and-torres-strait-islander-arts).

» An important report on the protection of Aboriginal heritage, knowledge and intellectual property was commissioned, called ***Our Culture Our Future: Report on Australian Indigenous Cultural and Intellectual Property***. The report (which was published in 1999) made several observations about the extent to which Indigenous heritage and culture need to be protected, including the rights to own and control Indigenous cultural and intellectual property, be recognised as the primary guardians and interpreters of their cultures, and authorise or refuse to authorise the commercial use of Indigenous cultural and intellectual property, according to Indigenous customary law.

>> A resale royalty scheme has been introduced to protect artists in Australia (that's all artists, not just Indigenous artists). This scheme was introduced because artists sometimes sell their work for a small sum compared with what it's worth several years later. The scheme was introduced in 2010 and entitles artists to receive a 5 per cent royalty from the sale price of certain works if they are resold. **Note**: The sale price of the work being resold has to be over $1,000 and the artist has to be alive or to have been dead for fewer than 70 years.

>> In 1992, a government-funded, not-for-profit organisation called Desart was established. This peak body represents desert art centres and, in particular, ensures that they employ good management practices and that artists are appropriately rewarded. Today, Desart represents over 34 independent Aboriginal Art and Craft Centres and represents over 8,000 artists.

TIP

Buying art from community art centres and reputable art fairs are good ways to ensure you are buying authentic Indigenous art and that the monies from the sale go back to the artist and the community. Many community art centres now have an online presence so you can learn more about the artists and their art.

REMEMBER

A sale of art doesn't automatically pass on the copyright. Artists in Australia can have Viscopy, a non-profit, artist-owned copyright collecting agency, manage their interests. Of the 6,000 members of Viscopy, 4,000 are Indigenous.

EDDIE BURRUP — OR ELIZABETH DURACK?

Australian artist Elizabeth Durack painted a series of paintings and exhibited under the name of Eddie Burrup. She created a profile for him as an Aboriginal man and had entered her artworks into Native Title Now, an exhibition open only to Indigenous artists. Two were selected for inclusion in the Telstra 13th National Aboriginal and Torres Strait Islander Art Awards. Durack confessed in the March 1997 issue of *Art Monthly* that the paintings were hers.

Before Eddie Burrup, Durack was recognised as an accomplished artist and had illustrated her sister's children's books. Durack defended her actions by explaining that she chose Burrup as 'her medium', inspired by her life experience, including her relationships with Aboriginal people. She described Eddie Burrup as 'a synthesis of several Aboriginal men I have known'.

Her actions caused anger in the Indigenous community, who thought her posing as an Aboriginal man and entering her artwork in competitions that were only for Indigenous artists was insensitive and misleading.

Chapter **17**

Singing and Dancing

As in all cultures, music and dance were a central and powerful part of traditional Indigenous cultural and spiritual life. But they were also a part of everyday life. Traditional music and dance are still practised and performed widely around Australia as part of ceremonial and spiritual life. Music had both a spiritual and educational role, performed in ceremony but also used to teach younger people about their responsibilities and their clans. Songs were accompanied by simple, rhythmic wood instruments that in some places included the didgeridoo, one of the world's oldest musical instruments.

Today, Indigenous people continue to use music as an important source of expression and storytelling. Particular genres of music such as country and western and, more recently, hip-hop, seem to have particularly captured the imagination of Indigenous people, who use their songwriting to describe life experiences. Contemporary Indigenous dance has grown steadily over the last few decades, with groups such as the Bangarra Dance Theatre lauded for their creative and artistic expression, as well as their role in carrying a spiritual and political message to their audiences.

In this chapter, I look at both traditional and contemporary Indigenous performing arts, focusing on music and dance.

Traditional Expression through Music and Dance

Music has a central role in traditional Aboriginal societies and cultures. As with other forms of creative expression, music is often linked with ceremonies and is integral to ancestry and kinship, the landscape and connection to country, the totemic systems and the animals of the area. Music is also connected with important events such as changes of season, water and rain, healing and triumph over enemies. Similar to cultural stories told through the oral storytelling tradition, Aboriginal music is handed down from generation to generation through performance. Songs can sometimes be built upon and developed over time and could be of sacred significance or for entertainment.

Dance also can tell a story, through movement — about the land, relationships between people, the journeys and lives of ancestors, and other culturally significant information. Ceremonies that focus on dance are often called *corroborees*. Clan groups would gather together for these important cultural and spiritual events.

Diverse Indigenous cultures across Australia have generated a wide variety of music and instruments; however, most music is rhythmic and accompanied by handclaps, body slaps and instruments (usually percussion instruments played by banging together, or sometimes the didgeridoo).

The sacred and the profane

Traditionally, certain music is reserved for specific types of ceremony while some music is open to anyone, as follows:

>> Sacred and secret music is only performed for sacred and secret ceremonies (sometimes in a particular place or for a special purpose). Some songs can be performed and heard only by men; other songs, often connected with reproduction, can be sung and heard only by women.

>> Semi-sacred music is performed in full only at an appointed ceremonial ground, and seems to have been sung by men while women danced.

>> Non-sacred music can be performed by anyone — men or women — at any time and any place. It's often performed at large gatherings or corroborees and often sung by women while men dance.

Banging out a rhythm

Indigenous people made musical instruments from the materials that were around them, most often wood. Percussion instruments were the most common, used to create rhythms to accompany singing and a beat for dancing. (The didgeridoo is an exception; it relies on rhythmic breathing to create its sound.) Many of the following instruments are used in modern music and dance, and have also been adopted by non-Indigenous performers:

>> **Bullroarer:** A simple wooden slat on a piece of cord is spun and whirled to produce a low-pitched roar. The sound was sometimes used to call people to ceremonies but is more usually associated with boys' initiation ceremonies.

>> **Clapsticks:** Two sticks of wood are banged together to create a rhythmic beat. The paired sticks can vary considerably in shape. Usually one long and slightly flattened stick is grasped in the middle and held flat. The other is more rounded, held towards the end and is used to beat the other.

>> **Didgeridoo:** The most famous instrument used in Indigenous music is the didgeridoo (also called the yidaki in eastern Arnhem Land) and it is one of the oldest musical instruments in the world. The instrument is made from a hollow branch of a tree, further carved by termites nesting in the wood. These branches are cut to length — about 1.5 metres long — making sure both ends are hollow. The mouthpiece is moulded with beeswax or tree gum. Didgeridoos were only played by men, and only used in the north of Australia, from Cape York to Arnhem Land and the Kimberley.

The didgeridoo's distinctive and melodic sound is made by blowing into the instrument with vibrating lips and then using a technique of circular breathing to achieve a continuous sound. Performers also employ techniques for creating harmonic, energetic and rhythmic patterns. During ceremonies, didgeridoos were used to create a constant hum in a deep note with rhythmic patterns and accents created by using the tongue and cheeks. Playing the didgeridoo requires skill and stamina, because the sound is sustained throughout the songs in the ceremony.

>> **Gum leaves:** A tree leaf (often of the eucalypt) is held against the lips and blown. The technique was usually used to imitate bird calls but in more recent times has also been used as a musical instrument to create a tune.

>> **Rasp:** A notched stick is scraped by a second smaller stick. This is different from clapsticks, most notably because the rhythmic sound is created by scraping rather than hitting the two pieces of wood together.

>> **Rattle:** Bunches of seed pods are shaken and used to make a rhythmic sound. This technique is found in Cape York.

>> **Skin drum:** A drum was a rare instrument in Indigenous communities. An hour-glass shaped drum made from lizard or goanna skin is used in ceremonies and dance in areas of Cape York.

Traditional songs

In Indigenous culture, songs were a central part of ceremonies and an important way of maintaining spiritual life. Songs related to mythical figures, the creation of the surrounding landscape, the journeys of ancestors, and other themes related to nature and the supernatural. Songs are constructed of many short verses that may tell a story of a particular place or event or have a strong educative value. They were a method of teaching about Indigenous culture and the environment, and a person's place in them.

Young children were taught songs about everyday tasks they were expected to perform and then, when reaching puberty, were taught what are known as karma songs. These songs are about the totems of the clan and the history and mythology of the group. Each clan's songs have distinctive and unique melodic formulas that allow them to be distinguished from the songs of other groups. Some songs are performed just as entertainment but the karma songs are of central importance to the cultural traditions of the group.

CULTURAL PROTOCOLS

When a man marries and takes on more responsibilities for family and clan, the karma songs are a central part of his education and believed to be his source of spiritual strength. His maturity can be measured in the knowledge he has acquired through songs and ceremonies.

Cultural dance

Traditional dancing is very energetic and usually done for ceremonial purposes. It was closely associated with song. The performances were associated with specific places, and dance grounds were often sacred places. Body decoration and specific gestures related to kin and other relationships all added to the ceremony and the performance. Different communities have different dances and they tell different stories. As with most Indigenous knowledge, the people who are the custodians of a particular story are the only ones allowed to perform those dances. Permission is needed before someone else can perform them. Dances have been passed on for centuries and generations, and remain important to Indigenous people today. Generally, dances, through movement, evoke particular stories or tasks — such as mimicking kangaroos or sharks, hunting with spears, paddling a canoe, or natural phenomena such as waves.

EVOLVING CEREMONY: THE KRILL KRILL

The Krill Krill ceremony is performed in the east Kimberley and has an interesting gene-sis. Aboriginal artist Rover Thomas (c. 1926 to 1998) lived in the Warmun community near Turkey Creek from the 1970s. The spirit of a woman he had a spiritual connection with revealed to him the songs and story that are the basis of the ceremony, which related to significant religious sites around the area. Thomas told the stories over several years, until they evolved into a ceremony of song and dance.

Thomas's uncle, Paddy Jaminji, painted the storyboards that are used in the ceremony — and these inspired Thomas and other community members to paint in a form that departed from traditional art on canvas, experimenting with landscapes painted on dismantled tea-chests. The number and combination of songs in the ceremony depends on where they are performed and who the audience is but the order of the movement across the landscape is maintained each time. The ceremony is an example of the continuation of an oral tradition of storytelling in evolving and eclectic creative ways.

Carrying a Tune: Contemporary Indigenous Music

Songwriting is a form of storytelling and many Indigenous people use music as a way of continuing a strong storytelling tradition from within their culture. Songs penned by contemporary Indigenous songwriters reflect a whole range of issues — the struggle for land rights and a treaty, Christianity, homelands, animals and Dreaming — and their songs often include traditional language words. But they are also often about love, lost love and unrequited love — themes universal to many songwriters.

Today, Indigenous musicians and performers have adopted many of the imported Western musical styles, sometimes mixing traditional instruments into their contemporary music. Contemporary Indigenous music is a fusion of many styles of music, with rock and country music being two of the most popular. Younger Indigenous people are also attracted to urban street music — such as rap and hip-hop — to express their experiences and aspirations.

Singers in the mainstream

A number of Indigenous Australians have achieved mainstream recognition in the music industry, with singers such as Jimmy Little, Archie Roach, Kev Carmody, Jessica Mauboy and country music star Troy Cassar-Daley some of the most successful. Particularly through the 1970s and 1980s, Aboriginal bands such as No Fixed Address, the Warumpi Band and Us Mob merged their experience with disadvantage and the political ambitions of the era into their music — a blend of different musical influences from rock, country and reggae. A new generation of Indigenous singers and songwriters have embraced the genres of heavy metal, hip-hop or rap. Of this same generation, some musical talents have emerged through song contests such as *Australian Idol* and gone on to enjoy commercial success.

The Torres Strait Islands also have a strong music tradition, with songs focused on the relationship with the islands and the sea. Torres Strait Islander musicians such as the Mills Sisters, Henry 'Seaman' Dan and Christine Anu have enjoyed popularity among wide audiences.

The strong storytelling theme in the lyrics of many Indigenous songs gives them not just educative and entertainment value. Some Indigenous people talk about music as a way of healing from the harder aspects of the lives they've led. Aboriginal singer-songwriter Archie Roach once said, 'I'm blessed that I have music. Some people don't have any outlet whatever for life's knocks and they're the people my heart goes out to. Music — to me — is a medicine'.

A BIG CAREER: JIMMY LITTLE

Jimmy Little's musical career spanned six decades. A Yorta Yorta man, he grew up on Cummeragunja Reserve on the Murray River (refer to Chapter 10). He left there in 1955 at the age of 18 to pursue his music career. By the time his single 'Royal Telephone' reached the top of the Australian music charts in 1963, Little had already released 17 previous singles. He continued to release hit music until 1974, with his song 'Baby Blue'. Little then tried his hand at acting, teaching and community work. He was NAIDOC Person of the Year in 1989.

In 2004, he released his 34th album, *Life's What You Make It,* a collection of contemporary songs by songwriters such as Elvis Costello and Bruce Springsteen that he uniquely interpreted. In 2004, Little had kidney failure and received a life-saving kidney transplant. The experience prompted him to establish the Jimmy Little Foundation to help other Indigenous Australians who suffer from kidney disease. Not surprisingly, Little was named a Living National Treasure and awarded the Order of Australia in 2004. Little retired from performing in 2010 and passed away in 2012.

Talent continues to run in Little's family. His daughter Frances Peters-Little is not only a singer-songwriter but also an historian and filmmaker. Grandson James Henry is also a singer-songwriter who sometimes performed with Little. And Jimmy's niece is famous Indigenous opera singer, composer and playwright Deborah Cheetham.

THE TALENTED YUNUPINGUS

Yothu Yindi is a band with Indigenous and non-Indigenous members. Formed in 1986, the founding Indigenous members were Yolngu men from near Yirrkala on the Gove Peninsula in the Northern Territory — Yothu Yindi means 'child and mother' in the Yolngu language. The band combines traditional Indigenous songs with pop and rock songs, and blends guitars and drums with traditional instruments. The group was led by singer and guitarist Mandawuy Yunupingu, not only a respected musician, but also the first Indigenous person to become principal of a school (he left this position to pursue his musical career). He was Australian of the Year in 1992. Now known as M Yunupingu, he passed away in 2013.

In 1991, Yothu Yindi achieved mainstream musical success with their song 'Treaty' and the album *Tribal Voice*. The group helped established the Yothu Yindi Foundation in 1990 to promote Yolngu cultural development, including producing the annual Garma Festival of traditional cultures. M Yunupingu's older brother, Galarrwuy Yunupingu, is chairman of the Yothu Yindi Foundation, was named Australian of the Year himself in 1978 and sometimes joined Yothu Yindi, playing the guitar.

Another member of Yothu Yindi was Geoffrey Gurrumul Yunupingu. An exceptionally gifted musician, he played guitar, drums, keyboards and didjeridoo, but it was the clarity and strength of his singing voice that was his most acclaimed talent. Born on Elcho Island in 1971, he taught himself how to play the piano and accordion at four, taking up the guitar the following year. Starting out in Yothu Yindi in 1989, he left in 1995 to found Saltwater Band. His first solo album, *Gurrumul*, was released in 2008. It won Best World Music Album at the ARIAs. He released three more albums, *Rrakala* (2011), *The Gospel Album* (2015) and *Djarimirri (Children of the Rainbow) (2018)*. Known after his death in 2017 as Dr G Yunupingu, at the time of his passing he was the most commercially successful Aboriginal Australian musician. That Geoffrey was also blind — a condition he had since birth — hadn't learned Braille and didn't use a cane or guide dog made his achievements all the more extraordinary.

Both types: Country and western

Although a range of musical genres has influenced Indigenous Australians, country music seems to have been a natural home for Indigenous musicians. The themes of connection to country, hardship in living off the land, rural poverty, the loneliness of heartbreak and the healing power of love all seem to have found a resonance with Indigenous storytellers. Indigenous country stars such as Dougie Young, Jimmy Little (who also enjoyed success on the pop charts), Col Hardy, Vic Simms, Gus Williams, Bob Randall, Warren H. Williams and Troy Cassar-Daley aren't just loved because their music is entertaining. Indigenous people also relate to the stories their songs tell and these artists, through their music, educate a wider audience about Indigenous culture and experience.

Clinton Walker's book, *Buried Country: The Story of Aboriginal Country Music*, is based on a documentary of the same name. Providing an account of six decades of Indigenous country music, it explains how, even though songs in this genre seem simple, they express complex emotions and worldviews.

TIP

For a great range of Indigenous artists, check out CAAMA Music. The label has been working with Indigenous artists for over 40 years and had developed talent from Central Australia and beyond — see caamamusic.com.au for more information.

Rock and pop

When Jimmy Little hit the number-one spot on the Australian music charts with his single 'Royal Telephone' in 1963, he was hailed as the first Indigenous pop star. He paved the way for Indigenous performers. In the 1970s and 1980s, Aboriginal rock bands such as the Warumpi Band, Coloured Stone, No Fixed Address and Us Mob started to hit the mainstream, attracting audiences through their tough lyrics, which spoke about fighting racism and overcoming disadvantage.

Many singers and songwriters have found country music the genre that attracts them. However, performers such as Archie Roach, the late Ruby Hunter, Bobby McLeod, Dan Sultan, Vic Simms and Kev Carmody have traversed many genres, including rock and pop music, giving voice to Indigenous experiences and perspectives through their music and lyrics.

COUNTRY'S GOLDEN BOY: TROY CASSAR-DALEY

Troy Cassar-Daley grew up in Grafton, New South Wales, and is an award-winning country musician. His first single, 'Dream Out Loud', was released in 1994 and reached the top position on the Australian country music charts. He released an album the following year and won the 1995 ARIA Award for Best Country Record (winning again in 2000, 2006 and 2009) and Best Male Vocalist at the 1996 Country Music Awards in Tamworth (and again in 1998, 2000, 2003, 2006, 2008, 2010, 2013 and 2016!). Cassar-Daley has won a total of 37 Golden Guitars at the Tamworth Country Music Awards, the APRA Country Song of the Year in 2008 and 2010, and 9 Deadly Awards. His albums include *Beyond the Dancing*, *True Believer*, *Big River*, *Long Way Home*, *Almost Home* and *I Love This Place*. In 2016, Troy released an autobiography and accompanying album, *Things I Carry Around*. In 2018, he released a *Greatest Hits* album.

ALL IN THE FAMILY: THE DONOVANS

The Donovans is an Indigenous country band made up mostly of brothers Michael, Ashley and Merv, with Troy Russell on drums. The family also includes Casey Donovan, daughter of Merv Donovan. In 2004 at the age of 16, Casey became the youngest winner of the second *Australian Idol* competition, and has since gone on to release solo albums and singles, star in theatre and musicals and reality TV. Singer-songwriter Emma Donovan is also a member of this famous musical family and sang with the Donovans at the age of seven. In 2000, she started Indigenous all-female band The Stiff Gins, leaving them in 2003 to pursue a solo career.

Aboriginal bands such as the Pigram Brothers from Broome and the Donovans from Sydney have audience appeal across Australia. Many mix traditional music with contemporary rock sounds: Yothu Yindi from Arnhem Land, Blekbala Mujik from Barunga and Nabarlek from the Manmoyi outstation in western Arnhem Land. Some mix their lyrics, using traditional language and English: Frank Yamma sings in English and Pitjantjatjara. And Saltwater — which included sometimes-solo performer Geoffrey Gurrumul Yunupingu — performed in a mixture of Yolngu Matha and English. David Hudson, an accomplished didgeridoo player, combines the traditional instrument with musical genres from classical to dance music.

Indigenous women have also used music as a vehicle for expression. Emma Donovan, Leah Flanagan, Kerrianne Cox, Marlene Cummins, Mo'Ju, Ursula Yovich, Thelma Plum and the late Ruby Hunter have all enjoyed success with audiences who relate to the powerful storytelling in their music. Indigenous all-female bands have enjoyed a popular following. Tiddas (*tidda* is Indigenous slang for 'sister') was a trio of Indigenous women from Victoria — Sally Dastey, Amy Saunders and Lou Bennett — who performed together in the 1990s and were loved for their rich harmonies. The Stiff Gins — Nardi Simpson and Kaleena Briggs, and previously Emma Donovan — hail from New South Wales.

While Indigenous artists once found themselves on the outside of the mainstream music industry due to the colour of their skin, today they not only have conquered every form of popular music genre, but are also running the show. Gadigal Music Label was a record label established by the Gadigal Information Service — which also runs Koori Radio and offers a recording studio for hire. So not only do they help record Indigenous music, but they can also put it on the air. Similarly, CAAMA Music Label is connected with CAAMA Radio, providing a place to record and disseminate the music of Aboriginal and Torres Strait Islander people.

REMEMBER The Black Arm Band is a group of Australian musicians — Indigenous and non-Indigenous — who perform together in the 'spirit and action of reconciliation'. The make-up of the band changes over time but it has been popular at festivals, when touring to remote and regional areas, performing and conducting community workshops. Indigenous musicians who have played with the Black Arm Band include Lou Bennett, Emma Donovan, Kutcha Edwards, Leah Flanagan, Jimmy Little, Amy Saunders, Dan Sultan, Bart Willoughby, Ursula Yovich, Geoffrey Gurrumul Yunupingu, Archie Roach and the late Ruby Hunter. Numerous non-Indigenous musicians perform with the band, and special guest artists have included Jimmy Barnes and Paul Kelly. The band won Band of the Year in the 2008 Deadlys.

Just a few of the best

Although many Indigenous bands have a strong following in the Indigenous community and on the country music, folk music and world music circuits, some recent chart toppers have emerged. These include Casey Donovan (see the sidebar 'All in the family: The Donovans), as well as the following:

>> **Jessica Mauboy:** Hailing from Darwin, Mauboy was the runner-up on *Australian Idol* contest in 2006 but has gone on to be the highest-selling female contestant from the show. Her music career since then has gone from strength to strength. She released her debut live album, *The Journey*, in 2007, which reached number four on the charts. To date she has released six top-10 albums and nine top-10 singles. Mauboy made her acting debut in the movie *Bran Nue Dae* in 2010 (see Chapter 19 for more on this film) and went on to star in *The Secret Daughter* in 2015. She competed for Australia in Eurovision in 2018. In 2019 she released her fourth studio album, *Hilda*, and it debuted at number one.

>> **Dan Sultan:** Sultan's music has been described as 'an electrifying romp through rockabilly, blues, country, soul and rock 'n' roll'. His 2009 album *Get Out While You Can* was one of the highest independent country music releases in Australia. He won two Deadly Awards in 2010 and ARIA Awards for Best Independent Artist, Best Blues and Roots Album and Male Artist of the Year. His 2014 album, *Blackbird*, won the ARIA award for Best Rock Album of the year. Dan appeared alongside Jessica Mauboy in the 2010 film *Bran Nue Dae* as Lester (see Chapter 19). His album *Killer*, released in 2017, was nominated for three ARIA awards. Sultan grew up in Williamstown, Melbourne, and is descended from the Arrernte and Gurindji people. Sultan started playing guitar when he was four years old and wrote his first song at the age of ten.

» **Archie Roach and Ruby Hunter:** Partners in life and in music, Roach and Hunter were a formidable duo. Archie Roach was born near Shepparton, in central Victoria, in 1956, but was taken from his family at the age of about four. He walked out of his foster home at the age of 15 and spent many years on the streets and searching for his family. He recorded his first album, *Charcoal Lane*, in 1990 to great acclaim. Roach writes songs about some of the difficult issues that face Indigenous people, and is a strong campaigner against excessive drinking and domestic violence. His song 'Took the Children Away' is about the moment he was taken away from his family and has become an anthem for members of the Stolen Generations. Archie released his biography, *Tell Me Why: The story of my life and music*, in 2019.

Ruby Hunter met Roach when she was just 16 and they were both homeless. Ruby was a Ngarrindjeri woman and a respected singer and songwriter in her own right, with albums including *Thoughts Within* released in 1995 and *Feeling Good* in 2000. She won Deadly Awards for Female Artist of the Year in 2000 and Outstanding Contribution to Aboriginal and Torres Strait Islander Music in 2003. She was deeply mourned when she passed away in 2010.

Hip-hop, rap and metal: Young people have their say

Hip-hop and rap (musical forms that spring from African-American performers from the United States) and their punchy, raw expression has attracted a fan base among younger Indigenous Australians, relating to messages about disempowerment in the system and reassertion of identity as a form of resistance or subversion. Young Indigenous performers are using these musical genres to put forward their views on the issues facing Indigenous young people, particularly in urban areas, and often focus on identity, urban poverty, and empowerment and disempowerment as themes in their work. Groups working with young people, such as Deadly Vibe, often include hip-hop and rapping as a way of fostering confidence and self-esteem.

Wire MC is a well-known hip-hop and rap performer from the Gumbaynggirr nation in north-eastern New South Wales. He has said that the MC stands for 'my cousin'. He has explained how he sees his music as a way of communicating: 'Hip-hop is the voice of the community, of the area. It helps you represent where you're from. It teaches you self-knowledge and self-awareness'. He has also explained how he sees this new form of musical expression as an extension of an older tradition: 'Hip-hop is the new clapsticks, hip-hop is the new corroboree'.

ALWAYS BLACK: A B ORIGINAL

A B Original is a hip-hop duo that brings together Briggs (Adam Briggs) and Trials (Daniel Rankine). Standing for Always Black Original, their music is feisty, political and passionate. Their single, *January 26*, which featured Dan Sultan, gave a frank view about having the day that the first colony was established as a national holiday. A multi-award winning album, *Reclaim Australia*, was released in 2016. They were awarded Songwriter of the Year at the 2018 APRA Music Awards.

Briggs, who also refers to himself as Senator Briggs, is also well known as a solo rapper, actor and television writer, and for his witty and insightful critiques of the issues facing Indigenous people in Australia. He has released three studio albums: *Blacklist* (2010), *Sheplife* (2014) and *Briggs for PM* (scheduled for 2021).

FROM THE TORRES STRAIT

As in other parts of Australia, music in the Torres Strait was a central part of spiritual and cultural life. Songs were a part of ceremonies and a key way of passing down cultural stories. However, many songs are unique to the Torres Strait and many relate to the relationship to the sea and its central place as a source of food and life. Today, over two-thirds of Torres Strait Islanders live on the Australian mainland and music is an important way through which they maintain their connection to country. Torres Strait Islanders also use contemporary song for storytelling and entertainment. Well-known Torres Strait Islander performers include

- Christine Anu, whose song 'My Island Home' has become an unofficial anthem for the Torres Strait Islands. 'Sunshine on a Rainy Day' was also a chart success. Her first album, *Styling Up*, went platinum. Anu also appeared in the movie *Moulin Rouge!*

- Henry 'Seaman' Dan, whose songs are a fusion of traditional Torres Strait Islander and pearling songs with jazz, hula and blues. Born in 1929, he continues to be a much-loved performer and his song, 'TI Blues' is a sentimental favourite in the Torres Strait.

- The Mills Sisters — Rita (guitar), Cessa (ukulele) and Ina (tambourine) — started singing in the 1950s and in the 1980s started to tour outside the Torres Strait.

- Mau Power is a hip-hop artist from Thursday Island. During a period of incarceration in 2001, he decided to focus on music and in 2019 released his third studio album, *Blue Lotus Awakening*.

Another important first wave hip-hop and rap group was The Last Kinection. Formed in 2006 in Newcastle, north of Sydney, its members were Jacob Turier (who also performs as DJ Jaytee) and siblings Joel Wenitong (who used to be in another hip-hop and rap band, Local Knowledge) and Naomi Wenitong (who enjoyed some chart success as part of a female rock duo performing as Shakaya). The trio said they were inspired to form the band after the death of four of their Elders (hence the word 'kin' in their name) and used their music to express their pride.

Other well-known Indigenous hip-hop and rap performers include Mau Power, South West Syndicate, Urthboy, Baker Boy, Nooky, Jimblah, Ebony Williams, Morganics, Brothablack and Munkimuk (also known as Munki Mark).

TIP

To find out more about the strong voices in Indigenous hip-hop, check out the anthology edited by Ellen van Neerven, *Homeland Calling: Words from a new generation of Aboriginal and Torres Strait Islander voices* (2020).

Heavy metal bands produce yet another form of expression through music. NoKTuRNL is a metal band led by Craig Tilmouth and Damian Young from Alice Springs. Their music has appeared in the movies *Radiance* and *Yolngu Boy*, and their album *Time Flies* was released in 2003.

Jumping into Modern Indigenous Dance

Many Indigenous dance groups in Australia perform to keep culture alive, passing on dances and the stories they represent to younger generations, and to teach non-Indigenous people about the diversity of Indigenous Australia. Dance remains an important way in which non-Indigenous people can learn about and experience Indigenous culture. In recent years, the focus on contemporary dance by Indigenous performers and choreographers has intensified. In particular, this focus has seen the establishment of a dance academy — the National Aboriginal and Islander Skills Development Association (NAISDA) — and the emergence of a national dance company with an international reputation — the Bangarra Dance Theatre.

Indigenous dance companies

Indigenous dance is very popular around Australia, and Indigenous dance companies give audiences an Indigenous cultural experience through the medium.

A NATIONAL DANCE ACADEMY

The National Aboriginal and Islander Skills Development Association (NAISDA) was established in 1975 to train Indigenous dancers. One of the driving forces was African-American dancer Carole Johnson. NAISDA grew the first Indigenous dance company — the Aboriginal Islander Dance Theatre (AIDT). AIDT disbanded in 1998 when artistic director Raymond Blanco left the company. NAISDA is now based in Gosford in New South Wales and produces graduates in all aspects of dance practice and performance, including arts management, music and film.

TIP

BlakDance is the peak body for Indigenous dance in Australia. It supports independent artists and small and emerging companies, embracing a philosophy of self-determination. (go to www.blakdance.org.au to find out more).

Some of the better known Indigenous dance companies are:

>> **Descendance Aboriginal and Islander Dance Theatre Company** performs both traditional and contemporary dance from Aboriginal and Torres Strait Islander communities. The company is Sydney-based but has toured internationally as well as extensively around Australia. It also creates performances with a range of influences fused with Indigenous dance, including flamenco, Indian, Native American and African.

>> **Nunukul Yuggera Aboriginal Dancers** from south-east Queensland performs dances from the Nunukul (also spelled Noonuccal), Yuggera (also Jagera), Yugimbir and Nugi clans. The company also has a strong emphasis on education and aims to improve the understanding of its audiences about the culture of the area as well as to educate younger generations of Indigenous people about their cultural heritage.

>> **Tjapukai Aboriginal Dance Theatre** has its home in the Tjapukai Aboriginal Cultural Park near Cairns and the small town of Kuranda. The group showcases the culture of the local area.

>> **Wadumbah Dance Group** showcases dances from Western Australia (the group is based in Perth), with a particular focus on those of the Noongar nation, the traditional owners of south-western Australia.

REMEMBER

Indigenous dance companies are not only dedicated to continuing cultural traditions and educating the broader community about Indigenous culture. They also provide employment opportunities for Indigenous people — as dancers, musicians, set and costume designers, and arts administrators — and they develop good role models for younger Indigenous people.

The Bangarra Dance Theatre

The Bangarra Dance Theatre (www.bangarra.com.au) is one of Australia's leading performing arts organisations (the word Bangarra is from the Wiradjuri language and means 'to make fire'). Established in 1989 under the guidance of Carole Johnson, Bangarra came into its own when Stephen Page became its artistic director in 1991. Performing creative and commercially successful programs nationally and internationally ever since, the organisation performs to over 50,000 people each year.

Bangarra's works combine traditional Aboriginal and Torres Strait Islander history and culture with contemporary dance styles. The company works with traditional dancers around Australia to ensure cultural protocols are observed when learning works from traditional dance. It also ensures the dancers return to country to show the finished production to the local community that helped foster it.

Stories are diverse and come from all over the country, including the Torres Strait Islands. *Bush* (2004) traced the journey of an older woman's spirit as she travels across her country. *Mathinna* (2008) is the story of an Aboriginal girl adopted into a white family who then finds herself caught between two cultures. 'ID', part of the 2011 *Belong* performance, was an exploration of the issues surrounding contemporary Indigenous identity. *Patyegarang* (2014) and *Bennelong* (2017) explored the lives of two important Aboriginal figures in the first years of the Sydney colony. *Dark Emu* (2019) explored the richness of Aboriginal and Torres Strait Islander knowledges.

REMEMBER

Some of Indigenous Australia's finest dancers have worked with the company, including the late Russell Page, Elma Kris, Yolande Brown, Jasmin Sheppard, Patrick Thaiday, Beau Dean Riley, Waangenga Blanco and Sidney Saltner. Senior Indigenous dancers from around Australia, including Kathy Marika and Djakapurra Munyarryun, mentor and work with dancers in the company. Alongside Stephen Page, Bangarra has seen the emergence of Indigenous choreographers Frances Rings, Daniel Riley and Elma Kris. In addition, the company has fostered talent in other aspects of dance production, including musical director David Page and set designer Jacob Nash.

Bangarra works collaboratively with other Australian performing arts companies (such as the Australian Ballet and Sydney Theatre Company), showcasing Australian dance talent and performing at important international events, such as the opening and closing ceremonies at the 2000 Sydney Olympic Games and the 2018 Commonwealth Games. Bangarra dancer Lillian Banks also featured in the 2020 ABC documentary *Freeman*, which was co-directed by Stephen Page.

THE PAGE BOYS

Stephen, David and Russell Page were born into a family of 12 children. They were born in Brisbane and are descended from the Nunukul (also spelled Noonuccal) people. The three brothers became key artistic forces within the Bangarra Dance Theatre and have worked more broadly in the Australian performing arts.

Stephen Page has been artistic director of the Bangarra Dance Theatre since 1991. After graduating from NAISDA in 1983, Stephen danced for the Sydney Dance Company and then in 1991 worked in choreography for the Sydney Dance Company, Sydney Theatre Company and the Australian Opera. He has been a driving cultural force within Bangarra but also continues to work collaboratively with other performing arts companies such as the Sydney Theatre Company and the Australian Ballet. He won a Helpmann Award in 2016. He was named New South Wales Australian of the Year in 2008 and presented the NAIDOC Lifetime Achievement Award in 2016. His son, Hunter Page-Lochard, has danced with Bangarra and is forging a successful career as an actor.

David Page has written the musical scores for Bangarra's major works and he creates the soundscapes that help make the Bangarra Dance Theatre a unique cultural experience. He studied at the Centre for Aboriginal Studies in Music at Adelaide University before joining his brothers in Sydney in 1989. David's music has been used in important ceremonial events such as the opening ceremony for the 2000 Sydney Olympic Games. David has contributed music to television and worked in collaboration with Indigenous filmmakers. He also received an award for his performance in the play *Page 8* — a coming-of-age story about his own life, told through spoken word, dance, home movies and music — and continues to perform to critical acclaim onstage. He was an Artist in Residence at the Bangarra Dance Theatre and his body of work made him one of the most prolific composers in Australia until his death in 2016.

Russell Page was the lead male dancer for the Bangarra Dance Theatre from 1991 until his death in 2002 at age 34. Russell was also a talented rugby league player but came to prominence as a dancer due to his charismatic stage presence. He performed at the opening ceremony of the Sydney Olympic Games in 2000 and had roles in film and television productions.

Torres Strait Islander dance

Torres Strait Islanders have a distinctive dance tradition. Their ceremonies include dances that reflect central aspects of Torres Strait Islander life. Costumes are also an important part of the cultural practice of dances of the Torres Strait and are often a testament to the people's relationship with the sea, sometimes including fishing implements or headdresses with shark motifs. The feather headdresses of the Saibai Islanders are also dramatic and distinctive, adding to the festive feeling of the dance performance. With two-thirds of Torres Strait Islanders now living on the mainland, the tradition of dance is taught in some schools — such as Djarragun College — with larger Torres Strait Islander student populations.

CULTURAL PROTOCOLS

The different islands have their own distinct dances. Mer, also known as Murray Island, in the eastern Torres Strait, has a unique shark dance known as the 'Baizam', a distinct style of dance known as Kab Kar, and costumes particular to their island, including the dhari headdress. This headdress is depicted on the Torres Strait Islander flag (refer to Chapter 2).

The closeness of the Saibai Islands to Papua New Guinea has influenced cultural practices there, seen in the use of long drums that are sometimes covered with sharkskin. These islands have distinctive dances, including the 'Maumatang', a warrior dance performed with bows and arrows and the 'Eagle Dance', where dancers use wooden wings and large headdresses, and perform with rapid head movements.

SHOWCASING INDIGENOUS MUSIC AND DANCE

Indigenous music and dance is often showcased in festivals — sort of modern-day corroborees. Many festivals in Australia — such as WOMADelaide, a festival dedicated to a 'World of Music, Art and Dance' — include a strong program of Indigenous performers. Several festivals focus on Indigenous culture, and key festivals include

- The Cairns Indigenous Art Fair, which celebrates art, dance, music and theatre

- The Barunga Cultural and Sports Festival, held near Katherine each year in June

- The Garma Festival, held in north-east Arnhem Land in the Northern Territory, one of the most famous Indigenous festivals. It's held at Gulkula, a beautiful stringybark forest with views to the ocean, and a site of importance to the Yolngu — it's said that an ancestor, Ganbulabula, created the didgeridoo (yidaki) here. The festival celebrates Yolngu culture — including music and dance — and allows visitors to experience all this on Yolngu country.

- The Laura Aboriginal Dance Festival, held on Cape York Peninsula every second year to celebrate language, song, dance and stories

- Yabun, held on Australia Day — or Invasion Day or Survival Day — in Sydney, a family-focused day, showcasing Indigenous music, dance, history, politics and culture

- The Coming of the Light Festival in the Torres Strait, marking the date of 1 July, the anniversary of the arrival of the London Missionary Society, bringing Christianity with them, with cultural ceremonies on the islands and the mainland

IN THIS CHAPTER

» Learning more about the importance of storytelling in Indigenous cultures

» Identifying books about Indigenous people

» Discussing the emergence of Indigenous authors in Australian literature

» Appreciating the current renaissance in Indigenous writing

» Being aware of the cultural sensitivities around Indigenous writing

Chapter **18**

Indigenous Literature: We've Always Been Storytellers

The past three decades have seen a renaissance in Aboriginal writing. Until colonisation, Indigenous languages were oral and then, from the late 1800s, anthropologists and others began to record some of them as written languages, albeit sometimes getting the subtleties a little wrong. Indigenous people are no longer content to let others write their languages or their stories for them, or to let others write about them.

Indigenous people are now using the written word — English, original languages and sometimes hybrids known as Aboriginal English, Kriol and Torres Strait Creole — to record their own lives, history and cultures. They have also moved into writing in a broad range of genres, from crime writing and commercial women's fiction to memoir and academic theses. Accompanying this development has been a greater assertiveness from Indigenous people and deeper consideration about the protocols that non-Indigenous people should use when writing about Indigenous peoples and their cultures. And, of course, much work is being done to improve literacy levels among the Indigenous community, particularly among children.

In this chapter, I examine this transition from oral to written languages, as well as the emergence of notable Indigenous authors and the publishing houses that have published them. I include information on some of the most notable Indigenous writers and poets, and their works. I also give a useful summary of the protocols established to protect Indigenous cultural content.

Moving From Oral to Written Traditions

Indigenous peoples have an oral tradition, so the fact that storytelling is a big part of life isn't surprising. Cultural stories — often referred to as *Dreamtime* or *Dreaming* stories — were told not for entertainment but to teach. The stories contained messages about morals, values, laws and responsibilities, and explained how the world was made, how different geographical features were formed, why animals had certain characteristics and where the boundaries of traditional lands were drawn. Refer to Chapter 4 for more on oral traditions and the Dreamtime.

Many observations have been made about the conflict between traditional oral cultures such as those of Aboriginal peoples and Torres Strait Islanders and the written traditions of European cultures. Courts of law, for example, sometimes struggle with what weight to give oral history from Aboriginal witnesses against the written accounts of anthropologists and historians.

But, when it comes to writing about Indigenous experiences and cultures, the adoption of the written word as a new way of communicating has been very positive. In similar ways, Aboriginal peoples and Torres Strait Islanders have also embraced other methods of storytelling such as filmmaking.

Many people feel this transition is a positive development because it allows Indigenous cultural stories and practices to be kept safely in archives. This became an important priority for Indigenous communities because the oral cultural tradition of older people handing down stories to younger people was disrupted by the process of colonisation, particularly by the policy of removing Indigenous children from their families. Because of this historical experience, Indigenous peoples have placed a great emphasis on the preservation of their cultures. Writing has provided a valuable way to make sure important cultural information isn't lost.

**MYTH
BUSTER**

Despite the tension between an oral tradition and writing, Aboriginal peoples and Torres Strait Islanders have embraced writing, seeing it as a way of continuing the tradition of storytelling.

**CULTURAL
PROTOCOLS**

In traditional Indigenous cultures, the telling of a Dreamtime or cultural story carried with it complex cultural protocols. Some stories contained information that could only be told to people initiated into the clan. Others related to 'men's business' and 'women's business' so couldn't be told to people of the opposite sex. For this reason, great sensitivity still remains over the telling of Dreamtime or cultural stories. Gaining permission from the people who are the custodians of those stories, before telling them to someone else, is important.

Writing about the 'Aborigine' in Australian Literature

Many people have been fascinated by Indigenous peoples and their cultures, and both have been the subject of novels by non-Indigenous people.

Sometimes non-Indigenous authors had negative views about Indigenous peoples and their cultures but on other occasions authors were motivated by good intentions, wanting to raise awareness about the plight of Australia's Indigenous peoples.

Ever since Indigenous characters first appeared in novels written by non-Indigenous people, Indigenous people have had strong reactions to how they're portrayed. The feeling that even sympathetic authors stereotyped Indigenous people and misrepresented Indigenous cultures contributed to the desire of Indigenous people to take up the pen and write their stories themselves.

White people writing about black people

Although Indigenous people featured prominently in the observations of colonists in diaries and other non-fiction forms of writing, exploring Indigenous characters in literature was something writers began to do more widely in the early 20th century.

The motivation for exploring the lives of Indigenous characters as part of a storyline was often motivated by sympathy of those writers for the marginalisation of Indigenous people in Australian society and the poor conditions that many Indigenous people lived in. These authors hoped that their work would reach an audience whose understanding about the issues facing Indigenous people would be deepened.

REMEMBER

Despite the good intentions of the authors, Indigenous people have been critical of the way they've been portrayed in literature written by white Australians, often believing that Indigenous characters are portrayed in one-dimensional or racist ways.

Here's a list of some noteworthy authors and their books that feature Indigenous characters:

» **Arthur Upfield (1890–1964):** The Bony detective series by Arthur Upfield comprises 29 books featuring a 'half-caste' Aboriginal detective, Napoleon Bonaparte, known as 'Bony'. Bony was an orphan who was later initiated into his mother's tribe. He became conscious of his heritage, living between the cultures of both black and white people, using his skills to help the police solve difficult cases.

In 1971, the books were made into a television series called **Boney**, with a second series the following year. The producers of the TV show angered Aboriginal people by using a New Zealander, James Laurenson, instead of an Aboriginal actor, to play the lead character. Laurenson was not aware of the controversy when he took on the role.

» **Katherine Susannah Pritchard (1883–1969):** Pritchard was a well-known journalist, feminist and founding member of the Communist Party of Australia. Pritchard wrote her novel **Coonardoo** in 1929 after visiting a cattle station in Western Australia. The novel focuses on the relationship between Hughie, the son and eventual owner of the property, and Coonardoo, an Aboriginal woman living on the property. The book makes a commentary about the way white cattle station owners treated Aboriginal women, and sought to make a case that people had a responsibility to look after Aboriginal people in a compassionate way.

» **Xavier Herbert (1901–1984):** Herbert's first book, **Capricornia**, published in 1938, was based on his experiences as a Protector of Aborigines in Darwin. Based on a fictional place called Capricornia, the book follows the fortunes of a series of characters but makes commentary about the attitudes and treatment of Aboriginal people by government bureaucrats (who, in this book, are seen as incompetent, negligent, uncaring and often cruel).

Herbert's later book **Poor Fellow, My Country** won the prestigious Miles Franklin award in 1975. (It's also often credited as the longest Australian novel, at more than 1,436 pages!) This book, like **Capricornia**, deals with the treatment of Aboriginal people and the relationships between black and white Australians. Herbert has been described as 'a visionary defender of Aboriginal rights who enjoyed talking like a racist'.

>> **Thomas Keneally (1935–):** Keneally is one of Australia's greatest writers. His novel ***The Chant of Jimmie Blacksmith***, published in 1972, tells the story of the title character, a 'half-caste' Aboriginal man who attempts to fit in to white society by becoming educated and marrying a white woman. Jimmie is constantly subjected to racism and in the end, trapped between two worlds, he snaps and embarks on a killing spree. ***The Chant of Jimmy Blacksmith*** was short-listed for a Booker Prize and made into a film in 1978 by Fred Schepisi, starring Aboriginal actor Tommy Lewis as Jimmie Blacksmith.

Keneally said subsequently, in 2000, that he would take a different approach if he were writing the same book now; he said he wouldn't presume to write from the perspective of an Aboriginal person, but instead he'd tell it through the eyes of the white characters. This is because he thought it was difficult, on reflection, to tell the story through the eyes of an Aboriginal person.

FINDING *THE SECRET RIVER*: KATE GRENVILLE

Australian author Kate Grenville's book *The Secret River* (2005) tells the story of William Thornhill who arrives in the Australian colony as a convict and takes over land for farming — despite the clear signs of Aboriginal occupation — and goes on to establish himself as a wealthy farmer and landowner. Inspired by Grenville's family history, the story is told from Thornhill's perspective but, due to Grenville's power as a writer, the book also provides evidence of the deep connection the Aboriginal people have to their country and of the violence inflicted upon them. Grenville is able to convey this without creating an Aboriginal character to explain it.

The book was turned into a play by Andrew Bovell in 2013 and also a television miniseries in 2015. In those, Aboriginal characters were introduced, developed by Indigenous creatives — writers, advisors and traditional owners — to include that perspective.

The sequel, *Sarah Thornhill* (2011), narrates the continuing family story from the perspective of William Thornhill's daughter. Grenville then explores the experiences of William Dawes, an engineer in the early days of the colony who was also an astronomer, in her 2008 book, *The Lieutenant*. It also includes the relationship Dawes developed with the Aboriginal people living near the colony. Grenville revisits the character of Dawes and the relationship the early colonists has with Aboriginal people in her book *A Room Made of Leaves* (2020), an historical novel based on the life of Elizabeth Macarthur (wife of pastoralist John Macarthur — refer to Chapter 8).

In *Searching for the Secret River* (2006), Grenville writes about the process of researching her family history as material for the novel.

Black people writing about black people

The first Indigenous people to pick up a pen and write their own stories were trailblazers. They showed Indigenous people that writing from an Indigenous perspective was possible and that they could take back control of the image of Indigenous peoples and the portrayal of their cultures. They were also able to give the wider community a chance to see, sometimes for the first time, a view of the world from an Indigenous perspective. Here are a few of those first Indigenous writers:

>> **David Unaipon (1872–1967):** Unaipon was a Ngarrindjeri man, a preacher and an inventor, and is also credited as the first Aboriginal person to publish a book. He wrote Aboriginal cultural legends and published booklets under his own name: *Hungarrda* in 1927, *Kinie Ger: The Native Cat* in 1928 and *Native Legends* in 1929. Unaipon published poetry in the 1930s and more books about Indigenous legends in the 1950s and 1960s. Unaipon's collected legends were also published in 1930 by William Ramsay Smith as *Myths and Legends of the Australian Aborigines* — but without any acknowledgement that it was Unaipon's work. Unaipon appears on the Australian $50 note.

>> **Jack Davis (1917–2000):** Jack Davis wrote about Aboriginal life, working and living on the land, the bush and Australian society. His autobiographical works — *Jack Davis: A Life Story* (1988) and *A Boy's Life* (1991) — have won critical acclaim. He also wrote for the stage and penned poetry.

>> **Oodgeroo Noonuccal (1920–1993):** Also known as Kath Walker, Oodgeroo Noonuccal was descended from the Noonuccal people of Stradbroke Island, Queensland. She published her first book of poetry in 1964, titled *We Are Going*. She was a trailblazer for Indigenous writing and also played an active life in Aboriginal cultural and political matters.

>> **Philip McLaren (1943–):** Phillip McLaren won the David Unaipon Award in 1992 for *Sweet Water: Stolen Land*, published the following year. He has written four subsequent books, including *Scream Black Murder*, a crime novel with an Aboriginal detective as the central character and set in the Aboriginal community of Redfern in Sydney.

>> **Sam Watson (1952–2019):** Sam Watson wrote *The Kadaitcha Sung*, published in 1990, as well as writing for the stage and screen. Watson was actively involved in political campaigns to protect the rights of Aboriginal peoples and Torres Strait Islanders.

Watson also bred some remarkable literary talent — his son, Samuel Wagan Watson, is an award-winning poet and his daughter, Nicole Watson, recently won the David Unaipon Award (see the sidebar 'David Unaipon Award Winners').

DAVID UNAIPON AWARD WINNERS

One of the most prestigious awards for Indigenous writing is the David Unaipon Award, part of the Queensland Premier's Literary Awards. David Unaipon was the first Indigenous author to be published so it is fitting that the award in his name is for unpublished authors. The Unaipon Award began in 1989 (the first winner was Graeme Dixon for **Holocaust Island**) and part of the prize is publication by the University of Queensland Press. The award has introduced many Indigenous authors to the Australian public, including these winners over a 20-year period:

- 1999: *Of Muse, Meandering and Midnight* by Samuel Wagan Watson
- 2000: *Bitin' Back* by Vivienne Cleven
- 2001: *The Mish* by Robert Lowe
- 2002: *Home* by Larissa Behrendt (that's me!)
- 2003: *Whispers of This Wik Woman* by Fiona Doyle
- 2004: *Swallow the Air* by Tara June Winch
- 2005: *Anonymous Premonition* by Yvette Holt
- 2006: *Me, Antman and Fleabag* by Gayle Kennedy
- 2007: *Skin Painting* by Elizabeth Eileen Hodgson
- 2008: *Every Secret Thing* by Marie Munkara
- 2009: *The Boundary* by Nicole Watson
- 2010: *Purple Threads* by Jeanine Leane
- 2011: *'Mazing Grace* by Dylan Coleman
- 2012: *Story* by Siv Parker
- 2013: *Heat and Light* by Ellen van Neerven
- 2014: *It's not just Black and White* by Lesley Williams and Tammy Williams
- 2015: *The First Octoroon or Report of an Experimental Child* by Andrew Booth
- 2016: *Dancing Home* by Paul Collis
- 2017: *Mirrored Places* by Lisa Fuller (published as *Ghost Bird*)
- 2018: *Making of Ruby Champion* by Kirstie Parker (yet to be published)

No prize was awarded for 2019 and, at the time of writing, the 2020 prize was yet to be announced.

>> **Kerry Reed-Gilbert (1956–2019):** Kerry Reed-Gilbert was a poet, advocate for Aboriginal rights and culture, and an educator. She published several books of poetry, including *Black Woman Black Life* in 1996 and *Talkin' About Country* in 2002. She also edited several collections of Indigenous writing and voices: *Message Stick: Contemporary Aboriginal Writing* (1997) and *The Strength of Us: Black Women Speak* (2000).

Establishing Indigenous Literature

Literature by Aboriginal people and Torres Strait Islanders is enjoying a renaissance, with a rich diversity of fiction, life stories and non-fiction being written by Indigenous authors. Poetry has also been a popular form of writing explored by Indigenous people.

Not surprisingly, as Indigenous writing has flourished, Aboriginal and Torres Strait Islander authors have diversified into writing in many different genres, including crime novels and commercial women's fiction (or 'chick lit').

Indigenous writing has been an effective way of drawing attention to the issues of Indigenous Australia, with books such as *My Place* by Sally Morgan and *Follow the Rabbit-Proof Fence* by Doris Garimara Pilkington enjoying commercial success, the latter also being adapted for a movie. Indigenous writing often appears on the reading lists of schools and universities.

REMEMBER

By the age of 15, one-third of Indigenous students don't have adequate skills and knowledge in reading literacy. Indigenous content in books can assist in engaging Indigenous kids in reading.

Breaking through with Indigenous novels

Some books by Indigenous authors have broken new ground either by enjoying unprecedented commercial or literary success, or by entering into a genre that Indigenous writing hadn't ventured into before.

Some important novels by Indigenous authors include

>> **Doris Garimara Pilkington, *Follow the Rabbit-Proof Fence* (1996):** Made into the movie *Rabbit-Proof Fence* by Phillip Noyce in 2002 (see Chapter 19), the story educated Australians — and people all around the world — about the policies that led to the Stolen Generations, which removed Aboriginal children from their families on the basis of their race.

- **Kim Scott, *Benang: From the Heart* (1999):** *Benang* won the Western Australian Premier's Book Awards Fiction Award in 1999 and the Miles Franklin Award in 2000. It was Scott's second novel. His 2010 novel, *That Deadman Dance*, also won the Miles Franklin Award.

- **Sally Morgan, *My Place* (1999):** Sally Morgan's book about her family history and the way they came to terms with their Indigenous identity became a bestseller. It won a Human Rights literature award.

- **Alexis Wright, *Carpentaria* (2006):** *Carpentaria* won the Vance Palmer Award for Fiction, the top fiction prize of the Victorian Premier's Literary Awards, a Queensland Premier's Literary Award and the Miles Franklin award in 2007. *Carpentaria* is both funny and profound and told from the perspective of an Aboriginal elder. Wright's style in this novel has been compared with Gabriel Garcia Marquez and Salman Rushdie. She won much critical acclaim for her 2013 novel, *The Song Book*.

- **Tara June Winch, *Swallow the Air* (2006):** After winning the David Unaipon Award in 2004, *Swallow the Air* went on to win the Victorian Premier's Award for a first book of fiction in 2006 and the Nita May Dobbie Literary Award in 2007. Winch's book focuses on the struggles of an Aboriginal family but most critics are drawn to the elegance of the writing. Her 2019 novel, *The Yield* won the Miles Franklin Award.

- **Anita Heiss, *Not Meeting Mr Right* (2007), *Avoiding Mr Right* (2008), *Manhattan Dreaming* (2010), *Tiddas* (2014), *Barbed Wire* and *Cherry Blossoms* (2016):** Anita Heiss is a prolific author and an active promoter of Indigenous writing. She has, through her books, created the unique genre of commercial women's fiction with Indigenous women as her main characters. Written for women, these books explore relationships but also deal with serious issues around racism and Aboriginal identity. Anita is an active champion for Aboriginal literacy projects.

- **Tony Birch, *Blood* (2011), *Ghost River* (2016), *The White Girl* (2019):** Tony Birch is a poet, essayist and writer of short stories and novels. He writes of the tenacity of Aboriginal people facing difficult life circumstances and creates strong, vivid characters. He is also known for his strong evocations of country. Tony also writes about environmental issues and is an historian. In 2017 he became the first Indigenous writer to win the Patrick White Award.

- **Melissa Lucashenko, *Mullumbimby* (2013), *Too Much Lip* (2018):** Melissa Lucashenko is a prolific novelist and essayist. Her stories of Aboriginal history and experience also explore connection to country and the strength of culture and family. *Mullumbimby* won the Victorian Premier's Literary Award for Indigenous Writing; *Too Much Lip* won the Miles Franklin Award. She is a founding member of Sisters Inside and works to protect the rights of women prisoners as well as being a strong advocate for the rights of Indigenous people.

Putting it into verse: Aboriginal poetry

Indigenous writers seem very comfortable in the genre of poetry and it's a popular form of written expression. Poetry is like songwriting, another form of expression popular with Aboriginal people and Torres Strait Islanders, so it's not surprising that Indigenous poets have flourished. In addition to Jack Davis, Oodgeroo Noonuccal and Kerry Reed-Gilbert (refer to the section 'Black people writing about black people', earlier in this chapter), here are just a few of the popular Indigenous poets:

>> **Herb Wharton (1936–):** Watson was a former stockman, drover and labourer who turned his hand to writing in the 1980s. He wrote novels, short stories and two books of poetry, ***Kings with Empty Pockets*** and ***Imba (Listen): Tell You a Story***, both published in 2003.

>> **Alf Taylor (1947–):** A member of the Stolen Generations, Taylor worked as a farm labourer before joining the armed services. He came to writing later in life, when he found acclaim as a poet. He released his most recent book of poetry, ***Long Time Now***, in 2007.

>> **Ali Cobby Eckermann (1963–):** Eckermann is an accomplished poet whose first poetry collection, ***Little Bit Long Time***, was released in 2009. Before then she had won several awards, including first prize in the ATSI Survival Poetry Competition in 2006 and the Dymocks Red Earth Poetry Award in the Northern Territory Literary Awards in 2008. She published a memoir, *Too Afraid to Cry*, in 2013 and another collection of poems, *Inside my Mother*, in 2015. In 2017 she won the Windham-Campbell Literature Prize for poetry.

>> **Romaine Moreton (1969–):** Moreton is a writer of poetry, prose and film, and a well-respected performance artist. She first published ***The Callused Stick of Wanting*** in 1996. It was republished in 2000 as part of an anthology titled ***Rimfire***. She published ***Post Me to the Prime Minister*** in 2004.

>> **Samuel Wagan Watson (1972–):** After winning the David Unaipon Award in 1999 for ***Of Muse, Meandering and Midnight***, Watson went on to win the 2005 New South Wales Premier's Literary Awards Kenneth Slessor Prize for Poetry Book of the Year for ***Smoke Encrypted Whispers***. Watson has written three other books: ***Itinerant Blues*** (2002); ***Hotel Bone*** (2001); and ***Three Legged Dogs, and Other Poems*** (2005). In 2017 Watson won the Patrick White Award

>> **Ellen van Neervan (1990–)** made a literary splash with her poetry collections *Comfort Food* (2016) and *Throat* (2020). Ellen is also an accomplished writer and her collection of short stories, *Heat and Light* (2014) won the David Unaipon Award and the NSW Premier's Literary Award.

>> **Alison Whittaker (1993–):** Whittaker published her first book of poems, *Lemons in the Chicken Wire*, in 2016 to critical acclaim. She received the Judith Wright Poetry prize in 2017 for her poem 'Many Girls White Linen'. *Blakwork* (2018) is a powerful mixture of poetry, prose and reflective pieces. She has been described as a powerful and important new voice.

LITERARY FRAUDS

Indigenous culture and writing has been the subject of literary fraud from time to time.

In 1990, American Marlo Morgan self-published a book called *Walkabout Woman: Messenger for a Vanishing Tribe*, in which she claimed that she had been kidnapped by Aboriginal people and taken to their Dreamtime cave in the Australian desert. The book was picked up by a large publishing house, HarperCollins, who retitled it *Mutant Message Down Under*. By this time, Aboriginal people were questioning Morgan's claims, especially her assertions that Aboriginal people communicated with her by telepathy. Morgan portrayed Aboriginal people as noble savages and childlike, which also offended Aboriginal people. HarperCollins had to publish the book as fiction but many readers continued to believe Morgan's claims. The book had originally had an endorsement by an Aboriginal man, Burnum Burnum, but he later retracted his support. Morgan finally admitted in 1996 that her work was fiction.

In 1994, Aboriginal publisher Magabala Books published the novel *My Own Sweet Time*, by an author believed to be an Aboriginal woman, Wanda Koolmatrie. After publication, it was revealed that Wanda was actually a white male writer, Leon Carmen. His book had won the Nita May Dobbie Award (an award that recognises the first publication of women writers). Carmen's actions angered members of the Indigenous community, who were critical of the attempt to try to publish writing using resources that were supposed to be supporting Indigenous writers unable to be published by large, mainstream publishing houses. The publisher withdrew the book and Carmen had to return his prize money.

Publishing Indigenous Stories

The emergence of Indigenous writers has also seen the emergence of publishers specialising in Indigenous literature and books about Indigenous people. Indigenous people originally found getting works published hard, because some mainstream publishers were sceptical about the potential for commercial success of Indigenous writing. In response, interest increased in establishing publishing houses that understood the issues around Indigenous writing and were committed to its development.

With these publishing houses established, they now play an important role in developing Indigenous writing and nurturing Indigenous writers. The main publishing houses include the following:

>> Aboriginal Studies Press (https://aiatsis.gov.au/about/what-we-do/aboriginal-studies-press) is the publishing arm of the Canberra-based

Australian Institute of Aboriginal and Torres Strait Islander Studies. This press publishes books on Indigenous culture and history, and life stories.

>> Black Ink Press (blackinkpress.wixsite.com/blackinkpress) is a community-based Indigenous publisher. It is based in Townsville, in north Queensland, and supports Indigenous writers. It has a focus on books for younger readers and on languages.

>> Fremantle Press (www.fremantlepress.com.au) is a small publishing house in Fremantle, Western Australia, that includes in its publication list a number of Indigenous authors, and books on Indigenous themes.

>> IAD Press (www.iad.edu.au/press), incorporating the Jukurrpa Books imprint, is an Indigenous-run publishing house established by the Institute for Aboriginal Development in Alice Springs, Northern Territory. It specialises in publications about Indigenous languages, as well as oral history, biography, fiction and children's books. It also has a focus on educational materials.

>> Magabala Books (www.magabala.com) is an independent publishing house, established through the Kimberley Aboriginal Law and Cultural Centre in 1987, soon becoming an Aboriginal Corporation in its own right. Based in Broome, Western Australia, Magabala publishes the works of Indigenous writers, including fiction, philosophy, poetry, children's books and social history.

Some mainstream publishers have a focus on Indigenous issues. The University of Queensland Press (www.uqp.uq.edu.au) in Brisbane publishes the winners of the David Unaipon Award (check out the sidebar 'David Unaipon Award Winners' earlier in this chapter) and has a special catalogue of Indigenous writing. Allen & Unwin (www.allenandunwin.com) in Sydney has also specialised in books about Aboriginal issues, culture and history.

Not Putting Your Foot in It!

Sometimes non-Indigenous people have misused Indigenous cultural content without fully understanding the proper *protocols* — ways of dealing with Indigenous cultural material and of interacting with Indigenous people and their communities, which are designed to promote ethical conduct. For example, some people have a misconception that Indigenous stories are in the public realm because they have no single 'author' and, therefore, require no permission for use or publication. This is definitely not the case, because they're owned by their respective communities. Some people, however, have deliberately disregarded both protocol and the law.

People have got into trouble writing about Indigenous cultures and characters in Australia in three ways:

>> Pretending to be an Indigenous author — and so writing from an Indigenous perspective — when not. This behaviour is literary fraud.

>> Telling Indigenous cultural stories without the proper cultural authority to tell them. Some cultural stories need to be told by the people who have the right to tell them — usually particular Indigenous people.

>> Writing characters that perpetuate stereotypes about Indigenous people and cultures. Writers get into trouble when they seek to write from an Indigenous perspective but don't have enough experience with Indigenous cultures and worldviews to make the characters authentic.

REMEMBER

Aboriginal authors such as Lisa Fuller (author of *Ghost Bird*) also caution against writing about Indigenous stories as containing myths and legends, when these stories are actually about cultural and spiritual beliefs.

CULTURAL PROTOCOLS

Guidelines to assist authors writing about Indigenous issues have been developed by the Australia Council for the Arts. You can download the publication, which gives very useful case studies and discussion, from the website at www.australiacouncil.gov.au by searching for *Protocols for Producing Indigenous Australian Writing*. The writing protocols identify nine principles for dealing with Indigenous cultural material and knowledge:

>> **Respect:** Use the material respectfully. Local community protocols relating to particular material should be understood and respected.

>> **Indigenous control:** Respect the principle of self-determination and ensure that Indigenous people retain control over cultural material. Consulting the appropriate individual or community about the use of their cultural heritage is important.

>> **Communication, consultation and consent:** Work closely with Indigenous people, talk with them and ensure they're consulted and consent to any use of their material. Consultation can be a slow process and needs a lot of time.

>> **Interpretation, integrity and authenticity:** Make sure that Indigenous cultural heritage is portrayed accurately and that Indigenous people won't be offended by the way the material is used.

>> **Secrecy and confidentiality:** Understand that some cultural material is secret and shouldn't be made public.

>> **Attribution and copyright:** Ensure that acknowledgement is given to people who have the rights to stories and ensure their copyright is protected.

>> **Proper returns and royalties:** Ensure that the publication of work that includes the knowledge and cultural property of Indigenous people gives an equitable share in the profits and royalties generated by the work.

>> **Continuing culture:** Maintain ongoing consultation about the use of material because Indigenous cultures are dynamic and changing.

>> **Recognition and protection:** Understand that some legal protections of Indigenous cultural heritage have been introduced and, in some instances, these may create issues over intellectual property to consider.

TIP

In seeking to build relationships or consult with Indigenous people about their culture and use of the culture in literary works, some key community organisations can be useful contacts, such as Aboriginal land councils, language centres and the Australian Institute of Aboriginal and Torres Strait Islander Studies.

FOUR QUICK FACTS ABOUT INDIGENOUS LITERATURE

Here are four facts about Indigenous literature that you might not know!

- Indigenous Literacy Day is celebrated on 1 September each year.

- The largest collection of Indigenous writing appears in *Macquarie PEN: Anthology of Aboriginal Australia*. It was published by Allen & Unwin in 2008.

- Several projects — such as the Literacy Empowerment Project, run by the Ian Thorpe Foundation, and the Indigenous Literacy Foundation — aim to assist Aboriginal and Torres Strait Islander children to read by donating books to their schools and communities. The Indigenous Literacy Foundation also produces and publishes books written by Indigenous people, in multiple languages.

- Five novels by Indigenous authors have won the prestigious Miles Franklin Award: Kim Scott's *Benang: From the Heart* (2000), Alexis Wright's *Carpentaria* (2007), Kim Scott again for *That Deadman Dance* (2011), Melissa Lucashenko's *Too Much Lip* (2019) and Tara June Winch's *The Yield* (2020).

IN THIS CHAPTER

» Beginning to share Indigenous stories on film

» Telling Indigenous stories from Indigenous perspectives

» Taking to the stage

» Appearing on television screens

» Broadcasting on Indigenous radio

Chapter **19**

Performance Storytelling: Film, Theatre, Television and Radio

With Indigenous culture's strong storytelling tradition, the leap by Indigenous people to use new methods and technologies to tell those stories was almost a given. Film, theatre, television and radio are all used successfully by Indigenous people to explore contemporary storytelling.

Not so long ago, Indigenous people felt the way they were portrayed in stories wasn't a true reflection of their lives, experiences, culture and worldviews, even if the portrait was attempting to be sympathetic.

Indigenous people prefer to tell their own stories their own way, and both electronic media and theatre have proved ideal vehicles. Although Indigenous storytellers often use humour to get their points across, they aren't afraid to tell stories of great tragedy as well. Through this work, Indigenous Australia has produced talented Indigenous directors, producers, writers and actors, who you get to meet in this chapter. These talented people not only give a voice to Indigenous people but also educate the wider community about Indigenous experience, perspectives and culture.

In this chapter, I also explore the more recent establishment of Indigenous media organisations such as the National Indigenous Radio Service (NIRS), Imparja and National Indigenous Television (NITV), which ensure that Indigenous people have control over the content they're creating, as well as its dissemination.

Acting the Part: Indigenous People in Films

Filmmakers have been interested in including Indigenous people and their stories in Australian films since the early days of the industry in Australia. But films such as the 1955 *Jedda* interpreted Indigenous peoples and their cultures through the eyes of European directors. The fact that filmmakers who sought to tell stories about Australia were drawn to Indigenous characters and themes is understandable, especially if they were exploring relationships to the land. Over time, stories about Indigenous people became more sympathetic and filmmakers worked with them on the stories.

Indigenous people also appeared as secondary characters in films such as *Crocodile Dundee* and *Priscilla, Queen of the Desert* to add a comic layer or to make a statement about Indigenous people's relationship with the land. But, inevitably, Indigenous people wanted to tell their own stories, in their own words, in their own style.

Films about Indigenous people

Indigenous people appeared in films from the earliest period of filmmaking. In the 1920s, movies were always from a non-Indigenous perspective, tending to stereotype Indigenous people and their culture. They were often portrayed as a menacing threat — as savages — or as mysterious and spiritual — noble savages. Whichever of these stereotypes the character fell into, they were one-dimensional and seen as inferior. *Heritage* (1935), for example, showed savage Aboriginal people attacking a homestead, and in *Uncivilised* (1936) and *Bitter Springs* (1950) they were seen as a violent force, a threat.

Many great Australian film directors have made a movie that has, at its heart, a story about Indigenous Australia: Fred Schepisi (*The Chant of Jimmie Blacksmith*), Baz Lurhmann (*Priscilla, Queen of the Desert* and *Australia*), Peter Weir (*The Last Wave*), Bruce Beresford (*The Fringe Dwellers*) and Phillip Noyce (*Backroads* and

Rabbit-Proof Fence). And, although these films weren't necessarily written to be critical of Indigenous people, Indigenous people haven't always been happy with how they were portrayed.

Jedda (1955)

The first movie with Indigenous people in its starring roles — Ngarla Kunoth (also known as Rosalie Kunoth-Monks) and Robert Tudwali — *Jedda* was also the first Australian movie to be shot in colour. Australian filmmaker Charles Chauvel had portrayed quite negative images of Indigenous people in earlier films such as *Heritage* (1935) and *Uncivilised* (1936). *Jedda* was Chauvel's final movie and it gained international attention.

The film tells the story of Jedda, an Aboriginal girl born on a cattle station but raised by the wife of the white station owner and taught European ways, forbidden to learn the culture of her own people. As a young woman, Jedda becomes intrigued by Marbuck — an Aboriginal man living a traditional life. She is lured to his camp and he abducts her. Marbuck is punished by his clan for bringing Jedda to their camp and is *sung*, a mystical practice that places a sort of curse on the recipient. He goes insane as a result of his tribal punishment and ends his life and Jedda's.

Although the audience is led to feel empathy with Jedda, the ending implies that Aboriginal people and their culture couldn't be 'civilised'.

Walkabout (1971)

This film was adapted from James Vance Marshall's novel of the same name, with Nicholas Roeg directing. The story is about the journey of two children, stranded in the Australian outback, who are assisted in finding their way back to civilisation by an Aboriginal boy, played by a young David Gulpilil.

THIS STAR STILL SHINES: ROSALIE KUNOTH-MONKS

Rosalie Kunoth-Monks appeared as Ngarla Kunoth in the famous 1955 film *Jedda* at the age of 14. She was born in 1937 at Utopia Cattle Station in the Northern Territory. She's now a highly respected Elder of her community and a strong advocate for her people. She has worked on a range of Indigenous issues with a particular focus on education. Kunoth-Monks is the Chancellor of Batchelor Institute of Indigenous Tertiary Education, an institution in the Northern Territory focused on the education of Indigenous people.

Their journey is set against a backdrop of the violent legacy of colonisation and the exploitation of the environment and Indigenous cultures. One of the strongest aspects of the film is the cinematography, which showcases the Australian landscape.

Backroads (1977)

Directed by Phillip Noyce, who later went on to direct *Rabbit-Proof Fence*, *Backroads* is a road movie that stars Aboriginal actors Gary Foley and Essie Coffey.

It tells the story of a white drifter — played by the iconic Australian actor, the late Bill Hunter — who has a chance encounter with an Aboriginal man. Together they steal a car and continue to steal as they travel. They're joined on the journey by other characters, including another Aboriginal man, the bored wife of a service station owner and a French backpacker. With this motley crew on the run from the police, the movie culminates with a deadly mix of boredom and violence.

One of the unique things about the film is the dialogue between the characters, who discuss Indigenous political issues and Indigenous culture.

The Last Wave (1977)

The main character in Peter Weir's movie *The Last Wave* is a white lawyer who defends two Aboriginal men accused of murder — related to a tribal punishment. Through a series of events and some bizarre dreams, he comes to understand that the men are keeping a secret that relates to the apocalyptic weather patterns that have started to occur.

The film stars Richard Chamberlain as David Burton, the white lawyer, and David Gulpilil as Chris Lee, a member of the Aboriginal clan. Although the film has a strong Indigenous storyline, the movie really relates to the main character, the white lawyer.

The Chant of Jimmie Blacksmith (1978)

Directed by Fred Schepisi, this movie was based on the 1972 novel by Thomas Keneally, who was inspired by the life of Aboriginal outlaw Jimmy Governor. (Refer to Chapter 18 for more information about Keneally's book and how he's said that he'd write it differently if he were writing it today.)

The film tells the story of Jimmie Blacksmith, a half-white and half-Aboriginal station worker. Raised by a Methodist minister, he finds himself estranged from his family. He marries a white servant, who becomes pregnant, but finds out later he isn't the father of her child. He is exploited as a worker and, although taught to try to attain the things that white society offers, he is denied being treated as an equal. Eventually he snaps and goes on a rampage of revenge.

The film — and the book — seeks to explain how an Aboriginal man, caught between white society and his traditional culture, could come to be so filled with rage. The movie was nominated for a Palme d'Or at the 1978 Cannes Film Festival. It stars Indigenous actors Tom E Lewis as Jimmie, Freddie Reynolds as his brother, Mort, and Steve Dodd as the wise Elder, Tabidji.

Manganinnie (1980)

Directed by John Honey, the film explores the Black Line of 1830, an attempt to exterminate the Indigenous people of Tasmania (refer to Chapter 7). Separated from her family, Manganinnie travels across the country — from the mountains to the coast — in search of her tribe, accompanied by a white girl. The two discover that the tribe has vanished. The film stars Mawuyul Yanthalawuy as Manganinnie.

The Fringe Dwellers (1986)

Acclaimed Australian director Bruce Beresford's first movie explores the difficulty faced by an Aboriginal family who want to leave their life on the fringe and shift into mainstream society. They move to a respectable suburb but the prejudice of the neighbours and the demands of kin responsibility make the adjustment difficult.

The movie attempts to explore the barriers to assimilation that Indigenous people experienced, leaving people caught between two worlds. The cast includes Indigenous actors Justine Saunders, Kristina Nehm, Kylie Belling, Bob Maza and Ernie Dingo. The movie was based on a novel by Nene Gare.

Babakiueria (1986)

Directed by Don Featherstone, the pretext of this satirical movie is that, instead of white people colonising Australia, the roles were reversed. The title is based on the word Aboriginal people believe the white people call their sacred space — which is, of course, the barbeque area. Starring Bob Maza as Minister for White Affairs, it uses humour to make a strong statement about the racist assumptions of dominant culture in Australia.

Yolngu Boy (2001)

Directed by Stephen Johnson and commissioned by the Australian Children's Television Foundation, this film tells the story of three young men from Arnhem Land who flee the police and head to Darwin. It attempts to highlight the contemporary issues facing Indigenous people and the way in which issues such as petrol sniffing are undermining the traditional cultural fabric of Indigenous communities. It stars Sean Munungurr, John Sebastian Pilakuwi and Nathan Daniels, and features music by Yothu Yindi (refer to Chapter 17 for information on this musical group).

Rabbit-Proof Fence (2002)

This film is based on the book *Follow the Rabbit-Proof Fence* by Doris Pilkington, a retelling of the story of Pilkington's mother and two other girls who, in the 1930s, ran away from an Aboriginal settlement to return to their families in the remote town of Jigalong. They walked for more than nine weeks, guided by a rabbit-poof fence, in order to return to their families.

In the movie, they are pursued by a white constable and an Aboriginal tracker, Moodoo, but the skills they had learned from their Aboriginal families before they were removed assist them in eluding their pursuers. Directed by Phillip Noyce, the film stars Everlyn Sampi, Daisy Kadibil and Tianna Sansbury as the three girls, Ningali Lawford (who also had her own stageplay, *Ningali*) and David Gulpilil.

Australian Rules (2002)

Based on the book *Deadly Unna?* by Phillip Gwynne and directed by Paul Goldman, this film is set in an isolated fishing town. The story examines the relationship between Indigenous people and the rest of the community. It explores personal relationships and racial tensions, with a focus on the way that football was often the place where racially divided towns united. The Indigenous stars are Luke Carrol and Lisa Flanagan.

The Tracker (2002)

Directed and written by Rolf de Heer, *The Tracker* is set in the outback in 1922. It tells the story of a racist policeman who uses the abilities of an Indigenous tracker, played by David Gulpilil, to find the Indigenous man accused of the murder of a white woman.

Ten Canoes (2006)

Rolf de Heer teamed up with Peter Djigirr to direct this film, the first feature film to be made entirely in an Aboriginal language — Yolngu Matha — though its narration, by David Gulpilil, is in English (a Yolngu Matha version is also available). Through transitions between the present and the past, it explores the Yolngu relationship to land, as well as kinship and human flaws. It interweaves two stories — the adventures of a Yolngu man, played by Jamie Gulpilil, who covets his older brother's wife and a story told to him about another young man whose desire for his brother's wife has tragic and unintended consequences. The wholly Indigenous cast are from the Arnhem Land communities of Ramingining and Maningrida.

THE QUINTESSENTIAL ABORIGINAL ACTOR: GULPILIL

David Gulpilil was born in 1953 in Arnhem Land in the Northern Territory. He has become the most prolific Indigenous actor in Australia. A Yolngu man, Gulpilil was raised in the bush and at a mission school in Maningrida, and initiated into his clan when he came of age. A skilled traditional dancer, it was this talent that caught the eye of filmmaker Nicolas Roeg, who cast Gulpilil in his 1971 film, *Walkabout*.

Gulpilil's screen presence brought him further attention. He went on to appear in many movies, including *Storm Boy* (1976), *The Last Wave* (1977), *Crocodile Dundee* (1986), *Rabbit-Proof Fence* (2002), *The Tracker* (2002), *Ten Canoes* (2006), *Australia* (2008) and *Charlie's Country* (2013) — for which he won the Best Actor award at the 2014 Cannes Film Festival. Gulpilil also appeared on television, including in the series *Boney*, about an Aboriginal detective, (1972 to 1973).

Gulpilil has also written two children's books based on Yolngu stories and continues to perform traditional dance. Perhaps the greatest Aboriginal actor to date, Gulpilil has also kept strong connections with his country and heritage, returning to his country to live a simple life as an Elder in his community. A documentary, *Gulpilil: One Red Blood*, was made about his life in 2003.

Taking Over the Camera

With storytelling such a central part of Indigenous cultures, it was only a matter of time before Indigenous people took over the camera so they could tell their stories themselves.

In 2000, the Message Sticks Indigenous Film Festival was established to showcase Indigenous films in the categories of drama, documentary, comedy and shorts. Curated by Indigenous filmmakers Rachel Perkins and Darren Dale, the festival was held at the Sydney Opera House. More recent festivals also celebrate Indigenous film, such as the inaugural BIRRARANGGA Film Festival, held at the Australian Centre for the Moving Image (ACMI) in Melbourne in 2019.

Indigenous filmmakers

Indigenous directors have emerged as some of Australia's greatest storytellers — using both documentary and drama. Here are just a few of them:

» **Wayne Blair** is an actor, writer and director. His first film was an adaptation of the play **The Sapphires** and starred Deborah Mailman, Jessica Mauboy, Shari Sebbens and Miranda Tapsell. More recently, he directed *Top End Wedding* (2019) starring Miranda Tapsell, and has directed episodes of *Mystery Road* and *Cleverman* for television. He has also worked in theatre, directing **The 7 Stages of Grieving**, written by Deborah Mailman and Wesley Enoch (see the section 'Must-see Indigenous plays', later in this chapter), and adapting Meme McDonald and Boori Pryor's award-winning novel, **Njunjul The Sun**, for Queensland's Indigenous theatre company.

» **Essie Coffey** was also known as the Bush Queen. From the town of Goodooga in north-west New South Wales, she was brought up in the bush and worked on cattle stations with her family. She married and lived on the banks of the Barwon River at Brewarrina, later moving to Dodge City, a reserve in West Brewarrina, where she raised eight children and ten stepchildren. She was a well-known country singer and songwriter and, in 1976, appeared in the Phillip Noyce movie, **Backroads**. She went on to direct the documentary, **My Survival as an Aboriginal** in 1978 and a sequel, **My Life as I Live It**, in 1993. She passed away in 1998.

» **Tracey Moffatt** is a well-known Aboriginal artist and photographer whose works are featured in art galleries around the world, including the Tate Gallery in London (refer to Chapter 17 for more on her artistic achievements). Her first film, the tongue-in-cheek **Nice Coloured Girls**, was released in 1987. She made another short film, **Night Cries: A Rural Tragedy** in 1989. **BeDevil**, which she directed in 1993, is said to be the first feature film by an Aboriginal woman. She went on to make several more short films, including **Heaven** (1997), **Lip** (1999), **Artist** (2000) and **Revolution** (2008).

» **Rachel Perkins** is a director, producer and writer. Her films include **Radiance** (1998), **One Night the Moon** (2001), **Bran Nue Dae** (2010) and *Jasper Jones* (2017). She also produced, directed and narrated the television series **First Australians** (2008) and directed the television series of *Mystery Road* (series 1, 2018) and *Total Control* (2019–2021). She is the daughter of Indigenous activist Charles Perkins. Along with producer Darren Dale, Rachel founded the first Indigenous production company, Blackfella Films.

» **Ivan Sen** made his debut feature film **Beneath Clouds** (2002) after working on numerous short films. He also has many documentaries to his credit. His second feature-length movie, **Dreamland**, was released in 2009 with **Toomelah** released in 2011, to great critical acclaim. He wrote and directed the Western-inspired movies *Mystery Road* (2013) and *Goldstone* (2016).

A DYNASTY OF SCREEN PIONEERS

Freda Glynn was a co-creator of the Central Australian Aboriginal Media Association (CAAMA). Her son, Warwick Thornton, is one of Australia's most successful directors, known for his films *Samson and Delilah* (2009) and *Sweet Country* (2017). Freda's daughter, Erica Glynn, is also an accomplished director and producer. Her film credits include *In My Own Words* (2017). Freda's grandchildren are also talented. Dylan River is an accomplished director, writer and cinematographer. His film credits include *Buckskin* (2013), *Finke: There and Back* (2018), *The Beach* (2020) and the television series *Robbie Hood* (2019). Freda's grand-daughter, Tanith Glynn-Maloney is a producer who has worked on *Robbie Hood* (2019) and *The Beach* (2020). Erica and Tanith produced a film, which Erica wrote and directed, on Freda Glynn's life story in 2019, *She Who Must be Loved*.

>> **Brian Syron** became the first Indigenous person to direct a full-length feature film when he made *Jindalee Lady* in 1992. Syron was born in Sydney. After ending up in Grafton Correctional Centre at the age of 14, no-one suspected that he would go on to have such an extraordinary life. He went to acting school and ended up studying in New York alongside Robert de Niro and Warren Beatty. Eventually returning home, Syron became a strong advocate for Indigenous human rights, helped establish the National Black Theatre in Redfern and worked with Indigenous prisoners, encouraging them to write plays. He established the Aboriginal Theatre Company with Robert Merritt, an Aboriginal playwright who penned *The Cake Man*.

>> **Warwick Thornton** is a cinematographer, director and screenwriter. His debut feature film *Samson and Delilah* (2009) was released to great critical acclaim. His film, *Sweet Country* (2017) was a cinematic triumph and highlights Warwick's exceptional talents as a cinematographer and director. He directed on the first season of TV's *Mystery Road*, and also directed *The Beach* (2020), a documentary about his retreat to a remote location with no power.

Noteworthy Indigenous films

As would be expected, the growing catalogue of Indigenous movies is a mix of different genres and styles. Here are a few noteworthy Indigenous films, directed by Indigenous directors — who are also noteworthy:

>> *Jindalee Lady* (1992) — directed by Brian Syron — the first full-length feature directed by an Indigenous person, tells the story of an Indigenous fashion designer who finds herself falling in love with another man during her

unhappy marriage to a white husband. With a strong female lead, the story explores the struggle for Aboriginal women to find respect and success in Australian society. It stars Lydia Miller in the title role.

» **BeDevil** (1993) — written and directed by Tracey Moffatt — is a trilogy of ghost stories ('Mister Chuck', 'Choo Choo Choo Choo' and 'Lovin' the Spin I'm In') that blend the imaginary and the real. It was the first full-length feature film made by an Aboriginal woman. Moffatt also stars in the movie, alongside Mawuyul Yanthalawuy, who also stars in **Manganinnie** (1980), **Women of the Sun** (1981), **We of the Never Never** (1982) and **A Waltz through the Hills** (1988).

» **Radiance** (1998) — directed by Rachel Perkins — tells the story of three sisters, successful opera singer Cressy, parental carer Mae, who looked after their ailing mother, and party girl Nona. The three unite for their mother's funeral and confront some family secrets. It stars Rachael Maza, Trisha Morton-Thomas and Deborah Mailman.

» **One Night the Moon** (2001) — directed by Rachel Perkins — tells the story of a white family living in the Flinders Ranges whose daughter goes missing on the night of the full moon. They fail to employ the skills of a black tracker, played by Kelton Pell, to assist in finding her, due to their own prejudices. Singer Ruby Hunter also makes an appearance in the film (refer to Chapter 17 for more about her). The story is based on a series of events that took place in 1932, depicted in a documentary, **Black Tracker**, made by Michael Riley in 1997.

» **Beneath Clouds** (2002) — written and directed by Ivan Sen — focuses on two teenagers who are leaving their country town for the city, hoping to find a better life. The film is a road movie and a coming-of-age movie that has universal themes that appeal to a broad audience. Its Indigenous star is Dannielle Hall.

» **Samson and Delilah** (2009) — directed by Warwick Thornton — depicts the lives of two Indigenous teens, played by Rowan McNamara and Marissa Gibson, living in a remote community. They steal a car and head to Alice Springs. The film is unflinching in its look at the issues facing Indigenous Australians, including the effects of petrol sniffing and sexual violence. It was co-produced by CAAMA Productions (see the section 'Indigenous media organisations' later in this chapter) and Scarlett Pictures.

» **Stone Brothers** (2009) — directed by Richard Frankland — is a comedy and a road movie that follows the adventures of Charlie (Leon Burchill) and Eddie (Luke Carroll) as they attempt to recover a sacred stone that has been entrusted to Eddie but which Charlie has lost. Frankland also wrote and directed the short film **No Way to Forget**, in 1996.

» **Bran Nue Dae** (2010) — directed by Rachel Perkins — is a musical set in Broome and tells the story of an Aboriginal boy's journey from a Catholic boarding school in Perth to his homeland. Along the way, he searches for his identity. The movie is based on a musical written by Aboriginal playwright Jimmy Chi, from his own experiences. The stageplay toured nationally from 1990. Jimmy Chi and local Broome band Kuckles wrote the musical score, with influences from traditional music, rock, blues and the Roman Catholic Mass. The film's Indigenous cast includes Rocky McKenzie, Jessica Mauboy, Ernie Dingo (in the role of Uncle Tadpole, which he played in the original stageplay), Deborah Mailman, Ningali Lawford (also in the stageplay), Dan Sultan and Stephen 'Baamba' Albert (who has also played Uncle Tadpole on the stage).

>> *Toomelah* **(2011)** — directed by Ivan Sen — interweaves the story of a 10-year-old boy (Daniel Connors) living on the Toomelah Mission, whose ambition to be a gangster sees him caught up in a drug turf war, and the story of his aunt, a member of the Stolen Generations, who returns home. The film was shown at the Cannes Film Festival. The cast members were all drawn from the Toomelah community.

>> *The Sapphires* **(2012)** — directed by Wayne Blair — based on a true story, tells the story of four Aboriginal singers in an all-girl group, The Sapphires, who travel to Vietnam to perform for the US troops. Starring Deborah Mailman, Jessica Mauboy and Shari Sebbins, the film speaks of the racism of the era but is also full of great musical numbers.

>> *Mystery Road* **(2013)** and *Goldstone* **(2016)** — directed by Ivan Sen — is based around the outback cop, Jay Swan, played by Aaron Pedersen. In *Mystery Road*, he investigates the murder of an Aboriginal girl. In *Goldstone*, Swan arrives at a town to investigate a missing person's case and uncovers a web of crime and corruption. Sen shoots both films in the Western genre making the most of the Australian landscape.

>> *Spear* **(2015)** — directed by Stephen Page — this film, in magic realism style, profiles the talents of the Bangarra Dance Theatre through a story of an Aboriginal man navigating ancient traditions and modern society. It stars Hunter Page-Lochard in the role of Djali.

>> *Sweet Country* **(2017)** — directed by Warwick Thornton — with a screenplay by Stephen McGregor and David Tranter, the film is set in the 1920s on the Northern Territory frontier and follows the events after an Aboriginal farm-hand shoots a white man in self-defence. It is based on a true story. It won the Special Jury Prize at the Venice Film Festival for Warwick Thornton.

>> *Top End Wedding* (2019) — directed by Wayne Blair — starring (and co-written by) Miranda Tapsell, the film follows the adventures of Lauren who, after she is engaged to Ned, must find her mother who has gone travelling somewhere in remote far north Australia, reunite her parents, deal with her family and arrange her dream wedding.

QUEEN OF THE SCREEN: JUSTINE SAUNDERS

Justine Saunders was one of the most prolific Indigenous actors to have worked on Australian stage and screen. She was the first Indigenous person to appear as a regular in a mainstream soap opera, *Number 96*, in 1976 and went on to appear in other television series, including *Prisoner* and *Heartland*. She also starred in the mini-series *Women of the Sun* and appeared in many movies, including *The Fringe Dwellers*, *The Chant of Jimmie Blacksmith* and *Jindalee Lady*.

Justine Saunders received a Medal of the Order of Australia for her services to the performing arts in 1991. She returned it in 2000 in protest at the way the federal government at the time continued to deny the existence of the Stolen Generations (refer to Chapter 9). Saunders herself was removed from her family as a child. She died in 2007.

REMEMBER

Stephen McGregor is a talented writer and director. He has worked on a range of television shows including *Art + Soul* (2010–2014), *The Warriors* (2017), *Blue Water Empire* (2019) and *Black Comedy* (2014–2020). He also directed the documentary *Servant or Slave* (2016). He wrote the screenplay for *Sweet Country* (2017) and has also written on the television series *Redfern Now* (2012) and *Mystery Road* (2018–2020).

REMEMBER

A new generation of Indigenous directors has also seen a new generation of Indigenous producers including Darren Dale, Mitchell Stanley, Dena Curtis, Pauline Clague and Tanith Glynn-Maloney. This means that the works are owned by Indigenous people ensuring more Indigenous control of Indigenous storytelling.

Telling it like it is: Documentaries

Film has been an effective vehicle for Indigenous stories but it has also been a powerful medium for exploring Indigenous reality.

Essie Coffey's *My Survival as an Aboriginal* was the first documentary directed by an Indigenous person and it details the realities of life for Indigenous Australians. Documentary filmmaking soon became a powerful vehicle to allow Indigenous people to highlight events and experiences that weren't being covered by the mainstream media.

Documentaries such as *Lousy Little Sixpence* exposed issues like the impact of the policy of removing children from their families and the failure to pay wages to Indigenous people — including children — who were sent out to work (refer to Chapter 9 for more on these issues). Exploring important key events, such as the freedom rides, the 1967 referendum, the Tent Embassy and the Mabo case, Indigenous filmmakers have brought their perspectives to a wider audience through the use of documentary filmmaking. Here's a sample:

>> *My Survival as an Aboriginal* **(1978)** — directed by Essie Coffey in collaboration with Martha Ansara — was the first documentary to give an Aboriginal perspective and worldview. Coffey shares her culture and community, and the harsh realities of her life, while making a powerful argument about the need to protect Indigenous cultures and rights.

>> *Lousy Little Sixpence* **(1983)** — directed by Alec Morgan and Gerry Bostock — tells the story of five children, now all Elders, who were stolen from their families and used as unpaid labour. It includes their narratives, old film and photographs, and tells a heartbreaking story in a simple way. The film became a way for many Australians who didn't know about the removal policy to understand its devastating effects.

>> *The Tent Embassy* **(1992)** — directed by Frances Peters-Little — is about this site of political activism outside Old Parliament House in 1972, which still stands today. The documentary explores the objectives and achievements of the Tent Embassy at the time and its legacy today. Chapter 12 examines the setting up of the Tent Embassy.

>> *Black Chicks Talking* **(2001)** — co-directed by Leah Purcell with Brendan Fletcher — is based on interviews with Indigenous women, including actress Deborah Mailman and former Miss Australia and politician Kathryn Hay. Purcell also produced a book and a stage production from the project.

>> *Vote Yes for Aborigines* **(2007)** — directed by Frances Peters-Little — is a documentary about the 1967 referendum and the campaign for Aboriginal citizenship rights that led up to it. It looks at the referendum's historical significance and contemporary legacy. Chapter 11 is devoted to this historic event.

>> *A Sister's Love* **(2007)** — directed by Ivan Sen — looks at the response of Aboriginal media personality Rhoda Roberts to the unsolved murder of her twin sister. Lois Roberts was last seen alive hitchhiking. Her body was later found in bushland. The film explores the power of family and the lasting impact of grief.

>> *The Intervention: Katherine NT* **(2008)** — directed by Julie Nimmo — follows the impact of the Northern Territory intervention on one community over the first year it was rolled out (refer to Chapter 14 for more on the intervention). It explores the lives of ordinary community residents and the various government and business workers who all come together to implement it.

- » ***Servant or Slave* (2016)** — directed by Stephen McGregor and produced by Mitchell Stanley — this powerful documentary follows the experiences of women who were removed from their families as children and forced to work as domestic servants with no remuneration, often subjected to psychological, sexual and physical abuse.

- » ***After the Apology* (2017)** — directed by Larissa Behrendt (me!) — follows the fight of three grandmothers to regain custody of their grandchildren after they are wrongfully removed. The film looks at the structural racism that sees Aboriginal children removed from their families at a greater rate and high-lights the need to have greater community control in the child protection space.

- » ***Black Divaz* (2018)** — directed by Adrian Russell Wills — follows six Aboriginal drag queens from around Australia as they compete in the inaugural Miss First Nations pageant.

REMEMBER

Two documentaries were released in 2019 that covered the relentless racial abuse by Australian Rules crowds of talented Aboriginal footballer Adam Goodes. *The Final Quarter* (2019) and *The Australian Dream* (2019) take unique but complemen-tary looks at this shameful episode but also highlight the quiet dignity with which Adam Goodes stands up to racism.

Treading the Black Boards

Performance has been a big part of traditional Indigenous cultures, and contem-porary Indigenous playwrights have sought to bring their stories to an audience through theatre. It has been a way of telling powerful personal stories — especially through one-person shows such as *Page 8* and *Little Black Bastard* — and exploring broader social issues like the exploitation of labour, poor living conditions and the legacy of removing Indigenous children from their families, such as in *The Cake Man* and *Stolen*.

In 1972, the National Black Theatre was established in Redfern. It marked a significant moment, when Indigenous people developed not only their own content but also their own theatre companies and spaces to showcase their work. Other Indigenous theatre companies — most notably Yirra Yaakin in Western Australia and Ilbijirri in Victoria — have followed in recent years.

The National Black Theatre

The Redfern community in Sydney was experiencing a politically vibrant time in 1972. The first Aboriginal medical service was being established, the first

Aboriginal legal service had also begun and four men from Redfern had gone to Canberra to set up the Aboriginal Tent Embassy.

At the time, street performance was part of the political movement of the community and, taking advantage of this momentum, creative figures such as Brian Syron, Gary Foley and Gerry Bostock moved for the creation of a black theatre group. African-American dancer Carole Johnson also began classes.

This movement brought together a dynamic range of Indigenous people and, through workshops on modern and traditional dancing, acting and playwriting, it helped develop a new generation of Indigenous talent.

The first performance of the embryonic National Black Theatre focused on the Gove land rights claim in the Northern Territory and was performed in the street. Other early performances included a dance program focused on the Tent Embassy and its reestablishment. A political revue called *Basically Black* was written and performed by a group that included Bob Maza, Gary Foley and Bindi Williams, and was directed by Ken Horler. The revue later toured the country and made a television show of the same name, although the material had to be toned down for television.

The National Black Theatre became a hub of many activities and an umbrella for many organisations, including a black casting agency. It also brought a focus on Indigenous arts policy.

In 1974, a building was provided and a 100-seat theatre built. It was given minimal funding from government. The first play to be performed there was Robert Merritt's *The Cake Man*, directed by Brian Syron. Merritt had written the play while in prison and was let out, under guard, to attend the opening night. A television production of the play was aired by the Australian Broadcasting Corporation (ABC) in 1977.

STALWARTS OF THEATRE: LESTER AND GERRY BOSTOCK

The Bostock brothers were both founding members of the National Black Theatre, with Gerry becoming a playwright and Lester producing. Lester later worked to establish Radio Redfern. He moved into filmmaking and television production, teaching at the Australian Film, Television and Radio School (AFTRS) and MetroScreen. Gerry went on to co-produce the influential documentary *Lousy Little Sixpence*.

With its funding cut in 1976, the Black Theatre closed the following year. However, people involved with it went on to write and perform other plays, make films and form other arts organisations such as the National Aboriginal Islander Skills Development Association (NAISDA), the Bangarra Dance Theatre and the Eora Centre, which specialises in providing professional development in the visual and performing arts. Refer to Chapter 17 for more on contemporary Indigenous dance.

REMEMBER

The Redfern Aboriginal community pushed to have the site of the National Black Theatre redeveloped. This finally occurred in 2008 and now houses the Gadigal Information Service and National Indigenous Television (see the sections 'Indigenous media organisations' and 'National Indigenous Television' later in this chapter).

Indigenous theatre companies

Since the advent of the National Black Theatre in 1972, several Indigenous companies have also sprung up. Here are a few of them:

>> **Nindethana Theatre** was established in Melbourne in 1972 by a group of Aboriginal people actively involved in the Aboriginal Advancement League. Its aim was to create Indigenous performances but also to encourage and promote Aboriginal dance, music, art, literature, film production and other such cultural activities in the community. The ensemble produced a version of *The Cherry Pickers*, by Kevin Gilbert, but dissolved in 1973.

>> **Ilbijerri Theatre Company** began in 1990, also in Melbourne. It's the longest running Indigenous theatre company and has Rachel Maza Long as its artistic director. Ilbijerri is a Woiwurrung word that means 'to come together for ceremony'.

>> **Yirra Yaakin** is a Perth-based theatre company formed in 1993. In addition to staging performances of Indigenous plays, it runs workshops for dance and theatre in the Indigenous community and provides arts residences. Yirra Yaakin means 'stand tall' in the Noongar language.

>> **Kooemba Jdarra** was a Brisbane-based company that, since its establishment in 1993, produced contemporary performances of the works of Indigenous people, such as eminent Indigenous writer Sam Wagan Watson (refer to Chapter 18), among other Indigenous authors.

Must-see Indigenous plays

Indigenous playwrights — and actors — have continued to write and perform on the stage. They tell moving, heart-warming stories about Indigenous experiences and worldviews in a medium that is often raw and stark.

Here are just some of the plays written by Indigenous people:

>> **The Cherry Pickers (1971)** was written by Kevin Gilbert in 1968 while he was in prison. It's credited as being the first Indigenous play. The story concerns itinerant rural workers and explores themes of dispossession, dislocation and family. It is also an honest exploration of issues such as alcoholism and violence.

>> **The Cake Man (1975)**, written by Robert Merritt, portrays the difficulties of life on a mission in western New South Wales. The play was written while Merritt was in Bathurst Correctional Centre and was first performed by the National Black Theatre in Redfern.

>> **Box the Pony (1997)**, co-written by Leah Purcell and Scott Rankin, is a semi-autobiographical play performed by Purcell. The one-woman show explores the life of an Indigenous woman growing up in Queensland.

>> **Stolen (1998)**, directed by Wesley Enoch and written by Jane Harrison, looks at the impact of the policy of removing children from their families on five Indigenous people who were taken away.

>> **The Keepers (1988)**, written by Bob Maza and performed at the Adelaide Fringe Festival and at Belvoir Street Theatre, was an exploration of the destruction of the Buandig people of South Australia and won Maza the National Black Playwright Award.

>> **What Do They Call Me? (1990)**, written by Eva Johnson, is a one-woman show that explores the impact of the policy of removing Indigenous children from their families through the eyes of a mother and her two daughters. She wrote several other plays, including **When I Die You'll Stop Laughing**, **Mimini's Voices** and **Faded Genes**.

>> **The Sapphires (2004)**, directed by Wesley Enoch and written by Tony Briggs, tells the story of The Sapphires, a singing group of four Indigenous women who tour Vietnam during the war. The original production included Deborah Mailman, Rachael Maza, Ursula Yovich and Lisa Flanagan. It was made into a movie by Wayne Blair.

>> **Page 8 (2005)**, co-written by David Page and Louis Nowra, and performed by Page, tells the story of his childhood as a singing and dancing child star growing up on a housing commission estate.

>> **Rainbow's End (2005)**, directed by Wesley Enoch and written by Jane Harrison, is set in 1950s northern Victoria. It creates a family snapshot through three generations — each represented by a richly developed female character — while also looking at the issues of housing and education.

>> **Little Black Bastard (2005)** was written and performed by Indigenous actor, director and choreographer Noel Tovey and tells of his extraordinarily brutal

childhood. Born into poverty in Melbourne, abandoned by his parents, physically and sexually abused by a foster parent, he ended up on the streets as a thief and child prostitute. By the age of 17 he was in jail. He went from there to become a dancer, actor and choreographer performing in the West End in London. The play is based on Tovey's biography of the same name.

» *Black Medea* **(2005)**, written and directed by Wesley Enoch, is an adaptation of the classical Greek play by Euripides, with the gods replaced by ancestral spirits. Medea betrays her heritage for the love of Jason. She leaves her desert home to marry a handsome, ambitious Indigenous man from the city. In doing so, she violates the kinship rules of her own people and compounds her crimes by selling knowledge of her land to mining companies. Her husband goes mad from his own demons and eventually throws Medea out of the house. Homeless and despondent, she murders her son as an act of revenge and despair. The cast included Margaret Harvey, Aaron Pederson and Justine Saunders.

» *The 7 Stages of Grieving* **(2008)** was directed by Wayne Blair and co-written by Deborah Mailman and Wesley Enoch. It is a one-woman play, starring Mailman, that explores episodes in the life of a character who represents every Indigenous woman. It uses humour and irony but also tells the story of a life dealing with racism, grief and reconciliation.

» *Jack Charles v The Crown* **(2010)** is a one-man play that tells the story of Jack Charles' life. It is an unflinching look at racism, systemic prejudice, street smarts, addiction and an embrace of life. The play was developed by the Ilbijerri Theatre Company.

» *Kill the Messenger* **(2015)** was written and performed by Nakkiah Lui. This powerful tale of Aboriginal people slipping through society's gaps was told with poignancy and humour, heralding Nakkiah's arrival as a presence on the Australian stage.

» *Barbara and the Camp Dogs* **(2017)** is a play with a great soundtrack written by Ursula Yovich and Alana Valentine about Barbara, an Aboriginal pub singer trying to make it in Sydney. Urusla played the title role of Barbara with Elaine Crombie playing her foster sister, Rene. It won four Helpmann Awards including Best Musical.

» *City of Gold* **(2019)**, written by and starring Meyne Wyatt, tells the story of the structural racism that defines life in a remote town like Kalgoorlie, while at the same time exploring the undercurrents of racism in the performing arts sector. Meyne's first screenplay, the play was influenced by real life events and experience.

TAKING THE STAGE: NAKKIAH LUI

Nakkiah Lui is an actor, comedian and writer. She has written a number of successful plays that have been put on by the larger theatre companies such as Sydney Theatre Company and Belvoir. These have included *Kill the Messenger* (2015), *Black is the New White* (2017) and *How to Rule the World* (2019). Nakkiah was a co-writer and starred in the sketch television show *Black Comedy* (2014–2020). She also wrote and starred in comedy television series *Kiki and Kitty* (2017). Nakkiah received the Nick Enright Prize for Playwriting in 2018 for *Black is the New White*.

THE RIGHT DIRECTION: WESLEY ENOCH

Wesley Enoch is one of Australia's best known, most successful Indigenous playwrights and directors. Enoch trained at the Queensland University of Technology, where he earned a Bachelor of Arts (Drama) and started the QUT Bonsani Commedia Troupe.

Enoch has written several plays, including *Black Medea*, inspired by the play by Euripides. He has directed theatre productions at the Sydney Theatre Company and Company B of Belvoir St Theatre, including *The 7 Stages of Grieving*, which he co-wrote with Deborah Mailman, and Jane Harrison's *Stolen*. He also debuted the work *I am Eora* at the Sydney Festival 2012, which brought together the stories of three Indigenous identities from the time of the establishment of the colony at Sydney Cove — the resistance warrior Pemulwuy; Bennelong, who lived between the new colony and his own community; and his wife, Barangaroo (all of whom are profiled in Chapter 6).

Enoch's work explores issues of Aboriginal identity and culture, and he has been a strong advocate for the establishment of a National Indigenous Theatre Company. Enoch was the Artistic Director of Queensland Theatre Company from 2010 to 2015 and, from 2015 to 2020, the Artistic Director of the Sydney Festival.

Appearing on Mainstream Screens

Throughout the 1950s and 1960s, more and more Australian households brought television into their lives. However, Indigenous people were absent from Australian television. As Indigenous actor and activist Gary Foley observed, at that time television spoke to 'the white, middle-class, patriarchal nuclear family and thereby excluded those that this audience saw as "other"'. So not only Indigenous Australians but also other parts of the community weren't seen on television, unless on current affairs or news shows.

By the 1970s, Indigenous actors made some rare appearances on mainstream television shows, such as police dramas *Division 4* and *Homicide*. However, Indigenous people were portrayed as victims or villains, one-dimensional caricatures rather than complex characters.

A production that was originally staged at the National Black Theatre in Redfern, *Basically Black*, which used comedy to make important statements about Indigenous experience, was adapted to become the first all-Indigenous television show, airing in 1972. Granted, its more cutting observations about racism in Australia had been removed.

Since then, Indigenous characters have started to appear in mainstream shows. Here are some of the Indigenous actors you may have seen regularly on television:

>> **Jack Charles** is an actor, musician and writer. He is best known for the one-man play *Jack Charles v The Crown* (2010), which talks about his life as a member of the stolen generation and of crime. His life, including his addiction to heroin, is recorded in the documentary *Bastardy* (2008). He has appeared on the screen in *The Chant of Jimmie Blacksmith* (1978), *Bedevil* (1993) and *Pan* (2015). He released an autobiography in 2020, *Jack Charles: Born-again Blakfella*.

>> **Rob Collins** has, since appearing in the television series *Cleverman* (2016–2017), built a career as one of Australia's busiest actors. He has had leading roles in *The Wrong Girl* (2016–2017), *Secret City* (2019), *Glitch* (2017–2019), *Total Control* (2019–2021) and *Mystery Road* (2020). Somehow, in between all of that, he has found the time to appear on the big screen in *Top End Wedding* (2019) and *Extraction* (2020).

>> **Ernie Dingo** has many movie credits, including ***Crocodile Dundee II*** and ***Bran Nue Dae***. But television is where he has most regularly worked, with appearances in ***The Flying Doctors***, ***Heartbreak High*** and ***Rafferty's Rules*** and as a host of the television program ***The Great Outdoors***. He also appeared in the first series of *Mystery Road*.

>> **Aaron Fa'aoso** is a Torres Strait Islander, Samoan and Tongan actor who is known for his roles in *RAN: Remote Area Nurse* (2006), *East West 101* (2007–2011) and *The Straits* (2012). He also proved his great comic timing in the sketch series *Black Comedy* (2014–2020). He has producing roles with *The Straits* and *Blue Water Empire* (2019).

>> **Gary Foley** appeared in the television series ***The Flying Doctors*** and ***A Country Practice***. Having begun his acting career with the National Black Theatre, he returned to the stage in 2011 with a play about his life simply — and aptly — titled ***Foley***.

- » **Ningali Lawford**, also known as Ningali Lawford-Wolf, premiered her one woman show, *Ningali*, in 1994. She made big screen appearances in *Rabbit Proof Fence* (2002), *Bran Nue Dae* (2009) and *Last Cab to Darwin* (2015). Her work on the small screen included *Little J and Big Cuz* (2017) and *Mystery Road* (2018). She sadly passed away while touring overseas with the play *The Secret River* in 2019.

- » **Bob Maza** appeared in many television series, including ***Bellbird*** and ***Heartland***. Born on Palm Island in north Queensland, his father was a Torres Strait Islander and his mother Aboriginal. He was also a playwright, with his work including ***The Keepers***, as well as movie credits including ***The Fringe Dwellers*** and ***Babakiueria***. He helped to establish the Nindethana theatre company and the National Black Theatre. He died in 2000.

- » **Deborah Mailman** was a regular in the popular television series ***Love My Way***, ***The Secret Life of Us*** and ***Offspring***, in addition to movie credits for ***Radiance*** and ***Bran Nue Da***e. She has also starred in the television series *Redfern Now*, *Cleverman* and ***Total Control***.

- » **Jessica Mauboy** rose to fame as a contestant on *Australian Idol* and has become one of Australia's most successful pop stars of her era. She has also carved out a career as an actress starring in *The Sapphires* (2012) and in the television series *The Secret Daughter* (2016–2017).

- » **Trisha Moreton Thomas** is an actress who wrote, starred in and produced the series *8MMM Aboriginal Radio* (2015). She played Mae in *Radiance* (1998) and Jan in the series *Total Control* (2019). She wrote and directed the documentary *Occupation: Native* (2017).

- » **Aaron Pedersen** began his acting career in ***Heartland***. He was in the popular television series ***Water Rats*** for two years and then starred in ***The Circuit*** and ***City Homicide***. He has defined the character of Jay Swan in the films *Mystery Road* and *Goldstone* and the subsequent television series, *Mystery Road*.

- » **Leah Purcell** is also an accomplished actress who has worked extensively, appearing on the big screen in films such as *Lantana* (2001), *Jindabyne* (2006) and *Last Cab to Darwin* (2015). On the small screen, she has appeared in series including *Fallen Angels* (1997), *Janet King* (2014–2017) and *Wentworth* (2018–2021). Leah also has had major success on the stage with her play *The Drover's Wife* (2016) which she wrote and starred in — and has also turned into a feature film that she directed!

- » **Justine Saunders** was the first Indigenous person to appear as a regular in a mainstream soap opera, ***Number 96***, in 1976 and went on to appear in other television series, including ***Prisoner*** and ***Heartland***. She also starred in the mini-series ***Women of the Sun***, many films and on stage.

- >> **Miranda Tapsell** co-wrote and starred in the film *Top End Wedding* (2019). She also appeared as Cynthia in *The Sapphires* (2012). Her television credits include leading roles in *Love Child* (2014–2017), *Newtown's Law* (2017), *Little J and Big Cuz* (2017) and *Doctor Doctor* (2018–2021). In 2020 she released a memoir, *Top End Girl*.

- >> **Meyne Wyatt** is an actor who wrote the critically acclaimed play *City of Gold* (2019). He has worked regularly on the stage including in the lead role of *Peter Pan*. He has also appeared in the television shows *Redfern Now* (2013) and *Mystery Road* (2018). In 2014, he joined the main cast of the show *Neighbours*, becoming the first Indigenous actor to do so since it began in 1985. And if that wasn't talent enough, in 2020, he won the Packing Room Prize in the prestigious Archibald Prize for his self-portrait.

Shows focusing on Indigenous issues, with a news and current affairs format, were developed on publicly funded television. These have included the ABC's *Message Stick* and SBS's *Living Black*. Several television series also focused on dramatic narratives about Indigenous people and issues — *Burned Bridge*, also known as *Heartland*, *The Circuit* and *RAN: Remote Area Nurse*.

The advent of National Indigenous Television (NITV) — an initiative that Indigenous people involved with filmmaking and media pushed for — has provided an opportunity for the development of more Indigenous content.

Notable Indigenous television shows

Many television shows have brought Indigenous issues to a broad Australian audience. Here are some of them:

- >> ***Basically Black*** **(1973)** was the first Indigenous show written and created by Indigenous people to appear on television. Based on a political review staged at the Black Theatre, writers and actors included Gary Foley and Bob Maza. The series was a searing satirical look at racism in Australia with cheeky and sophisticated humour with some elements censored by the ABC. It remains a classic.

- >> ***Women of the Sun*** **(1981)** was a groundbreaking television mini-series, originally broadcast on SBS television and later on the ABC. It contained four discrete stories set in different periods, looking first-contact in the 1820s, frontier violence in the 1860s, life on the reserves in the 1930s and contemporary issues in the 1980s. It stars Naykakan Munung, Yangathu Wanambi and Gordon Lunyupi, with appearances by Essie Coffey, Justine Saunders and Bob Maza.

» **Message Stick (1999 to 2018)** showcased documentaries either made by Indigenous filmmakers or about Indigenous people. It aired on the ABC. Indigenous producers Grant Saunders and Miriam Corowa created the show but it also showcased the work of other Indigenous producers such as Darlene Johnson and Kelrick Martin. Presenters also included Aden Ridgeway, Trisha Moreton Thomas, Rachael Maza and Deborah Mailman.

» **Bush Mechanics (2001)** originally screened on the ABC. This unique series was developed by Warlpiri Media, based in the Central Australian community of Yuendumu. It follows the adventures of a group of men from the community on their travels through the desert, in the last episode driving to Broome in the Kimberley, across the Tanami Track. Along the way they have to solve their car troubles through innovative mechanical repairs. It also integrates stories and reflections of people from the area, giving a rich view of Warlpiri life. The show stars Francis Jupurrula Kelly, who co-directed it with David Batty (Kelly had established Warlpiri Media in the early 1980s — see the next section), with a cameo performance from Stephen 'Baamba' Albert, of **Bran Nue Dae** fame, as Jungala the Rainmaker in Episode 4.

» **Living Black (2003 to present)** is a current affairs program that focuses on the issues affecting Indigenous Australians. Hosted by Karla Grant and airing on SBS, the program seeks to educate a broad audience about issues that don't always get an airing on mainstream television.

» **Heartland (2003)**, also known as **Burned Bridge**, is set in a small coastal town and focuses on the mysterious death of an Aboriginal girl, the boyfriend accused of her murder and the two people who believe he is innocent. It stars Ernie Dingo, Cate Blanchett, Justine Saunders, Bob Maza and Rachel Maza, and includes appearances by Aaron Pedersen, Lillian Crombie, Lydia Miller and Luke Carroll.

» **RAN: Remote Area Nurse (2006)** is based in the Torres Strait Islands and highlights some of the distinctive aspects of Torres Strait Islander culture. As the title implies, it follows the life of a remote area nurse working in the island communities. The show deals with cultural conflict, alcohol abuse, family dramas and the challenges of the environment. It aired on SBS and its Indigenous stars include Charles Passi, Luke Carroll, Margaret Harvey, Jimi Gela, Belford Lui and Dan Mosby. Locals also performed as extras and assisted with production.

» **The Circuit (2007)** starred Aaron Pedersen as an Indigenous lawyer who moves to the Kimberley area to work on the court circuit. The series also has appearances from Kimberley actors Stephen 'Baamba' Albert and Ningali Lawford. Indigenous filmmaker Catriona McKenzie directed the series. A second series aired in 2009.

>> *First Australians* **(2008)** is a landmark documentary directed by Rachel Perkins and Beck Cole and with producers including Darren Dale. Each episode covers a period of Australia's colonial history with a focus on the characters who experienced historic events.

>> *8MMM Aboriginal Radio* **(2015)** is a six-part comedy series set at a local Aboriginal radio station that looks at the issues that face the station along with the broader issues facing the community in Alice Springs. It shows the tough, systemic issues facing the characters and their families, and the way they are faced with innovation and humour. The series stars Trisha Moreton Robinson, Shari Sebbins and Elaine Crombie and was directed by Dena Curtis.

>> *Black Comedy* **(2014–)** is a sketch comedy show that has been a showcase for Indigenous writing and comedy performance. It has included standout performances by Nakkiah Lui, Steven Oliver, Adam Briggs, Elizabeth Wymarra, Bjorn Stewart and Aaron Fa'aoso.

>> *The Gods of Wheat Street* **(2014)** is more than just a family drama. It mixes social realism with magic realism to create a unique Indigenous story. Written by Jon Bell, it stars Kelton Pell as Odin Freeburn and also stars Leah Flanagan, Shari Sebbens, Rarriwuy Hicks, Ursula Yovich and Miah Madden. It was directed by Wayne Blair, Catriona McKenzie and Adrian Russell Wills.

>> *Art + Soul* **(2010–2014)** this series, narrated by curator Hetti Perkins, explores contemporary Aboriginal and Torres Strait Islander art through the themes of Home + Away, Dreams + Nightmares and Bitter + Sweet. The show was directed by Warwick Thornton and Steven McGregor.

>> *Redfern Now* **(2012–2013)** is a ground-breaking series with each episode a stand-alone story based around the inner-city suburb of Redfern. It provided a platform for Indigenous writers, directors and actors.

>> *Cleverman* **(2016–2017)** was created by Ryan Griffin. It is set in the near future and sees creatures from ancient mythology seeking a way to co-exist in the modern world. The series cleverly explores ideas of racism and xenophobia. Directed by Wayne Blair and Leah Purcell, it stars Hunter Page-Lochard, Rob Collins, Rarriwuy Hick, Tasma Walton and Jada Alberts.

>> *Mystery Road* **(2018–2020)** is a series based on the character Detective Jay Swan, played by Aaron Pedersen, a role he also played in the 2013 Ivan Sen film of the same name and its follow up, *Goldstone* (2016). Directed by Rachel Perkins, Wayne Blair and Warwick Thornton, Jay Swan's investigations go beyond the superficial to uncover deeper systemic corruption and injustice.

>> *Total Control* **(2019–2021)** stars Deborah Mailman as Senator Alex Irving who is parachuted in to parliament by Prime Minister Rachel Anderson, played by

Rachel Griffiths. Alex struggles to get outcomes for her community as she navigates the shady world of political self-interests and corruption. Rob Collins plays her brother, Charlie. Rachel Perkins directed the first season of the show.

>> **The Beach (2020)** is six-part television series that follows director Warwick Thornton as he retreats to a remote beach for several months and, without power, has to go back to basics. The series also showcases the work of cinematographer Dylan River.

Indigenous media organisations

Indigenous people have become more prevalent on Australian television screens but Indigenous people were always interested in making their own content and controlling its distribution.

Urban communities such as Redfern had a great interest in developing media organisations, and some remoter communities also saw the advantages of being able to broadcast their own content on radio or television.

A report commissioned by the federal government in 1984 — *Out of the Silent Land* — focused on the impact of satellite on remote areas in the central parts of Australia. As a result, the Broadcasting for Remote Aboriginal Community Scheme (BRACS) was introduced, with the purpose of giving people access to and control of their own media services by supplying basic production and broadcasting equipment. Communities could receive mainstream content off satellites or produce their own instead. The scheme became the Remote Indigenous Broadcast Service in the mid-2000s.

STAN GRANT JR: A GLOBAL VOICE

Stan Grant Jr is ABC's International Affairs Analyst. After beginning his career as a newsreader and radio presenter, he became a television presenter on Australian commercial and public broadcasters. He has worked internationally, including a period as a journalist and correspondent for CNN. A sought-after opinion maker, his books, *Talking to my Country* (2016) and *Australia Day* (2019), have been best sellers. He also wrote and narrated the documentary *The Australian Dream* (2019) about the racial abuse of AFL star Adam Goodes and wider racism in Australia.

THE NEWS PRESENTERS AND PRODUCERS

Karla Grant presents *Living Black*, SBS's Indigenous news and current events program. She has hosted the show since 2004. Before then, from 1994, she was a producer, reporter, director and presenter on the SBS show *ICAM*, its first Indigenous current affairs show.

Brooke Boney started as a political reporter for NITV and SBS before becoming a newsreader on ABC's Triple J. In 2018, she became the entertainment reporter on the popular morning program *Today*, on Channel 9, making her the first Indigenous Australian to land such a high-profile job on a mainstream show.

Miriam Corawa is a broadcaster, producer and presenter. She co-hosts the ABC News 24 Weekend Breakfast program, and has worked on programs across the ABC and SBS, including *World News Australia* and *Message Stick*. She has co-hosted special events such as the 2008 Apology to the Stolen Generations.

Lorena Allam is a journalist who was a producer and presenter with the ABC for over 20 years before becoming the Indigenous Affairs editor at *The Guardian Australia*. She presented and produced the Indigenous arts and culture program *Awaye!* for over 14 years as well as worked on other Radio National Shows. Lorena Allam also worked outside of broadcasting at the Australian Human Rights Commission on *Bringing Them Home*, the report of the National Inquiry into the Separation of Aboriginal and Torres Strait Islander Children from Their Families, released in 1997. Since moving to *The Guardian Australia*, Lorena has been nominated for several Walkley Awards, winning the All Media: Innovation category in 2018 as part of the team who worked on the *Deaths Inside: Indigenous deaths in custody* project.

Indigenous-controlled media companies have flourished across Australia, using both radio and television to tell their stories and maintain their culture and languages:

>> **Central Australia Aboriginal Media Association (CAAMA)** was established in 1980 by John Macumba and Freda Glynn — both Indigenous — and Phillip Batty. CAAMA's work is driven by its vision to promote Indigenous culture, language, dance and music. CAAMA's radio network is broadcast on 8KIN FM. It has a music label, CAAMA Music, as well as a film and television production company, CAAMA Productions, that produces programs about Indigenous culture and issues.

>> **Goolarri Media Enterprises** was set up in 1991 and operates in Broome, Western Australia. It develops media content and also supports the development of Indigenous musicians in the area.

>> **Imparja Television** broadcast its first show, an Australia versus Sri Lanka test cricket match, in 1988. Imparja is a private company owned by Indigenous people in the Northern Territory and South Australia. By 2008, its audience had grown to over 430,000, and it now services over 700,000 people. It also broadcasts NITV (see the next section) on its second channel.

>> **Pilbara and Kimberley Aboriginal Media (PAKAM)** is an association of Indigenous producers and broadcasters in the Pilbara and Kimberley regions of Western Australia. It supports 12 remote radio and television stations and 8 town-based radio stations. It covers an area of over a million square kilometres. PAKAM also has a training program that it runs in conjunction with Goolarri media.

>> **PY Media** started in the Ernabella community in north-western South Australia as Ernabella Video and Television (EVTV). PY Media was developed in 1987 to deliver content developed by the local Indigenous community across the Anangu Pitjantjatjara Yankunytjatjara (APY) Lands.

>> **Warlpiri Media** is based at Yuendumu in Central Australia. Warlpiri people began experimenting with video production and established the first Aboriginal television station in Australia in 1983. The community also established its own media organisation, the Warlpiri Media Association, to undertake these activities. It created the popular, quirky television show *Bush Mechanics*, which aired on the ABC.

REMEMBER

In remote communities that became involved with video production in the early 1980s, the community could decide whether to broadcast its own materials or material from elsewhere. From 1987, BRACS was rolled out to 103 communities to enable the transmission of locally produced radio and television. Today, 71 remote Indigenous communities have a community broadcasting licence that enables them to broadcast their own radio and television content locally. Another 76 communities have a television licence that allows them to retransmit material. Indigenous Community Television (ICTV) was developed in 2001 as a way for remote communities across Australia to share their videos. It was one of the organisations that supported the establishment of National Indigenous Television (NITV).

National Indigenous Television

In 2004, a committee was formed to oversee the establishment of a national Indigenous television service. At the time, research estimated that only two hours per week of Indigenous programming aired on Australian television.

The initiative was supported by Indigenous media organisations such as Goolari Media Enterprises, ICTV, Warlpiri Media, CAAMA and Imparja, which were determined to see more Indigenous content developed for and broadcast on television.

In 2005, the federal government funded the development of NITV. On 13 July 2007, NITV was launched. Originally airing on Imparja's second channel, it was picked up by Foxtel and Austar, as well as several community television channels. It was re-launched in December 2012 by SBS as a free-to-air channel.

NITV has provided a platform for established talent and led to the development of new talent within the industry, including new producers and new on-screen talent. Here are some of the television shows developed and screened on NITV:

- **The Barefoot Rugby League Show** was a weekly show focused on rugby league, co-hosted by Brad Cooke and Tony Currie. It looked at the premier games in the NRL (National Rugby League) and at grassroots football competitions and their players. It paid tribute to Indigenous players of earlier years, as well as the star players of today. The show ran until 2010. In 2017, a new show was launched to cover NRL from an Indigenous perspective. **Over the Black Dot** is hosted by George Rose, Timana Tahu and Dean Widders.

- **Family Rules** is a reality television show featuring the Rule family, a charismatic and inspiring family of nine sisters — and one amazing mother! These are women who are great role models as they navigate the world and stay strong in their culture.

- **Letterbox** was a game show for children that taught spelling and grammatical skills, focused on children between the ages of 10 and 12.

- **Little J and Big Cuz** is an animated children's show that teaches values of community, family and self-respect. Little J is five and Big Cuz is nine, and they live with their nan and Old Dog. The characters are voiced by a range of high-profile Indigenous actors, including Deborah Mailman, Miranda Tapsell, Aaron Fa'aoso, Shari Sebbins and Ningali Lawford. Episodes are also dubbed in Indigenous languages to assist with bilingual education.

- **The Marngrook Footy Show** was a weekly show that discussed the news in Australian Rules football. The show was initially developed for radio by Grant Hansen in the mid-1990s. It easily lent itself to being turned into a television show when the opportunity arose. It was seen on NITV, ABC2 and SBS, still co-hosted by Grant Hansen, until 2019. It included general commentary about the sport with a focus on the performance of Indigenous players. The show ran for 12 years.

- **The Point** is a current affairs show that was originally anchored by Stan Grant Jr when it first aired in 2016. It remains an important source of news from an Indigenous perspective, and is hosted by John Paul Janke and Rachael Hocking.

>> **Yaarnz** told unique stories in short vignettes from all over the country. Hosted by Paul Sinclair, it provided a platform for many people to get their stories, achievements and points of view to a larger audience.

Getting onto Mainstream Airwaves

Indigenous community broadcasting has been a popular way for communities to communicate, and to promote their languages and cultures.

Some 50 years after the first Australian radio broadcast, the first Indigenous-produced radio programs went to air, in 1972. The broadcasts were on 5UV in Adelaide and on 4KIG FM, the station of the Townsville Aboriginal and Islander Media Association (TAIMA) in Mount Stuart.

Although the 1970s saw the first development of Indigenous broadcasting, it wasn't until the 1980s that it really began to flourish. Today, over 120 Indigenous radio stations operate and, in addition to community radio, national broadcaster the ABC carries Indigenous-focused shows.

REMEMBER

The first broadcast by the ABC of an Indigenous program occurred in 1981 in Alice Springs. This was extended to north Queensland in 1983. Today, ABC Radio's main Indigenous show is *Awaye!* hosted and co-produced by Daniel Browning. It focuses on the arts, politics and diversity of Indigenous cultures.

National Indigenous Radio Service

The National Indigenous Radio Service (NIRS) is a national service residing in Brisbane. It provides 24-hour Indigenous-focused broadcasting, including news and current affairs, but allows other broadcasting services to pick up this content.

In this way, local communities can provide 24-hour broadcasting while allowing them to put local content on the airwaves when they want to. This means that local radio stations with few resources can run full-time, and it also gives local people the opportunity to use the radio station when they want.

At the time of writing, over 130 Remote Indigenous Broadcasting Services units, 23 local radio stations and 120 community radio stations can receive NIRS content.

Koori radio

Here are some of the Indigenous radio stations on air at the time of writing:

» **CAAMA Radio:** CAAMA's radio network is broadcast on 8KIN FM. (Refer to the section 'Indigenous media organisations', earlier in this chapter, for more on CAAMA.)

» **Koori Radio:** The Gadigal Information Service was established in 1993 as a result of the determination of the Indigenous community to develop an Indigenous-controlled and operated media organisation in Sydney. In 2001 — after a six-year campaign — Gadigal Information Service was granted a full-time broadcasting licence for Koori Radio. It is the only Indigenous radio station in Sydney. You can find it at 93.7 FM and it can be heard in the Sydney Metropolitan area, the Blue Mountains, the Central Coast and Wollongong.

» **Radio Goolarri:** After broadcasting on the ABC for up to 25 hours a week, this service got its own broadcasting licence and started going to air 24 hours a day through the Broome and Kimberley area. It focuses on local content and culture and is an arm of Goolarri Media.

» **Radio Larrakia:** This station promotes the language and culture of the Larrakia people in Darwin and the surrounding region. Established in 1998, it now broadcasts 24 hours a day in 26 languages.

IN THIS CHAPTER

» Looking at sporting traditions and traditional sports

» Competing in the mainstream

» Claiming a first in cricket whites

» Boxing above their weight

» Excelling in all kinds of football

» Succeeding in every sporting sphere

Chapter **20**

Indigenous People and Sport

I f anything transcends race, intolerance or discrimination, it's sport. Indigenous peoples were excluded from many aspects of Australian life but sportspeople overcame those barriers to achieve in their chosen fields. In some areas, they're underrepresented — such as cricket and golf — but in others — such as football and boxing — they almost dominate the scene.

The revival of traditional Indigenous games is a strong indicator that Indigenous cultures can survive. In this way, traditional games are not only helping Indigenous people stay fit; they're also a way of keeping culture strong.

Indigenous people have had a high profile in all kinds of Australian sport. From boxing legends such as Lionel Rose to Olympian runner Cathy Freeman and stars across all codes of football, Indigenous people have made their mark on the sporting field.

In this chapter, I look at both traditional and modern sports, and Indigenous sportspeople who have made, and are making, their mark today.

A (Traditional) Sporting Life

Indigenous people, as hunters and gatherers, lived active lives. Everyday activities such as spearing and digging required physical fitness, and clans would travel across their country walking great distances all the time.

Recreation in traditional life was focused on games that included elements of friendly rivalry and competition, instilling concepts of teamwork and loyalty. Games also encouraged a show of skill, strength and stamina, improving skills like spear throwing and hand–eye coordination. Traditional games include a range of ball games, bat-and-ball games, wrestling games, water games, games where a target had to be hit, tag games and hide-and-seek games. The most well-known traditional sports are *marngrook*, a type of football, and *coreeda*, a game that combines wrestling and dance. Many of these games disappeared as the colonisation of Australia occurred and traditional recreational activities were replaced by participation in other sports.

Marngrook

Marngrook — which means 'game ball' — is credited by many as providing some of the rules for what's now known as Australian Rules Football or, affectionately, Aussie Rules. It was a traditional game played by Aboriginal people of regions across Victoria and The Riverina in south-west New South Wales. The game was played with a ball about the size of an orange and made from possum skin stuffed with pounded charcoal and/or grass. The ball was kicked and caught but wasn't supposed to touch the ground. Teams were made up of a large number of players and membership was based on a player's totem. (The Warlpiri nation, north-west of Alice Springs, had a similar game. They called it *pultja*.) The *Marngrook Footy Show*, which took its name from the game and aired on NITV, ABC2 and SBS, also focused on Indigenous participation in Australian Rules Football.

In 2002, the Australian Football League (AFL) teams of the Sydney Swans and Essendon Football Clubs started to compete for the Marn Grook Trophy. This match is traditionally played annually by the two teams, providing an opportunity to showcase Indigenous talent in the game. In 2020, Fremantle competed against the Sydney Swans for the first time for this trophy, and the match was played in Perth.

Coreeda

Coreeda is often described as a wrestling game but it includes elements of traditional dance as well as combat. Played as a team sport, it combines three segments of dance with a fourth of fighting. It replaced traditional spearing punishments in parts of New South Wales and the dance is said to be based on the movements of the kangaroo when it fights.

Competitors can only touch the ground with their hands and feet and have to stay within a circle. The third dance segment sees the competitors trying to push each other outside of the circle or make each other touch the ground with a part of their body other than their hands or feet. The winner of this dance component can choose the position he starts in for the fourth combat component. In the combat stage, one person is inside the circle and his opponent outside it. The person within the circle is the defender and the person on the outside is the attacker. The attacker tries to force the defender outside the boundary of the circle by pushing him. The defender tries to resist the attacker from within the circle. Competitors then swap positions.

Today, the game is played in quarters and with time limits. Competitors get points in each quarter. The game is played in teams, with individual scores added together. Teams are made up of six competitors of different weight divisions; these divisions are named after species of kangaroos or wallabies, with teams then further divided into two moieties, black and red. The revival of coreeda is still relatively new and Indigenous wrestlers Shane Parker and Stephan Jaeggi have been ambassadors for the game.

Other traditional Indigenous games

In 2008, the Australian Sports Commission produced a resource called *Yulunga: Traditional Indigenous Games*, which details the rules of many traditional Indigenous games. *Yulunga* means 'playing' in the Gamillaroi language. Today, some schools and Indigenous community organisations, such as land councils, run programs to teach children how to play traditional Indigenous games.

Apart from marngrook and coreeda, other games focused on aspects such as spear throwing, boomerang throwing and diving. Here's just a sample of some of those games:

>> **Battendi** was played in South Australia by the Kaurna people and was a spear-throwing game that tested accuracy and distance.

>> **Boomerang games** tested skill with boomerang throwing. Although boomerangs used for hunting weren't always designed to come back, returning boomerangs were often used for entertainment and sport.

>> **Buroinjin** was played by the Kabi Kabi people of southern Queensland and was said to be similar to basketball but made with a ball made of kangaroo skin and filled with grass.

- » **Kalq** was played in the Cape York region, with men using a woomera to project a spear towards the next player in a circle, who used the woomera to deflect the spear from that player. Younger men used spears with blunted ends until their skill levels improved!

- » **Keentan** is a game where two teams try to keep a ball between their own players and try to take it off the players of the other team. The ball was made from possum, wallaby or kangaroo hide and tied with twine. The game has been likened to basketball. It was played in parts of Queensland. Keentan means 'play' in the Wik-Mungkan language.

- » **Koolchee** used small balls of about 10 centimetres diameter and made of sandstone, mud or gypsum. Players rolled the ball on the ground between two teams and the aim was to hit the balls of the other team. The game has been likened to lawn bowls.

- » **Murrumbidgee** is played by throwing stones into the water and then diving to catch them before they reach the bottom.

- » **Parndo** was played in South Australia by the Kaurna nation. It was a kicking and passing game played with a ball made of possum skin. In Kaurna, parndo means 'ball to play with'.

- » **Taktyerrain** is a combat game in which players throw toy spears. It was a way for children to practise for adult life. The spears were made from light sticks or grass. This word means 'to fight' in the Wembawamba language of Victoria.

- » **Tarnambai** was played on the Tiwi Islands. Children tossed the seed heads of spinifex grass and then tried to catch them as the wind blew them along the beach. Tarnambai means 'running'.

- » **Walle ngan werrup** was a game of hide and seek played by children pretending to be on a kangaroo or emu hunt.

- » **Wana** was played by the Noongar people of north-west Western Australia. A stick was placed in the ground and a player had to defend it with her digging stick (a wana) as other players tried to hit it. The game has been likened to French cricket.

- » **Yiri** was played in the Ulladulla area on the southern coast of New South Wales. It involved throwing a spear at a moving target such as bark placed in running water. Yiri means 'to throw'.

Torres Strait Islanders also used games for skills development and recreation. Here are a few of them:

- » **Kai** was played by having a number of players standing in a circle singing the 'kai wed' song as they hit a 'ball', trying to keep it in the air by using the palm of one hand. The thick, roundish red fruit of the kai tree was used as a ball because it was quite light when it was dry.

>> **Kokan** used a small ball (a kokan), probably made from reeds and long leaves. Played on the beach, the aim was to hit the kokan with a bat or club made from bamboo. It has been described as a kind of hockey.

>> **Kolap** was an object-throwing game that used beans of the Kolap tree.

Playing Them at Their Own Games

Indigenous people are often thought to be natural sportsmen and sportswomen. Although no evidence suggests Indigenous people are predisposed genetically to be better skilled at sport, plenty of evidence does exist that they're good athletes and they like playing sport.

From the first Indigenous cricket team that toured England in 1868, Indigenous people have shown they can excel at sports in the national and international arena. Boxers and footballers in every code have also ably demonstrated their athletic prowess. In just about every sport, from tennis to motor racing, Indigenous stars have carved a niche. The later sections of this chapter detail the specific sports and athletes. Many of these athletes have played a leadership role in the development of younger Indigenous players in the sport.

Getting in and having a go

In 2017, Michael Dockery and Sean Gorman released a report that looked at participation in sport, particularly the AFL. They found a strong link between playing sport and wellbeing. Some of their findings include:

>> For Aboriginal and Torres Strait Islander children, 46.6 per cent had played sport in the last 12 months.

>> Around 65,000 Indigenous Australians participated in sport, other than as a player.

>> Mental health is estimated to be higher among Indigenous men and women who participate in organised sport.

>> The most popular sports played by Indigenous boys are Australian Rules Football (17 per cent), rugby league (16 per cent) and soccer (11 per cent).

>> The most popular sports played by Indigenous girls are netball (13 per cent), swimming (7 per cent) and basketball (7 per cent).

Because of the recognised health benefits of participation in sport, physical activity is encouraged among Indigenous people, who have poorer health levels than other Australians. Participation in sport is also seen as a way to bring Indigenous and non-Indigenous people together, as well as to build confidence and self-esteem among Indigenous young people.

Teaching through sport

Some sporting programs have been used to provide incentives to young Indigenous people to stay in school and to give them exposure to good role models. For example, the Clontarf Academies for boys and the Role Models and Leaders Academy for girls use sport to encourage Indigenous students to stay at school. The first Clontarf Academy was set up at Perth's Clontarf Aboriginal College in 2000. By 2020, 122 Clontarf Academies had been set up within 135 schools across Western Australia, Northern Territory, Victoria, New South Wales, Queensland and South Australia. The Role Models and Leaders Academy has built up to 46 Academy sites across Western Australia, Northern Territory, Queensland and New South Wales, supporting 2985 girls.

Strong role models — often footballers who have had successful careers on the field — work in the programs. The programs focus on the interest young people have in sport but they also aim to teach students about the importance of learning, leadership, healthy lifestyles and making sensible life choices.

The National Aboriginal Sporting Chance Academy (NASCA) was founded in 1995 to mentor young Indigenous people in sport. It also offers academic and health programs and helps to send famous Indigenous athletes to Indigenous communities, to promote healthy lifestyles and to give them additional training in various sports such as rugby league, Aussie Rules, cricket and basketball.

READY, SET, GO

The GO Foundation was started by AFL stars Adam Goodes and Michael O'Loughlin. It focuses on education and provides opportunities for Indigenous children from kindergarten to university, including cultural mentoring, homework support, leadership training, STEM training and employment opportunities. Scholarships support a range of student needs, including providing laptops, internet access, sporting equipment and excursions. To find out more about the good work the foundation does, GO to www.gofoundation.org.au.

Slipping on the Whites: Cricket

From the early 1860s, cricket matches had been played between Indigenous people and Europeans in western Victoria. An all-Aboriginal cricket team was the first Indigenous sports team to tour internationally. Later, restrictions on movement limited the ability of Indigenous people to participate in representative cricket, but Indigenous people continued to play the sport.

These racial barriers continued to prevent talented Indigenous cricketers from playing representative cricket up until the end of the 20th century. Despite the skills of players such as Eddie Gilbert and Vince Copley, it wasn't until 1996 that an Indigenous cricketer — Jason Gillespie — was selected for the Australian test team. Today, Indigenous players at the highest levels of the game are more common.

The first Indigenous cricket team

An all-Aboriginal team was put together and played a match at the Melbourne Cricket Ground on Boxing Day in 1866. They came from the western districts of Victoria. The team then played matches in Sydney and Brisbane, and the idea of touring the team to England took shape, although raising the money for the tour took some time.

The team of 13 that arrived in London in May 1868 was coached and managed by Charles Lawrence. Indicative of the time, the men on the team had English nick-names, as well as traditional names. A massive crowd of 20,000 people turned out to watch the first match. Over the course of the six-month tour, the team played 47 matches. The results surprised many who thought the team would be inferior to the English stars of the game. They won 14 matches, lost 14 and drew 19. The most outstanding player was all-rounder Johnny Mullagh, who scored 1,698 runs and took 245 wickets.

The members of the team also put on displays of boomerang and spear throwing at the end of the game. One player, Dick-a-Dick, held a narrow shield and repelled cricket balls that he invited the crowd to throw at him. Sadly, King Cole died of tuberculosis early on in the tour, and Sundown and Jim Crow returned to Australia before the tour was finished due to ill health.

When the team returned to Sydney in February 1869, they played a match against a military team and then were disbanded. Many of the players disappeared into obscurity. Mullagh went on to play for the Melbourne Cricket Club and represented Victoria against a visiting English team in 1879. Johnny Cuzens also played for Melbourne as a professional before going bush in 1870. He is believed to have died the following year. The only other player to appear again in representative cricket was Twopenny, who played for New South Wales against Victoria in 1870.

PAYING HOMAGE TO THE 1868 CRICKET TOUR

Several Indigenous cricket teams have followed that first team's tour to England, on a sporting pilgrimage. In 2001, an Indigenous cricket team calling themselves the Downunders played nine one-day games in England, with four specifically commemorating the 1868 tour.

In 2009, 14 Aboriginal players aged 16 to 26 left Brisbane, Queensland, on 20 June, following in the footsteps of the 1868 tour. They played 11 matches within a month and some were on the same grounds where the earlier tour had been played. This tour was a success, too: The team won 8, lost 3 and drew 1 of their 12 games.

In 2018, to commemorate the 150th anniversary of the tour, Cricket Australia sent a men's team and a women's team to England. They played a series of matches during the first two weeks of June, and four of these matches were played at the same venues used 150 years ago.

Participation in cricket by Indigenous people was curtailed by a change of law in 1869 in Victoria that made it illegal for Indigenous people to travel out of Victoria without approval from the government minister.

Indigenous cricketers today

The segregation of Indigenous people on reserves, as well as other social barriers that existed in Australian society for most of the 20th century, prevented Indigenous people from playing representative cricket. Cricketers such as Jack Marsh (the first Indigenous cricketer to play at first-class level, from 1900 to 1903 for New South Wales), Eddie Gilbert and Vince Copley, who had great skills, found themselves excluded from the sport on a national level, though Gilbert did play at state level. Bernie Lamont, Jeff Cook and Dan Christian also played at state level. Dan Christian, described as a natural all-rounder, became the first Indigenous person to play for Australia in Twenty20 cricket when selected in 2010.

To date, the most successful Indigenous male cricket player is Jason Gillespie. In 1996, he played for the Australian cricket team and thus became the first male Indigenous player to play at that level. (The first Australian test team played in 1877; it took well over 100 years for an Indigenous person to be selected for the national team, which highlights the barriers Indigenous players faced in the game.) Gillespie played 71 test games for Australia, retiring in 2008 after playing at international level for 14 years, taking 259 wickets.

Women's cricket

Indigenous women have also been attracted to the game of cricket. Faith Thomas (her maiden name was Choulthard) played test cricket for Australia in 1958. Considering the first Indigenous man wasn't selected for the Australian team until 1996, Thomas was a real groundbreaker in the game. Thomas was the first Indigenous woman to earn national honours. Female cricketers Edna Crouch and Mabel Campbell were both inducted into Queensland's Indigenous Hall of Fame.

Today, a new generation of Indigenous women are embracing the game. The most successful female Indigenous player to date is Ashleigh Gardner who, at the age of 18, captained the National Indigenous women's squad on a tour to India and soon after became the second Aboriginal woman to play test cricket for Australia. She has played for Australia in international test, one-day and Twenty20 competitions. She made her test debut playing against England in 2019 and in 2020 was part of the winning Australian team in the T20 Women's World Cup. This team chose to wear a uniform designed by Indigenous artists.

REMEMBER

Although she is better known for her accomplishments on the tennis court, Ashleigh (Ash) Barty also played cricket in the Women's National Cricket League and played for the Brisbane Heat in the inaugural Women's Big Bash League.

SHOWING UP BRADMAN: EDDIE GILBERT

In 1931, Indigenous cricketer Eddie Gilbert made cricket history when he famously became the only bowler to knock the bat out of Sir Donald Bradman's hands, bowling him out for a *duck* — a score of zero. Bradman said later that the six deliveries he faced from Gilbert in that match were the fastest he'd experienced in his career.

Gilbert was born in Queensland and taken from his family at the age of three to Barambah Aboriginal Reserve, now known as Cherbourg. He took up cricket at a young age and developed into an exceptionally talented fast bowler. Gilbert claimed the skill in his flexible wrist was developed from boomerang throwing. He played for Queensland from 1931. In the 23 matches he played at representative level, he took 87 wickets. Because of the laws of the day, Gilbert had to get written permission from the government to travel from his Indigenous reserve each time he played a representative match. He retired in 1936 and returned to his community. He died in 1978, aged 72, after years of battling alcoholism and substance abuse. Gilbert is a member of Queensland's Indigenous Hall of Fame.

Stepping Up in the Boxing Ring

Boxing was a popular sport in Australia from the 1920s to the 1960s. During this period, tent boxing became a common form of entertainment throughout rural Australia. Travelling troupes of professional boxers travelled the outback, following the agricultural fairs and carnivals, where they erected large tents and took on anyone who wanted to enter the ring, and Indigenous boxers had the chance to become stars. Although many Indigenous boxers got their first shot in the boxing tents, others also took to boxing through more conventional means, producing some of Australia's finest title fighters.

The boxing tents

Roy Bell, Jimmy Sharman and Fred Brophy ran the boxing tents. Jimmy Sharman Senior established the Sharman tent in 1911, and then his son, Jimmy Sharman Junior, took over the business in 1955 and ran it until 1971, when the sport was heavily regulated due to safety concerns. The tent visited 45 to 50 different locations every year. Fred Brophy's boxing tent is the last surviving tent boxing troupe in the world.

The tents — and the sport of boxing — offered an opportunity for money and upward mobility, and a small victory over powerlessness. Boxing also offered a chance for dignity and collective pride as Aboriginal people barracked for their heroes. But exploitation of black boxers also existed, with managers taking crippling percentages. In some places, they were still treated differently from other Australians, with regulation of their movement and wages. These tents included many Indigenous boxers, such as Dave Sands — a leading contender for the world middleweight title before dying in a car accident at the age of 26. In a career lasting only eight years, Sands had 110 fights. He won 97 (63 by knockout), lost 10 and had 1 draw.

Title fighters

Boxing has been a popular choice of sport for Indigenous athletes, both professional and amateur. The first Aboriginal person to become a national boxing champion was Queensland middleweight Jerry Jerome, in 1913. In 1968, Lionel Rose achieved hero status for both black and white Australians when he won the world bantamweight title in Tokyo against Fighter Harada. More than 250,000 people lined Melbourne streets to welcome him back from Japan. Another of the best known Indigenous boxers was Tony Mundine, who competed in four different weight divisions. His son Anthony is also a champion boxer. (See the sidebar

'The Mundines' for more on these athletes.) And the interest in boxing extends beyond the gloves. Chris Collard was the first Indigenous person to win a world kickboxing title. In 1999, he won the world middleweight kickboxing title.

Here are just a few Indigenous people, including Rose, who've made a name in the boxing ring:

- **George Bracken**, who was born on Palm Island in 1935, won the Australian lightweight title in 1955. Hampered by undiagnosed hepatitis, he was arrested on a fake charge in Innisfail in 1957 and was beaten by police for an hour. Bracken was an outspoken advocate for the rights of Indigenous people. He spoke out against the conditions on reserves, racial prejudice, the lack of educational opportunities, and for an insurance scheme for black athletes.

- **Dave Sands** had 97 wins and only 10 losses and 1 draw when he was killed at the age of 26 in an accident. He's still considered one of the most talented Indigenous boxers even with his life tragically cut short.

- **Ranold (Ron) Richards** won three Australian titles (middleweight, light heavyweight and heavyweight) and a British Empire (middleweight) title. He retired from boxing in 1945 with a career of 142 fights and more than 60 knockout victories. By 1946, Richards was broke and he was charged with vagrancy in 1947. Richards was inducted into the Australian National Boxing Hall of Fame in 2003 and into the Queensland Indigenous Sporting Hall of Fame in 2010.

- **Jeff 'Mitta' Dynevor** was one of the first two Indigenous people (along with high-jumper Percy Hobson) to win a Commonwealth Games gold medal when, in 1962, he won in the bantamweight division.

- **Wally 'Wait-awhile-Wal' Carr** fought 101 matches between 1971 and 1986 in a range of divisions. In 2010, he was inducted into the Australian National Boxing Hall of Fame.

- **Frank Roberts**, at the age of 21, was one of Australia's first Indigenous Olympians when he competed as a welterweight at the Tokyo Olympic Games in 1964.

- **Lionel Rose** was the first Indigenous Australian to win a world title in boxing when he became the world bantamweight champion in 1968. By that time, he already had several Australian bantamweight titles under his belt. Rose was born in Gippsland into poverty; his father, Roy, a regular of the boxing tents, looked after his early training. He won the Australian amateur flyweight title at 15.

    Rose was Australian of the Year in 1968 and appointed a Member of the Order of the British Empire (MBE) in the same year. He refused to travel to

South Africa when invited in 1970. Due to the apartheid system that existed there, he would have had to travel as an 'honorary white', which he refused to do. He retired from boxing that year, but remained a strong advocate for Indigenous rights throughout his life. After his career in the ring, he embarked on a singing career.

» **Hector Thompson**, born in Kempsey, New South Wales, won 73 fights (including 27 knockouts); he lost 12 fights and drew 2.

» **Chris Collard,** also known as 'the Aboriginal Warrior', spent his 18th birthday in prison. Five years later, he became the World Kick Boxing Champion, the first Indigenous person to claim the title. Now that's turning your life around!

» **Bradley Hore** represented Australia in two Olympic and two Commonwealth Games. After retiring from boxing in 2016, he started the charity Keep Your Hands to Yourself.

THE MUNDINES

Tony Mundine, born in Baryulgil in New South Wales, won 20 of his first 21 bouts, including the Australian middleweight title. He won eight straight knockouts, winning the Australian heavyweight title in 1972. He added the Commonwealth light heavyweight title in 1975 and, in 1981, he won the Australian heavyweight, cruiser and light heavyweight titles. He retired in 1984 with a record of 80 wins (64 knockouts), 15 losses and one draw. He is the only Australian boxer to fight in four separate weight divisions! Mundine was awarded the Order of Australia (OAM) in 1986.

His son is one of Australia's most charismatic boxers and a superb athlete: Anthony Mundine — affectionately known as 'The Man' — is a two-time champion having won both the World Boxing Association super middleweight and the International Boxing Organization middleweight divisions. He also played rugby league for the St George Dragons and represented New South Wales in the State of Origin. When other representative opportunities didn't eventuate in rugby league, he raised racism as a possible explanation. This theory is shared by some and contested by others.

Anthony left football in 2000 and entered the world of competitive boxing. Trained by his father, Mundine fought his first professional boxing match in July 2000 at the age of 25. He fought his first world title after only ten professional bouts. Mundine went on to claim the title of World Boxing Association super middleweight champion in 2003. Mundine was named Aboriginal and Torres Strait Islander Person of the Year in 2000 and won the Deadly Award for Male Sportsperson of the Year in 2003, 2006 and 2007. After his last fight in 2019, he had a record of 48 wins (28 by knockout) and 10 losses.

>> **Damien Hooper** represented Australia in the 2012 Olympics and caused controversy when he stepped into the ring with a T-shirt that had the Aboriginal flag on it. The Australian Olympic Committee demanded an apology. Hooper replied: I'm representing my culture, not only my country'.

>> **Jamie Pittman** turned professional after representing Australia at the 2004 Summer Olympics. He has a record of 25 bouts (22 victories, 11 knockouts, 3 losses). He has turned his talents to coaching and in 2019 was named National Futures Coach for Boxing Australia.

We Love Our Footy!

Indigenous sportsmen have been prominent across all codes of football in Australia — Australian Rules, rugby league, rugby union and soccer. Codes have also been keen to develop younger Indigenous players and to use high-profile Indigenous players as role models for Indigenous young people. Many Indigenous people see football as a community sport. Crowds gather to watch their team, and football games and carnivals become important social and cultural events.

REMEMBER

The skill shown by Indigenous players means they play with non-Indigenous players and for non-Indigenous fans and, therefore, are seen as breaking down racial barriers. At the same time, however, they can be subjected to racist abuse from crowds and other players. Sometimes they're stereotyped as natural athletes and other times as high risk, because they're assumed to be more prone to anti-social behaviour. Breaking down these stereotypes is another task that falls to high-profile football players.

Australian Rules Football

Australian Rules Football originated in south-eastern Australia but is played all over Australia. It's a popular sport in Indigenous communities across Australia: In 2020, of the total AFL player base, 10 per cent identified as Indigenous.

Research by Michael Dockery and Sean Gorman in 2017 showed that: almost 50 per cent of Indigenous men aged 15 to 19 living in AFL states (Victoria, South Australia, Western Australia, Tasmania and the Northern Territory) played the game, and its popularity is even greater away from major cities. The study also found that children who played football were less likely to have learning difficulties due to poor health, and that boys living in remote areas who played AFL had 20 per cent lower truancy rates.

One of Australia's most successful football clubs is St Marys Football Club, created in 1952 in Darwin, Northern Territory, to give Indigenous people a place to play football and socialise — at the time, Indigenous people were banned from being in the city after 6 pm. One of the club's impressive records is a winning streak of 50 consecutive games, beginning in 1994. By 2020, the club had won 903 out of 1,254 games and only collected their first 'wooden spoon' (finishing on the bottom of the ladder) in 2019 — maintaining a 72 per cent winning ratio!

On Elcho Island (off the coast of Arnhem Land), over 800 people play the game. This is about a third of the population and makes it the place with the highest AFL participation rate in Australia.

Each year, one round of the AFL is the Indigenous Round, intended to acknowledge and celebrate Indigenous footy players. This round traditionally culminates with the 'Dreamtime at the 'G' clash at the Melbourne Cricket Ground, always played between the Richmond and Essendon football clubs. (In 2020, round 13 saw the first-ever 'Dreaming in Darwin' game, still played between Richmond and Essendon.)

Here's a list of some of the best known Indigenous Aussie Rules players:

>> **Eddie Betts** joined Carlton in 2004 and played for Adelaide between 2014 and 2019 before returning to Carlton in 2020. In his time at Adelaide, he was the leading goalkicker in 2014, 2015, 2016 and 2017. He had the goal of the year in 2015, 2016 and 2019.

>> **Shaun Burgoyne** was with Port Adelaide from 2002 to 2009 before moving to Hawthorn in 2010. In 2017, he was named captain of the Australian International Rules football team. He has been a strong supporter of other Indigenous players and was an inaugural member of the Indigenous Players Advisory Board when it was established in 2011 and became its chair in 2016.

>> **Barry Cable** played and coached in the Western Australian Football League and Victorian Football League. He also coached in both competitions. He debuted with Perth Football Club in 1962 and ended his playing career in 1979 at East Perth. During that time, he played 383 games and scored 508 goals. He was named in the Indigenous Team of the Century and is named in the Sport Australia Hall of Fame and the Australian Football Hall of Fame — Legend. Legend indeed!

>> **Troy Cook** played 301 games between 1993 and 2010, with 108 games for the Perth Demons, 43 for the Sydney Swans, and 150 for the Fremantle Dockers. He has also represented Western Australia.

>> **Graham 'Polly' Farmer** played a key role in the 1963 Geelong Cats premiership win. He played 392 games and was selected in the AFL Team of the Century. He was also selected as the vice-captain of the West Australian Team of the Century and the captain of the Indigenous Team of the Century. He went on to coach Geelong, West Perth and Western Australia's first State of Origin team. In 1971, he became the first footballer to receive an MBE.

>> **Lance 'Buddy' Franklin** played with Hawthorn from 2005 to 2013 then moved to the Sydney Swans in 2014. He was a six times leading goal kicker during his time at Hawthorn and was the leading goal kicker his first five years at the Swans. He scored the AFL goal of the year in 2010 and 2013 and was consistently named in the All Australian team.

>> **Adam Goodes** played with the Sydney Swans and won two Brownlow Medals (2003 and 2006), is a four-time All-Australian team member and a member of the Indigenous Team of the Century, and has represented Australia internationally. He played his 250th game in 2009. He retired in 2015, having played 372 games.

>> **Joe Johnson** is thought to be the first Indigenous Australian to play in the Victorian and Australian Football Leagues. He played for the Fitzroy Football Club in 1904 and Brunswick Football Club in 1907.

>> **Michael Long** began his football career with the famous St Marys Club in Darwin. In 1989, he started playing for Essendon, playing 190 games for the club. He was inducted into the AFL Hall of Fame in 2007. He has been a strong spokesperson on Indigenous issues and rights.

>> **Andrew McLeod** played a record 340 games in the AFL competition before retiring in 2010. He captained the 2008 Dream Team.

>> **Peter Matera** played over 253 games for the West Coast Eagles in the 1990s. He was often admired by commentators of the game for his skills. He had seven siblings, and two of his brothers — Wally and Phillip — also played in the AFL.

>> **Stephen Michael** played for South Fremantle from 1975 to 1984, kicking 231 goals. He won the Sandover Medal twice (1980 and 1981) and represented Western Australia on 17 occasions. Despite lucrative offers from the Victorian competition, he always refused and didn't leave his home state.

>> **Michael O'Loughlin** was selected for the Indigenous Team of the Century and twice represented Australia. He was only the third Indigenous person in the AFL to play 300 games.

>> **Maurice Rioli** played 118 games for the Richmond Tigers between 1982 and 1987. He was a three-time All Australian and won a Norm Smith Medal in 1982. He later moved from the football field into the political arena when, in 1992, he won a seat in the Northern Territory Legislative Assembly. Sadly, Rioli passed away in December 2010, aged just 53.

- ≫ **Gavin Wanganeen** was nicknamed the 'Indian Rubber Man' because he was so flexible. In 1990, aged just 17, he began his AFL career playing for Essendon. He played 127 games for that club, went on to play 173 for Port Adelaide and 8 for South Australia. This track record made him the first Indigenous player to reach 300 AFL games. In June 2010, he was inducted into the Australian Football League Hall of Fame.

- ≫ **Neil 'Nicky' Winmar** became a symbol of Indigenous pride with his powerful reaction to racist taunts. In 1993, after a match-winning performance for St Kilda against Collingwood, hardcore Magpies fans were yelling racist comments at him (as they had for the whole game). Winmar famously lifted his jumper and pointed to his black skin. This became an iconic moment for the Aboriginal community.

- ≫ **David Wirrpanda** made his debut at the age of 16 years for the West Coast Eagles. He played 227 games for the club before retiring in 2009. He represented Australia in international matches against Ireland and was awarded the inaugural AFL Community Leadership Award in 2003. He established the David Wirrpanda Foundation to help underprivileged young people.

REMEMBER

After calling out a young spectator for racial abuse in 2013, Adam Goodes was subjected to on-going and relentless abuse from crowds, particularly in 2015. Some have pointed out a correlation between Adam Goodes speaking out about Indigenous issues and becoming more of a role model for Indigenous Australians and the abuse from crowds. This shameful episode in AFL history was documented in the documentaries *The Final Quarter* (2019) and *The Australian Dream* (2019). In April 2019, on the eve of the premiere of *The Final Quarter*, the AFL and all of its 18 clubs issued an unreserved apology for the sustained racism and events that drove Goodes out of the game, and their failure to call it out.

REMEMBER

In 1995, the AFL introduced *Rule 30: A Rule to Combat Racial and Religious Vilification*, the first rule of its kind in Australian sport. It was brought in as a result of the use of racial abuse as an on-field tactic used against Indigenous players.

REMEMBER

AFL Women's is the league for female players. It is enjoying increasing popularity and has expanded from 8 teams in 2017 to 14 teams in 2020. Of the 2017 AFL Women's players, 4 per cent were Indigenous, a lower percentage than in the men's league (10 per cent) but the numbers are growing, with talented players such as Ally Anderson (Brisbane), Cassie Davidson (Fremantle) and Aliesha Newman (Melbourne).

HAVING A KRAK

Jim Krakouer played for Claremont in 1977 before moving to North Melbourne in 1982 and then St Kilda in 1990. By the time he retired in 1991, he had played 235 games and scored 450 goals. His son, Andrew Krakouer, was also a talented player who played for Richmond and Collingwood, winning the Sandover and Simpson Medals in 2010. Jim's brother, Phil Krakouer, was also an outstanding footballer who played for Claremont (1978–1981), North Melbourne (1982–1990) and Footscray (1990–1991). During this time, he kicked 423 goals across 238 games.

Rugby league

Rugby league was introduced to Australia in 1907, and strong evidence exists that it was first played just a year later in 1908 in Cherbourg, a small Aboriginal mission in Queensland. Today, Indigenous people continue to excel in the sport. In the National Rugby League (NRL), 12 per cent of the players are of Indigenous heritage. Some key events in Indigenous rugby league include

>> **1908:** George Green, thought to be the first Indigenous footballer to play in competition, played for the Eastern Suburbs and North Sydney teams between 1908 and 1922. His true heritage was never established. Although it's hard to know for sure, more Indigenous rugby league players were probably involved in the game in the early years, but many disguised their heritage for fear of facing prejudice and racism.

>> **1930:** Indigenous communities started their own league clubs. The Tweed Heads All Blacks and the Redfern All Blacks became more than just sporting organisations; they played political, social and cultural roles in their local communities.

>> **1960:** Lionel Morgan was the first Indigenous person to play rugby league for Australia. He was often subjected to racist abuse from the crowds who also threw objects at him while he was on the field.

>> **1973:** Arthur Beetson became the first Indigenous player to captain an Australian rugby league team. That same year, the first Indigenous side toured internationally, to New Zealand.

>> **2008:** Australia's national rugby league team had five Indigenous players on their team of 13.

>> **2020:** Josh Addo-Carr lifted his shirt before the Indigenous All-Stars match against the Maori All-Stars, emulating the classic display of pride shown by AFL legend, Nicky Winmar, and reminding audiences of the importance of standing up to racism.

Here are just some of the famous Indigenous rugby league players:

>> **Arthur 'Big Artie' Beetson** was a rugby league player for Queensland, playing representative football from 1964 until 1981. In 1973, when he captained the Kangaroos (the national rugby league team), he became the first Indigenous player to captain Australia in any major sport. He also captained Australia in 1974, 1975 and 1977. He went on to coach Australia, Queensland, Eastern Suburbs (Brisbane), the Redcliffe Dolphins (Brisbane) and the Cronulla-Sutherland Sharks (Sydney). Beetson was inducted into the Australian Rugby League Hall of Fame in 2003. He passed away in 2011 and his life was celebrated with a state funeral.

>> **Preston Campbell** played for Cronulla, Penrith and the Gold Coast between 1999 and 2011. In 2001, he was awarded the Daly M medal. In 2008 he received the Ken Stephen Medal for his work with Indigenous communities, on and off the field.

>> **Larry Corowa** played league for Balmain in the 1970s and continued his career into the 1990s. He was an Australian international and New South Wales interstate representative.

>> **Laurie Daley** played mainly in the 1990s, representing Australia in rugby league on 31 occasions and captaining the team once. He was named in the list of Australia's 100 Greatest Rugby League Players (1908 to 2007), and chosen for the first rugby league Indigenous Team of the Century in 2008.

>> **Justin Hodges** started playing for the Brisbane Broncos in 2000 before moving to the Sydney Roosters in 2002. He returned to the Broncos in 2005 and played with them until he retired in 2015, captaining the team during his last year. He played for Queensland and Australia, and in the Indigenous All Stars team.

>> **Greg Inglis** played for the Melbourne Storm before joining the South Sydney Rabbitohs in 2011. He was awarded the Golden Boot in 2009 by *Rugby League World* magazine as the world's best player that year. Inglis played representative matches for Queensland and Australia.

>> **Cliff 'God' Lyons** played for Manly during the 1980s and 1990s and played more than 300 first-grade games. He won a Clive Churchill Medal in 1987, when Manly won the final. He went on to also win two Dally M Medals in 1990 and 1994. Lyons made his State of Origin debut in 1987. In 1990, he played his first game for Australia in international tests.

>> **Latrell Mitchell** was selected for the Australian Schoolboys team in 2014. He played for the Sydney Roosters from 2016 to 2019 before moving to South Sydney in 2020. He played in the Indigenous All Stars and for Australia in 2018 and 2019.

- **David Peachey** played 255 NRL games — for the Cronulla Sharks, Widnes Vikings (in the English Super League) and South Sydney Rabbitohs — before retiring from elite rugby league in 2007. During his career, he scored 468 points, including 117 tries. He was awarded Sportsman of the Year in 2002. He also played State of Origin and represented Australia.

- **Steve Renouf** played for the Brisbane Broncos from 1988 to 1999 before playing two seasons in England with the Wigan Warriors. Over his career, he scored over 185 tries over 242 games. He played representative football for Queensland and was named in the Australian team each year from 1992 to 1998. He was named in the Indigenous Team of the Century.

- **Eric Robinson** played for the South Sydney Rabbitohs in the 1960s but he left a legacy to the game that went beyond his own career. One of his sons, Ricky Walford, played first grade for St George. Three of his grandsons — Travis Robinson (Cronulla Sharks), Reece Robinson (Brisbane Broncos) and Nathan Merritt (South Sydney Rabbitohs) — also played in the NRL.

- **Wendell Sailor** is a Torres Strait Islander who debuted in 1993 and played a total of 222 games of league for Brisbane, the Dragons and St George Illawarra, as well as representing the Queensland Reds in rugby union. He represented Australia in both codes, playing 14 rugby league and 37 rugby union representative matches. After playing rugby union from 2001 to 2006, Sailor returned to rugby league in May 2008.

- **Dale Shearer** played rugby league in the 1980s and 1990s and is remembered for his record of being the top try-scorer in State of Origin history (12 tries and 6 goals). He also represented Australia in international test matches (scoring 12 tries and 9 goals).

- **Eric Simms** played rugby league for South Sydney in the 1960s and 1970s. He won four premierships while playing for South Sydney and was the top point scorer for four consecutive seasons. He played 206 first-grade games, scoring a total of 1,841 career points. Even though he retired from the field decades ago, some of his club records still stand: Most number of goals in a season (112 goals and 19 field goals), most career field goals (86) and most field goals in a game (5).

- **Gorden 'Raging Bull' Tallis** played rugby league from 1992 to 2004 for St George Dragons and the Brisbane Broncos. He captained Australia, Queensland and the Brisbane Broncos (with whom he won three premierships).

- **Sam Thaiday** played 308 games for the Brisbane Broncos between 2003 and 2018. He played representative football for Queensland and Australia. He was also named in the Indigenous All Stars team from 2010 to 2016. He was awarded Daly M Second Rower of the Year in 2010 and 2011 and the Ken Stephen Memorial Award in 2011.

>> **Johnathan Thurston** started his career with the Canterbury Bulldogs in 2001, before moving to the North Queensland Cowboys in 2005. Thurston won two Dally M Medals for best player in 2005 and 2007, and in those same years won the Dally M Medal for best halfback (which he also won in 2009). Not surprisingly, he was named as halfback in the Indigenous Team of the Century in 2008.

>> **Ricky Walford** played most of his career for St George Illawarra Dragons. He played representative football for New South Wales in the State of Origin and in the Aboriginal side that toured Tonga in 1990. After retirement, Walford became the Indigenous Development Manager at the Australian Rugby League.

REMEMBER

The NRL Women's Premiership features the best female players. Four clubs fielded teams in the inaugural 2018 season: Brisbane Broncos, Sydney Roosters, St George Illawarra Dragons and New Zealand Warriors. Indigenous players for these teams included Taleena Simon (Sydney Roosters), Amber Pilley (Broncos) and Shakiah Tungai (Dragons).

REMEMBER

In November 2009, the NRL announced its first Indigenous All Star team. The team played against the NRL All Stars on 13 February 2010 to mark the two-year anniversary of the federal government's apology to the Stolen Generations. The Indigenous All Stars won 16–12. A women's game was first played in 2011 between Indigenous players and a side made up of Australian representatives and rising talents. The All Star's (men and women) continue to play a match every year at the start of the season, now playing an All Star Maori team.

IT'S A KNOCKOUT!

The New South Wales Annual Aboriginal Rugby League Knockout began in 1971. Also known as the NSW Koori Knockout, it has grown over the years into a three-day event, held in October, and is one of the biggest social events on the calendar for the Aboriginal community in New South Wales. Although originally held in Sydney, it became the custom, after Kempsey won in 1975, that the winning team would host the competition the following year. This tradition has seen the knockout held around the state. The founders of the competition — including former St George Dragon's player Bob Morgan — saw it as an opportunity to showcase the talent in the Aboriginal community, especially in more remote country towns, which may have been overlooked by the talent scouts for the large Sydney-based clubs. In 2007 and 2008, and then every year since 2012, the event also included a women's Knockout.

RUGBY IN REDFERN

Redfern is well known for its Indigenous community, and many rugby league initiatives have come from, or connected themselves to, this area of Sydney.

The Redfern All Blacks is the oldest Aboriginal rugby league football club in Australia. Although officially founded in 1944, the origins of the club can be traced back to the 1930s. The club was started by Aboriginal players as a response to not being accepted to play with other clubs in the local south Sydney area. Over the years, many players for the Redfern All Blacks came from around Sydney and from small country towns with large Aboriginal populations such as Walgett, Kempsey and Cowra.

The Redfern All Blacks are a feeder club for the South Sydney Rabbitohs, who are based in Redfern, and consequently have a very strong connection to the Indigenous community.

The South Sydney Rabbitohs formed in 1908 as one of the founding members of the New South Wales Rugby Football League. The Rabbitohs and the Sydney Roosters are the only foundation clubs still in the league. Souths has produced Indigenous players such as Eric Simms and Nathan Merritt, and continues to be home to some of the best Indigenous players in the game including Greg Inglis, Latrell Mitchell and Cody Walker.

An Indigenous Team of the Century was named in 2008. It included many well-known players such as Arthur Beetson, Laurie Daley, Greg Inglis and Sam Thaiday. In 2020, A Dream Team of the past 20 years was named: Greg Inglis, Nathan Blacklock, Latrell Mitchell, Justin Hodges, Laurie Daley, Johnathan Thurston, Andrew Fifita, Nathan Peats, Caral Webb, Gordon Tallis, Sam Thaiday and Greg Bird.

Rugby union

Indigenous players have made their mark on the game of rugby union, as well as other rugby codes. However, union hasn't had the same popularity as rugby league and Australian Rules within the Indigenous community.

Frank Ivory was the first Indigenous person to play representative rugby union when he played for Queensland in 1893–94. Lloyd McDermott was the first to play for Australia when he was selected for the national team in 1962. Other Indigenous players who have represented Australia include Lloyd McDermott, Mark Ella, Glen Ella, Gary Ella, Lloyd Walker, Andrew Walker, James Williams, Wendell Sailor and talented twins Anthony Fainga'a and Saia Fainga'a.

SPORTING GREATNESS: THE ELLA FAMILY

The Ella family (Mark, Gary and Glen) has left a great mark on rugby union. All three played test matches for Australia and Glen's twin brother, Mark, played for Australia in 25 tests, captaining 9 of them. Despite his exceptional skills as a player and being offered large sums of money to continue playing, he retired in 1984, aged 25.

The Ella brothers were occasionally subjected to racial abuse from crowds, and some speculation remains that Mark lost the captaincy of the Australian team because he was Indigenous. However, Mark's abilities were admired by many. He was inducted into the International Rugby Hall of Fame in 1997 and the Australian Rugby Union Hall of Fame when it was established in 2005.

But the sporting accolades for the Ella family don't end there — the boys weren't the only talents in the Ella family. Their sister, Marcia Ella-Duncan, achieved sporting success in her own right, playing netball for Australia in the 1986 tour of England and then at the Tri Nations with New Zealand and Jamaica. She also played for the Australian team in the World Tournament in Glasgow, 1987.

Lloyd McDermott ('Mullenjaiwakka') was a rugby union player for the Wallabies in the 1960s. Born in Queensland, his father battled to give him an education and McDermott attended Queensland University, studying law. He played two Australian tests against New Zealand in 1962. During the 'apartheid era' in South Africa, he withdrew from playing for the Australian team rather than play as an 'honorary white'. In 1972, he joined the New South Wales Bar as a barrister, and he was named a Queensland Great in 2016. He passed away in 2019 but the foundation he established, the Lloyd McDermott Rugby Development Team, continues his legacy of promoting rugby union and Indigenous rights.

Soccer

Soccer has produced a few Indigenous stars over the years, though its popularity among Indigenous communities has begun to increase only recently. Here are a few Indigenous soccer stars of note (who have all enjoyed distinguished careers outside of their sporting successes):

>> **John Moriarty** graduated from Flinders University a few years after his cousin Charles Perkins (see next point). He played for South Australia and was chosen for the Australian team to Asia in 1961 (this tour never went ahead, however, because Australia was banned from international matches by FIFA, the Federation Internationale du Football).

- **Charles Perkins** is perhaps the most famous Indigenous soccer star. At the age of 21 he was one of the most highly paid soccer players in Australia, when he left to play in the English league. While there, he decided he would study at university, because football provided him with the means of paying for tuition. Perkins became vice-president of the Australian Soccer Federation in 1987. For more on Perkins' political career, refer to Chapter 11.

- **Harry Williams** was the first Indigenous person to play for Australia at international level when he was chosen for the national team in 1970. He played 17 internationals and 26 other representative games between 1970 and 1978, including 6 World Cup games in 1977.

REMEMBER

Indigenous people who've played soccer have observed that they experienced much less discrimination against them than in other football codes, particularly among immigrants from European countries. But fewer players flocked to this code of football, tending to prefer the 'glamour game' of Aussie Rules. Charles Perkins once said that he wasn't welcomed by Australian society but was more welcomed by ethnic groups and found the Aboriginal–ethnic relationship in soccer to be a good one. In 2016, the Football Federation Australia launched the National Indigenous Football Championships.

Indigenous Australians continue to have a presence in the game:

- **Travis Dodd** played 137 matches for Adelaide United before moving to Perth Glory in 2011. When he played his 100th match in 2009, he became the second Aboriginal person to reach this milestone. In 2006, Dodd became the first Aboriginal soccer player to score a goal for Australia.

- **Jade North** joined the Brisbane Strikers in 1998 at the age of just 16. He represented Australia at the 2004 and 2008 Olympics, and by June 2011 had represented Australia 34 times.

- **Kyah Simon** played for Sydney FC in the W-League. She joined the team in 2009 after a year playing for Melbourne Victory. In 2011, she was named Player of the Year, Young Player of the Year and Player's Player of the Year. She has also played in the United States and for Australia in the FIFA Women's World Cup. In the 2015 World Cup, the women's team became the first Australian team, male or female, to win a knockout stage match at a World Cup when they defeated Brazil by a score of 1–0 — with Simon scoring that winning goal.

- **Lydia Williams** played for Canberra United FC in the W-League. She joined the team in 2008. Since then, she has played in the United States and represented Australia. She now plays for Arsenal in England and in 2019 published a children's book *Saved!!!*

TIP

Indigenous historian – and sports enthusiast – John Maynard released an updated second edition of his book *The Aboriginal Soccer Tribe* in 2019. It's a comprehensive account of the Indigenous contribution to the game.

Track and Field

Indigenous people have traditionally excelled as athletes, so it's not surprising that many of Australia's track and field events have been won by Indigenous people. Here are some of the Australia's Indigenous Olympians and world champions:

>> **Cathy Freeman** won gold in the 400-metre sprint at the Sydney Olympics in 2000. She'd won the silver medal four years earlier. Cathy also won 400-metre medals at the 1997 and 1999 world championships, and won four Commonwealth Games titles in the 200-metre and 400-metre events (in 1994), and in the 100-metre and 400-metre relays (in 1990 and 2002).

>> **Benn Harradine** holds the Australian and Oceania records for discus throwing. He was the first Indigenous field athlete to represent Australia at the Olympic Games when he was selected in 2008.

>> **Percy Hobson**, a high-jumper, was the only Indigenous track and field athlete to win a gold medal in the Commonwealth Games when he took the honours at the 1962 Perth games. He remained so until Cathy Freeman won the gold at the 1990 Commonwealth Games (she was on the relay team).

>> **Patrick Johnson** is a sprinter who, in 2003, became the first Australian to break ten seconds (9.93) for the 100-metre sprint — the 17th fastest man in history. He also won the men's 100-metre open at the 2006 Telstra A-Series.

>> **Nova Peris-Kneebone** represented Australia on the women's hockey team at the 1996 Olympics. There, she became the first Aboriginal Australian to win an Olympic gold medal. Also a talented athlete, at the 1998 Commonwealth Games in Kuala Lumpur, she won the 200-metre sprint and was a member of the 100-metre winning relay team. Nova Peris, as she later became known, was the first Indigenous woman to sit in Federal Parliament when she was brought in to fill a Senate vacancy for the Australian Labor Part in 2013.

>> **Joshua Ross** won the Stawell Gift (a 100-metre race) in 2003. As a sign of his talent as an athlete, it took less than a year of participating in competitive athletics before he was ranked number six on the all-time-greatest list. When Ross retired in 2009, he was ranked as the third-fastest Australian of all time over 100 metres, having run it in 10.08 seconds. He represented Australia at the 2004 Olympic Games, at the World Championships in Athletics in 2005 and 2009, and at the Commonwealth Games in 2006.

>> **Kyle Vander-Kuyp** set the Oceania record for 110-metre hurdles in 1995. He competed at the 1996 and 2000 Olympic Games, and the 1994 and 1998 Commonwealth Games.

REMEMBER

After her career as an elite athlete, Cathy Freeman established a Foundation to work with Indigenous children in remote Aboriginal communities. Focused on education and excellence, the Foundation works with Indigenous children to develop academic skills, build self-esteem and develop other activities that promote wellbeing and success. To find out more about Cathy's good works, you can visit www.cathyfreemanfoundation.org.au.

Championing Other Sports

As with every community around the world, the Indigenous community enjoys, participates in and excels at a range of sports. Across Australia, Indigenous communities engage with sports as diverse as basketball, netball, hockey, golf and surfing. Within these sports, the Indigenous community has produced some notable champions. Some of these have achieved elite international success, such as tennis player Evonne Goolagong-Cawley. Other sports have a growing following among Indigenous people, including golf and surfing.

All-rounders at basketball

Basketball is an increasingly popular sport in Australia, and Indigenous people have excelled in it. Here are some of the notable players:

>> **Michael Ah Mat** represented the Northern Territory at the 1959 Australian championships, playing 588 games over 20 seasons. In 1964, he became the first Indigenous person to represent Australia at the Olympic games — and the first Northern Territorian to do it, too! In 1979, he retired from basketball and died of a heart attack in 1984 at the age of 41. He was inducted into the Australian Basketball Hall of Fame in 2010.

>> **Rohanee Cox** played in the Women's National Basketball League (WNBL). She won the Eddie Gilbert Medal in 2008 and was a member of the silver-winning Australian women's team at the 2008 Olympic Games. She holds the impressive record of having represented Australia more than 100 times.

>> **Tyson Demos** grew up in Wollongong and played in the National Basketball League for the Wollongong Hawks.

- **Nathan 'Baby Shaq' Jawai** was part of the 2009 Australian men's basketball squad. He was the first Indigenous Australian to be selected into the NBA, in 2008, by Indiana Pacers but was traded to the Toronto Raptors that same year. In 2011, he played for the Serbian team KK Partizan, going on to play for Spanish and Turkish teams. In 2016, he returned to playing in Australia (and the club he began his career with).

- **Danny Morseu** was the first Torres Strait Islander to represent Australia when he qualified for the national team in the 1980 Olympics in Moscow. He also played with the Australian team in the 1984 Olympics in Los Angeles. He was the first Indigenous person inducted into the NBL Hall of Fame in 2002.

- **Patrick Mills** represented Australia at the 2008 Olympics. He was selected by the Portland Trailblazers in the 2009 NBA draft. In 2012, he signed with the San Antonio Spurs, and was still playing with them in 2020.

Excelling at netball

In 1987, Marcia Ella Duncan became the first Indigenous person to represent Australia internationally in netball. She continued to be involved with the sport as a coach and administrator for the Randwick team, training them for the State Championships. She also helped found the Pearlers Netball Club in 2004. The club, based in the inner western suburbs of Sydney, focuses on getting women from disadvantaged backgrounds into the sport and specifically targets involvement from Indigenous girls.

Several programs have been developed to promote the sport to younger Indigenous women. For example, an Australian Indigenous Schoolgirls Netball team, the Budgies, have been competing in the Trans-Tasman International Challenge since 2009 and the New South Wales Echidna's Indigenous Schoolgirls Netball team has been competing in national selections since 2005.

Indigenous players have made their mark on the game, including Nicole Cusack, Bianca Giteau (nee Franklin) and Stacey Campton who, after a successful playing career, went on to umpire.

REMEMBER

Rose Damaso has represented the Northern Territory in softball, hockey, netball and basketball — one athlete representing her state 36 times across four different sports, an astonishing record!

A few out of the box

Here's just a sample of some Indigenous people who have excelled at their chosen sport and achieved outstanding success:

>> **Beach volleyball:** Taliqua Clancy represented Australia in the 2016 Olympics, the first Indigenous Australian to represent Australia at that level in the sport. As a show of her pride, she painted the flag on her fingernails for the Olympic matches. She won silver in the sport in the 2018 Commonwealth games.

>> **Golf:** May Chalker won the Western Australian women's golf championship and was the captain of the state team in 1982. She represented her state six times during her career.

Scott Gardner became the first Indigenous person to earn a PGA Tour card. He had played the European Tour in 2001 to 2003 and then the Nationwide Tour for nine years winning the Chatanooga Classic in 2010, participating in the US PGA tour in 2013.

>> **Hockey:** Des Abbott played more than 80 times for Australia, including his selection for the Australian men's hockey squad in the 2010 Commonwealth Games in Delhi. His cousin, Joel Carroll, also represented Australia internationally in hockey.

>> **Motocross:** Chad Reed excelled in the sport of motocross. Born and raised in Kurri Kurri in the Hunter Valley, New South Wales. Chad won two Supercross championships before racing overseas. He moved to the United States in 2002 and won the 2004 AMA Supercross championship; he was runner-up in the same competition in 2005 and 2006. Reed only retired from racing in 2020.

>> **Softball:** Stacey Porter was first selected for the national softball team in 2002 and captained the Australian women's team in 2010 at the International Softball Federation's world championships in Venezuela. At the 2004 Olympics, the team won silver and followed this performance with a bronze medal at the 2008 Olympics.

>> **Surfing:** Indigenous surf carnivals are becoming more popular. The numbers attracted to the sport are assisted by initiatives such as the Indigenous Surfing Programs run by Surfing New South Wales and Surfing Victoria. These programs promote the sport, as well as the importance of education and of a healthy lifestyle. Here are a few noted Indigenous surfers:

• **Ginava Henare** won the women's championship at the 2010 Indigenous Classic.

• **Russell Molony** won his seventh Indigenous Classic in 2011 and, as a result, was ranked in the world's top 225.

- **Dale Richards** won the Quicksilver Pro in 2007 and joined the world's top 45 professional surfers.
- **Mark 'Sanga' Sainesbury**, an Aboriginal man from New South Wales, surfed on the professional tour in the 1980s. He died of an aneurysm in the early 1990s while surfing.

Other notable Indigenous surfers include Andrew Ferguson (Coffs Harbour), Barry Chanel (La Perouse), Dean McLeod, Eric Mercy (also Coffs Harbour), Gus Ardler, Joel Slabb (Fingal), John Ardler, John and Gary Brown, Kenny Dann (Western Australia), Lara Haddon, Steven Williams and Todd Roberts (Wreck Bay).

» **Tennis:** Evonne Goolagong-Cawley is not only a famous Indigenous Australian sportsperson, but she also one of Australia's most famous sportspeople! A world-class athlete, she won a total of 14 Grand Slam titles — four Australian Open, two Wimbledon and one French Open, six in women's doubles and one in mixed doubles.

During the 1950s and 1960s, when Goolagong-Cawley was a child, Aboriginal people still lived in harsh conditions and experienced discrimination. In this climate, it is remarkable that Goolagong-Cawley became such a success. She was able to play tennis because a white man, Bill Hurtzman, saw her peering through the fence at the local courts and encouraged her to come in and play. Things really changed for her when, in 1967, the proprietor of a tennis school in Sydney travelled to Goolagong-Cawley's home town of Barellan after being told about her skills. He was impressed and convinced her parents to allow her to move to Sydney. There, she attended school and continued to train. She was named Australian of the Year in 1971, awarded an MBE in 1972 and made an Officer of the Order of Australia (AO) in 1982.

Ashleigh ('Ash') Barty is the second Indigenous Australian to reach the No.1 women's singles ranking. After winning the US Open doubles title in 2018, she won the singles title in the 2019 French Open. She serves as a National Indigenous Tennis Ambassador for Tennis Australia. Her down-to-earth attitude has made her a fan favourite. She played professional cricket during a hiatus from tennis between 2014 and 2016. She was named Young Australian of the Year in 2020.

» **Volleyball:** Dalma Smith was one of Australia's talented volleyball players. She was selected for the senior team to represent Australia in 1985, including at the World Championships Qualifying Tournament in Melbourne.

CELEBRATING SPORT THROUGH FESTIVALS

Many Indigenous sportsmen and sportswomen haven't just excelled at their sport but have also sought to increase the number of Indigenous people — especially young people — who play. One way to do that is through sports carnivals or festivals. In 2008, the Australian Indigenous Games Foundation was established with the purpose of hosting a national Indigenous games event.

Here's a list of popular festivals from around Australia that culture and sport:

- **The Aboriginal Power Cup** was created in April 2008. Indigenous students must attend at least 70 per cent of their classes to participate in the cup, so the festival is used as an incentive!

- **The Barunga Festival** is named after its host town, about 80 kilometres south-east of Katherine, and is the largest annual festival in the Northern Territory. It is held over the Queen's Birthday long weekend in June. The local Jawoyn community use the festival to celebrate their culture. Throughout the festival, sports competitions and events such as spear making and spear throwing are held.

- **The Ella 7s Rugby Union Carnival** is an annual event held in Coffs Harbour, New South Wales, and started in 2009. It was named after the Ella brothers and is aimed at promoting rugby union to Indigenous players. The tournament includes men's and women's games.

- **The Foley Shield** was started in 1948 and is held in far north Queensland with teams from the Torres Strait and Cape York. It is auspiced by the Queensland Rugby League. After a period of 'hibernation' in the mid-2010s, the competition was revived in 2017.

- **The Generation Cup,** for netball, softball and football, has been held in Launceston, Tasmania since 1995 and is hosted by the Tasmanian Aboriginal Centre.

- **The Indigenous Reconciliation Rugby League Carnival** started in 2009 in Rockhampton, Queensland, and now involves 24 rugby league teams.

- **The Island of Origin Series Rugby League Carnival** is held on Badu Island and has been going since 1985. Many players and supporters travel by small boat to get there. The unpredictable seas and tides can prevent people from getting to the carnival — or delay their leaving!

- **The Newcastle Koori Netball Tournament** began in 1999 and aims to increase participation by Indigenous women in the sport. The competition attracts players and teams from all across New South Wales.

(continued)

(continued)

- **The New South Wales Aboriginal Rugby League Knockout Carnival** was first held in 1971 in St Peters, Sydney, with eight participating teams. Teams represent Indigenous communities across New South Wales, and the carnival has grown to be one of the biggest Indigenous social, cultural and sporting events in Australia, with its family-friendly feel and rules about being alcohol-free. The winning team gains the right to hold the next knockout, so the tournament has been held in various locations across the state.

5

Dealing with Current Issues

Explore some of the historical reasons for Indigenous disadvantage — including lower levels of literacy, higher levels of unemployment and incarceration, higher levels of poverty, overcrowded houses and lower levels of home ownership.

Understand attempts to address Indigenous disadvantage through laws and government policies.

Look at some concrete examples of programs and policies that have worked to improve Indigenous disadvantage — most of them simple but clever ideas that have been devised by communities working to solve problems themselves.

Chapter **21**

Closing the Gap: Health, Housing, Education and Employment

ndigenous people make up 3.3 per cent of the Australian population. Yet, on all social indicators, they don't have the same opportunities or living standards as other Australians.

Australian governments have developed policies in relation to Indigenous people. From assimilation through to practical reconciliation, none of these strategies has been successful in creating equality. The key strategy developed now is to Close the Gap on Indigenous disadvantage.

All the socioeconomic factors that affect the lives of so many Indigenous people — poor health, literacy and numeracy, housing, education and income — create a cycle of poverty. Poor health, which can be exacerbated by poor-quality housing and overcrowding, affects the ability to engage in education and employment. This, in turn, leads to lower incomes, and makes housing and health care harder to afford.

Indigenous people continue to search for and implement the best solutions to these intractable problems, and effective ways to break the cycle. These include establishing Indigenous medical services to better provide more targeted health care to Indigenous people and their communities, training more Indigenous doctors, implementing programs designed to keep children interested in school and providing support for Indigenous businesses.

In this chapter, I take a look at the key federal government policies of the past that have been implemented in relation to Indigenous people. I then look at some of the statistics and highlight the disparity between Indigenous and non-Indigenous Australians, while also looking at the enormous efforts being made by Indigenous people themselves to effect positive change.

Looking Back at Past Government Policies

Government policies concerning Indigenous peoples were often shaped by what governments thought was in the best interest of Indigenous peoples at the time, even though, looking back now, it's clear that the policies weren't. These past policies were also shaped by other interests, such as the demand for farming land, and ideologies, such as the idea that Indigenous people were inferior to white people.

When the colonies in Australia were established, the British government had difficulty controlling how policies were implemented across the different colonies. Therefore, local opinions and the priorities of the settlers shaped the government's approach to Indigenous peoples. However, across the country (and through both the 19th and 20th centuries), an era of protection and assimilation was established with policies such as removing Indigenous children, denying the right to vote and refusing to grant equal wages.

It wasn't until the 1967 referendum, when the responsibility for Indigenous policy was also given to the federal government, that it became a national focus. (Refer to Chapter 11 for more information.)

The Whitlam government started a policy of self-determination in 1972. This policy remained in various forms (although never quite reaching a form of self-determination the way Indigenous people wanted) until the election of the Howard government, when the policy of self-determination was eroded and replaced with a period of 'practical reconciliation' and a focus on addressing the disparities between Indigenous and non-Indigenous Australians.

Moving from 'amity' to 'practical reconciliation'

The following provides a little more detail on how the various policies relating to Indigenous peoples played out:

>> **'Amity and kindness':** Governor Phillip was ordered by his superiors in Britain to deal with Aboriginal people in the new colony with 'amity and kindness'. Phillip was given no direct instructions to form treaties or details on what rights of Aboriginal people were to be recognised. Colonial law was imposed and Aboriginal people were expected to follow it. The colonies were left to implement cordial relationships with the Aboriginal people, but they were much more influenced by local factors rather than policies created back in Britain. The relationship with Aboriginal people focused on conflict over land and resources. The Aboriginal population was also heavily affected by disease (as discussed in Chapter 7) and numbers dwindled significantly, disrupting traditional practices and kinship systems.

>> **Protection:** By the 1880s, large tracts of land had been taken from Aboriginal people and they had been pushed onto reserves, as part of the **protection** policy, and other marginal places within society. (Refer to Part 2 for more information about this period in Australia's history.) Governments believed that Indigenous people had to be protected because, at the time, they assumed (based on the dramatic decreases in Indigenous populations since 1788), that Indigenous peoples were dying out. (Chapter 10 discusses the protection policy in more depth.)

The reserves where Indigenous people were corralled were heavily regulated by white managers; the food and housing were substandard and educational opportunities were minimal. Marriage, work and movement around the country were all regulated, and the policy of removing Indigenous children from their families started to be implemented on a larger scale (refer to Chapter 9 for more about the Stolen Generations). Of course, Indigenous populations didn't die out; instead, they began to grow.

>> **Assimilation:** Becoming a formal government policy in the 1950s, *assimilation* policy had actually been influential well before then; the policy maintained that the best way for Indigenous peoples to be accommodated in Australian society was to demand that they give up their cultures, languages and traditions, and instead live like white people. (Chapter 10 gives more detail about the assimilation policy.) The policy focused on Indigenous children, especially 'half-castes', and removed children from their families, either

sending them to institutions where they could learn 'white ways', or adopting them into white families. Removing Indigenous children from their families (discussed in detail in Chapter 9) was the most obvious, and cruellest, aspect of the assimilation policy. Racism and exclusion was so entrenched in society that many Indigenous people were denied the benefits of citizenship that other Australians had — much the same as under the protection policy.

REMEMBER

Indigenous people were told that they had to behave more like white people, but were constantly denied basic rights — so 'behaving more like white people' became impossible. In addition, Indigenous people were proud of their identity and culture, and didn't want to give it up. Towards the end of the 1960s, people started to talk about *integration* instead of assimilation; this was the idea that Indigenous peoples could keep their cultures and still integrate into broader Australian society — much as non-British immigrants were beginning to do, and had done in increasing numbers since the end of World War II.

» **Self-determination:** The 1967 referendum results (refer to Chapter 11) meant that the federal government now had some responsibility for Indigenous issues and began to formulate national policies. Introduced as a policy by the Whitlam government in 1972 (as a reaction to the assimilation policy), *self-determination* (the right of all peoples to 'freely determine their political status and freely pursue their economic, social and cultural development') influenced government policy on Indigenous people until the Howard government was elected in 1996. Self-determination, in the Australian context, was taken to mean that Indigenous people should be part of developing policies that affected them and in the establishment of community organisations that could work on their behalf. (Self-determination policy is discussed in further detail in Chapter 22.)

» **Practical reconciliation:** The Howard government came to power in 1996 and clearly didn't have the same views on Indigenous affairs as did the previous Labor governments. So, John Howard announced that his government would adopt a policy of ***practical reconciliation***, with the primary focus for his government on improving practical issues such as health, housing, education and employment outcomes. In order to achieve this, the government embraced concepts of shared responsibility and mutual obligation, such as services or infrastructure being offered to Indigenous communities in exchange for behavioural changes, such as sending children to school. You can read more about practical reconciliation in Chapter 14.

Closing the gap

When Kevin Rudd came to power in 2007 as the leader of the new Labor government, he set the stage for a change of Indigenous policy by making an important symbolic statement — an apology for the removal policy (refer to Chapter 15).

The focus of the Rudd and Gillard Labor governments was on 'closing the gap' between Indigenous and non-Indigenous Australians on a range of social indicators, with a report card on closing the gap presented during the first sitting week of each year's parliament.

The original Close the Gap target areas were:

>> Halve the gap in child mortality rates for Indigenous children under five by 2018

>> Ensure 95 per cent of all Indigenous four-year olds enrolled in early childhood education by 2025

>> Close the gap between Indigenous and non-Indigenous school attendance by 2018

>> Halve the gap for Indigenous children in reading, writing and numeracy within a decade by 2018

>> Halve the gap for rates of Indigenous Australians aged 20 to 24 attaining Year 12 or equivalent by 2020

>> Halve the gap in employment outcomes between Indigenous and non-Indigenous Australians by 2018

>> Close the life expectancy gap by 2021

By 2020, only the targets for early childhood education and Year 12 attainment were on track.

REMEMBER

The Close the Gap agenda was a new approach to Indigenous Affairs. However, in other ways, such as continued support for welfare quarantining and other aspects of the Northern Territory intervention, the Rudd and Gillard government's policies didn't shift from those of the previous government. (See Chapter 15 for more on the intervention.)

Closing the Gap Reboot

After the continual failures to make any significant headway on most of the Close the Gap targets, the Morrison Government revealed new and expanded Close the Gap targets in 2020.

As part of this reboot, a National Agreement on Closing the Gap was developed between the Australian government and Aboriginal and Torres Strait Islander peak bodies. This means a closer relationship between government and

Indigenous community-controlled organisations — seen as a positive step in making progress.

The new targets include

- ›› Close the gap in **life expectancy** within a generation by 2031

- ›› Increase the proportion of Aboriginal and Torres Strait Islander babies with a **healthy birthweight** to 91 per cent by 2031

- ›› Increase the proportion of Aboriginal and Torres Strait Islander children enrolled in **early childhood education** (the year before school starts) to 95 per cent

- ›› Increase the proportion of Aboriginal and Torres Strait Islander **children assessed as developmentally on track** in the five areas of physical health and wellbeing, social competence, emotional maturity, language and cognitive skills, communication skills and general knowledge to 55 per cent by 2031

- ›› Increase the proportion of Aboriginal and Torres Strait Islander people aged **20 to 24 attaining Year 12 or equivalent qualification** to 96 per cent by 2031

- ›› Increase the proportion of Aboriginal and Torres Strait Islander people aged 25 to 34 years who have **completed a tertiary qualification** (Certificate III and above) to 70 per cent by 2031

- ›› Increase the proportion of Aboriginal and Torres Strait Islander youth (15 to 24 years) who are in **employment, education or training** to 67 per cent by 2031

- ›› Increase the proportion of Aboriginal and Torres Strait Islander people aged 25 to 64 who are **employed** to 62 per cent by 2031

- ›› Increase the proportion of Aboriginal and Torres Strait Islander people living in appropriately sized (not overcrowded) **housing** to 88 per cent by 2031

- ›› **Reduce the incarceration rate** of Aboriginal and Torres Strait Islander adults by at least 15 per cent by 2031

- ›› Reduce the rate of Aboriginal and Torres Strait Islander young people (10 to 17 years) in **detention** by 30 per cent by 2031

- ›› Reduce the rate of over-representation of Aboriginal and Torres Strait Islander children in **out-of-home care** by 45 per cent by 2031

- ›› A significant and sustained reduction in **violence and abuse** against Aboriginal and Torres Strait Islander women and children towards zero

- ›› Significant and sustained **reduction in suicide** Aboriginal and Torres Strait Islander people towards zero

>> A 15 per cent increase in Australia's landmass subject to Aboriginal and Torres Strait Islander people's **legal rights or interests** and a 15 per cent increase in areas covered by Aboriginal and Torres Strait Islander people's legal rights or interests in the sea by 2030

>> A sustained increase in number and strength of Aboriginal and Torres Strait Islander **languages** being spoken by 2031

Four Priority Reforms have also been identified to assist with reaching the Close the Gap targets:

>> Strengthen and establish formal partnership and decision-making

>> Build the Aboriginal and Torres Strait Islander community-controlled sector

>> Transform government organisations so they work better for Aboriginal and Torres Strait Islander peoples

>> Improve and share access to data and information to enable Aboriginal and Torres Strait Islander communities to make informed decisions

Examining Health Issues

A key indicator of the difference between the health of Indigenous and non-Indigenous people is the difference in life expectancy between the two groups. The life expectancy for Indigenous males is 71.6 years (versus 80.2 years for non-Indigenous males), and for Indigenous females is 75.6 years (versus 83.4 years for non-Indigenous females). Part of the reason for the difference is that the health of Australians as a whole has improved over recent decades, especially with advances in medicine and treatment of diseases, but the health of Indigenous peoples hasn't improved at the same rate.

Discussing particular medical issues for Indigenous people

The top four most common health problems for Indigenous people are circulatory diseases, cancer, respiratory diseases and diabetes. But Indigenous people face many other particular medical problems, as outlined here:

>> **Eye and ear health:** Ear and eye infections are found in higher rates among Indigenous communities. When untreated, these infections can lead to long-term damage. Sadly, higher rates of blindness and deafness among Indigenous children are caused by preventable diseases, including the following:

- Trachoma has been prevalent in Indigenous communities around Australia. Although treatable, without medical attention it leads to blindness. An Australian government 2018 study showed prevalence of active trachoma in at-risk communities had fallen since 2009.

- Otitis media, a disease of the inner ear, can lead to hearing loss and deafness if left untreated. Occurring three times as often among Indigenous children under 15 years than in the rest of the Australian population, it has been identified as a factor that impacts on the participation and learning ability of children in the classroom.

>> **Disabilities:** Of the total Indigenous population, 7.8 per cent have a level of disability that requires assistance on a consistent basis; this is twice the rate of the total Australian population. The First People's Disability Network is a community-controlled organisation that advocates for and supports Indigenous people with disabilities and their carers (see fpdn.org.au for more information).

>> **Infant mortality:** Percentage-wise twice as many infants are born in the low birth weight range (less than 2,500 grams at birth) to Indigenous mothers than to non-Indigenous mothers. Two to three times as many Indigenous infants die before their first birthday than non-Indigenous babies. Factors that contribute to higher rates of infant mortality within Indigenous communities include poor health of mothers, due to factors such as lack of nutrition and smoking, and overcrowding and poor housing.

>> **Infectious diseases:** Some infectious diseases are much more prevalent in the Indigenous community than in the rest of the Australian population:

- Hepatitis B is detected in the Indigenous population at five times the rate of the overall Australian population (including Indigenous people).

- Meningococcal disease and chlamydia are detected in the Indigenous population at eight times the rate of the Australian population as a whole.

- Tuberculosis is detected in the Indigenous population at 1.6 times the rate of the total Australian population.

The dramatic increase in infectious diseases in Indigenous communities is linked to lower levels of hygiene (from poor water and sewerage infrastructure), overcrowding in houses and lack of access to medical services.

>> **Mental health:** Indigenous people suffer higher rates of mental illness than the rest of the Australian population, with the rate of hospitalisation for mental illness five times higher for Indigenous men and three times higher for Indigenous women. Indigenous people are three times more likely to be hospitalised for self-harming.

Several lifestyle factors complicate the health of Indigenous people:

MYTH BUSTER

>> **Alcohol:** Overall, the Indigenous population consumes less alcohol per capita than the general Australian population but a higher level of excessive drinking occurs among the group that does drink. In fact, Indigenous people are more likely to abstain from alcohol than the general Australian population, especially in more remote areas.

>> **Obesity:** Of Indigenous people aged 15 and over, 69 per cent are overweight or obese. The rate for men is about the same as for the general Australian community but Indigenous women are one and half times more likely to be overweight or obese than other Australian women.

>> **Smoking:** The proportion of smokers in the Indigenous population is almost three times that of the non-Indigenous population. Even though rates of smoking have decreased among Australians overall in the last three decades, the rate of smoking among Indigenous people remains high.

Watching the emergence of Indigenous medical services and professionals

Inequality in standards of health is partly a result of lack of access to primary health care. Historically, Indigenous people weren't given adequate access to doctors — they were, for example, given medical attention on the verandahs of hospitals but not allowed in the beds in the wards. The long-term effect of this discrimination in the provision of health services meant that Indigenous people had poorer health levels, and this was further compounded by poorer access to doctors and hospitals.

PRE-CONTACT LIFESTYLES WERE HEALTHIER

Historians believe that Indigenous Australians had better levels of health before 1788. Indigenous peoples enjoyed traditional diets made up of food that was hunted, fished or gathered. Much of this food was rich in vitamins and minerals. No processed food was included in the diet and little fat, only unprocessed sugars and no alcohol. Hunting and gathering lifestyles necessarily involve a lot of physical activity and also include a range of natural remedies (refer to Chapter 4 for more in Indigenous diets and medicines).

Many of the diseases that plagued European countries at the time — such as scarlet fever, tuberculosis, syphilis and measles — didn't exist in Australia. So, when the Europeans arrived and brought their diseases with them, these new diseases had a devastating effect on the Indigenous peoples, who had no immunity to them. Smallpox, measles, whooping cough and influenza were particularly lethal.

The impact of these diseases led to a drastic drop in numbers in the Indigenous population. This meant that the social structures of Indigenous communities were severely disrupted. Health was further affected by the impact of European settlement, particularly farming practices that destroyed traditional food bases. So, from the earliest days of the colony, a cycle of poor health began in Indigenous communities.

By the 1970s, Indigenous communities became interested in establishing their own medical services as a way of circumventing the racism they experienced in the mainstream health system. People also believed that Indigenous health services were better placed to specifically target the health issues unique to particular Indigenous communities. Staffed by Indigenous people, as well as experienced doctors and nurses, the Indigenous health services were well placed to treat local community members.

The first Indigenous-controlled medical service opened in 1971 in Redfern, and the service has grown rapidly since then; as with other Indigenous medical services, the Aboriginal Medical Service Cooperative in Redfern has expanded to include primary and preventative health care programs and a dental clinic. Specific programs target nutrition, health-worker education and immunisation. Many services are also provided in remote and regional communities, often as a result of the initiative of local communities.

Eventually, these Indigenous community-controlled medical services and health organisations established a peak body: the National Aboriginal Community Controlled Health Organisation (NACCHO). The body started in 1976 as the National Aboriginal and Islander Health Organisation (NAIHO) and today represents over

140 health services (you can visit the website at www.naccho.org.au). The Torres Strait Islander community has also established its own culturally appropriate health services to specifically meet the community's needs.

REMEMBER

Aboriginal women were trained as nurses from the 1960s but the increasing number of Indigenous people trained as doctors is a more recent development. The Australian Indigenous Doctors Association (AIDA) was established in 1998, with the aim of improving the health and life outcomes of Indigenous people. AIDA advocates for improvements in Indigenous health, provides expert advice to government and health bodies, and encourages Indigenous people to become doctors. It provides support to Indigenous medical students and works closely with medical schools within Australian universities.

Here's a list of some leading Indigenous people in the medical profession:

>> **Ian Anderson** is Deputy Vice-Chancellor (Student and University Experience) at Australian National University. In 2017, he was appointed Deputy Secretary of Indigenous Affairs in the Department of Prime Minister and Cabinet, and was Deputy Chief Executive of the National Indigenous Australians Agency. He also held leadership roles at the University of Melbourne, and worked in the health field for over two decades as a health worker, health educator and general practitioner, including as the CEO of the Victorian Aboriginal Health Service. He has chaired numerous health working parties, boards and research programs.

>> **Ngaire Brown** is a medical practitioner with qualifications in medicine, public health and primary care. A founding member of AIDA, she has worked to ensure culturally relevant approaches to child and adolescent wellbeing, and a cultural determinants approach to Indigenous health and wellbeing. As well as undertaking an extensive research program, Professor Ngaire Brown also has made significant contributions to research process and health policy and practice.

>> **Pat Dudgeon** was the first Aboriginal psychologist and was the inaugural Chair of the Australian Indigenous Psychologists Association. Not surprisingly, she is considered one of the founding figures of Indigenous psychology. She has also been a leader in the higher education field.

>> **Jilpia Nappaljari Jones** was one of the first nurses employed at the Aboriginal Medical Service in Redfern when it opened in 1971. She was born in the Kimberley, Western Australia, but taken from her mother and raised in Queensland. She later worked as the registered nurse on the National Trachoma and Eye Health Program (NTEHP) with Fred Hollows during the 1970s and 1980s. While travelling with the program, she was reunited with her mother, through a chance encounter. Jilpia went on to undertake ophthalmologic training at the prestigious Moorefield Eye Hospital in London. After retiring from nursing, she graduated

from the Australian National University with a Bachelor of Arts and worked on a history of the NTEHP from an Aboriginal perspective. She received the Order of Australia for services to ophthalmology and birthing choices in 1995.

» **Kelvin Kong** was the first Indigenous person to become a surgeon when he qualified as a Fellow of the Royal Australasian College of Surgeons, specialising in otolaryngology (head and neck surgery) in 2006. He is now also Conjoint Associate Professor at the University of Newcastle and board member for the National Centre of Indigenous Excellence. The Kong family have been trailblazers in the medical profession. Kelvin's mother was a nurse. His sister Marlene is a general practitioner and his sister Marilyn became the first Indigenous obstetrician and gynaecologist.

REMEMBER

A key strategy in dealing with the difference in health standards between Indigenous communities and the rest of Australia is to have Indigenous people more closely involved with the delivery of medical services and involvement in the medical profession, especially as doctors and nurses.

FRED HOLLOWS AND THE TRACHOMA PROJECT

Fred Hollows was originally from Dunedin in New Zealand and graduated from the medical school at Otago University. He then studied ophthalmology in the United Kingdom and went on to work for three years as an Ophthalmic Registrar in Cardiff, Wales.

In 1965, Hollows moved to Sydney to become Associate Professor of Ophthalmology at the University of New South Wales. He visited towns in rural New South Wales and was shocked by the poor eye health among Indigenous people in those communities, particularly from trachoma.

He helped establish the Aboriginal Medical Service in Redfern in 1971 and began travelling to Indigenous communities with a team of colleagues to survey and provide eye care services. Hollows started the National Trachoma and Eye Health Program (NTEHP) as a vehicle for carrying out this work. He and his team visited over 465 communities, screened 100,000 people, treated 27,000 people for trachoma and performed 1,000 eye operations. In 1992, the Fred Hollows Foundation was established to ensure his work would be ongoing. He passed away in 1993, but left a lasting legacy.

The Australian Medical Association (AMA) has also been active in recent years in advocating for improvements in Indigenous health. The AMA recommended the following, in order to improve the disparity between health standards in Indigenous and non-Indigenous Australia:

>> Establishment of a national network of centres of excellence in Indigenous health, as hubs for training and research for best-practice Indigenous health care

>> Funding to improve access of Indigenous people to medical specialists and tertiary health services

>> Grants provided for enhancing infrastructure and services delivered by Indigenous medical services

>> Increased spending over the next ten years to non-government organisations and community groups, to increase availability of health resources in Indigenous communities by building knowledge, skills and partnerships

The AMA supported the goal of closing the gap in life expectancy, and halving the gap in Indigenous mortality rates for children under 5.

When the Morrison government released its new Closing the Gap goals, the AMA stated it was 'hopeful that this unique partnership between Aboriginal and Torres Strait Islander people and governments will provide a pathway for governments to achieve tangible improvements in life expectancy and other key health indicators for Indigenous Australians'.

The AMA's viewpoint indicates that it doesn't see any quick solutions but that what is needed is long-term investment.

Looking at Housing Problems

Good housing is an important part of ensuring a healthy environment. Some of the chronic health problems in Indigenous communities, especially infectious diseases, are caused or exacerbated by poor-quality housing and overcrowding; these are environments where poor hygiene and inadequate water and sewerage infrastructure is common. (Refer to the preceding section for more discussion about these health issues.)

An important aspect of housing and its links to health is the number of people living in a dwelling. Overcrowding is a problem in the Indigenous community, bringing many associated health and social problems. The statistics show that, on average, 3.4 people live in Indigenous households, compared with 2.6 people in total Australian households. The number increases in remote areas, where Indigenous households have an average of 5.3 people per household. Across Australia, 78.9 per cent of Indigenous people are adequately housed compared to 92.9 per cent of non-Indigenous people. In Western Australia, 75.2 per cent of Indigenous people live in adequate housing compared to 95.5 per cent of non-Indigenous people; in the Northern Territory, only 38.4 per cent of Indigenous people live in adequate housing compared to 90.2 per cent of non-Indigenous people.

While only 3.3 per cent of the population, over 29 per cent of Indigenous Australians aged over 15 have been homeless at some time compared to 13 per cent of non-Indigenous Australians.

REMEMBER

Given the health problems that can occur with overcrowding or poor-quality sewerage and no clean water, of particular concern is that over 16 per cent of houses where Indigenous children live have been classed as being of poor quality. In addition to health problems, children have difficulty studying and being school-ready in environments that are overcrowded or have poor infrastructure. For example, poor water quality and sewerage can lead to problems with hygiene that lead to a greater risk of infectious diseases. Ear infections can impede the ability for children to hear in class and make it harder for them to engage in school and to learn.

TRADITIONAL (AND NOT-SO-TRADITIONAL) HOUSING

Indigenous communities around Australia had different forms of traditional housing. These ranged from lean-tos made of stringybark (more of a windbreak) to round dwellings made of thatched grass, trees or spinifex, and stone huts in the colder climates of the country. Traditional communities knew where the closest water sources were but also knew how to collect water by evaporation. Techniques were also developed to filter water such as by straining it through spinifex grass.

With the establishment of towns and pastoral properties as European settlement spread through Australia, camps of Indigenous people (who had been pushed off their traditional lands) developed around the fringes of settlements. Dwellings were made of any available material, such as bark, hessian bags, wood and corrugated iron. The floors were either dirt or made of pieces of linoleum or carpet. This type of housing and living arrangement was common up until the 1960s (when Indigenous people were still excluded from entering towns during certain times).

Figures from 2018 showed 38 per cent of Indigenous people owned their own home (compared to 66 per cent of non-Indigenous people) and 57 per cent rented (36 per cent were private renters and 21 per cent were in social housing).

The lower rates of home ownership among Indigenous Australians can be explained by a number of factors. In some remote communities, large numbers of houses don't exist. (Indigenous people in remote areas are even less likely to own their own homes than in urban or rural areas.) Housing is also expensive (both in remote areas and in the cities) and affordability in relation to income is an issue. In addition, Indigenous people are more likely than other Australians to have irregular employment or income streams, which makes home ownership difficult.

As well as having too many people in a dwelling, poor infrastructure in housing — such as sewerage and water problems, leaking roofs and rising damp — can also cause health problems. In a 2014–2015 National Survey, one in five Indigenous Australians were living in a house that did not meet acceptable standards. In remote areas, 27 per cent lived in houses that lacked basic household facilities and 31 per cent were in dwellings that did not meet acceptable standards.

Overall the Australian Institute of Health and Welfare has noted that compared to all other Australians, Indigenous Australians are

>> Half as likely to own their own home

>> Ten times as likely to live in social housing

>> Three times more likely to live in overcrowded housing

>> Nine times more likely to access services for homelessness

ALICE SPRINGS TOWN CAMPS

Several town camps were developed around Alice Springs for Indigenous people who had been excluded from mainstream services in the town. The camps were often clusters of people from the same language area and over time they developed into permanent communities. The residents of the 18 camps established a community organisation called Tangentyere Council to advocate on their behalf in the 1970s. The council worked to get the residents legal ownership over the land they were camping on — though they were forced to lease the land back to the government in 2007 (refer to Chapter 14) — and to assist in getting essential services such as water and electricity. The council also runs a range of services, such as a breakfast program at Yipperinye school, a night patrol, an art centre, a community banking facility and a 'work for welfare' employment program. The population of the town camps averages around 2,000 but can reach up to 3,500 when particular events are held, such as sports events or meetings.

To help improve access for Indigenous people to quality housing, various Indigenous housing companies have been established; some land councils also own housing stock that they rent to Indigenous tenants. *State owned and managed Indigenous housing* organisations (SOMIH) and *Indigenous community housing organisations* (ICHOs) hold housing stock designated especially for Indigenous people. However, many problems exist; the accommodation held by these community-controlled organisations isn't without the issues of overcrowding, maintenance and repairs:

>> Often the organisations have little money (usually less than mainstream public housing organisations) and struggle to maintain the houses. The houses are usually of poor quality and need costly maintenance, and the tenants are often living in poverty — so collecting rent can be an issue.

>> The housing organisations are also required (under federal government policy) to lease back their land to the government in order to access funding for housing repairs. Some communities take a strong philosophical view that the land is theirs and they don't want to lease it back to the government but want to keep control over it — which then means that not as much funding is available for continuing repairs.

Learning about Education Issues

Good education is key for socioeconomic advancement, a pathway to employment and an important prerequisite to being able to fully participate in many levels of society. But, on this important indicator, Indigenous children fall behind their non-Indigenous counterparts because they have poorer levels of literacy and numeracy, poorer attendance rates at school and poorer achievement rates; they're less likely to finish high school and much less likely to attend university. These differences start to occur very early on in the educational pathway and the differences only become greater as students move further through the education system.

REMEMBER

Much consideration has been given to why Indigenous children don't go to school as regularly as their non-Indigenous counterparts and why they don't have the same levels of academic achievement. The main reasons Indigenous children don't stay in school include

>> A curriculum that doesn't engage them

>> Health problems — especially ear infections — making hearing and learning difficult

>> Lack of educational infrastructure in schools in certain areas (not enough books, chairs, desks and teachers)

>> Overcrowding at home (no environment in which to study and be school-ready)

>> Poor quality of teaching in certain locations

>> Teachers having low expectations of Indigenous students

>> An unfriendly culture at the school that makes students feel alienated

In the following sections, I look at specific problems in Indigenous education at each of the three levels of schooling (primary, secondary and tertiary), and also examine the benefits of vocational education and training for Indigenous youth.

Primary education

Indigenous students fall behind their non-Indigenous counterparts early on. In terms of literacy and numeracy levels expected for their age, Indigenous students perform more poorly than other Australian children, and this gap in learning begins in the earliest years. Some headway has been made on closing this gap — partly because Indigenous preschool enrolments have increased to 84.6 per cent in 2018 from 76.7 per cent in 2016, and partly because rates for Australian students overall have dropped, from 91.9 per cent in 2016 to 88.8 per cent in 2018.

Although the Close the Gap target to halve the gap for Indigenous children in reading, writing and numeracy within a decade had not been met by 2018, some improvement had been made in this area. The gap narrowed across all year levels by between 3 and 11 percentage points. Between 2008 and 2018, the number of Indigenous students in Year 3 exceeding the national requirements in reading increased by 20 per cent.

Even so, by 2018, one in four Indigenous students in Years 5, 7 and 9 and one in five in Year 3 remained below the national minimal standards in reading. Between 17 and 19 per cent of Indigenous students were below the minimum standards in numeracy.

REMEMBER

Literacy rates are poorest among Indigenous students in remote areas. This is due to a range of factors, including the difficulty of attracting and retaining teachers, and the lack of investment in educational infrastructure such as classrooms and desks. In remote areas, adults often don't have good levels of literacy, which makes it difficult for parents to support their children through their education.

BILINGUAL EDUCATION

Children learn best when taught in the language they speak at home. For some Indigenous children, English is their second language. This is a challenge for their teachers.

Just one example is the school community at Areyonga, west of Alice Springs and the most northern Pitjantjatjara community. Children are first taught to read and write, speak and listen in Pitjantjatjara but, at the same time, they're taught in English. When they're older, they have half their lessons in reading and writing English with the remainder of the time concentrating on Pitjantjatjara literacy. From the age of 13, students then study only in English. Local Elders are a consistent part of the program, teaching in the school.

In 2008, the Northern Territory government, supported by the federal government, mandated that all schools must give instruction in English for the first four hours of the day. This decision effectively closed bilingual education in remote Indigenous schools. The challenges facing bilingual education stem from their resource-intensive nature, including the time that teachers need to develop their skills in the local Indigenous language (meaning spending time in the community). However, it has been difficult to attract teachers to remote communities in the Northern Territory; on average, teachers posted to those communities stay about 15 months.

Disengagement with the school system also occurs early on. About 88 per cent of Indigenous five year olds attend school regularly, compared with 95 per cent of non-Indigenous children. In 2019, the attendance rate for Indigenous primary students overall was 85 per cent, compared with 94 per cent of non-Indigenous children. Very few Australians have never attended school (just 0.9 per cent) but 2.5 per cent of Indigenous people have never been to school.

Secondary education

More Indigenous students stay on to Year 10 and Year 12 than a generation ago but the retention and completion rates are much lower for Indigenous Australians than for all other Australians. A gap still exists: 63.2 per cent of Indigenous 20 to 24-year olds had a Year 12 equivalent in 2016 (up from 39.4 per cent in 2001). This is compared to 88.5 per cent for their non-Indigenous counterparts (up from 77.6 per cent in 2001).

Attendance rates for Indigenous students remain lower for non-Indigenous students (82 per cent compared to 92 per cent in 2019). By Year 10, Indigenous students attend school 72 per cent of the time on average, a gap of around 17 percentage points.

The key to keeping children in school and improving attendance rates is to build up the relationship between the community and the school. A great example of how this works comes from Chris Sarra, who was the principal of Cherbourg State School, Queensland, in the late 1990s. The school had over 250 students, many of them from disadvantaged Indigenous backgrounds. Sarra transformed the performance of students through programs to improve school attendance and to increase the community's involvement in the school. Sarra went on to establish the Stronger Smarter Institute at the Queensland University of Technology to continue this work on a larger scale. Sarra's work operates on the assumption that Indigenous children need to understand that they can achieve academic excellence, but they must be confident. The program builds self-esteem through assisting children to be proud of their Indigenous heritage. The Institute also delivers leadership programs to school principals and other educators, and supports leadership in education in Indigenous communities. In this way, the Institute focuses on building the capacity of teachers and schools on the one hand, and communities and parents on the other.

Another program that assists Indigenous youth to complete high school and make transitions to tertiary study (through building confidence and aspirations) is the Australian Indigenous Mentoring Experience. AIME was started by Jack Manning Bancroft, an Aboriginal man, and provides a six-year mentoring program for Indigenous students while they're attending high school. Students start in Year 7 and can remain on the program all the way through to Year 12. AIME links university student volunteers with Indigenous students so that they can form one-on-one mentoring relationships.

Tertiary education

Between 2008 and 2018, the number of Indigenous students enrolled in Universities had doubled.

In 2001, 18 per cent of Indigenous Australians aged 25 to 34 had a qualification of Certificate III or higher, compared to 49.2 per cent of the total Australian population. By 2016, 42.3 per cent of Indigenous people in that age group had a tertiary qualification, a large increase but still behind the 72.0 per cent of the total population.

The number of Indigenous people studying at university is continually increasing (10,440 students were enrolled in 2009; by 2013 there were 13,781) but the total number of Australians attending universities has increased at an even greater rate — so, in fact, the percentage of Indigenous students as part of the total student population was 1.8 per cent in 2007 (less than parity of 3.3 per cent).

Fewer Indigenous students completing high school means that fewer Indigenous students are ready to be accepted into university. But, within the Indigenous student population at universities, larger numbers of mature-aged students have come back to study after leaving school early.

REMEMBER

Most universities have programs that acknowledge that Indigenous students in the past weren't encouraged to complete high school and go to university, and so provide bridging courses designed to give Indigenous people a pathway into university. Whereas 82 per cent of all Australian university students enter tertiary education through their previous educational attainments, only 46 per cent of Indigenous students enter tertiary education this way, with the remainder gaining entry through bridging courses.

Today, Indigenous students study in all areas but are more likely to be studying in the areas of law, social sciences, education and health. Numbers are much smaller in areas such as medicine, science, engineering, economics, accounting and architecture.

Indigenous students overall degree completion rates have increased; however, these rates still sit at less than 50 per cent. In comparison, 74 per cent of their non-Indigenous peers complete their studies. Most Indigenous students cite financial and academic reasons for leaving university; many also have children, which can increase financial pressures. Universities have responded to this lower completion rate by establishing programs that provide support to Indigenous students and create a space within the campuses that's culturally welcoming.

Also increasing is the number of Aboriginal people and Torres Strait Islanders enrolling in and completing postgraduate studies at Australian universities. Table 21-1 shows Indigenous tertiary enrolments by course level.

TABLE 21-1

Indigenous Tertiary Enrolments by Course Level

Level of Course	2008	2017	Growth
Enabling course	871	1,749	101%
Non-award qualification	50	97	94%
Bachelor degree	6,352	13,528	113%
Post graduate course work	1,138	2,372	108%
Post graduate research	393	590	50%

PROVIDING TERTIARY INDIGENOUS EDUCATION

Two education providers stand out for their commitment to Indigenous tertiary education.

Tranby Aboriginal College was established in Glebe, Sydney, in 1958, making it the oldest Indigenous education provider in Australia. Tranby delivers courses in a cultural environment that's friendly for Indigenous students, who come from across the country to study there. Courses include leadership programs for women and young people, community management, Indigenous history and culture, and legal studies. Tranby specialises in teaching Indigenous people who have had a limited secondary education, and provides these students with an opportunity to study again.

Batchelor Institute of Indigenous Tertiary Education was established in 1999 in the Northern Territory, though it had its origins back in the 1960s, and started teaching programs as Batchelor College in 1982. It attracts Indigenous people from all over the country but has a particular focus on students from rural and remote parts of Australia. Batchelor has developed a process of teaching that's culturally appropriate for people who may have had little opportunity to complete secondary education. Batchelor also focuses on teaching traditional knowledge, especially Indigenous languages. The Institute is located at Batchelor, about 100 kilometres south of Darwin, but also holds classes in Alice Springs, Katherine and Tennant Creek.

Interestingly, the Indigenous student population at university has a higher percentage of mature-age women than the general student population; 64 per cent of Indigenous students are women whereas, in the general student population, women are 55 per cent of all students.

Importantly, the number of Indigenous people employed in universities has also increased (by 72.6 per cent between 2005 and 2017; academic staff increased by 55 per cent over that period). This has also meant the inclusion of more Indigenous perspectives across all disciplines. However, this means that Indigenous staff still make up only about 1 per cent of the workforce at universities.

When Rebecca Richards enrolled in a Masters of Philosophy in Material Anthropology and Museum Ethnography at Oxford University in 2011, she became the first Indigenous Australian to receive the prestigious Rhodes scholarship.

Vocational education and training (VET)

Indigenous people are much more likely to pursue further studies at a tertiary institution such as TAFE and agricultural colleges rather than a university. They are more likely to take a TAFE pathway than their non-Indigenous counterparts (19.8 per cent compared to 9.8 per cent). One of the main functions of the vocational education and training (VET) sector is to train apprentices.

Indigenous students make up 3.7 per cent of the student population in the VET sector, in areas as diverse as plumbing, horticulture, hairdressing and hospitality. The learning pathway through VET doesn't always require completion of high school. However, the VET sector can be a pathway to further studies. Within the VET sector, Indigenous students are less likely to be studying for higher level qualifications — 44 per cent of Indigenous students in VET courses are studying for Certificate I or II qualifications (compared with 22 per cent of non-Indigenous students), but only 13 per cent are studying for Certificate IV qualifications (compared with 21 per cent of non-Indigenous students).

About 28 per cent of young Indigenous graduates studying Certificate I and II go on to further study.

Education as a step up the ladder

Education is a vehicle to better opportunities. Indigenous people with higher levels of schooling are more likely to be in full-time employment than those with lower levels of attainment. The percentage of Indigenous youth (aged 15 to 24) engaged with education, employment or training is 57.2 per cent compared to 79.6 per cent for their non-Indigenous counterparts.

Indigenous people who have completed Year 12 are more likely to have very good health, and lower levels of psychological stress. Completing Year 12 means a person is less likely to smoke and consume large amounts of alcohol. They're also less likely to have a range of diseases than Indigenous people who leave school before Year 10 — including diabetes, kidney disease and cardiovascular disease.

And each Indigenous person who graduates from university is changing the socioeconomic future for themselves, their family and their community.

Working on Employment Problems

Indigenous people experience higher levels of unemployment than non-Indigenous Australians, with unemployment traditionally sitting at 8 per cent compared with 3 per cent unemployment for non-Indigenous Australians.

Employment for Indigenous people is at just 51 per cent (with 46 per cent not in the workforce), compared with 75.7 per cent employment (and 35 per cent not in the workforce) for non-Indigenous people. The Close the Gap target is to increase Indigenous employment to 62 per cent by 2031.

Indigenous employment strategies have been developed to try to increase the number of Indigenous people in the workforce and programs have been implemented in parts of the country — particularly remote areas — where not enough jobs are available for everyone. For example, a large number of Indigenous people were employed under work-for-welfare schemes — such as the Community Development Employment Projects (see the sidebar 'Working for welfare payments' and refer to Chapter 14 for more on this scheme). However, the abolition of these schemes has increased Indigenous unemployment rates, particularly in remote areas.

When employed, Indigenous people are much more likely to work in low-skilled occupations (78 per cent), such as labouring and trades, than other Australians in the workforce (60 per cent) and twice as likely to work part-time (75 per cent) compared with other Australians in the workforce (39 per cent). You can see a notable gender difference within the statistics of Indigenous employment: Indigenous women are much more likely to be working in professions (15 per cent) than Indigenous men (8 per cent), but this difference is not quite as pronounced in the non-Indigenous workforces (23 per cent of women and 17 per cent of men).

Realising why employment issues exist for Indigenous people

Low levels of Indigenous employment have a historical context. Indigenous people had a long history of being excluded from the workforce by often being paid with rations and kept as a pool of cheap labour. Indigenous girls were trained to become domestic staff and boys to undertake manual labour.

When it was finally made law in the 1960s that Indigenous people had to be paid equal wages in the pastoral industry, many lost their jobs (refer to Chapter 8 for more detail). Tracking of Indigenous employment statistics from the 1970s to the 1990s shows that the levels of employment for Indigenous people actually worsened and that they were much more likely to be long-term unemployed. Most disturbingly, Indigenous labour trends often operate counter to the economic cycle; at moments when the economy improves, Indigenous employment levels don't automatically follow.

Several factors contribute to the high levels of unemployment in Indigenous communities, including poor skill levels and low levels of education (such as lower literacy rates), health problems, contact with the criminal justice system and geographical remoteness from jobs. Indigenous people are much less likely to be employed in rural and remote communities, especially by private industry.

REMEMBER

Systemic racism has also caused issues with employment. In the past, Indigenous people were excluded from accessing adequate health services, unable to attend school, weren't allowed to live in towns and were overlooked by employers because of the colour of their skin. This racism was particularly entrenched in rural and remote areas. In the 1970s, discriminating against people on the basis of their race became illegal, in the provision of medical, housing and other services, and in employment.

More recent times have seen a greater push to increase the numbers of Indigenous people working in the private sector. Indigenous people have also established their own businesses as a way of participating in the economy (see the next section).

WORKING FOR WELFARE PAYMENTS

Finding jobs in rural and remote areas can be even more difficult than in urban areas. The Community Development Employment Projects (CDEP) scheme was established to allow Indigenous people on welfare to work.

Under CDEP, participants were paid an extra amount on top of their unemployment benefits for undertaking work and training in local Indigenous community organisations. The scheme was used by community organisations that couldn't afford additional staff, with participants doing a range of activities, from garbage collection to maintaining community buildings and running small enterprises, such as orchards and land management. The CDEP scheme not only employed people within areas where no other jobs are available, but also provided services and activities in communities that don't otherwise have them.

Although the program was originally thought to be a pathway towards paid employment, this isn't the reality, because there simply aren't enough jobs in some of the communities where the program operated. The program certainly increased the number of Indigenous people working, though most of the scheme provided part-time employment. This was especially so in remote and rural areas.

In recent years, the scheme was abolished in urban and some rural areas and people in the Northern Territory were moved from working on a CDEP-based job to receiving welfare payments. The program was replaced with the Community Development Program, a work-for-the-dole scheme that requires unemployed people to work five hours a day, five days a week in supervised work or training.

Running Indigenous businesses

In recent years, Indigenous people have increasingly sought to participate in the economy by starting their own businesses. In 2016, a conservative estimate placed the number of Indigenous owned businesses at 17,900. Figures also show the number of Indigenous people running their own businesses is increasing.

In the Australian workforce, 17 per cent of people are self-employed. Of the employed Indigenous workforce, 6 per cent are self-employed (just under 7,000 people). Of those self-employed Indigenous people, 89 per cent are based in the major cities or rural areas and 11 per cent in remote areas.

One way communities have often become successful in business is by establishing community stores to offer better quality food and other products to their communities. Art collectives are another way in which Indigenous communities are seeking better economic outcomes for their work. Indigenous people are also pursuing business opportunities in areas such as mining, eco-tourism, fashion and textiles, legal services, cultural consulting and land management.

REMEMBER

An important strategy for supporting Indigenous business has been procurement strategies implemented through government departments, large businesses and organisations such as universities. These strategies prioritise sub-contracting through Indigenous-owned companies. The federal government launched its procurement policy in 2015 and in its first five years saw contracts of more than $3.14 billion made with Indigenous controlled businesses. An expanded policy was launched in 2020.

Support is given to Indigenous business through a variety of organisations:

>> **Indigenous Business Australia** (IBA; www.iba.gov.au) was established to provide assistance to Indigenous people to establish and grow their own businesses.

The IBA also has a Business Development and Assistance Program that provides financing and business support services. To qualify, the business must have at least 50 per cent Indigenous ownership and have the capacity to meet a business consultant's costs. Most of the successful businesses supported by the IBA are in mainstream industries — such as hairdressing, car repair, building trades and manufacturing — and also in cultural businesses based on Indigenous art and crafts. IBA also offers a home ownership scheme that assists Indigenous Australians to buy their own homes.

>> **Supply Nation** (www.supplynation.org.au) connects verified Indigenous businesses with people seeking to engage with their services. This has been an important initiative in facilitating companies and organisations seeking to

implement Indigenous procurement strategies and targets. It also helps to highlight the diversity and increasing growth of Indigenous businesses across Australia.

>> **The Tribal Warrior Association Inc** (www.tribalwarrior.org) is a Sydney-based community cultural tourism business that runs cultural cruises around Sydney Harbour. The organisation is also a maritime education facility that targets Indigenous people with low incomes and limited formal education, and trains them to gain various commercial maritime licences, thereby increasing their potential for employment. Tribal Warrior also provides a drug counselling and rehabilitation program and provides Indigenous cultural learning programs.

No new Stolen Generations: Keeping Indigenous Children with their Families

Since the apology delivered to the members of the Stolen Generations in 2007, the rates of Aboriginal children being removed from their families has increased, almost doubling in the ten years since then. By 2018, Indigenous children were 5.5 per cent of the total number of Australian children but made up 37.3 per cent of the children in out-of-home care. They are 10.2 times more likely to be in out-of-home care than non-Indigenous children. When Indigenous children are removed, they are increasingly less likely to be placed with Aboriginal and Torres Strait Islander family members or carers. In 2018, only 45 per cent of Indigenous children who were removed were placed with family. (This was down from 49.4 per cent in 2017.) These are alarming trends — especially with so much information available now about the negative social and psychological impacts on Indigenous children brought up away from their culture.

This alarming trend has continued even after the release of the *Bringing them Home* report, with recommendations that included the implementation of a principle of self-determination and the implementations of a Child Placement Principle.

A key explanation for the statistical trend is that Indigenous children have been deemed neglected because they live in poverty — that is, a household being overcrowded or short on food is equated with neglect. A further recurring issue is that many child protection workers are still not Indigenous and make cultural assumptions where they assume neglect — for example, Indigenous children are often brought up communally and then judged as neglected because they spend nights at the homes of different family members. These workers can also sometimes make biased decisions — for example, a child underweight is deemed neglected but later found to have had a medical condition. The linking of neglect with poverty is troubling since one in three Aboriginal children live in poverty and 25 per cent of Indigenous people experiencing homelessness are children.

Another systemic problem is that state child protection services are often under-resourced, so most of the effort goes in to child removal with little effort on supporting families in crisis or restoring children to families after a period of crisis.

REMEMBER

The Aboriginal Child Placement Principle states that where an Indigenous child needs to be removed from their family, they should be placed with an extended family member. If that isn't possible, they should be placed with another Indigenous family within their community. Where that isn't possible, they should be placed with an Indigenous family. Finally, if that isn't possible, the child should be placed with a non-Indigenous family but a cultural plan should be in place. This is great as a principle, and it has been put into legislation or the regulations of each Australian state and territory; however, child protection agencies struggle to implement it.

TECHNICAL STUFF

The Indigenous community–controlled sector is really important in the child protection space. Given that child protection is a state-based issue, state bodies such as the Victorian Aboriginal Child Care Agency (VACCA), AbSec in NSW and the Queensland Aboriginal and Torres Strait Islander Child Protection Peak (QATSICPP) play an important role. A national coalition of these organisations exists in SNAICC: National Voice for Our Children. This sector is better able to understand the family and cultural circumstances of Indigenous children, and is also better placed at finding extended family and community placements for children who do need to be removed. They also focus on family support and family reunification.

The Indigenous community–controlled organisations have advocated for policy changes through their Family Matters campaign (www.familymatters.org.au). A key strategy advocated for changing the trend is to implement the child protection principle and further implement the recommendations of the *Bringing Them Home* report, particularly the recommendation of self-determination.

REMEMBER

Some positive steps have been taken in attempting to turn the statistics around. After much lobbying from the Aboriginal community–controlled sector through their Family Matters campaign, an indicator was included in the 2020 Close the Gap targets that focuses on ensuring children are not over-represented in the child protection system. Even though child protection is a state issue, this inclusion has made the issue a national priority.

In addition, both Victoria and South Australia have a dedicated Commissioner for Aboriginal Children and Young People. Victoria and Queensland have made the strongest commitment to giving more control over to community-controlled organisations. In Queensland, 33 Family Well-being Services and 12 family participation programs are now delivered by the community-controlled sector. In Victoria in 2019, 46 per cent of Indigenous children on a care order were managed by a community-controlled organisation.

Chapter **22**

Working In the System and Changing the System

The Australian legal and parliamentary systems are the framework through which laws and policies are made and enforced. Based on the British legal and political system, the Australian system from the start failed to recognise the laws and governance structures of Australia's Indigenous peoples, instead providing a basis for laws that regulated their lives.

Aboriginal people and Torres Strait Islanders continue to be over-represented in the courts and prisons, despite a Royal Commission into Aboriginal Deaths in Custody that detailed entrenched racism within the legal system and made hundreds of recommendations to improve the situation. The focus on Black Lives Matter in Australia has put a further spotlight on the way the legal system continues to discriminate against Indigenous peoples.

Law reform to protect the rights of Indigenous peoples has remained an important issue in Australia. In this chapter, I also look at efforts to change the playing field with proposed changes to the Constitution through the referendums of 1967 and

1999 and beyond. And I look at the calls that are still being made for constitutional reform that will not only benefit and protect Indigenous rights, but also provide greater benefits to all Australians, regardless of race.

To round off this chapter, I look at the continued political aspirations for self-determination and the evidence that this really is the best strategy for better outcomes for Indigenous people and their communities.

Black Lives Matter: Indigenous People and the Criminal Justice System

Aboriginal people and Torres Strait Islanders have a complex relationship with the criminal justice system. They are over-represented in custody and also over-represented as victims of crime. The problem for Indigenous people is that police tend to use arrest for minor offences, and they tend to use it more frequently in their apprehension of Indigenous people than they do with non-Indigenous people. Additional issues arise when Indigenous offenders appear before the courts and are sentenced. I look at all of these issues in the following sections.

But first, I look at the largest and most comprehensive inquiry into the relationship between Indigenous people and the criminal justice system: The Royal Commission into Aboriginal Deaths in Custody, which reported in 1991.

Examining the Royal Commission into Aboriginal Deaths in Custody

The Royal Commission into Aboriginal Deaths in Custody was established in 1987 and reported to the federal parliament in 1991. The Commission was generated by activism from Aboriginal organisations, Aboriginal Legal Services, and the families of those who had died in custody and their supporters.

From the early 1980s, a number of deaths that had occurred in police and prison custody increased concern among Aboriginal communities across the country about the way Aboriginal people were treated by police or while in prison. For example, the deaths of John Pat in Western Australia, who died after a pub brawl involving police, and Eddie Murray in New South Wales, who was picked up by police for public drunkenness and was subsequently found hanging in a police cell, were particularly disturbing.

The Commission investigated the deaths of 99 Indigenous people in custody. A key finding was that the high number of Indigenous deaths in custody was directly related to the over-representation of Indigenous people in custody. That is, they died at the same rate as non-Indigenous prisoners but, because so many Indigenous people were in custody, the actual number of Indigenous deaths in custody was higher. The Commission concluded that every one of the 18 deaths that had been investigated in New South Wales, Victoria and Tasmania (the rest were in the other states and territories) was 'potentially avoidable and in a more enlightened and efficient system . . . might not have occurred'. The report also stated that many of the people whose deaths had been investigated shouldn't or need not have been in prison in the first place.

The recommendations of the Royal Commission

Many of the recommendations of the Commission specifically addressed issues related to the way that Indigenous people were dealt with by police. It found that many Indigenous people were

>> In custody for minor offences (such as public order offences — swearing and being drunk), which non-Indigenous people wouldn't usually be held in police custody for

>> Refused bail (in higher numbers than non-Indigenous people) while waiting for their court appearance — and a number of deaths had occurred while they were on remand

>> Given harsher sentences than non-Indigenous people for similar offences

>> More likely to be living in poverty, and that this lower socioeconomic state contributed significantly to their increased contact with the criminal justice system

>> More likely to have been removed from their families as children (the Commission found that this was true in almost half of the cases investigated and a similar proportion had been arrested for a criminal offence before they were 15 years old)

In general, those who died in custody had early and repeated contact with the criminal justice system.

The Royal Commission came up with 339 recommendations to improve the justice system, including some broader ideas for improving the relationship between Indigenous people and the criminal justice system. These recommendations included

AN ELDER'S DEATH IN CUSTODY

Long after the 1991 report of the Royal Commission into Aboriginal Deaths in Custody, Mr Ward, an Aboriginal Elder, was arrested on the night of 25 January 2008 in Laverton, about 900 kilometres north-east of Perth. He was refused bail, so the next day he was transported to Kalgoorlie, 360 kilometres south of Laverton, to attend court the following week. For the drive, he was placed in the back of an ageing police van in 42-degree heat and given only a 600-millilitre bottle of water.

The two people driving the van didn't make any comfort stops or check on Mr Ward during the trip. Mr Ward collapsed in the back of the van and was taken to Kalgoorlie Hospital, but he wasn't able to be revived. He had died of heatstroke, but he also had third-degree burns to his upper torso, after falling onto the hot surface of the cell he was locked in during the drive.

A subsequent inquiry found that the two prison officers, the prisoner transport company and the Western Australian Department of Corrective Services were collectively responsible for his death. Two years later, the Director of Public Prosecutions decided not to lay charges against the two security guards after noting that he couldn't determine if they had colluded while giving evidence.

>> Better education of police and judicial officers, including judges, about the most appropriate way to deal with Aboriginal people and Torres Strait Islanders

>> Educational programs that would inform the wider Australian population about the issues facing Aboriginal people and Torres Strait Islanders, as well as improve understanding about their culture and history

>> Empowerment of Indigenous people through self-determination and reconciliation

>> Improved educational and employment opportunities

>> Improved health care and housing conditions

Deaths in custody since the Royal Commission report

Despite the investigations of the Royal Commission, strong evidence exists that many of the recommendations have been ignored. Aboriginal people and Torres Strait Islanders have continued to die in police custody, sometimes in controversial circumstances. Since the Royal Commission into Aboriginal Deaths in Custody and up to June 2020, at least 437 Indigenous people have died while in custody. Many of those died in circumstances similar to those deaths that were investigated as part of the Royal Commission, further evidence of the impact of its recommendations being ignored.

To find out more about Indigenous deaths in custody since the Royal Commission, you can visit the Guardian Australia's award-winning, interactive, online database that personalises these deaths (go to www.theguardian.com/au and search for 'deaths in custody database').

The number of deaths in custody continues to increase due to the overall over-representation of Indigenous people in custody, the rate of which continues to rise. At the time of the Royal Commission in 1991, Aboriginal people and Torres Strait Islanders made up 14 per cent of the prison population and were 15 times more likely to be in prison than non-Indigenous people. By 2020, over 27 per cent of the prison population was made up of Aboriginal people and Torres Strait Islanders. In December 2019, 2,536 Indigenous people were in prison per 100,000 adults; for the non-Indigenous population, this was 218 per 100,000.

The increased momentum behind the Black Lives Matter movement, sparked by the death in May 2020 of African-American man George Floyd in Minneapolis after a police officer knelt on his neck, turned a spotlight back on the issue of deaths in custody in Australia. Floyd's death, and his cries that he couldn't breathe, had a particular resonance with the case of David Dungay that was being investigated through a coronial inquest in 2020 at the time. Dungay had died in Long Bay jail in 2015 after guards rushed into his cell to stop him eating biscuits, dragged him to another cell, and held him face down and injected him with a sedative. He claimed over twelve times that he couldn't breathe. His family have campaigned for charges to be brought in following his death but without success.

Indigenous women and the criminal justice system

Indigenous women are over-represented as offenders at even higher rates than men. They make up 34 per cent of the total female prison population. In addition, they are also much more likely to be the victims of violent crime. For example, Indigenous women are

» Over 10 times more likely to be a victim of homicide than other women in Australia

» Forty-five times more likely to be a victim of domestic violence than non-Indigenous women

> » Close to 11 times more likely to be victims of violent crime than non-Indigenous women

> » More than twice as likely to be the victim of sexual assault than non-Indigenous women

> » Seven times more likely to suffer grievous bodily harm in an assault than non-Indigenous women

> » Thirty times more likely to hospitalised for assault than non-Indigenous women in Australia

A TRAGEDY THAT COULD HAVE BEEN AVOIDED: MS DHU

Ms Dhu was a 22-year-old woman who died in Port Hedland police station in Western Australia. She was arrested for the non-payment of a fine on 2 August 2014, when the police had been called to her home during a domestic violence incident (her partner had breached an apprehended domestic violence order). She was in custody for four days due to the debt. During that time, she complained of pain and was twice taken to the Hedland Health Campus where she was judged to be exaggerating. On 4 August, she was unable to stand. Police handcuffed her, assuming she was still faking her condition, and took her to the hospital. She was pronounced dead shortly after arriving there. The cause of death was sepsis and pneumonia (completely treatable if detected) caused by an infection due to her ribs being broken by her partner three months earlier.

An internal police investigation found that 11 officers failed to comply with regulations and a coronial inquest determined that her treatment had been 'unprofessional and inhumane'. But hospital staff were also at fault, influenced by their own biases about Indigenous people.

The case was a reminder that the Royal Commission into Aboriginal Deaths in Custody had recommended that people should not be locked up for non-payment of fines. Much concern was also expressed about women being arrested for associated minor offences when police are called to a situation where the women are the victim of domestic violence incidents.

This was also a case that echoed deaths investigated by the Royal Commission that were due to negligence and racial bias in the provision of medical services to Indigenous people in custody.

Stopping the cycle: Indigenous young people and incarceration

Aboriginal people and Torres Strait Islanders have a greater likelihood of being sentenced to imprisonment than non-Indigenous offenders, but the rates are even higher for young people. Indigenous young people are 24 times more likely to be in the criminal justice system than non-Indigenous young people. Indigenous men are twice as likely to be in prison as in university.

A high correlation exists between the number of children in juvenile detention and the number who are in out-of-home care. When young people act out in their families, strategies for dealing with their behaviour include being grounded or some other type of punishment. But when children are in out-of-home care, their misbehaviour is more often criminalised — an outburst of anger can lead to charges of assault or damage to property, for example — and, as a result, they are more susceptible to ending up in juvenile detention. This is another reason why decreasing the rates of child removal from Indigenous families is important. It is another way of keeping Indigenous children from falling in to the criminal justice system.

In July 2016, footage was broadcast of the treatment of children in the Don Dale Youth Detention Centre in the Northern Territory. This included children being stripped, hosed down, restrained and hooded. As a result, the Royal Commission into the Protection and Detention of Children in the Northern Territory was set up. Finalising its work in 2017, it concluded that youth detention centres were not fit for accommodating — let alone rehabilitating — young people. They also found that children were subject to verbal abuse, physical control and denied human needs such as water and toilets. It also recommended the closure of the Don Dale facility. The Commission also concluded that the child protection system did not adequately protect vulnerable and at-risk children and families. The system is under-resourced and the Commission recommended the establishment of at least 20 Family Support Centres across the Territory.

In 2018, a year after the Northern Territory Royal Commission finished its work, it was estimated that all children in the Northern Territory juvenile justice system were Indigenous. That's 100 per cent.

Inspecting the relationship between Indigenous people and police

Two-thirds of the deaths investigated by the Royal Commission into Aboriginal Deaths in Custody occurred in police custody rather than in prison. This was because police were using their powers to arrest and hold Aboriginal people and

Torres Strait Islanders in police cells for minor offences, particularly public order offences such as public drunkenness.

Key recommendations of the Royal Commission were to decriminalise public drunkenness, provide sobering-up shelters, change practices relating to arrest and bail (particularly for minor offences) and to provide alternatives to the use of police custody.

Despite the subsequent decriminalisation of public drunkenness in most states and territories, many Indigenous people still come into contact with the criminal justice system because of the public consumption of alcohol. In part, these problems are related to the use of *protective detention* (where people are locked up when they're intoxicated), the use of local council by-laws prohibiting public alcohol consumption, and other such legal restrictions (for example, the Northern Territory's law prohibiting alcohol consumption within two kilometres of licensed premises and penalties associated with breaches of Queensland's alcohol management plans).

Several recommendations of the Royal Commission called on governments to fund non-custodial alternatives for Aboriginal people and Torres Strait Islanders detained for drunkenness, to place a statutory duty on police to use alternatives and to negotiate with Indigenous communities to find acceptable plans for public drinking. Despite the common perception that Indigenous people have a problem with alcohol (see Chapter 25), many Aboriginal communities haven't waited for governments to act, and have established their own drying-out shelters and safe houses to assist with managing issues around drunkenness. In the Northern Territory in particular, many communities had, from the 1980s, made the decision to be 'dry' and to regulate alcohol consumption.

Aboriginality as a relevant factor in sentencing was considered in *R v Fernando*. There, the court developed what became known as the Fernando Principles. These principles state that the same sentencing principles are to be applied to everyone and that a person's Aboriginality won't excuse an offence, though the court can take into consideration the socioeconomic circumstances of the Aboriginal community if it's relevant to the offence. Application of the principles has generally been accepted but the extent to which they are taken into account is a matter for the magistrate or judge hearing a particular case.

The question is often asked: Why do incarceration rates continue to rise despite the Royal Commission into Aboriginal Deaths in Custody? The simple answer is that the extensive recommendations the Commission came up with (a complex range of solutions, including education programs, preventative programs, and changes to police practices and sentencing policies) haven't been implemented. While state and territory governments continue to get 'tough on crime', policies such as making the conditions for giving bail tougher work against reducing the number of Indigenous people in custody. What have been most effective in reducing the contact Indigenous people have with the criminal justice system are community-developed solutions such as community policing, circle sentencing and Aboriginal courts (examined in the following sections).

Targets in the Close the Gap agenda to decrease incarceration rates of Indigenous adults and children were introduced in 2020.

Several reform proposals are aimed at reducing the over-representation of Indigenous people in the criminal justice system and deaths in custody. These include:

>> Implementing the recommendations of the Royal Commission into Aboriginal Deaths in Custody

>> Introducing justice reinvestment strategies that redirect funding from prisons to programs that will prevent crime or offer alternatives to incarceration (check out Just Reinvest for a good example of this type of approach: www. justreinvest.org.au)

>> Ensuring adequate funding of Indigenous legal services and community-controlled child protection agencies

THE BOWRAVILLE MURDERS: ELUSIVE JUSTICE FOR ABORIGINAL VICTIMS OF CRIME

In the summer of 1990–1991, three Aboriginal children were murdered on the Bowraville Mission — Colleen Walker-Craig (16), Evelyn Greenup (3) and Clinton Speedy-Duroux (17). Despite concern by the families that the disappearances were out of character, the police did not take these concerns seriously until Clinton's body was found several weeks later. Evelyn's remains and Colleen's clothes were subsequently found on the same stretch of road. A NSW Parliamentary Inquiry later highlighted problems with the police investigation, caused by racial bias and an historical and antagonistic relationship between the police and the local Aboriginal community. The failures in the investigation frustrated the ability to present all the evidence in court against the non-Indigenous man who had been charged with the murders of Clinton and Evelyn.

The cases remain evidence of the way in which, while Indigenous people are over-represented in the criminal justice system, often for summary offences, justice for them when they are victims of crimes is elusive. The families of the Bowraville children have still not given up fighting for their day in court.

>> Creating an independent body to oversee investigations into Indigenous deaths in custody

>> Providing culturally appropriate support for Indigenous victims of crime

>> Removing the practice of imprisonment for summary offences, including fine default, and taking a medical approach to substance addiction rather than criminalising it

>> Providing alternatives to incarceration, such as community service

>> Increasing support for treatment of mental health issues

TIP

Change the Record (changetherecord.org.au) is a campaign aimed at reducing the incarceration rates of Indigenous Australians. It also puts together resources about the issue.

Recognising customary law and sentencing

The Australian legal system has strong cultural differences from Indigenous methods of dispute resolution, as shown in Table 22-1.

The Australian Law Reform Commission undertook the first major inquiry into Indigenous customary law and issues of recognition in 1986. Its recommendations about sentencing included that legislation should provide for the consideration of the customary law of the Indigenous offender's or victim's community, where relevant.

TABLE 22-1 **Indigenous Dispute Resolution System Compared with the Australian Legal System**

Indigenous Dispute Resolution	Australian Legal System
Emotional response	Controlled response
Oral	Written
Disputants live together	Disputants often strangers
Experience as training	Formal legal training
No rules of evidence	Strict rules of evidence
Process in front of community and family	Process in front of strangers
Disputants speak	Use of advocates
Time not an issue	Deadline intensive
Informal	Formal
Communal	Hierarchical

A report from the New South Wales Law Reform Commission in 2000 recommended that evidence concerning customary laws of both the offender and the victim should be taken into account in sentencing. As a result of this report, New South Wales courts may now take into account customary law when sentencing an offender, in one of two ways: When the offender has been or will be subject to traditional punishment, or when customary law may explain the reason for a particular offence. Two principles apply when the courts take into account traditional punishment:

>> Courts are required to consider all the relevant facts, including those that only arise as a result of a person's membership of a particular group. Traditional punishment only exists by reason of the offender's Aboriginality.

>> **Double jeopardy** (the principle that a person shouldn't be punished twice for the same offence) needs to be considered. Although the court may not condone traditional sanctions that are unlawful, it may acknowledge the inevitability of the punishment taking place.

REMEMBER

Governments are responsible for making laws, and the courts are part of the process of enforcing the law. However, communities have also come up with their own solutions to try to deal effectively with offending. Indigenous communities, in particular, have looked at ways to deal with members of their own communities who break the law. For example, circle sentencing and Aboriginal courts (Koori courts, Murri courts and Nunga courts) have been established for Indigenous offenders in Victoria, Queensland, South Australia, the Australian Capital Territory and New South Wales over the last decade. More recently, similar developments have occurred in the Northern Territory and have been recommended in Western Australia.

I look at circle sentencing and Aboriginal courts in the next sections.

Circle sentencing

Circle sentencing was developed in Canada as part of the court process in that country. The process of circle sentencing still results in convictions and criminal records for offenders but invites community involvement. The usual process is as follows:

1. Participants are welcomed to the circle by community Elders and the judicial officer; those attending introduce themselves and explain why they are present.

2. The facts of the case are presented to the circle by the prosecutor, and the defence is then allowed to comment.

3. **Following a period of discussion, participants develop a sentence plan, which the judge uses to sentence the offender.**

The judge is also free to ignore the sentencing circle recommendations, but must impose an appropriate sentence (which is still subject to court sentencing guidelines).

Circle sentencing has operated for Indigenous offenders in a number of areas in New South Wales since 2002. The objectives of circle sentencing include the inclusion of members of Indigenous communities in the sentencing process and the reduction of barriers between Indigenous communities and the courts. Circle sentencing also aims to provide more appropriate sentencing options for Indigenous offenders, more effective support for victims of offences by Indigenous offenders and the reduction of reoffending in Indigenous communities.

REMEMBER

Circle sentencing is designed to increase the awareness of Indigenous offenders of the consequences of their actions on their victims and the Indigenous communities to which they belong. An evaluation of circle sentencing in Nowra, New South Wales, found that circle sentencing not only had all the effects mentioned here, but also led to improvements in the level of support for Indigenous offenders, promoted healing and reconciliation, and generally empowered Indigenous people in the community.

Aboriginal courts

Indigenous courts (also known as Koori courts, Murri courts and Nunga courts) typically involve an Indigenous Elder or justice officer sitting on the bench with a magistrate. The Elder advises the magistrate about cultural and community issues relating to the offender. Indigenous courts can only sentence Indigenous offenders who have pleaded guilty to an offence.

Offenders may receive customary punishments or community service orders as an alternative to prison. The offender may have a relative present at the sitting, with the offender, a relative and the offender's lawyer sitting together at the bar table. The magistrate may ask questions of the offender, the victim (if present), and members of the family and community to assist with sentencing options. The conditions placed on sentences may involve offenders meeting with Elders or a community justice group on a regular basis and undertaking courses, programs or counselling relevant to their particular needs. For example, sentences (particularly probation orders and intensive correction orders) often require offenders to spend time with Elders, attend counselling or programs to address specific issues (such as domestic and family violence, and alcohol or drug abuse), or attend Indigenous men's groups or other support groups.

Changing the system from within

A growing number of Indigenous people are graduating with law degrees. In 2016, a national survey saw 621 solicitors identify as Indigenous, 1.2 per cent of the profession (53 per cent were women and 47 per cent were male). This is well under population parity but shows an exponential growth since Pat O'Shane became the first law graduate in 1976.

Here are some further firsts from Indigenous people in law:

>> The first Indigenous barrister was Lloyd McDermott

>> The first Indigenous person appointed Senior Counsel was Tony McAvoy SC in 2015

>> Pat O'Shane became the first Indigenous person to become a magistrate in 1986 (another first for him)

>> Bob Bellear was the first Indigenous person appointed as a judge in 1996, when he was appointed to the District Court

>> Matthew Meyers was the first Indigenous person appointed to a Federal Court in 2012

>> The first Indigenous person to graduate from Harvard Law School was me, in 1994 with a Masters and again in 1998 with a Doctor of Juridical Science!

Several Indigenous law firms have also been established including Terri Janke & Associates and Chalk & Behrendt (that's my brother!). In 2020, Sonja Stewart became the CEO of the NSW Law Society, the first Indigenous person — and first woman — to lead the professional body.

Reading the Australian Constitution: A Framework for Laws and Policies

The Australian Constitution sets out our system of government, defining the powers and relationships among the three arms of government — the *executive*, the *judiciary* and the *legislature* — and it also defines the way that power is distributed between the federal government and state and territory governments. (For more information on how the political system works in Australia, refer to *Australian Politics For Dummies* by Nick Economou and Zareh Ghazarian, also published by Wiley Publishing Australia.)

The Constitution does its work in a mechanical and practical way, and doesn't make for very inspiring reading! But this foundational document does contain many of the values that the drafters of the original document wanted to instil into it, revealing a lot about the kind of Australia our founding fathers wanted for us, our community today and, in particular, the relationship between Indigenous and non-Indigenous people. At the time the Constitution was drafted, in 1891, Indigenous peoples were excluded from participating in the drafting process. Beliefs of white racial superiority, as well as the belief that Indigenous people would eventually die out, were rife at the time the Constitution came into force in 1901. While these views don't appear expressly in the text of the Constitution, it isn't hard to see the intentions of those who wrote the Constitution.

The drafters of the Constitution believed that parliament should make the decisions about rights protections (as in, which people are recognised and the extent to which they are protected). They discussed whether they should include basic human rights within the Constitution itself, but rejected this option, preferring instead to leave the founding document mostly silent on these matters. Ensuring that the Australian states would have the power to continue to enact laws that discriminated against people on the basis of their race was considered desirable. The power to make discriminatory laws was considered necessary for discriminating against not only Indigenous people, but also other races. For example, special rules regulated the movement of Chinese Australians, which had become general practice during the gold rushes.

For Indigenous peoples, the Australian Constitution, as it was originally drafted, symbolised three things:

>> The modern Australian state was founded without any involvement of Indigenous peoples in the process and, therefore, represented the way in which they were marginalised within Australian society.

>> Indigenous peoples were given no recognition, within the document, of their unique place as the traditional owners of the country.

>> By leaving the Constitution silent about rights, Australians had to rely on governments to protect them. For Indigenous Australians, this trust in the benevolence of government would leave them vulnerable to exploitation and the breach of their human rights.

The 1967 referendum

The Federal Council for Aboriginal Advancement (FCAA) emerged in the 1950s as the first national representative body for Aboriginal people. It later became the Federal Council for the Advancement of Aborigines and Torres Strait Islanders

(FCAATSI). As the dominant voice on Indigenous rights until the late 1960s, FCAATSI's agenda focused on 'citizenship rights', but it also called for other special rights for Indigenous peoples. FCAATSI became a driving force in the call for an amendment to the Constitution that would provide protection to Indigenous peoples. (You can read lots more about events leading up to the 1967 referendum in Chapter 11.)

The referendum in 1967 was one of only eight that have led to changes to the Constitution and had the most resounding endorsement, winning over 90 per cent of voters and carrying in all six states. At a time when many parts of Australia were actively practising segregation, this was an extraordinary result. This support reflected a high-water mark for the relationship between Indigenous and non-Indigenous people.

MYTH BUSTER

Perhaps because of the focus on citizenship rights in the decades leading up to the referendum, and because the rhetoric of achieving equality for Indigenous people was used in 'vote yes' campaigns, inevitably, the mistaken perception that the constitutional change allowed Aboriginal people to become citizens and have the right to vote became entrenched. In fact, the referendum achieved neither of those things.

When voting yes in the 1967 referendum, Australians voted on two specific areas:

>> To allow for Indigenous peoples to be included in the census

>> To give the federal parliament the power to make laws in relation to Indigenous people

Aboriginal people quickly became disillusioned by the lack of change that followed from the referendum — specifically the continued discrimination and the poor socioeconomic conditions of their communities. They rejected the notion of assimilation, but embraced the idea of equal rights and equal opportunities for Aboriginal peoples and Torres Strait Islanders. In this environment, a new generation of activists was created whose protests culminated in the establishment of the Aboriginal Tent Embassy on the lawns of what is now Old Parliament House. From there, the modern land rights movement was formed (refer to Chapter 12).

The failure of the referendum to effect real change to their circumstances created a new momentum in the political activism of Indigenous peoples. They continued to campaign for changes to the legal system to create equality for Indigenous peoples and recognise and protect their rights (refer to Chapter 13). And they continued to highlight how the 1967 referendum hadn't actually changed the way the Constitution, as it was originally drafted, failed to recognise the unique status and place of Indigenous peoples in Australia, and continued to leave the recognition and protection of their rights to the benevolence of government.

The 1999 referendum

In 1999, the Howard government set up a referendum to gauge whether Australians wanted their country to become a republic. The government decided to add to the referendum a question asking whether a *preamble* (introductory statement) should be inserted into the Constitution. The wording of the preamble proposed by Prime Minister John Howard, though it wasn't actually part of the referendum question, included the following:

. . . honouring Aborigines and Torres Strait Islanders, the nation's first people, for their deep kinship with their lands and for their ancient and continuing cultures which enrich the life of our country . . .

However, it was stipulated that the preamble, if passed, would have no legal force and couldn't be used in constitutional or statutory interpretations. In other words, it would have no legal weight. The Preamble was rejected by Australians at the referendum, held on 6 November 1999.

Proposing Legal and Constitutional Reform

Social justice for Aboriginal people and Torres Strait Islanders can be achieved through three key areas of constitutional reform:

>> Acknowledging the unique place and role of Aboriginal people and Torres Strait Islanders in Australia in the Constitution, the nation's founding document

>> Modernising or updating the Constitution so that it provides stronger protection of human rights

>> Providing an opportunity, by working in an inclusive way to achieve constitutional change, to engage in a nation-building process that was not undertaken when the Constitution was first drafted

Considering changes

Proposed changes for the Australian Constitution to better recognise and protect Indigenous Australians include

>> **A new preamble to the Constitution:** A preamble sets the tone for the rest of the document. In the Constitution, a new preamble that recognises the unique place of Aboriginal peoples and Torres Strait Islanders would offer an opportunity to articulate as a nation our shared goals, principles and ideals. If recognition of prior sovereignty and prior ownership were contained in a constitutional preamble, courts may be able to read the Constitution as clearly promoting Indigenous rights protection.

>> **Substantive changes to the sections of the Constitution:** By referendum, sections of the founding document can be changed to provide stronger protections for Indigenous rights.

>> **A Bill of Rights:** Very few human rights are protected by the Australian Constitution. Those that appear in the text have been interpreted in court in a minimal manner (although members of the High Court have implied some rights, this is a precarious approach to rights protection). A Bill of Rights that granted rights and freedoms to all people of Australia (Indigenous and non-Indigenous) would be a non-contentious way to ensure some Indigenous rights protection.

TECHNICAL STUFF

Public discussion needs to be focused on whether we should have a constitutional or a legislative Bill of Rights. A *legislative* Bill of Rights is, as the name suggests, in legislation and can be overridden or repealed. A *constitutional* Bill of Rights is included in the Constitution and can be only be altered by a referendum. For some, a legislative Bill of Rights is viewed as an interim step towards a constitutionally entrenched Bill of Rights.

REMEMBER

Some of the steps to improve the Australian rights framework for Indigenous people outlined in the preceding list — such as a constitutional preamble and a Bill of Rights — would have benefits for all Australians.

Some of the 'substantive changes' to sections of the Constitution that have been suggested over time are

>> **Including a non-discrimination clause in the body of the Constitution:** Such a clause could enshrine the notion of non-discrimination, but must adhere to the principle that affirmative action mechanisms aid in the achievement of non-discrimination (which is consistent with international human rights standards).

>> **Adding specific constitutional protection:** An amendment could be made to the Constitution to specifically provide for Indigenous rights. For example, in Canada (a country with a comparable history and relationship with its Indigenous communities to Australia), the *Constitutional Act 1982* added a provision to its Constitution, acknowledging the rights of their native peoples.

>> **Repealing Section 25 of the Constitution:** This particular section permits discriminatory laws in relation to voting, allowing states to pass legislation to prevent people of a specific race from voting. Though the clause isn't used, some people wish to remove it because it's seen as a reminder that the original document was drafted in a time when theories of white supremacy and endorsed racially discriminatory practices were persuasive.

Responding to the Uluru Statement

Constitutional change became a focus again in 2010 (refer to Chapter 15) but, since its release in 2017, the leading proposal has been the Uluru Statement from the Heart.

Advocates for the statement have focused on the inclusion of a First Nations Voice to Parliament in the Australian Constitution. This is described as a representative body giving Aboriginal and Torres Strait Islanders a say in law and policy affecting them.

The Uluru Statement and a First Nations Voice to Parliament has not been adopted as official government policy and no clear timetable for a proposed Constitutional referendum on the issue has been set. However, a co-design process was started by Minister for Indigenous Australians Ken Wyatt in 2019 to develop local, regional and national elements of an Indigenous voice to government. It may be that such representative structures are put in place in legislative form, without Constitutional protection.

Scrutinising Self-Determination and Self-Representation

Indigenous peoples were subjected to racially discriminatory laws and policies that, even if well-intentioned, had devastating results, such as the removal of children and non-payment of wages. But, from the moment that the First Fleet arrived in 1788 to establish a penal colony in Sydney Cove, Indigenous peoples have continued to assert their identity as distinct peoples. They have asserted their right to take responsibility for and control of their own lives and the policies that affect them, and have organised community and national organisations to represent their interests.

Self-determination – more than a principle

The concepts of *self-determination* and *sovereignty* have pervaded the expression by Aboriginal people and Torres Strait Islanders of their political aspirations.

The belief that Aboriginal peoples and Torres Strait Islanders remain sovereign peoples flows from the fact that Indigenous peoples have never formally ceded their land and continue to feel distinct identities and distinct histories. But, in their political language and aspirations, Indigenous peoples attach a unique interpretation to the term 'sovereignty' that differs from what it means under international law. The Indigenous Australian interpretation includes concepts such as representative government and democracy, the recognition of cultural distinctiveness and notions of the freedom of the individual, which are embodied in liberalism. These claims seek a new relationship with the Australian state, with increased self-government and autonomy for Indigenous peoples, though not the creation of a new country.

Another reason exists to embrace self-determination as a principle, other than the fact that it is an inherent human right and a political aspiration of Indigenous people. Research consistently shows that the more Indigenous people lead the identification of the priorities in their community — and the development of policies, delivery of services and design of programs — the better the outcomes. This is because they are best placed to understand the issues in their communities and the solutions that will work the best. They can use their informal networks to work across agencies and services and they are able to ensure that the most vulnerable in the community are involved rather than falling through the cracks.

TECHNICAL STUFF

Many Indigenous peoples across the world haven't been considered as 'peoples' within the principle of self-determination under international law. They continue to find it hard to fit their claims into the definition that requires them to show distinct territorial boundaries, since much of their land was stolen during the colonisation process. They're also unable to justify the violation of the principle of non-intervention, because most live in countries that have recognised, legitimate governments. Therefore, Indigenous peoples remain under the control of their colonising state for rights protection and steps towards autonomy. The International Covenant on Civil and Political Rights (ICCPR) and International Covenant on Economic, Social and Cultural Rights (ICESCR) both state that the principle of 'self-determination' applies to all 'peoples'. By asserting that Indigenous people aren't 'peoples', they're stopped from being able to claim the right to 'self-determination' under international law.

Self-representation

Aboriginal peoples and Torres Strait Islanders have formed several organisations to represent them and provide a collective voice. Some of the organisations were created by legislation but became a vehicle used by Indigenous people. Others have been created independent of government. Here's a look at each organisation:

- >> **The Aboriginal and Torres Strait Islander Commission (ATSIC)** was established in 1990 under legislation that was passed through federal parliament the year before. ATSIC set up a national board and a system of regional bodies that consisted of elected representatives. It had a range of responsibilities, including advocacy on behalf of Indigenous peoples, monitoring the performance of government and administering a housing, infrastructure and work-for-welfare program. The Howard government removed ATSIC's powers when it came to office in 1996; the coalition had never supported the principle of an organisation that represented Indigenous peoples and had argued strongly against its establishment when the legislation was originally passed by the Hawke government. ATSIC was abolished in 2005 after a political agreement between the Howard government and the then leader of the opposition, Mark Latham. (Refer to Chapters 13 and 14 for more on ATSIC.)

- >> **The National Congress of Australia's First Peoples** was established in 2009, with its first election in 2011. Established as a lobbying body to represent its members, its stated aims were to advocate for Indigenous rights and to work towards the social, economic, cultural and environmental future of Australia's Indigenous peoples. The Congress was a non-government body with over 2,000 members, although it received funds from the federal government to support its operations until 2013. It was then required to be economically self-sufficient. However, it was defunded by the federal government and ceased operations in 2019. (Refer to Chapter 15 for more on the Congress.)

- >> **The New South Wales Aboriginal Land Council** (established in 1983) was formed as part of state land rights legislation that provided a mechanism for Aboriginal people in New South Wales to claim back traditional land now owned by the Crown and not needed for an essential public purpose (refer to Chapter 12). The state land council consists of elected representatives from across the regions of New South Wales and the system also has a network of 121 local land councils — all elected by the local membership — that deal with local issues and hold land for local communities. It has a $2 billion portfolio of land and a $680 million capital fund that finances its operations and provides scholarships for its members and their children, as well as providing money for repairs and infrastructure on Aboriginal reserves in New South Wales.

  Today, it has over 23,000 members (one in three Aboriginal people in New South Wales are members), meaning the largest representative structure with elected representatives is not a national body but a state one. The land council is also a strong advocate on Indigenous issues and attends United Nations forums to represent the views of its members.

A common level of aspiration for representation is at the regional level. As mentioned in the preceding list, the regional council structure in ATSIC was effective and heavily utilised. Operating at the regional level allows for a large enough group to be influential but ensure the focus is local enough to appreciate the distinct local cultures and needs. Some examples of regional-level organisations are

>> **The Gunditjmara Nation:** These traditional owners have developed their own system of decision making in a way that also embodies the ideas of nation building and developing systems of self-governance and which fits in with the cultural values of the nation. They have established the Gunditj Mirring corporation under the *Native Title Act 1993 (Cwth)*, which is governed by Full Group meetings that bring together the traditional owners for a monthly cycle for discussion and decision making. This then binds the Gunditj Mirring in representing the interests of the nation as a whole. The corporation also operates culturally significant sites at places such as Lake Condah Aboriginal Mission and Lake Gorrie.

>> **The Murdi Paaki Regional Assembly:** This is a representative structure that represents the members of 16 communities in north-west NSW. Its membership of Community Working Parties and the MPRA determine the priorities in their area and work with government and service providers. It evolved out of the ATSIC Murdi Paaki Regional Council, led by the Community Working Parties. Be inspired by their work at www.mpra.com.au.

>> **The Ngarrindjeri Regional Authority:** This is an example of a community-designed self-governance model. Formed in 2007, the Ngarrindjeri nation in South Australia designed the structure with no involvement from government. It includes the values by which the Ngarrindjeri want to be ruled by. One of those principles is the NRA Yarluwar Ruwe Program, which guides the direction of the NRA and ensures that cultural and environmental aspects are integrated into its work. It has resulted in a range of caring for country projects and cultural and education programs. The Ngarrindjeri have also developed their own protocols for making agreements or contracts with people. Kungun Ngarrindjeri Yunnan — or 'listen to what Aboriginal people have to say' — are agreements that structure negotiation and consultation, with principles including the recognition of Ngarrindjeri rights and interests and the importance of cultural knowledge.

These regional structures are not only structures that allow regional communities and individual Indigenous nations to focus on the issues relevant to them. They also provide an important interface between the community and state and federal governments. Governments can be confident when dealing with these regional representative bodies that they are engaging in a legitimate consultative process.

TECHNICAL STUFF

Important research undertaken by the Harvard Project on American Indigenous Economic Development (the Harvard Project), established in 1987, looked at why some Native nations in the United States do well and why others fail. The major finding of the research was that no correlation existed between the resources and wealth of the tribe and its ability to tackle socioeconomic and other issues. Native nations with a lot of resources could be living in poor conditions but tribes with few resources could be doing well. The critical factor, the research found, in determining the success or failure of a Native nation was their governance system. The Harvard Project established that the necessary elements included

>> The ability for Native nations to make their own decisions (sovereignty)

>> Assertions of sovereignty to be backed by capable institutions of governance and stable decision making (institutions)

>> The institutions to be structured so they reflect the contemporary cultural values of the individual Native nation (cultural fit)

>> Leaders who introduce new knowledges and experiences and inspire action (leadership)

Working within the existing process

Indigenous people have also sought to make change by working within the political process, joining political parties and being elected to Parliament. Neville Bonner was the first Indigenous person to enter parliament when he became a senator for Queensland in 1971. A member of the Liberal Party, he became an independent in 1983, his last year in Parliament.

Here are some other note-worthy Indigenous politicians:

>> In 1999, Aden Ridgeway, a member of the Australian Democrats, was elected to the Senate, representing New South Wales.

>> Ken Wyatt was the first Indigenous person to be elected to the House of Representatives, when he became the Member for Hasluck in 2010.

>> The first Indigenous woman in federal parliament was Nova Peris, when she became a senator for the Northern Territory in 2013 as a member of the Australian Labor Party. She left the parliament in 2016.

>> Linda Burney (Australian Labor Party) became the first Indigenous woman in the House of Representatives when she became the member for Barton in 2016.

In 2020, federal parliament included five Indigenous members: Ken Wyatt, Linda Burney, Senator Malarndirri McCarthy (for the Northern Territory; ALP), Senator Patrick Dodson (for Western Australia; ALP) and Senator Jackie Lambie (for Tasmania; Independent).

Representation has also increased in state and territory governments. Of note are the following:

>> Adam Giles became Chief Minister of the Northern Territory leading a Country Liberal Party government in 2013.

>> Ernie Bridge was the first Indigenous Cabinet minister in an Australian government when he became the Western Australian Minister for Water Resources, the North-West and Aboriginal Affairs in 1986.

>> Marion Scrymgour was the first female minister in 2003 as part of the Northern Territory government.

>> John Ah Kit and his daughter Ngaree Ah Kit were the first Indigenous father and daughter to serve in a parliament, both in the Northern Territory. John Ah Kit served from 1995 to 2005; Ngaree Ah Kit was elected in 2016.

LINDA BURNEY: WORKING INSIDE AND OUTSIDE THE SYSTEM

Linda Burney has had a distinguished career as a politician in both the NSW state and federal parliaments. She was the first Indigenous person to serve in the NSW parliament when she was elected as the Member for Canterbury in 2003. In 2011, after the Australian Labor Party lost government in 2011, she became Deputy Leader of her party. She became the National Vice President of the ALP in 2006.

She moved from state to federal politics in 2106 when she was elected the Member of Barton in a by-election and became the first Indigenous woman elected to the House of Representatives.

Before her career as a politician, Linda Burney had been active in the reconciliation process and was an Executive Member of the National Council for Aboriginal Reconciliation. But she also worked at the community level on education policy, becoming President of the Aboriginal Education Consultative Group in NSW and then became Director-General of the Department of Aboriginal Affairs. She's made a contribution inside and outside the system — and she's still going strong!

6

The Part of Tens

Explore a list of ten important cultural sites that are must-sees and ten of the exciting 'firsts' achieved by Indigenous people in Australia.

Help debunk ten myths about Indigenous people and their cultures.

Understand ten (plus one!) important legal decisions about Indigenous people and their rights.

IN THIS CHAPTER

» Visiting the icons of the red heart and the Top End of the Northern Territory

» Discovering the gorges of the west and the rainforests of the east of northern Australia

» Marvelling at the archaeological finds of Lake Mungo

» Investigating sites of southern Australia

» Honouring the protest at Old Parliament House

Chapter **23**

Ten Important Indigenous Cultural Sites

ustralia's Indigenous peoples have sacred sites all over the country, many of them not accessible to visitors. The sites listed in this chapter can be visited for a unique cultural experience. These sites are as naturally beautiful as they are spiritually important — and deserving of a visit if you have the chance. Most of these sites have Indigenous-owned tourism businesses operating that can provide information on the cultural significance and particular bush tucker and medicines in the area. In this chapter, I've included sites from all over Australia, from Tasmania in the south to far north Queensland and across the country to the Kimberley in northern Western Australia.

Uluru, Northern Territory

Uluru is an enormous sandstone outcrop 335 kilometres south-west of Alice Springs. It's about 9.4 kilometres around the base, 3.6 kilometres long, 2 kilometres wide and about 345 metres high. According to the Anangu people, the traditional owners of the area, Uluru represents the rainbow serpent, a creation spirit, and is considered to be a site of fertility. It's seen as both a male and female spirit, and considered to be both mother and father. Caves inside the rock are covered with paintings that show that this is an area of special spiritual significance.

The best time to see Uluru is at sunset, when the colours of the rock change from red to purple. The rock is also stunning after heavy rain, as large amounts of water cascade off the sides.

REMEMBER

Uluru is a sacred place to Aboriginal people and they found it offensive that people climbed over it. The area was returned to the Anangu in 1985 but is leased back as a national park (Chapter 3 gives more detail on this arrangement). The Uluru climb closed permanently on 26 October 2019.

Kata Juta, Northern Territory

About 40 kilometres to the west of Uluru is another stunning natural outcrop, Kata Juta. Also known by the European name of 'the Olgas', Kata Juta — and Uluru — started as sediments in an inland sea. Kata Juta covers an area of over 22 square kilometres and contains 36 domes, with the highest point being Mount Olga, over a kilometre above sea level and over 546 metres above the surrounding plateau.

More than 300 million years ago, the sediments were pushed upwards above sea level. During this shift in the landscape, the force created cracks and fissures. Erosion over millions and millions of years has left the formations that look so stunning today. Like Uluru, they are especially beautiful at sunset, when the colours of the rocks change dramatically as the sun sinks below the horizon. They are thought to be 500 million years old.

Nitmiluk, Northern Territory

In 1978, the Jawoyn people of the Katherine area made a land claim over country that included the Katherine Gorge National Park. After negotiations between the Jawoyn, the Northern Land Council and the Northern Territory government, the land was leased back to the government and the Nitmiluk (Katherine Gorge) National Park established. Katherine Gorge is a series of 13 gorges carved by a river over a billion years, creating a spectacular natural landscape with dramatic cliffs and sandy beaches. *Nitmiluk* means 'cicada place' and the area has spiritual significance for the Jawoyn people.

Windjana Gorge, Western Australia

Windjana Gorge, in the Kimberley region of north-western Australia, was carved out of the Napier Range by the Lennard River over 300 million years. The walls are 30 to 100 metres high and the gorge is over 100 metres wide. The name of the gorge is believed to be a misspelling of Wandjina, a very important spiritual being of the Kimberley region. The traditional owners, the Bunuba, tell a creation story of how a large serpent carved the gorge. The gorge also provided protection for Bunuba resistance fighter Jandamarra in the late 1800s (refer to Chapter 7). The area is now part of a national park that was created in 1971 and is home to freshwater crocodiles.

Daintree Rainforest, North Queensland

The Daintree Rainforest is more than 135 million years old, the oldest tropical rainforest in the world. The area has a rich history of Indigenous culture that dates back thousands of years. The area is also rich with wildlife and natural beauty. It contains 30 per cent of the frog, reptile and marsupial species in Australia and 65 per cent of Australia's bat and butterfly species. Situated north of Mossman, Queensland — and about 100 kilometres north of Cairns — the area was made into a national park in 1981 and was given World Heritage Site listing in 1988. Many of the natural features that appear on the landscape — as well as the areas that provide sources of water or constant supplies of food — have spiritual significance for the traditional owners of the area, the Eastern Kuku Yalanji.

Mungo National Park, New South Wales

Some 900 kilometres west of Sydney, near Mildura in Victoria's north-west, lies the World Heritage–listed Willandra Lakes region, comprising 17 dry lakes, including Lake Mungo. In 1969, a skeleton, given the nickname of 'Mungo Lady', was discovered. In 1974, a second skeleton, 'Mungo Man', was found and added to other evidence that showed that Aboriginal people had occupied the area for thousands of years. Scientists have applied various dating methods to the remains, resulting in different estimates of their age, though it was discovered both were ritualistically buried. Consensus was achieved through a collaborative effort in 2003, dating the skeletons at around 40,000 years. Since then, children's footprints have been discovered in solidified clay and sand, and dated to over 40,000 years ago. Three Aboriginal nations are actively involved with the management of Mungo National Park — the Mutthi Mutthi, the Paakantyi and Ngyiampaa nations.

Yeddonba, Victoria

Yeddonba Aboriginal Cultural Site sits near the twin New South Wales and Victorian border towns of Albury and Wodonga, about 300 kilometres north of Melbourne. The site showcases artworks of the Duduroa clan of the Pangarang. The area, including several important water sources, was of special significance to the Pangarang clans. The Yeddonba area is related to a Dreamtime story about the Tasmanian tiger, the totem of the people here, and rock art depicts images that relate to this story. The paintings have been dated to about 2,000 years ago. Given that the Tasmanian tiger (the thylacine) is depicted in ancient rock art way up in Arnhem Land, finding the animal related to a Victorian site is perhaps unsurprising, as the island state of Tasmania was once linked by a land bridge. On another interesting note, the ochre in the paintings has been sourced to South Australia, indicating past trade connections between the two regions.

Ngaut Ngaut, South Australia

The Ngaut Ngaut Aboriginal Site is situated near Mannum in South Australia, on the land of the Nganguraku people, and is the place of the Black Duck Dreaming. The area is rich with Aboriginal rock art and cultural stories. Today, the site has been developed with a boardwalk that allows visitors to walk over land occupied tens of thousands of years ago.

Wybalenna, Tasmania

Wybalenna is on Flinders Island and of special cultural significance to the Palawa people. Unlike other places that have a long cultural history, the importance of Wybalenna has occurred over recent times. In the 1830s and 1840s, more than 200

Aboriginal people from Tasmania were kept on the island in terrible conditions and it was seen as a place of attempted social, cultural and spiritual genocide. Although the area has a tragic history, many Aboriginal people see it as an important spiritual place. The area was handed back to the Palawa in 1999. They believe that the return of the land can allow them to ensure that this spiritual resting place will be cared for and its history never forgotten.

The Aboriginal Tent Embassy, Canberra

On Australia Day in 1972, four Aboriginal men who had travelled from Sydney set up a protest camp on the lawns of Parliament House and declared it to be the Aboriginal Tent Embassy (refer to Chapter 12). Over the next few months, thousands of people — black and white — came from all over the country to join their demonstration, capturing national and international attention, before being dispersed by police in July. The site was reestablished in 1992 and remains a reminder of an important historical political movement. Makeshift buildings still exist on the original site.

IN THIS CHAPTER

» Looking at some remarkable firsts in the 18th and 19th centuries

» Discovering Indigenous Australian icons of the 1960s

» Getting serious in the 1970s

» Taking it to great heights in the 1990s

» Breaking new ground in the 21st century

Chapter **24**

Ten Indigenous Firsts

Australia has provided far from a level playing field to its Indigenous peoples. Breaking through the barriers of racial inequality and prejudice, and socioeconomic factors, is no easy feat. But Indigenous people are doing just that and achieving more and more in sport, the arts and the professions.

Lack of educational opportunities meant that firsts in the professions have been a long time coming, with the first Indigenous law graduate arriving in 1976 and the first Aboriginal surgeon in 2006! Some firsts are great achievements for any Australian but, in the Indigenous community, each time someone breaks through a new barrier to achieve a first, that person becomes a role model to others in the community — especially young people — to show what's possible.

In this chapter, I list ten significant firsts for Indigenous peoples.

The First Indigenous Australian to Visit Great Britain: 1793

The first Aboriginal person to take the long journey to Great Britain was Bennelong. He sailed there with Governor Phillip, departing in December 1792. Bennelong's original contact with Phillip was Bennelong's capture in 1789, when Phillip had grown impatient with the slow progress of building relationships with the local Aboriginal community.

Bennelong remained in the colony and adopted some of the habits and customs of the British, dressing in their clothes and learning their language. He returned to his clan in 1790 and frequently appeared at Sydney Cove to ask after the Governor. In 1791, a hut was built for him at what is now Bennelong Point, the site of the Sydney Opera House.

Bennelong and another Aboriginal man called Yemmerrawanne accompanied Governor Phillip on his return to London, where they were introduced to King George III. The stay in England didn't appear to be an altogether happy one for Bennelong, with him suffering from the cold and homesickness. He returned to the Sydney colony with Governor Hunter in 1795. He died in 1813. Refer to Chapter 6 for more on his life.

The First Indigenous Cricket Team Tour: 1868

In 1868, a team of 13 Aboriginal cricketers from Victoria sailed to England. They were, in fact, the first Australian cricketers to tour England as a representative team. In a tour that lasted six months, they played 47 two-day games. At the completion of each game, the team showcased their skills at throwing spears and boomerangs.

The coach and manager of the team was Charles Lawrence but the star was perhaps Muarrinim (sometimes referred to as Unaarrimin), a player also known as Johnny Mullagh, who scored 1,698 runs and claimed 245 wickets on the tour. He went on to play for the Melbourne Cricket Club, though most of the other players who toured on this historic visit didn't continue with professional cricket.

The team impressed the English with their stamina. It was remarked in one newspaper, *Sporting Life*, that 'no eleven in one season ever played so many matches so successfully — never playing less than two matches in each week, frequently three, bearing an amount of fatigue that now seems incredible'. Refer to Chapter 20 for more on this momentous sporting feat.

The First Indigenous 'Pop Star': 1963

Musician Jimmy Little was said to be the first Indigenous pop star when his song, 'Royal Telephone', went to the top of the music charts in 1963. Little is a Yorta Yorta man who grew up on Cummerangunja Reserve. He moved to Sydney in 1955 and began his recording career in 1956.

He started to record hit songs with 'Danny Boy' in 1959 and 'El Paso' the following year. After 17 singles, 'Royal Telephone' reached number one on the charts. He continued to record songs, with his final hit from that era in 1974, 'Baby Blue'.

He turned his hand to acting and then released his 14th album in 1994, and in 1999 he was inducted into the ARIA Hall of Fame. In 2004, he released *Life's What You Make It*, featuring poignant covers of contemporary songs. Little passed away in 2012.

The First Indigenous Person to be Australian of the Year: 1968

Champion boxer Lionel Rose was named Australian of the Year in 1968 — at the age of 20 — the first Indigenous person to receive that honour. He was awarded a Member of the Order of the British Empire (an MBE) that same year!

Born in the town of Warragul, in Victoria, Rose became a bantamweight boxer and, in another first, was the first Indigenous Australian to win a world title in the sport. Rose had developed his skills when he joined his father on the boxing tent show circuit.

He won his first Australian title — amateur flyweight — in 1963, at the age of 15, and the Australian bantamweight title in 1966. He won the world title in 1968 challenging Fighter Harada in a match played in Tokyo. After his boxing career was over, Rose embarked on a singing career. He passed away in 2011.

The First Indigenous Person to be Elected to the Australian Parliament: 1971

Neville Bonner was the first Indigenous Australian to take a seat in the federal parliament. Elected from Queensland, Bonner was a senator from 1971 until 1983. He was born at Franklin Island, a small settlement on the Tweed River in northern New South Wales, in 1922. He started out doing various labouring jobs — stockman, canecutter and ringbarker.

He spent 16 years on the Palm Island Aboriginal Reserve after he married and moved there with his wife in 1943. Many credited this experience as giving him many skills that helped him in political life. It certainly spurred him to want to change the circumstances in which Aboriginal people were living.

He left Palm Island and joined OPAL — the One People of Australia League (refer to Chapter 10). Although seen as a more conservative reform movement, OPAL focused on the welfare, housing and education of Indigenous people. Bonner entered politics in 1967, when he joined the Liberal Party. After his death in 1999, he gained numerous posthumous honours, including a scholarship in his name to support Indigenous Australians studying politics or a related field.

The First Indigenous Lawyer: 1976

The first Indigenous Australian to become a lawyer was Patricia O'Shane, who graduated from the University of New South Wales and became a barrister in 1976. In 1981, she moved from legal practice to run the New South Wales Department of Aboriginal Affairs but returned to the law when she was appointed as a magistrate in 1986.

O'Shane was born in northern Queensland, in the town of Mossman. She often talked about the way in which she saw and experienced discrimination, and it shaped her determination and her advocacy. She was a gifted student, attending school in Cairns and being awarded a Teacher Scholarship at the Queensland Teachers Training College and the University of Queensland. She graduated and taught at primary and high schools before winning a federal government study grant to study law in 1973.

The First Indigenous Person to Make a Feature Film: 1992

The first Indigenous person to make a feature film was Aboriginal actor and teacher Brian Syron. His movie *Jindalee Lady* starred two Aboriginal actors, Lydia Miller and Michael Leslie. Born in Sydney, Syron went on to have an extraordinary life for someone from humble beginnings.

In 1961, Syron travelled to Europe and worked as a model for designers such as Dior and Cardin. Later that year, he moved to New York, after being accepted into the prestigious acting school run by Stella Adler. Classmates included Robert de Niro and Warren Beatty. He then spent a year studying his craft in London and returned to the United States to work in theatre and to teach.

Despite such opportunities, Syron was drawn back home to work with Aboriginal people, returning to Australia in 1967. Syron worked actively in the arts sector, continuing to act in theatre, film and television, directing theatre productions, teaching acting to a new generation of Aboriginal actors and working with Aboriginal writers. He helped establish the Aboriginal Theatre Company in 1981.

Syron spent two years making *Jindalee Lady*. It premiered in 1992. In another first, Syron asked Bart Willougby to write the score for the movie, making him the first Indigenous person to compose, play and direct the music track to a feature film. Chapter 19 has more on Indigenous filmmaking.

The First Indigenous Surgeon: 2006

Dr Kelvin Kong, a Worimi man from the Newcastle area, became the first Indigenous person to be qualified as a surgeon when, in 2006, at the age of 32, he became a fellow of the Royal Australasian College of Surgeons. He was a graduate of the University of New South Wales and helped to establish a pre-medical program there to encourage other Indigenous people to study medicine.

Based at the University of Newcastle's School of Medicine and Public Health, he has been involved in running clinics for various Aboriginal medical services. He also assisted in the establishment of a professional body for Indigenous doctors — the Australian Indigenous Doctors Association (AIDA) — and has worked on health policy advocacy for Indigenous Australians. His twin sisters, Marilyn and Marlene, are also doctors!

The First Indigenous Senior Council (SC): 2015

Tony McAvoy SC became a barrister in 2000 and worked extensively in the area of native title. He has also worked in the areas of environmental law, human rights, discrimination law, criminal law and coronial inquests. He was appointed Senior Council in 2015, the first barrister to reach that elevated position. Tony was the co-Senior Council assisting the Royal Commission into the Protection and Detention of Children in the Northern Territory in 2016. He has been an outspoken advocate on the protection of Indigenous rights in the legal system.

Active in trying to improve the profession from within, Tony McAvoy SC co-chairs the Indigenous Legal Issues Committee of the Law Council of Australia, is the Chair of the NSW Bar Association's First Nations Committee and is a trustee of the NSW Bar Association's Indigenous Barristers Trust.

The First Indigenous Minister for Indigenous Australians: 2019

Ken Wyatt, a member of the Liberal Party, became the first Indigenous person to be elected to the House of Representatives. He came to politics after a career working in Indigenous education and health. His electorate, Hasluck, is in Western Australia, and he increased his margin in the 2019 election. After that election, he became the first Indigenous person to hold the Ministry for Indigenous Australians. He also became the first Indigenous person to sit in the Cabinet, the focal point of decision making in public. Ken has maintained his interest in Indigenous health and education as a Minister. He has also been active in the Aged Care portfolio.

REMEMBER

In 2016, Linda Burney became the first Indigenous woman to sit in the House of Representatives. A member of the Australian Labor Party, she represents the seat of Barton in New South Wales. She is the Shadow Minister for Indigenous Australians and Shadow Minister for Families and Social Services.

Chapter **25**

Ten Myths about Indigenous People

Stereotypes about Indigenous people are numerous, and some are surprisingly well entrenched in some sectors of the Australian community. Many of the people who hold these views have possibly never met an Indigenous person, let alone understood the issues that Indigenous people grapple with every day.

From the thinking that all Indigenous people have a problem with alcohol to the belief that they're a dying race or have a violent culture, these stereotypes are offensive and, as with most generalisations, aren't true.

So, in this chapter, I debunk a few . . .

'Indigenous People Have a Problem with Alcohol'

Indigenous people drink less than the general Australian population. Among Indigenous men, 35 per cent don't drink at all, whereas only 12 per cent of the total Australian population abstain from consuming alcohol. In the Northern Territory, 75 per cent of the Aboriginal population doesn't drink alcohol.

Among the population that drinks, some people do have problems with excess drinking that cause further problems for their communities. However, no evidence exists that Indigenous people are less biologically able to handle alcohol.

'Indigenous People Are a Dying Race'

Indigenous populations are increasing. Compared with the rest of the Australian population, Indigenous people have more children and have a much larger proportion of young people in their populations. Refer to Chapter 2 for more information about population statistics.

In addition, as discrimination against Indigenous people has become less entrenched, more Indigenous people are choosing to identify themselves as Indigenous. In earlier times, such an admission may have seen them confined to reserves and needing permission to work and to marry.

'Indigenous People Who Live in Urban Areas Have Lost Their Culture'

Even in heavily populated cities, Indigenous people retain strong memories and oral histories of their stories, history and culture. In Sydney, for example, rock paintings and carvings are plentiful around the harbour and the local community remembers where the important sites for birthing, burial and other traditions are. In addition, they still have the same values that are a strong part of Indigenous cultures — respect for country, respect for the wisdom of Elders and a belief in the concepts of reciprocity and interconnectedness.

'Indigenous People Were Killed Off in Tasmania'

It was believed that the Indigenous people of Tasmania died out with the death of an Aboriginal woman, Truganini, in 1876. She was thought to be the sole returnee from the Flinders Island mission where Tasmanian Aboriginals were sent for resettlement.

Although both the forcible and passive removal of Aboriginal people from Tasmania resulted in a severe fracturing of traditions and languages, an Aboriginal population has survived and continues to remind the larger population of their existence, history and culture. Chapter 7 has details of the colonisation process in Tasmania.

'Indigenous People Are Addicted to Welfare'

Increasing employment is a widely shared aspiration in Indigenous communities around Australia. However, unemployment among the Indigenous population is around three times the national average. Not surprisingly, in remote areas not as many jobs are available as in more populated areas and unemployment rates tend to be higher. In these areas, where work-for-the-dole schemes have been established, the opportunities created have had a high take-up.

Other factors contributing to the high level of unemployment in the Indigenous community are the low levels of education in some Indigenous communities and lingering prejudice among some non-Indigenous employers who prefer not to hire Indigenous people. Refer to Chapter 21 for more on employment and education.

'Too Much Money Is Spent on Indigenous People'

Identifying Indigenous-specific spending is difficult, because costs are allocated throughout all portfolios. According to a 2017 Australian Productivity Commission report on Indigenous expenditure by the Australian government, however, an estimated $6 billion was spent by federal, state and territory governments on targeted programs for Aboriginal and Torres Strait Islander Australians. In comparison, non-Indigenous people cost governments $522.7 billion.

Considering the low education levels, the overcrowding and the lower life expectancy that are constant features of Indigenous communities, this allocation isn't enough to meet those pressing needs. And the remote location of some communities increases costs further.

Groups such as the Australian Indigenous Doctors Association and the Australian Human Rights Commission agree. Indigenous people say that money spent needs to be spent properly, with less of it channelled into expensive, inefficient bureaucracy. Recent government policies are addressed in further detail in Chapters 13 to 15 and Chapter 22.

'Real Indigenous People Live in Remote Areas'

The largest Indigenous populations are in the cities. Of the total population of Indigenous people in Australia, 31 per cent live in major cities, 22 per cent live in inner regional Australia, 23 per cent in outer regional Australia, 8 per cent in remote Australia and 16 per cent in very remote Australia.

People don't stop being Indigenous because they adopt a more western lifestyle; cultures can coexist. The legal definition provided by the Federal Court declares a person is Indigenous when that person:

>> Is of Aboriginal descent or Torres Strait Islander descent

>> Identifies with the culture

>> Is accepted as being Indigenous by the community in which he or she lives

This definition applies whether an Indigenous person lives in the city or the country. Chapter 2 has more information about this definition. Where people live doesn't make them more or less Indigenous.

'Indigenous Organisations Mismanage Money and Are Prone to Nepotism'

Accountability requirements imposed on Indigenous corporations, statutory authorities and grants are often greater than their non-Indigenous counterparts.

Indigenous organisations such as the New South Wales Aboriginal Land Council manage a portfolio of more than $700 million and $2 billion worth of land. Strong governance mechanisms are in place to ensure transparency in decision-making processes, and all members of its elected arm undertake governance training so they are clear about the difference in responsibilities between a board member and a staff member.

Another organisation, the Aboriginal and Torres Strait Islander Commission (ATSIC), which was disbanded in 2004, was constantly accused of lacking accountability but was the only statutory body at the time with its own internal audit section. It was also reviewed satisfactorily by external assessments and investigations. Refer to Chapters 13 and 14 for more information about ATSIC.

'Indigenous Culture Is Violent and Accepts Abuse of Women and Children'

Sexual abuse of women and children has never formed part of traditional cultural practices and is considered abhorrent by Indigenous men and women of all generations. Sexual abuse and violence are behaviours that are learned, and studies and reports have found them to be generational and cyclical; abusers have often been victims of abuse themselves. Today, many initiatives — some led by Indigenous men — speak out against violence towards and abuse of Indigenous women and children.

The colonisation of Australia left a legacy of abuse in many Indigenous communities. In 1898, a Northern Territory judge proposed laws to prohibit European settlers from kidnapping Aboriginal children 'for the purpose of having carnal knowledge or intercourse' on stations far away from their homelands.

The recent report on abuse in the Northern Territory by Pat Anderson and Rex Wilde, *Little Children are Sacred*, observed that the sexual abuse of children was not only perpetrated by Aboriginal people. The report said, 'The phenomenon knows no racial, age or gender borders. It is a national and international problem'. Refer to Chapter 14 for more on this report.

'Indigenous Self-Determination Has Been Tried but It Has Failed'

Self-determination is a concept that is recognised as a human right and describes the ability of people to determine their own future. It's gauged by the extent that people feel they have control over the political processes that affect them. Refer to Chapters 15 and 22 for more on the concept and the realities of self-determination.

For a brief period, Indigenous affairs in Australia had the title of 'self-determination' but that title has since been officially abandoned by the Australian government. During the so-called period of self-determination, the approach was one of top-down decision-making, where governments controlled policy-making and program development and delivery, and Indigenous people had no influence on the decisions made about them. They were also not encouraged to find solutions to the problems affecting their communities — even though many communities came up with strategies independent of government funding and interference.

REMEMBER

Self-determination is a concept that promotes Indigenous people leading policy development and program implementation. The top-down approach of governments seems to be a direct contradiction of this concept.

Self-determination has never been properly tested in Australia, even though previous governments have adopted the term to describe their approach. This has created the myth that self-determination has been tried but failed.

Chapter **26**

Ten Key Legal Decisions (Plus One to Keep an Eye On)

ndigenous peoples had their own complex laws and systems of governance — and still do in many places — but, when the officers of the First Fleet arrived in 1788, they brought the laws of the British with them. From 1836, this new legal system — and the courts that were a part of it — established that, as far as the courts were concerned, Indigenous people were considered to be British subjects and, therefore, required to obey — or be protected by — British laws. This assumption provided no place for the recognition of Indigenous law within the system. This system remained in place when Australia became a federation in 1901.

However, Indigenous peoples have often sought to have their rights recognised or to exercise them by using the Australian legal system. Two areas of particular focus for legal action have been attempts to establish rights to traditional land and claims for compensation for the removal of Indigenous people from their families.

In this chapter, I look at some of the most well-known legal cases involving Indigenous people, starting with a murder trial in 1836, through to Bruce Trevorrow's

2007 case, claiming compensation for unlawful removal from his parents. Finally, I provide an insight into the Timber Creek Case from 2019, which may end up having far-reaching effects.

R v Jack Congo Murrell: 1836

The case of *R v Jack Congo Murrell* was a trial in the New South Wales Supreme Court in which an Aboriginal man was accused of killing another Aboriginal man. The accused claimed that he wasn't subject to British law and that his own customary law should be used to hold him to account.

The Court didn't accept this argument and held that Aboriginal people were bound by the laws of the colony for any offence committed within it. In so finding, the court reversed a finding in 1827, *R v Ballard*, in which it had been held that that offences committed by Aboriginal people against other Aboriginal people — such as murder — were subject to Aboriginal customary law.

The Gove Land Rights Case: 1971

In late 1968, the traditional owners of the Gove Peninsula, in Arnhem Land, brought a case against the Nabalco Corporation in the Supreme Court of the Northern Territory. Nabalco had secured a 12-year bauxite mining lease from the federal government and the Aboriginal applicants argued that they enjoyed legal and sovereign rights over their land. They wanted to be able to occupy that land on the basis of having title to it without interference.

The case of *Milirrpum v Nabalco Pty Ltd* became known as the Gove land rights case because it was the first litigation by Aboriginal people to try to establish recognition of a title to their traditional land. Justice Blackburn, although personally sympathetic to the Aboriginal plaintiffs, found that no Aboriginal or native title existed because Australia had been claimed using the fiction of *terra nullius* (the conviction that Australia was an 'empty land'). See the section 'The Mabo Case: 1992' later in this chapter for the overturning of this belief.

Blackburn noted that, even though the claim of terra nullius wasn't true in fact, it was how the Australian law treated the matter — it was a legal fiction! Justice Blackburn was supportive of the establishment of a land rights system. Although the case wasn't successful, it did lead to the establishment of the Woodward Royal Commission and, in 1976, Northern Territory Aboriginal land rights legislation was passed by the federal government.

Koowarta v Bjelke-Petersen: 1982

John Koowarta, a Wik man of the Aurakun region of Cape York Peninsula, in north Queensland, and a number of other stockmen had planned to purchase the Archer River station, which covered much of the Wik peoples' traditional homeland, using funds from the Aboriginal Land Fund Commission. The Queensland government tried to block the purchase. It had a policy against allowing Aboriginal people to own large tracts of land.

Koowarta complained that the government's action was discriminatory and breached the *Racial Discrimination Act 1975* (Cwlth). The Queensland government objected and took the matter to the High Court, complaining that the federal anti-discrimination legislation wasn't constitutionally valid.

The majority of the High Court found that the Discrimination Act was valid because it was an incorporation of Australia's obligations under international law — as a signatory of the Covenant to Eliminate All Forms of Racial Discrimination. It decided that the federal parliament could intervene by using the power that it had to make laws about 'external affairs', such as international treaties.

So, the sale could proceed; however, Queensland Premier Joh Bjelke-Petersen declared the property to be a national park — now known as the Mungkan Kandju National Park — to ensure that no-one could ever own it. In October 2010, Premier Anna Bligh announced that 750 square kilometres of the park would be given over to the Wik-Mungkana peoples as freehold land.

The Mabo Case: 1992

Mabo v Queensland (No 2) — the Mabo case — was brought by Eddie Mabo, David Passi and James Rice, Meriam people of Murray Island (Mer) in the Torres Strait. In this important case, the High Court overturned the legal fiction of terra nullius that had been part of Australian law since the Gove land rights case (described earlier in this chapter). The Court found that Indigenous people held a native title over their traditional land if they could show a continual connection to or occupation of their land and that title hadn't been extinguished by the valid exercise of governmental powers.

In response to the case, the Keating government passed the *Native Title Act 1993* (Cwlth) and established the National Native Title Tribunal to facilitate native title claims by Indigenous people across the country who might want to assert a native title interest in their traditional land.

The Wik Case: 1996

The Wik and Thayorre people are traditional owners of parts of western Cape York Peninsula. They claimed native title over two areas of leased land — Holroyd River Holding and Michellton Pastoral Leases. In *Wik Peoples v the State of Queensland*, they claimed that their native title in that land wasn't extinguished by the granting of the various leases but those native title rights continued and coexisted with the pastoral leases.

The High Court agreed with them and found that native title rights could coexist, depending on the terms and nature of the particular pastoral lease. Where a conflict of rights existed, the rights under the pastoral lease would extinguish the remaining native title rights. The decision in the case led to changes to the *Native Title Act 1993* (Cwlth) that extinguished some native title rights but gave native title holders the ability to negotiate Indigenous Land Use Agreements between them and other interests.

Kruger v Commonwealth: 1997

A group of Northern Territory Aboriginal people, led by Alec Kruger, began legal proceedings that challenged the constitutional validity of the *Aboriginals Ordinance Act 1918* (NT). Sections of the Ordinance made the Chief Protector of Aborigines their legal guardian and gave them extensive powers, including the discretion to undertake the care, custody and control of any 'aboriginal or half-caste', and this included the power to remove them to any reserve or 'aboriginal institution' — including mission stations, schools, reformatories, orphanages or other institutions. (Refer to Chapter 9 for more on this and other similar legislation around the country.)

The plaintiffs challenged the constitutional validity of the Ordinance on several grounds, including that it infringed their implied constitutional right to legal equality, violated their implied constitutional right to freedom of movement and association as well as violating an implied constitutional right to freedom from genocide. The plaintiffs further contended that the Ordinance violated the express protection of freedom of religion enshrined in Section 116 of the Constitution. They sought damages for these breaches. In 1997, the High Court rejected the plaintiffs' claims on all grounds.

The Hindmarsh Island Bridge Case: 1998

A dispute developed between developers of a bridge and the Indigenous community of the Hindmarsh Island area in South Australia. A group of Ngarrindjeri women claimed it was a 'secret women's business' site. To settle the dispute, the Howard government passed the *Hindmarsh Island Bridge Act 1996* (Cwlth), which allowed construction to go ahead by suspending rights under heritage protection and racial discrimination legislation.

The Ngarrindjeri challenged the legislation in the High Court, in *Kartinyeri v Commonwealth*, on the basis that it was discriminatory to declare that the Heritage Protection Act applied to sites everywhere but on Hindmarsh Island. They also argued that when the Australian people voted to give the government the power to make laws for Indigenous peoples in the 1967 referendum (refer to Chapter 11), it was with the understanding that the power would be used only to make laws that were beneficial to Indigenous peoples.

The High Court rejected the latter argument, holding that the Constitution didn't restrict the Commonwealth parliament to making beneficial laws and, if it could legislate for a particular benefit, it could also repeal the legislation and take that benefit away. The bridge was completed in March 2001.

Gunner and Cubillo: 2000

Lorna Cubillo and Peter Gunner were both taken from their families when they were children. They both commenced proceedings against the Commonwealth, claiming damages for wrongful imprisonment and deprivation of liberty, negligence, breach of statutory duty (obligations imposed by legislation) and breach of fiduciary duty (obligations of trust and confidence). They said that they were prevented from returning to their families, were made to live among strangers, in a strange place, in institutions that bore no resemblance to a home. They also said they suffered psychiatric injury and lost the culture and traditions of their families.

In *Gunner v Commonwealth; Cubillo v Commonwealth*, a single judge of the Federal Court found against the plaintiffs on the basis that sufficient evidence didn't exist to support their claims. That decision was later upheld in an appeal to the Full Federal Court. (Refer to Chapter 9 for details about the Stolen Generations.)

The Yorta Yorta Case: 2002

The Yorta Yorta people claimed native title over an area of land and waters in northern Victoria and southern New South Wales. Justice Olney, of the Federal Court, originally dismissed the claim on the basis that the Yorta Yorta people hadn't met the evidentiary standard necessary to establish native title over the area. He found that the Yorta Yorta people had ceased to occupy their traditional lands in accordance with their traditional laws and customs long before. He said, 'The tide of history has indeed washed away any real acknowledgement of their traditional laws and any real observance of their traditional customs'.

The Yorta Yorta appealed and eventually the High Court handed down its decision in 2002, upholding the decision of the Federal Court. The Court found that, when establishing whether laws and customs are 'traditional' for the purposes of native title, laws and customs must be like those practised at the time the British claimed sovereignty over the land. It also declared the need to show that an acknowledge-ment and observance of laws and customs has occurred on a substantially unin-terrupted basis since sovereignty. The Court noted that an attempt by the Yorta Yorta people to revive laws and customs that had been effectively lost at some point in the past wasn't sufficient to establish native title.

The Yorta Yorta people were understandably upset about this finding and believed the court had looked at their culture in a time warp instead of understanding that their culture — like European cultures — evolved over time. In many cases, claim-ants may find it difficult to produce the oral and historical evidence necessary to meet the criteria set down by the High Court, especially in areas that have been subjected to intensive European settlement.

The Trevorrow Case: 2007

In 2007, Justice Thomas Gray of the South Australian Supreme Court awarded Bruce Trevorrow compensation of $525,000 for injuries and losses he suffered after being separated from his parents as a baby, and as damages for his unlawful removal and false imprisonment. The Court later awarded another $250,000 as a lump sum in lieu of interest payments on the original award.

Trevorrow had been sent to hospital in 1957 at the age of 13 months and was listed as a 'neglected child — without parents' by staff. This wasn't the case, as the court established, but Trevorrow was taken from the hospital and placed with a foster family. During this process, no paperwork was completed to document Trevorrow's removal from his family. Trevorrow's mother made numerous 'clear and consistent' attempts to try to get him back; however, the Aborigines Protection Board didn't allow her to be reunited with her son.

Trevorrow's father died without ever seeing him again. Trevorrow was finally reunited with his mother in 1966, when he was 10 years old, and he moved to be with her permanently in 1967. He later exhibited a range of behavioural problems that, it was found, were the result of his time away from his family. Unable to settle back into his family, he ended up in a series of boys' homes and other institutions, and with other foster parents.

In February 2008, the South Australian government lodged an appeal against the decision to award him compensation. Five months later, on 20 June 2008 — and with the appeal still pending — Bruce Trevorrow died of a heart attack, aged 51. In 2010, the court dismissed the appeal and upheld the compensation award.

The Timber Creek Case: 2019

In 2019, the High Court of Australia found that compensation was payable for the loss of exclusive possession when native title is extinguished. It was a significant finding, even though it only relates to native title that was extinguished between 1975 (when the Racial Discrimination Act was passed) and 1993 (when the Native Title Act validated extinguishment of native title). However, a lot of native title was extinguished during that time.

In this case, representatives of the Ngaliwurru and Nungali lodged an application for compensation against the Northern Territory for the impact of pastoral leases, public works and other acts that extinguished or impacted on their native title in the town of Timber Creek. The court awarded $2.9 million in compensation.

In awarding compensation, the High Court awarded an amount for spiritual or cultural loss (in this case, $1.3 million) and an amount for economic loss $1.6 million). Subsequent payouts will need to be determined with regards to each individual situation, and with consideration of the type of act that extinguished native title, its timing, the identity of the claimants, their connection to country and the impact the extinguishment had on that relationship.

This right to compensation in these circumstances was considered a part of the *Native Title Act 1993* that was 'sleeping'. The Timber Creek Case has now woken it up. It can be expected that more compensation claims will be forthcoming, particularly in the Northern Territory, Queensland and Western Australia.

Glossary

Aboriginal English: A version of English that encompasses some regional Aboriginal words but also applies particular meaning to other words of English, spoken across Australia.

Aboriginal person: A person who is of Aboriginal descent, identifies as Aboriginal and is accepted as Aboriginal by the Aboriginal community in which he or she lives. See also *blood-quantum*, *Indigenous person*, *Torres Strait Islander*.

acknowledgement of country: A common protocol whereby an Aboriginal or non-Aboriginal person holding an event acknowledges the *traditional owners* of that land. See also *welcome to country*.

ALS: Aboriginal Legal Service.

AMS: Aboriginal Medical Service.

Anangu: An *Aboriginal person* from Central Australia.

ATSIC: The Aboriginal and Torres Strait Islander Commission, established in 1990 as a nationally elected body to represent and support Indigenous regional communities; abolished in 2004.

ATSIS: Aboriginal and Torres Strait Islander Services, established in 2003 to administer *ATSIC* programs, replaced in 2004 by the Office of Indigenous Policy Coordination (OIPC).

blood-quantum: An outdated method of categorising Aboriginal or Torres Strait Islander people according to the proportion of Aboriginal or Torres Strait Islander heritage they have, using such terms as 'half-caste' and 'quadroon', which may be considered offensive. See also *Aboriginal person*, *Indigenous person*, *Torres Strait Islander*.

boomerang: A curved wooden tool used for hunting or as a weapon; returning and non-returning varieties.

bush tucker: Plants and animals gathered for food.

canoe tree: A tree with a visible scar in the bark from where a canoe was carved out of the bark.

clan: Small extended family group of about 40 to 50 people, part of a larger language group called a *nation*.

clapstick: A musical instrument comprising two wooden sticks, usually of different shapes, that are banged together to create a rhythmic beat.

coreeda: A traditional Indigenous game encompassing dance and combat.

corroboree: An important cultural or spiritual event celebrated through music and dance at a gathering of clan groups or nations.

Day of Mourning: The 1938 Australia Day protest in Sydney that marked the beginning of the Indigenous rights movement; later known as Aborigines Day and overseen by *NAIDOC*.

Dreaming tracks: The pathways taken by spiritual ancestors as they travelled across the landscape, creating its features, during the *Dreamtime*. See also *songlines*.

Dreamtime: Also called the Dreaming, the term given to the period when the world was created, with spiritual ancestors journeying across the landscape, along *Dreaming tracks*, creating its features; central to Aboriginal worldviews and spirituality.

Elder: An *Aboriginal person* or a *Torres Strait Islander* who has earned and is afforded the respect of the community, often then referred to as Aunty or Uncle.

firestick farming: The systematic use of fire to clear undergrowth and encourage regrowth to attract fauna.

freshwater people: Those who live in inland areas.

gubba: An *Aboriginal English* term used to refer to white people; from 'governor'.

history wars: Also called the culture wars; refers to a period in the 1990s when historians and others became embroiled in debate over Aboriginal history, particularly the number of people killed on the frontier.

Indigenous Land and Sea Corporation (ILSC): A body set up in 1995 to assist *Indigenous people* to acquire and manage land through a land fund; originally known as the Indigenous Land Council (ILC).

Indigenous person: Used in Australia to describe *Aboriginal peoples* and *Torres Strait Islanders* together. Some people prefer the term 'First Nations'.

karma songs: Traditional songs about the totems, history and mythology of a particular *clan*, used to educate children approaching puberty.

kinship system: A social division within some clans that defines the relationships between the people of the clan, usually giving a specific name to all members of that group. See also *skin name*.

Koori: An *Aboriginal person* from New South Wales or Victoria; also spelled as Goori.

Kriol: A hybrid language comprising English and a local Aboriginal dialect.

land rights legislation: Legislation enacted in states and territories in response to a social and political movement that evolved from the 1960s to the 1980s to include people from a broad spectrum of society. See also *native title legislation*.

marngrook: A traditional game involving kicking and leaping for a ball of possum skin encasing pounded charcoal and/or grass; believed to be the precursor to Australian Rules Football.

Murri: An *Aboriginal person* from Queensland or northern New South Wales.

NACCHO: National Aboriginal Community Controlled Health Organisation; the national leadership body for Aboriginal and Torres Strait Islander health.

NAIDOC: Originally NADOC, the National Aborigines Day Observance Committee (it became NAIDOC in 1991 to recognise Islanders too) was formed to celebrate Aborigines Day, as the *Day of Mourning* became known. It is now a week-long celebration held from the first Sunday in July each year and the whole week is known as NAIDOC.

nation: A large language group with responsibility for a specific area of country. See also *clan*.

National Sorry Day: A day of acknowledgement of the tabling in parliament of the *Bringing Them Home* report of the inquiry into the *Stolen Generations*, celebrated on 26 May since 1998.

native title legislation: Federal legislation enacted through the judicial recognition of native title in the Mabo case in 1992. See also *land rights legislation*.

1967 referendum: Referendum to change the Constitution to give the federal government the ability to make laws for *Indigenous people*, under the *races power*, and for them to be counted in the census.

Noongar: An *Aboriginal person* from southern Western Australia.

Nunga: An *Aboriginal person* from southern South Australia.

Palawa: An *Aboriginal person* from Tasmania.

pastoral lease: A form of land tenure, unique to Australia, where land settled by *squatters*, for the purpose of agriculture or sheep or cattle breeding, is converted by the government to a lease agreement, with the government retaining ownership.

Protector of Aborigines: A powerful position, also often incorporating a Chief Protector, created from the late 1830s in each of the states and the Northern Territory under the auspices of protection of Aboriginal rights and welfare (but in practice used to control the lives of Aboriginal people).

races power: Section of the Constitution that gives the federal government the ability to make laws for any specific race; changed in the *1967 referendum* to remove the exclusion of *Indigenous people*, so the federal government could make laws for Indigenous people.

rasp: A musical instrument comprising a notched stick that is scraped by a second smaller stick to produce a rhythmic sound.

saltwater people: Those who live in coastal areas.

Shared Responsibility Agreement: A type of agreement between government and *Indigenous* communities, endorsed by the *National Indigenous Council*, based on the concept that to receive services, communities had to agree to certain behavioural changes or standards.

skin name: A name given to every member (often with variations for male and female) of a kinship group within a *clan*; also called a kinship name.

songlines: The routes taken for cultural exchange of ideas, songs and ceremonies between *nations*, often following *Dreaming tracks*.

sorry business: Ceremonial practices surrounding a funeral.

Stolen Generations: The generations of children removed from their families as a result of government policies that promoted assimilation.

Survival Day: Term given by many people to Australia Day, commemorated on 26 January as the anniversary of the proclamation of the first British colony at Sydney Cove in 1788; also known as Invasion Day.

terra nullius: A phrase applied in legal terms in Australia until 1992 that implied Australia was vacant and without government at the time of possession by the British, later acknowledged as a 'legal fiction'.

totem: An animal, plant or landform believed to be ancestrally related to a person.

traditional owner: An *Aboriginal person* or a *Torres Strait Islander* who's acknowledged as being of direct descent of the original custodians of an area of land. See also *acknowledgement of country*, *welcome to country*.

Torres Strait Islander: A person of the Torres Strait Islands north of Cape York Peninsula in Queensland. See also *Aboriginal person*, *Indigenous person*.

welcome to country: A common protocol whereby *traditional owners* welcome people onto their land. See also *acknowledgement of country*.

woomera: A particular type of spear-thrower used as a multipurpose tool for hunting, chopping wood, cutting tree branches or chopping meat.

Yolngu: An *Aboriginal person* from central or eastern Arnhem Land in the Northern Territory; the nation of that region.

Index

About the Author

Larissa Behrendt AO is of Eualeyai and Kamillaroi descent, peoples of the north-western New South Wales. She is Distinguished Professor of the Jumbunna Institute of Indigenous Education and Research at the University of Technology, Sydney.

She graduated with a Bachelor of Laws and Bachelor of Jurisprudence from the University of New South Wales and was the first Aboriginal Australian to graduate from Harvard Law School when she gained her Master of Laws in 1994 and Senior Doctorate of Jurisprudence in 1998.

Larissa is a member of the Academy of Social Sciences of Australia and of the Australian Academy of Law.

She is the author of several books on Indigenous legal issues. She won the 2002 David Unaipon Award and a 2005 Commonwealth Writers' Prize for her novel *Home*. Her novel, *Legacy*, won a Victorian Premier's Literary Award in 2010. She is also a filmmaker and won the Australian Director's Guild award for Best Direction in a Feature Documentary for her film *After the Apology* in 2018.

Larissa is a Board Member of the Australian Museum, the Sydney Community Fund and Sydney Festival. She is Chair of the Cathy Freeman Foundation and is a former Chair of the Bangarra Dance Theatre. She was the inaugural chair of National Indigenous Television Ltd.

She was named as 2009 National Aborigines and Islanders Day Observance Committee (NAIDOC) Person of the Year and 2011 New South Wales Australian of the Year. Larissa was awarded an AO in 2020 for her work in Indigenous education, law and the arts.

Author's Acknowledgements

With thanks to everyone at Wiley (especially Ingrid Bond, Francesca Tarquinio, Charlotte Duff and Lucy Raymond). Special thanks to editor Kerry Davies for the expertise she provided in the first edition of the book. Thanks also to Amanda Porter and Terry Priest. Also sincere thanks to Michael McDaniel, my mother Raema Behrendt and my husband Michael Lavarch.

Dedication

To my mother, Raema Behrendt, who taught me the importance of knowledge and education, encouraged me to dream big and supported me when I did.

Publisher's Acknowledgements

Some of the people who helped bring this book to market include the following:

Acquisitions, Editorial and Media Development

Project Editor: Tamilmani Varadharaj

Acquisitions Editor: Lucy Raymond

Editorial Manager: Ingrid Bond

Copy Editor: Charlotte Duff

Production

Graphics: SPi

Proofreader: Susan Hobbs

Indexer: Estalita Slivoskey

The author and publisher would like to thank the following organisations for their permission to reproduce copyright material in this book:

- Cover image: © Daphne Marks / Copyright Agency, 2020

- Page 34: Unpublished paper 'Aboriginal Citizenship Conference' by Professor Peter Read, ANU, February 1996

- Page 77: National Archives of Australia. NAA: A6135,K10/12/74/9. © Commonwealth of Australia National Archives of Australia 2019.

- Page 92: NLA.PIC-AN24526893 Engraving by James Neagle. Reproduced with permission from the National Library of Australia. © Commonwealth of Australia National Archives of Australia 2019.

- Page 95: State Library of Victoria; Accession No: 30328102131553/7, Image No: pb000329

- Page 96: © Keith Barnes / Shutterstock.com

- Page 103: State Library of Victoria; Accession Number: H14164; Image Number: b28462

- Page 126: State Records Authority of New South Wales

- Page 136: © Newspix / News Ltd

- Pages 151-152: From Prime Minister Kevin Rudd, MP — Apology to Australia's Indigenous peoples; Wednesday, February 13, 2008, Parliament of Australia, Department of Parliamentary Services

- Page 185: *Charles Perkins returning home after studying at Sydney University, circa 1963.* Copyright photograph by Robert McFarlane, courtesy Josef Lebovic Gallery.

- Page 202; Table 12-1: *Resolving Indigenous Land Disputes*, Larissa Behrendt and Loretta Kelly, The Federation Press, 2008, p. 40. Reproduced with permission.

- Page 220: From Prime Minister Paul Keating, MP, Redfern Park address, 10 December 1992

- Page 229: NLA.PIC-AN24526893 Photograph by Loui Seselja. Reproduced with permission from the National Library of Australia.

- Pages 229-230: Council for Aboriginal Reconciliation, 27 May 2000

- Pages 270-272: Uluru Statement, https://ulurustatement.org/

- Page 281: © Newspix / Brenton Edwards

- Page 288: © Newspix / Mark Calleja

Every effort has been made to trace the ownership of copyright material. Information that enables the publisher to rectify any error or omission in subsequent editions is welcome. In such cases, please contact the Permissions Section of John Wiley & Sons Australia, Ltd.

Printed and bound by CPI Group (UK) Ltd, Croydon, CR0 4YY
29/03/2021
00590113-0001